Investment Strategies in the Age of Technological Innovation and Emerging Markets

Liao Faxing
Chengdu International Studies University, China

Ooi Kok Loang
Universiti Malaya, Malaysia

IGI Global
Scientific Publishing
Publishing Tomorrow's Research Today

Vice President of Editorial	Melissa Wagner
Managing Editor of Acquisitions	Mikaela Felty
Managing Editor of Book Development	Jocelynn Hessler
Production Manager	Mike Brehm
Cover Design	Phillip Shickler

Published in the United States of America by
IGI Global Scientific Publishing
701 East Chocolate Avenue
Hershey, PA, 17033, USA
Tel: 717-533-8845
Fax: 717-533-8661
Website: https://www.igi-global.com E-mail: cust@igi-global.com

Library of Congress Cataloging-in-Publication Data

Names: Liao, Fa Xing, 1990- editor. | Ooi, Kok Loang, 1994- editor.
Title: Investment strategies in the age of technological innovation and emerging markets / [edited by] Fa Xing Liao, Ooi Kok Loang.
Description: Hershey, PA : IGI Global Scientific Publishing, [2025] | Includes bibliographical references and index. | Summary: "The principal objective of this book is to furnish a comprehensive examination of how technological innovation is reshaping investment strategies within the context of emerging markets"-- Provided by publisher.
Identifiers: LCCN 2024055160 (print) | LCCN 2024055161 (ebook) | ISBN 9798369385838 (hardcover) | ISBN 9798369385845 (paperback) | ISBN 9798369385852 (ebook)
Subjects: LCSH: Investments--Technological innovations.
Classification: LCC HG4515.5 .I56 2025 (print) | LCC HG4515.5 (ebook) | DDC 332.6--dc23/eng/20250202
LC record available at https://lccn.loc.gov/2024055160
LC ebook record available at https://lccn.loc.gov/2024055161

British Cataloguing in Publication Data
A Cataloguing in Publication record for this book is available from the British Library.

Table of Contents

Detailed Table of Contents

The digital era has revolutionized nearly every aspect of financial markets, from how investors interact with financial instruments to how trades are executed. Behavioral finance, a field that explores how psychological factors influence financial decision-making, must now consider the profound impact of digital technologies. As financial technology (FinTech) platforms, social media, and algorithmic trading gain prominence, understanding investor behavior in the digital age becomes increasingly crucial. This chapter examines the role of digital advancements in shaping behavioral biases and market psychology, and their implications for both individual investors and the broader financial system.

This study examines the impact of AI, machine learning (ML), and blockchain on investment strategies. Using a mixed methods approach with survey data from 90 financial professionals, secondary data, and 12 case studies, the study employed SWOT analysis, percentile method, chi-square, and Kruskal-Wallis H-test for analysis. Findings reveal that 38.9% of respondents find traditional strategies less effective compared to modern approaches. Technological innovations have notably improved portfolio performance and risk management. A substantial 77.8% believe these technologies have transformed traditional strategies. However, data security remains a major concern for 70% of respondents. The study underscores the importance of AI, ML, and blockchain in modernizing investment strategies and highlights the need for robust security measures and further research on long-term impacts. It offers actionable recommendations for investors, policymakers, and researchers to leverage these technologies effectively.

Artificial intelligence (AI) in Fintech refers to the extensive or widespread application of AI in the functioning of financial institutions and related businesses. The focus is on AI techniques such as Deep Learning, Robotics, the Internet of Things (IoT), Image Processing, Artificial Neural Networks (ANN), Wireless Sensor Networks, and Machine Learning (ML). FinTech's use of AI has revolutionized the industry by bringing cutting-edge technologies that improve decision-making, expedite procedures, and offer customers individualized services. There are many different applications in the financial sector due to the combination of AI and FinTech. This chapter addresses AI techniques and their applications in the various functional areas of the fintech industry. Benefits, challenges, case studies, and success stories were also discussed.

This study focuses on the ways that technological developments have changed market dynamics, decision-making procedures, and investing patterns. The rapid development of fintech, algorithmic trading, big data analytics, and artificial intelligence (AI) has had a profound effect on how investors research markets, obtain information, and make financial decisions. The democratization of access to financial data brought about by technology allows individual investors to engage in markets that were previously controlled by institutional players. Although technology improves accessibility and efficiency, the results indicate that it also adds complications that call for a more thorough comprehension of investor behavior in a tech-driven financial environment. The study's conclusion suggests directions for future investigation into reducing the psychological risks connected to technology-driven financial decision-making.

In today's ever-evolving financial landscape, the integration of behavioral finance into investment strategies is increasingly critical. This chapter explores how insights from behavioral finance can be effectively applied by stakeholders to enhance investment decision-making in emerging markets characterized by technology and innovation. These markets, which present both unique opportunities and challenges, demand a nuanced and comprehensive understanding of the psychological and behavioral traits of investors. By offering pragmatic insights into cognitive biases, heuristics, and emotional influences, the chapter aims to equip stakeholders—including investors, financial advisors, and policymakers—with the essential tools and techniques needed to successfully navigate these complex markets.

This study investigates the cognitive and emotional factors influencing collective investment behaviors in stock markets, focusing on how biases such as overconfidence, loss aversion, social influence, and the fear of missing out (FOMO) contribute to herding behavior. Behavioral finance suggests that cognitive and emotional stimuli can lead to investment patterns that deviate from rational decision-making models. By examining how these psychological triggers interact in financial markets, the study addresses gaps in understanding the combined effect of biases on collective market behavior. The findings emphasize the importance of comprehending these biases to mitigate their negative impact on market efficiency and stability, particularly in a technology-driven trading environment. Future research should explore cross-cultural influences and the role of technology in intensifying herding dynamics.

future predictions, this article aims to equip investors, policymakers, and financial professionals with the insights needed to navigate the ever-evolving ETF landscape.

Investment decisions are influenced by a large number of factors beyond pure rational analysis. The study explores the mediating effect of regret aversion bias and herding bias on investment experience and investment decisions. The study aimed to understand the effect of parallel mediation on the relationship between the dependent and the independent variable. The sample of the study included 212 individual investors from India. The Structural Equation Modeling (SEM) is used to understand the mediation effect. It was found that the herding bias significantly impacts the relationship between investment experience and investment decision. However, regret aversion bias does not mediate the relationship. The study contributes to the existing body of knowledge by understanding how behavioral biases and experiences interact to shape investment behavior.

Sustainable and Ethical Investment is a growing investment approach that considers Environmental, Social, and Governance (ESG) factors alongside financial returns. By aligning investments with personal values, investors can contribute to a positive impact on society and the environment while potentially earning competitive returns. Technological advancements like AI, blockchain, and renewable energy technologies are reshaping the landscape of ethical investment, enabling data-driven investing and creating new investment opportunities. This chapter covers the key aspects of sustainable and ethical investment, including ESG factors, technological advancements, and the benefits of integrating sustainability principles into investment strategies. The integration of sustainability principles into investment strategies is becoming increasingly essential for long-term value creation and a more resilient future.

Preface

In the financial landscape of today, the pace of change is dizzying, driven by transformative technologies, unprecedented access to data, and the meteoric rise of emerging markets. Investors are no longer operating in a world defined solely by balance sheets, price-to-earnings ratios, and traditional risk metrics. Instead, they face an era of unparalleled complexity, where decisions are influenced as much by the psychology of crowds and the speed of algorithms as by fundamental financial principles. *Investment Strategies in the Age of Technological Innovation and Emerging Markets* is not just a guidebook; it's a narrative journey through this new financial terrain, one that invites readers to rethink, reimagine, and redefine what it means to invest in the modern world. It challenges the reader to go beyond familiar paths and explore uncharted territories, merging the disciplines of technology, psychology, and economics in a way that feels as thrilling as it is essential.

As this book unfolds, it becomes clear that traditional investment models no longer suffice. In the past, finance rested on assumptions of rationality and order, assuming that markets functioned like well-oiled machines where every cog played its part predictably. But modern finance is anything but predictable. In a world marked by complexity and constant innovation, we can no longer rely solely on models built for a bygone era. Instead, this book introduces readers to the science of behavioral finance, which recognizes the profound influence of human psychology on market behavior. This shift to understanding the psychological triggers and biases of investors—from fear and greed to overconfidence and herding—marks a revolution in finance. Through this lens, readers will see how emotions, cognitive shortcuts, and social pressures shape investment decisions in ways that are sometimes beneficial but often detrimental.

Today, the relevance of this topic is unmistakable. Financial markets are more interconnected than ever, and the rapid advancement of technology has fundamentally reshaped how investors interact with those markets. Emerging markets, once seen as the "wild frontier" of finance, have now stepped into the spotlight, offering high-growth opportunities that are increasingly drawing the attention of global investors. In regions like Southeast Asia, Africa, and Latin America, technological innovation and economic expansion are creating a dynamic blend of opportunities and challenges. This book situates itself at this crucial intersection, where behavioral finance, technological tools, and emerging market dynamics converge. It explores how investors can navigate this unique landscape responsibly and strategically, using new tools and insights to capitalize on high-growth opportunities while managing the unique risks that these markets entail.

The target audience for this book is as diverse as the world it describes. For scholars and academics, it provides a rigorous analysis of the latest theories in finance, behavioral science, and technology. Professors, researchers, and students in finance, economics, and psychology will find this book to be a valuable addition to their libraries, offering fresh perspectives and real-world applications that enhance academic discourse. Practitioners in the finance industry, including asset managers, financial analysts, and portfolio strategists, will find actionable insights that bridge the gap between theory and practice, translating complex concepts into strategies that can be implemented in the real world. Institutional investors, fund managers, and policymakers will discover a framework for understanding the long-term implications of emerging market growth and technological innovation on financial stability and regulatory policy. Finally, individual investors and students, whether they are seasoned market players or newcomers, will benefit from the accessible language and engaging narrative that demystify the complexities of modern finance, offering a roadmap for making sound, strategic choices in an increasingly volatile world.

The book's structure is meticulously designed to guide readers on a journey from foundational insights to sophisticated strategies, each chapter building upon the last to construct a holistic view of today's investment landscape. *Behavioral Finance in the Digital Era*, the opening chapter, serves as the cornerstone of this exploration. Here, readers are introduced to the psychological principles that drive investor behavior, including cognitive biases such as confirmation bias, loss aversion, and overconfidence. In an era dominated by digital communication and social media, these biases are not only present but often amplified. This chapter sets the stage by revealing how digital platforms can fuel both optimism and panic in an instant, making understanding human psychology more essential than ever for any investor seeking stability in turbulent times.

The second chapter, *Technological Innovation in Investment Strategies*, examines the rise of artificial intelligence, blockchain, and machine learning as transformative forces in finance. These technologies have shattered traditional barriers, granting investors unprecedented access to data and analytics. For the first time in history, the average investor has tools at their disposal that rival those of major financial institutions. This chapter dives deep into how investors can harness these technologies to uncover patterns, predict trends, and automate decisions, but it also issues a warning against over-reliance on machines. True financial acumen, this chapter argues, requires blending the predictive power of technology with human intuition and judgment.

The Transformative Role of Artificial Intelligence in Fintech goes a step further, examining how AI is specifically reshaping the fintech industry. This chapter takes readers into the world of machine learning algorithms, natural language processing, and data mining, showcasing how these tools enable real-time analysis of market sentiment, financial news, and even social media chatter. With AI-powered tools, investors can analyze vast amounts of data in ways that were previously unimaginable. Robo-advisors, sentiment analysis platforms, and predictive algorithms are democratizing finance, offering personalized advice and insights once reserved for the elite. However, this chapter also encourages readers to approach AI with a critical eye, exploring both its transformative potential and its ethical implications.

A Critical Review of the Influence of Technology on Financial Decision-Making and Investor Psychology, the fourth chapter, explores the interplay between technology and psychology. It addresses the double-edged sword of digital tools—while they offer data-driven insights, they also risk exacerbating biases and fueling herd behavior. In an age where social media platforms can ignite market panics or rallies within hours, understanding this relationship is vital. This chapter invites readers to reflect on the balance between embracing technology and maintaining a healthy skepticism, cautioning against becoming slaves to algorithms and the "wisdom" of the online crowd.

In *Behavioral Finance Approaches to Investing in Technology-Driven and Emerging Markets*, we enter the realm of high-growth regions with unique market dynamics. Emerging markets, with their mix of high potential and high risk, present a different set of psychological challenges. Cultural factors, investor sentiment, and economic conditions create distinctive behavioral patterns that traditional Western models fail to capture. This chapter equips readers with the behavioral finance tools they need to understand and navigate these regions effectively, offering strategies that account for both the risks and rewards of investing in developing economies.

The sixth chapter, *Cognitive and Emotional Triggers of Collective Investment Patterns in Stock Markets*, delves into the powerful social forces that drive collective investment behavior. Herding, contagion, and emotional influence are examined in detail, showing how market trends can emerge and evolve due to shared psychological responses. Drawing on historical examples and real-world data, this chapter illustrates the conditions under which collective behavior can drive markets to soar or collapse, offering investors insights into how to anticipate and respond to these dynamics.

Investor Biases and Reaction Dynamics: Exploring the Psychological Mechanisms Behind Market Fluctuations offers a focused exploration of individual biases—like anchoring, mental accounting, and the disposition effect—and their effects on market movements. This chapter provides readers with practical tools for identifying and mitigating these biases, empowering them to make rational, disciplined decisions, especially in volatile environments where emotions run high.

The book's examination of biases continues in *Bias-Driven Trading Patterns: Exploring the Influence of Sentiment and Anchoring on Market Liquidity*, which addresses how sentiment and anchoring affect market liquidity. Through case studies and analysis, readers will learn how to recognize and adapt to these patterns, understanding liquidity as not just a financial measure but as a reflection of investor psychology.

The Role of Heuristics in Shaping Investment Strategies: Analyzing Bias-Driven Decision-Making in Volatile Markets explores how mental shortcuts—heuristics—can be both a blessing and a curse. While they simplify decision-making, they can also lead to systematic errors. This chapter offers a nuanced view of heuristics, helping readers identify when these shortcuts enhance decision-making and when they might lead to costly mistakes.

With *Emerging Market Dynamics and Their Impact on Ethical Investment Behavior: A Case Study on Investment Strategies in Ethiopia*, the book pivots to socially responsible investing. Using Ethiopia as an example, this chapter discusses the challenges and opportunities of investing in emerging markets with a conscience. It underscores the importance of balancing financial returns with social impact, providing readers with a framework for evaluating ethical considerations in unfamiliar markets.

In *Exchange-Traded Funds (ETFs): Redefining Financial Instruments in the 21st Century*, readers will find an in-depth look at ETFs, an essential tool for modern investors. This chapter explains how ETFs offer diversified exposure, reduce costs, and add flexibility to portfolios, making them invaluable in both stable and volatile markets. From sector-specific ETFs to ESG-focused funds, readers will learn how to leverage these instruments to align with their investment goals.

Investment Experience on Investment Decisions: The Mediating Role of Regret Aversion and Herding Biases examines how past experiences and emotions shape decisions, especially through regret aversion and herding behavior. By recognizing these influences, experienced investors can refine their strategies, learning from their own mistakes while avoiding the traps of overconfidence and crowd psychology.

The final chapter, *Investment Strategies in the Age of Technological Innovation and Emerging Markets: Sustainable and Ethical Investment Approaches*, synthesizes the insights from the entire book, urging readers to embrace a more holistic view of investing. This chapter emphasizes the alignment between financial success and social responsibility, discussing how investors can contribute to sustainable development without sacrificing returns. Here, readers will find practical advice on measuring impact and performance side by side, reinforcing the idea that financial growth and positive change are not mutually exclusive.

In conclusion, *Investment Strategies in the Age of Technological Innovation and Emerging Markets* is a comprehensive roadmap for anyone seeking to understand and thrive in the new age of finance. By blending behavioral insights, technological advancements, and practical strategies, it offers readers a blueprint for informed, ethical, and adaptable investing. This book is not merely a guide; it's an invitation to think critically, act responsibly, and embrace the potential for financial decisions to drive meaningful change in the world. As you immerse yourself in these pages, may you find not only strategies for wealth creation but also a deeper understanding of the forces that shape our global economy and the role you play in it. Welcome to the future of finance.

Chapter 1
Behavioral Finance in the Digital Era

Asheetu Bhatia Sarin
https://orcid.org/0000-0001-5321-1969
VIPS, Guru Gobind Singh Indraprastha University, India

ABSTRACT

The digital era has revolutionized nearly every aspect of financial markets, from how investors interact with financial instruments to how trades are executed. Behavioral finance, a field that explores how psychological factors influence financial decision-making, must now consider the profound impact of digital technologies. As financial technology (FinTech) platforms, social media, and algorithmic trading gain prominence, understanding investor behavior in the digital age becomes increasingly crucial. This chapter examines the role of digital advancements in shaping behavioral biases and market psychology, and their implications for both individual investors and the broader financial system.

INTRODUCTION

Behavioral finance challenges the traditional notion that investors act rationally, as proposed by classical financial theories such as the Efficient Market Hypothesis (EMH). According to the EMH, investors process all available information logically, leading to asset prices that reflect the true value of securities. However, behavioral finance argues that real-world investors often deviate from this ideal due to cognitive biases and emotional influences, which can result in irrational decisions and market

DOI: 10.4018/979-8-3693-8583-8.ch001

inefficiencies. Instead, it highlights how cognitive biases and emotions can lead to irrational investment decisions, ultimately influencing market outcomes.

Cognitive biases, such as overconfidence, loss aversion, and anchoring, often cause investors to misjudge risks, overestimate their knowledge, or cling to previous beliefs despite new information. For example, loss aversion suggests that investors feel the pain of losses more acutely than the pleasure of gains, leading them to hold on to losing stocks for too long or sell winning ones too quickly—a phenomenon known as the disposition effect. Emotions also play a significant role in shaping investor behavior. Fear and greed can drive market trends, creating periods of excessive optimism or pessimism. During market bubbles, for instance, investors may become overly confident, buying overvalued assets in the hopes of quick profits, only to panic and sell off in a downturn.

This divergence from rational decision-making introduces inefficiencies into the market, as prices may temporarily deviate from their intrinsic values. As a result, behavioral finance provides a more nuanced understanding of market dynamics by accounting for human psychology, helping explain phenomena like stock price anomalies, market bubbles, and crashes. This perspective also opens the door to strategies for mitigating the impact of biases, such as using automated tools or decision frameworks to reduce emotional reactions in trading.

This chapter examines the intersection of behavioral finance and technology, highlighting the role of digital innovations in reinforcing irrational behavior, such as herding and overconfidence, while offering solutions to counteract these biases. By integrating insights from psychology, technology, and finance, this research sheds light on how digital transformation is reshaping investment behaviors and the broader financial markets.

MEANING OF BEHAVIORAL FINANCE

In any economy, investors can be categorized into two types: rational and irrational. According to Nofsinger (2001), rational investors make decisions based on objective, unbiased data and information, which allows for more logical and reliable predictions. In contrast, irrational investors rely on instinct and follow the crowd, often engaging in herd behavior, as described by Thaler (1985). The main impact on the global economy in the past is from various crises which were controlled by the economists on the influential seats of the government institutions. Psychologists Daniel Kahneman and Amos Tversky made huge contributions to behavioral psychology literature in the 1970s and worked to give rise to Behavioral Finance. The main aim of this topic is to study how people behave in any given financial environment. Therefore, it can be termed as a vertical of finance that studies and helps to analyze the behavior of agents in the financial stock market across the globe. Therefore, it can be said that behavioral finance is about identifying and explaining inefficiencies and mispricing in financial markets. As per behavioral finance, the explanation of irrational investors can be drawn on human cognitive-behavioral biases ranging from sociology, psychology, and anthropology.

Kahneman and Tversky (1979) introduced a descriptive model of decision-making under risk, known as Prospect Theory. They discovered that individuals tend to underweight outcomes that are only probable compared to those that are certain. Additionally, they found that people often disregard elements that are common to all potential outcomes being considered. According to Prospect Theory, value is attributed to "gains and losses" rather than to overall final assets, with decision weights substituting probabilities. The value function is based on deviations from a reference point, typically showing concavity for gains i.e. risk aversion, and convexity for losses i.e. risk-seeking behavior, with losses generally felt more intensely than equivalent gains i.e. loss aversion. Additionally, decision weights are often lower than the corresponding actual probabilities. The theory anticipates a distinct fourfold pattern in risk attitudes:

i. Risk aversion for gains with moderate to high probabilities and for losses with low probabilities, and
ii. Risk-seeking behavior for gains with low probabilities and losses with moderate to high probabilities.

In their 1982 paper, Tversky and Kahneman introduced the concept of framing, demonstrating that the psychological principles influencing how people perceive decision problems and evaluate probabilities and outcomes lead to predictable changes in preferences depending on how the problem is framed (Tversky & Kahneman, 1982). Bondt & Thaler (1985) found that individuals tend to overreact to unexpected, dramatic news events, leading to significant inefficiencies in the stock market. They also introduced the idea of mental accounting, which refers to the cognitive processes individuals and households use to organize, evaluate, and track their financial activities. Furthermore, Thaler (1985) developed a new model of consumer behavior centered on mental accounting.

Tversky & Kahneman (1986) argued that, due to framing and prospect theory, the rational theory of choice does not provide an adequate foundation for a descriptive theory of decision making as seen in Figure 1 below.

Figure 1. Value function in prospect theory

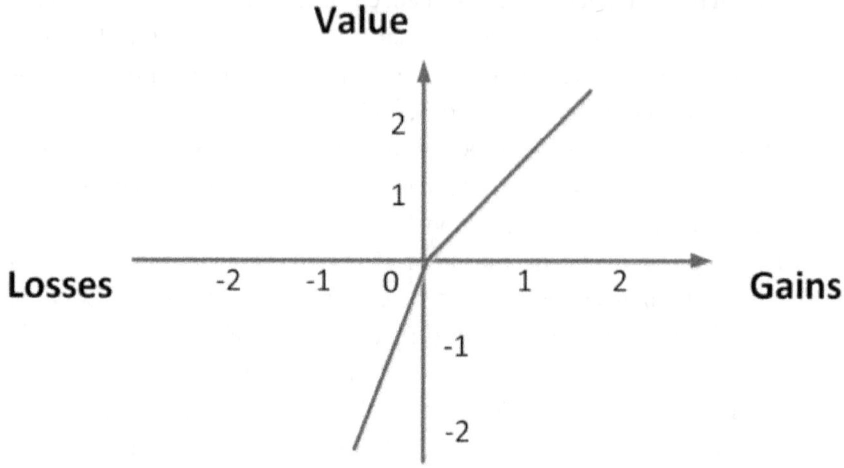

Source: Tversky and Kahneman (1986)

Several experiments demonstrated by Kahneman, Knetsch, and Thaler (1990) identified that loss aversion persists in market settings where there is an opportunity to learn.

Figure 2. Integration vs. segregation

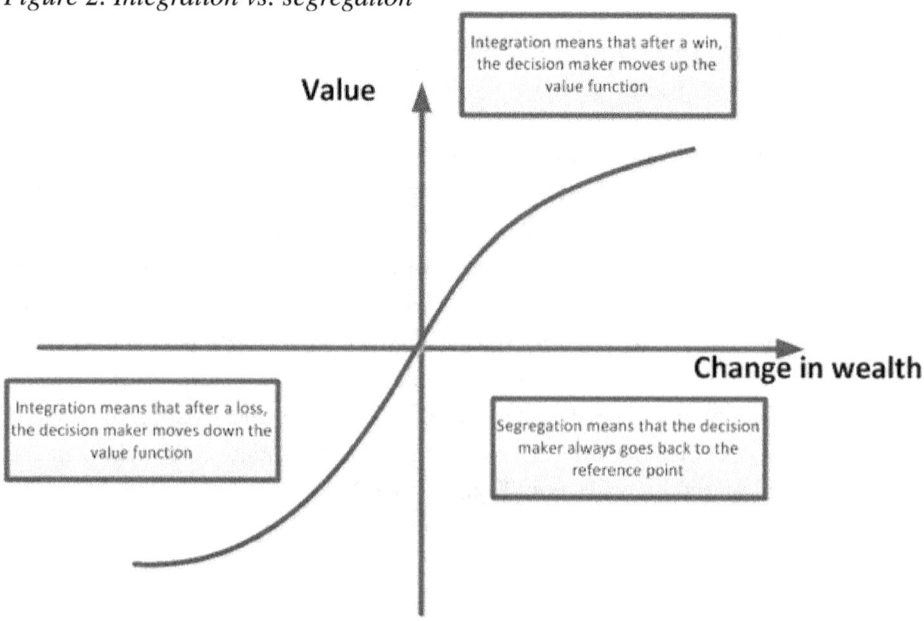

Source: Author

Tversky& Kahneman (1991) developed a reference-dependent model of riskless choice, with the vital supposition of this theory being loss aversion, which indicates that "losses and disadvantages" have a more significant impact on preferences than "gains and advantages". Tversky & Kahneman (1992) employed cumulative rather than separable decision weights to its original prospect theory, which applies to uncertain as well as to risky prospects with any number of outcomes, and it lets different weighting functions for gains and for losses as seen in Figure 3 below.

Figure 3. Weighing functions

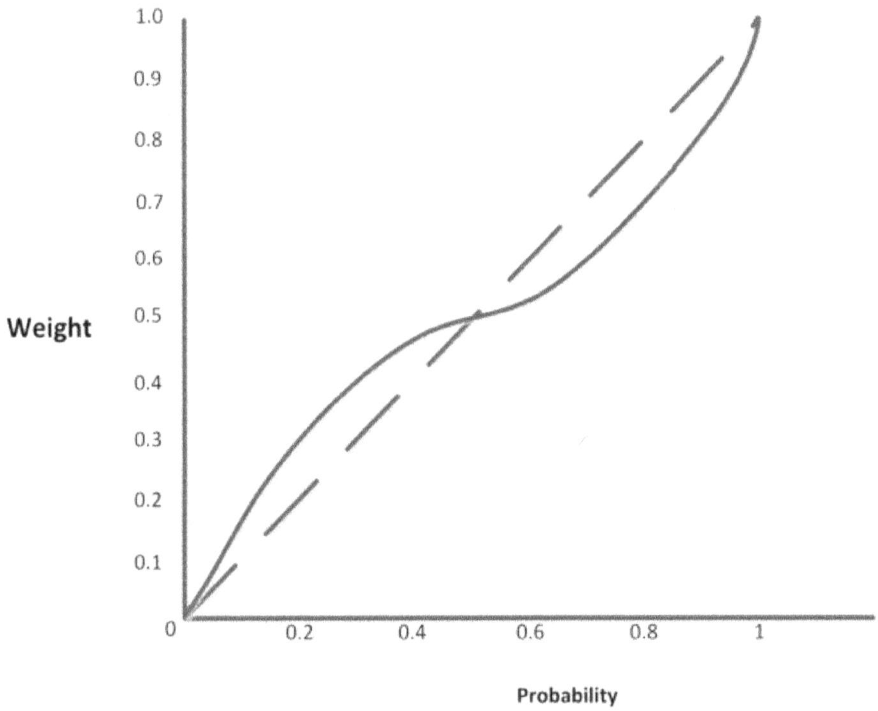

Source: Tversky and Kahneman (1992)

Plous (1993) provided a thorough overview of the field of psychology, focusing on the social factors involved in processes of decision-making. He stated that the strategy of value involves buying stocks that are priced low relative to earnings, dividends, book assets, or other measures of fundamental value. In contrast, Lakonishok et al. (1994) assessed that value strategies tend to generate higher returns because they take advantage of the sub-optimal behaviors displayed by the average investor. Grinblatt et al. (1995) examined the behavior of mutual funds and identified trends related to momentum strategies and herding. Gigerenzer (1996) critiqued the study of heuristics and biases in judgment, arguing that, contrary to the criticisms, frequency judgments—not just subjective probabilities—are susceptible to significant and systematic biases. Barberis et al. (1998) introduced a model of the sentiment of investors that demonstrated how stock prices tend to underreact to news, such as earnings announcements while overreacting to sequences of positive or negative news.

Fama (1998) defended the EMH, arguing that stock prices often overreact to information just as frequently as they underreact. This assertion was notable because under-reactions and over-reactions appear to occur under different circumstances and timeframes. Odean (1998) provided evidence for the disposition effect, which describes investors' propensity to sell attractive investments too quickly while holding onto losing/ non-attractive investments for an extended time. Kahneman et al. (1998) introduced a theory of security markets that focuses on investor overconfidence regarding the accuracy of private information and biased self-attribution. According to this theory, fluctuations in investors' confidence are influenced by their investment outcomes, resulting in both underreactions and over-reactions in the market.

Thaler (1999) reviewed the literature on mental accounting and concluded that it has a significant impact on decision-making. Odean (1999) found that trading volumes in equity markets are excessively high, suggesting that overconfidence may be a contributing factor. He also presented evidence of the disposition effect, which results in profitable stocks being sold too quickly and unprofitable stocks being held onto for too long. Additionally, Hong & Stein (1999) created a model of a market consisting of 2 groups of bounded informed investors. They are 'news watchers' and 'momentum traders' which leads to underreaction at short horizons and overreaction at long horizons. Lee and Swaminathan (2000) showed that past trading volume provides an important link between 'momentum' and 'value' strategies and these findings help to reconcile intermediate-horizon 'under reaction' and long-horizon 'overreaction' effects. Barber & Odean (2001) stated that men trade 45 percent more than women and thereby reduce their returns more so than do women and conclude that this is due to overconfidence.

Barberis and Huang (2001) compared two forms of mental accounting by incorporating loss aversion and narrow framing into two asset-pricing frameworks: individual stock accounting and portfolio accounting. Gilovich and Griffin (2002) recognized six general-purpose heuristics and six special-purpose heuristics. The special-purpose heuristics include attribution substitution, outrage, prototype, recognition, choosing by liking and choosing by default. In contrast, general-purpose heuristics impact factors such as availability, causality, fluency, similarity, and surprise. Two heuristics have been replaced: representativeness has been substituted by attribution substitution (which includes both the prototype and similarity heuristics), and anchoring and adjustment have been replaced by the affect heuristic. Besedes et al. (2012) indicated that the probability of a person selecting the optimal option declined as the number of options increased and this decline was more pronounced for older subjects. The study concluded that heuristics differ by age with older subjects relying more on sub-optimal decision rules.

Common behavioral biases include:

1. **Overconfidence:** Investors tend to overestimate their knowledge or predictive abilities, often leading to excessive trading or risk-taking.
2. **Loss Aversion:** The tendency to fear losses more than valuing equivalent gains, leading investors to hold on to losing positions too long or sell winners prematurely.
3. **Herd Behavior:** Investors may follow the crowd, leading to market bubbles or sudden downturns, particularly when uncertainty is high.
4. **Mental Accounting**: Investors compartmentalize their financial decisions, often leading to irrational investment behavior by treating different types of assets differently.

These behavioral tendencies were identified long before the digital age. However, the rise of digital platforms and tools has not only amplified some of these biases but also introduced new behavioral dynamics.

DIGITAL TECHNOLOGIES AND THEIR IMPACT ON INVESTOR BEHAVIOR

The Role of Fintech Platforms

Fintech platforms have revolutionized the way individuals interact with financial markets, fundamentally reshaping the field of behavioral finance. By leveraging technology, these platforms are not only democratizing access to financial services but also addressing common cognitive and emotional biases that influence investor behavior. However, they also risk exacerbating certain biases by making financial decisions more immediate and frequent.

FinTech has transformed the operational, collaborative, and innovative landscape of businesses, particularly in the financial transactions and finance sectors. Ryu (2018) characterizes FinTech as a disruptive and innovative financial service offered by non-financial companies, where information technology plays a critical role (Yang et al. 2023). Moreover, FinTech includes *"innovations in financial divisions that feature technology-enabled business models capable of facilitating disintermediation, revolutionizing the creation and delivery of products and services by existing firms, addressing privacy, regulatory, and law-enforcement challenges, opening new avenues for entrepreneurship, and fostering opportunities for inclusive growth"* (Dhar & Stein, 2017). Key digital innovations such as artificial intelligence, blockchain, machine learning, cryptocurrencies, and technology-driven business models are vital to the growth and evolution of the FinTech industry (Yang et al. 2023). Khan et al. (2022) studied ninety-one Fintech papers sourced from five databases, investigating the challenges and growth of Fintech in the Gulf Cooperation Council regions. They concluded that Fintech presents considerable research opportunities, given its potential to offer a wide range of financial services worldwide. Similarly, Ahmi et al. (2020) used the Scopus database to conduct a bibliometric analysis of Fintech research, identifying key trends in the field. They observed that, although Fintech is a relatively new concept, it emphasizes the crucial role of technology in the financial services sector. Furthermore, Liu et al. (2024) identified a significant increase in Fintech-related studies, particularly in reputed journals, after studying five hundred and eighteen research papers published between 2008 and 2021 from 4 academic databases. They concluded that Fintech and banking, Fintech development, and Fintech adoption, all will be future research areas and there will be a rise in the number of published articles.

The digital financial sector is experiencing a significant transformation, driven by technological advancements and changing consumer behaviors. The global fintech market is projected to grow from approximately $200 billion in 2020 to over $500 billion by 2027, reflecting a compound annual growth rate (CAGR) of around 20%. Adoption rates are also rising, with a survey by Accenture revealing that 64% of consumers are using at least one fintech service, particularly among younger generations like millennials and Gen Z. Venture capital investment in fintech startups reached a record $44 billion in 2020, showcasing strong investor confidence in the sector's growth and innovation potential. Additionally, the digital payments market is expected to surpass $10 trillion by 2025, fueled by an increasing preference for contactless and mobile payment solutions. Many countries are implementing new regulations to promote fintech innovation while ensuring consumer protection and financial stability, such as open banking initiatives. Furthermore, the rise of blockchain technology and cryptocurrencies has created new opportunities and challenges within the financial sector. On March 14, 2024, the total market capitalization of cryptocurrencies surpassed $2.5 trillion, with Bitcoin reaching a record high of $73,750 and achieving a market capitalization of $1.44 trillion (Forbes, 2024). This increase was driven by several factors, including the approval of Bitcoin exchange-traded funds (ETFs) in the United States, which enhanced investor confidence and led to significant capital inflows in the market. Additionally, favorable regulatory developments and greater institutional adoption further propelled the rise in cryptocurrency valuations during this time (Forbes, 2024). Together, these factors illustrate the rapid evolution of the digital financial landscape and the transformative impact of technology on traditional financial services.

Fintech platforms have lowered the barriers to entry for investing, saving, and borrowing, empowering retail investors to participate in financial markets that were traditionally accessible only to institutional or high-net-worth individuals. With the advent of commission-free trading apps like Robinhood and Revolut, even those with minimal capital can invest in stocks, cryptocurrencies, or fractional shares. This democratization enhances participation but also introduces millions of inexperienced investors to complex markets, where behavioral biases may influence their decisions. Fintech platforms often incorporate behavioral nudges, a concept from behavioral economics, to guide users toward better financial decisions. For example-Round-up features on apps like Acorns encourage users to save by automatically investing spare change from everyday purchases. Automatic rebalancing on robo-advisor platforms helps users avoid common pitfalls such as holding onto poorly performing assets due to loss aversion. These features leverage technology to subtly encourage better financial habits, which can counteract impulsive or emotional decision-making.

Fintech platforms can both mitigate and exacerbate common behavioral biases, influencing how users make financial decisions. Many fintech platforms use automation to help reduce biases like loss aversion or mental accounting. For example, robot advisors like Betterment or Wealthfront automatically rebalance portfolios and enforce a diversified investment strategy, thus minimizing the emotional influence that can lead to poor timing decisions or chasing past performance. Fintech platforms provide users with real-time data and personalized insights based on their spending or investment patterns. This helps reduce biases such as overconfidence by presenting a more accurate picture of their financial health and market conditions. Apps like Mint and YNAB give users a clear overview of their finances, thus helping them avoid confirmation bias, where they might selectively focus on positive information that supports their existing beliefs. Many fintech platforms use gamification techniques, which can trigger fear of missing out (FOMO) and encourage herding behavior. For example, apps like Robinhood use push notifications and flashy visuals to celebrate trades, reinforcing frequent trading. This approach can lead to impulsive decision-making based on short-term market movements rather than long-term strategy.

Additionally, the social features on platforms like eToro, which allow users to copy the trades of popular investors, can encourage herding and increase susceptibility to the bandwagon effect, where individuals follow the crowd without conducting their analysis. By making trading as simple as swiping on a smartphone, fintech platforms can exacerbate overconfidence bias. Investors may believe that because they have access to more information and tools, they are better equipped to make winning trades, despite lacking deep financial expertise. This increased accessibility can lead to excessive risk-taking without a clear understanding of the markets.

Fintech platforms have enabled real-time trading and financial management, allowing users to react immediately to market changes. However, the immediacy of decision-making can amplify emotional reactions, leading to behavior that is driven by short-term emotions rather than long-term financial goals. Instant Access to Markets: With fintech platforms offering real-time access to financial markets, users are more likely to make impulsive decisions based on emotional reactions to news, social media, or market trends. The ability to execute trades instantly on platforms like Robinhood or Weibull can lead to panic selling during market downturns or chasing gains during market rallies. This behavior is often driven by recency bias, where individuals place too much emphasis on recent events, leading to poor investment outcomes. Many fintech apps use push notifications to alert users about market movements, price changes, or trade opportunities. While these notifications keep users engaged, they can also trigger emotional reactions and reinforce short-termism, where users prioritize immediate gains over long-term strategy. This environment can fuel biases like myopic loss aversion, where individuals focus excessively on avoiding short-term losses, leading to suboptimal investment decisions.

Fintech platforms have increasingly integrated behavioral nudges into their design to help users overcome biases and improve their financial outcomes. By using insights from behavioral finance, these platforms can subtly influence user behavior in positive ways. Many fintech platforms encourage automatic savings and investment strategies to help users overcome the inertia associated with decision-making. For example, apps like Digit and Qapital automatically save money for users based on algorithms that analyze spending patterns. These features combat present bias, where individuals prioritize immediate consumption over future savings, by making saving effortless and automatic. Fintech platforms often set up goal-oriented savings features, where users can save for specific milestones (e.g., a vacation, down payment on a house). This approach appeals to the mental accounting bias by compartmentalizing finances and giving users a tangible reason to save. By setting clear savings targets, fintech platforms can help users prioritize long-term financial goals over impulsive spending.

Fintech platforms often use gamification techniques to encourage users to save more, invest wisely, or manage their debt. Gamification, which is primarily shaped by the socio-technical knowledge and commercial practices of digital marketing and UX/UI design (Cochoy et al., 2020), intersects with two broader economic-theoretical discourses that offer somewhat opposing views on socio-economic behavior. The first is rooted in behavioral science, viewing gamified techniques as part of choice architecture that nudges, incentivizes, and rewards rational user behavior. The second discourse stems from humanistic design, which sees gamified techniques as a means of creating positive and meaningful user experiences. This could include:

1. **Reward Systems:** Some apps offer small rewards or achievements for reaching savings milestones, paying down debt, or sticking to a budget. This positive reinforcement can counteract loss aversion, where individuals are more focused on avoiding losses than achieving gains.
2. **Leaderboards and Social Proof:** Platforms that incorporate social features, like Acorns' comparison tools or Step's peer savings goals, encourage competition or social proof. This can be beneficial when it comes to promoting financial discipline, as users are motivated by their peers' success in saving or investing, creating positive herding behavior in areas like savings.

The rise of big data and machine learning in fintech platforms has allowed for a more personalized approach to finance, which can help mitigate certain behavioral biases. Platforms like Betterment and Wealthfront provide personalized investment strategies based on individual goals, risk tolerance, and time horizons. By automating portfolio management, these platforms remove the emotional element of investing, helping users avoid overconfidence, regret aversion, or the tendency to make reactive decisions during market volatility. Fintech apps like YNAB and Mint provide users with spending insights based on their financial behavior. By offering real-time data on where and how money is spent, these apps help users overcome self-control biases and status quo biases, where individuals may fail to make necessary adjustments to their spending or investment habits. Fintech platforms also use machine learning algorithms to offer tailored financial products, such as loans or investment portfolios that suit a user's financial profile. This can reduce information overload and help users make more informed decisions by providing clear, personalized recommendations based on data, thus countering the choice overload bias, which can lead to decision paralysis.

Despite their benefits, fintech platforms can also introduce new challenges for behavioral finance by making it easier to engage in speculative, risky behavior or overreact to market noise. The ease of trading on fintech platforms, combined with social media influence and real-time updates, can lead to excessive speculative trading. The disposition effect, where investors sell winning stocks too early and hold on to losing stocks for too long can be exacerbated by the constant access and feedback loop provided by these platforms. Fintech platforms are tightly intertwined with social media, which can lead to herd behavior and the amplification of narrative bias. Platforms like Reddit's WallStreetBets have shown how social media-driven investment trends can lead to massive market volatility, as seen in the GameStop saga in early 2021. This social media-driven investing environment can create bubbles or extreme losses as investors flock to trendy stocks without understanding the underlying fundamentals. Algorithmic trading, including high-frequency trading (HFT), has become a dominant force in modern financial markets. While algorithms can remove human emotion from the trading process, they also interact with human behavior in unexpected ways. Automated trading systems help eliminate human biases like fear and greed by adhering strictly to predetermined rules. However, they can also cause herd-like movements when multiple algorithms follow similar strategies. Flash crashes, where market prices drop rapidly within seconds, are often linked to the actions of algorithms reacting to market signals at high speeds. While these are typically short-lived, they can cause panic among retail investors, amplifying emotional responses.

SOCIAL MEDIA AND ONLINE COMMUNITIES

Online communities have had a profound impact on investor behavior, particularly with the rise of platforms like Reddit, Twitter, and various financial forums. These communities serve as hubs for the exchange of ideas, tips, and market sentiment, often shaping the investment decisions of large groups of individuals. One of the key effects is the amplification of herd behavior, where investors follow the crowd based on popular discussions or trends within the community. For instance, the GameStop saga, fueled by Reddit's WallStreetBets, demonstrated how collective action in online spaces can lead to extreme price volatility, driving stock prices up or down independent of company fundamentals.

These forums also tend to reinforce confirmation bias, as users seek out information that aligns with their pre-existing beliefs while dismissing contrary views. Additionally, social media discussions often create fear of missing out (FOMO), pushing investors to make impulsive decisions to capitalize on perceived market opportunities. While these platforms democratize access to financial insights and enable retail investors to challenge traditional market players, they also heighten emotional decision-making, potentially leading to irrational investments and market instability. Consequently, while online communities empower investors with information, they also introduce new behavioral risks that can significantly influence market outcomes.

Case Studies

1. Tesla

Tesla, the electric vehicle (EV) manufacturer led by Elon Musk, became one of the most valuable companies in the world by 2024, with its stock price experiencing unprecedented growth. From 2019 to 2021, Tesla's stock surged over 1,000% and as per reports it is forecasted a 30% growth in 2025, capturing the attention of both institutional and retail investors. During this period, Tesla became a focal point for speculative trading, driven by a combination of investor enthusiasm, media coverage, and behavioral biases. This case study examines how behavioral finance influenced Tesla's stock rise, with a focus on the role of social media, retail investors, and the digital trading platforms that facilitated this frenzy.

Tesla's growth trajectory has been fuelled by its innovation in the EV market, its charismatic CEO Elon Musk, and its ambitious vision for the future of transportation and clean energy. By the end of 2019, Tesla had already gained a loyal following among investors and tech enthusiasts, but it was in 2020 that the stock price took off, rising from $86 (adjusted for stock splits) in January to over $700 by December.

Several factors contributed to this meteoric rise, including Tesla's inclusion in the S&P 500, growing demand for electric vehicles, and Musk's public presence on social media. Retail investors, particularly those trading on platforms like Robinhood, were key drivers of this surge, often fueled by excitement and behavioral biases.

Tesla's stock surge between 2019 and 2021 was marked by several key behavioral biases that influenced the decision-making of retail investors:

Overconfidence and the Cult of Elon Musk

Overconfidence was prevalent among Tesla's retail investors, many of whom believed that Tesla was destined to dominate the automotive industry and that Elon Musk could do no wrong. Musk's frequent communication with his followers on Twitter, where he often made bold predictions and announcements, reinforced the belief that Tesla's growth was unstoppable. Investors were confident that Tesla's stock would continue to rise, leading them to take increasingly larger positions, often without fully understanding the company's financials or risks. The "cult of Elon Musk" phenomenon amplified this overconfidence. Musk's public persona, which combined charisma, technological vision, and a penchant for controversy, endeared him to a large fanbase. Many investors equated Musk's success with Tesla's future performance, often viewing him as a visionary who could defy traditional business norms and market expectations.

FOMO (Fear of Missing Out)

As Tesla's stock price soared in 2020, many retail investors were driven by FOMO, particularly those new to the stock market. Stories of individuals making massive profits on Tesla fueled the desire to get in on the action, even when the stock seemed overvalued by traditional metrics. Social media platforms like Twitter, Reddit, and YouTube were flooded with Tesla-related discussions, stock analysis, and memes, all of which amplified the fear of missing out on potentially life-changing gains.

Herding Behavior

Tesla's stock surge was also driven by herding behavior, where investors followed the crowd rather than conducting their independent analysis. Tesla became one of the most discussed stocks on Reddit's WallStreetBets, with countless posts advocating for buying the stock due to its potential for further gains. Retail investors, often influenced by social media trends and viral posts, bought Tesla shares en masse, reinforcing the upward momentum of the stock price. Additionally, Tesla's inclusion in the S&P 500 in December 2020 created a sense of validation for the company's long-term viability, further encouraging investors to join the bandwagon. This event attracted both retail and institutional investors, but retail investors, in particular, viewed it as a sign that Tesla was now a mainstream investment opportunity.

Anchoring

Anchoring played a key role in how investors evaluated Tesla's stock price. Many retail investors anchored their expectations to Tesla's previous price highs and expected similar performance in the future, even when the stock became significantly overvalued based on traditional financial metrics. For example, after Tesla's stock split in August 2020, many investors expected the stock to quickly return to its pre-split highs, even though the split itself did not change the underlying value of the company.

Confirmation Bias

Confirmation bias, the tendency to seek out information that supports existing beliefs, was prevalent among Tesla's retail investors. Many investors selectively consumed news and analysis that reinforced their bullish views of the company while dismissing or ignoring negative reports, such as concerns over Tesla's valuation or competitive threats from other automakers. Social media platforms and online forums, where Tesla bulls congregated, became echo chambers that further entrenched these optimistic views.

The digital era played a critical role in Tesla's stock surge, with social media platforms and digital trading apps enabling retail investors to drive much of the momentum behind the stock. Elon Musk's use of Twitter was a significant factor in Tesla's rise. Musk frequently tweeted about Tesla's future, shared company updates, and even made controversial statements that influenced the stock price. For example, in May 2020, Musk tweeted that Tesla's stock price was "too high," causing a temporary dip in the price. However, this event did little to dampen investor enthusiasm, as the stock quickly recovered. Musk's tweets became part of the broader narrative around Tesla, and many retail investors looked to his Twitter account for signals about the company's future. This direct communication with investors created a sense of proximity between Musk and Tesla shareholders, further fueling the loyalty of his fanbase.

Reddit's WallStreetBets community played a central role in driving interest in Tesla's stock. The forum, known for its irreverent tone and aggressive investment strategies, became a hub for Tesla bulls who shared memes, analysis, and success stories about their Tesla investments. Posts encouraging users to buy Tesla stock, often framed in humorous or exaggerated terms, contributed to the herding behavior that drove the stock's upward trajectory. The community also reinforced a sense of camaraderie among Tesla investors, many of whom viewed their investments as part of a larger narrative of disrupting traditional industries and supporting a cleaner future. This collective enthusiasm often drowned out more cautious or skeptical voices, reinforcing the behavioral biases of overconfidence and FOMO.

Robinhood and other commission-free trading platforms played a significant role in Tesla's retail-driven surge. The ease of access to Tesla's stock, combined with the ability to buy fractional shares, made it possible for even small retail investors to participate in the stock's rise. Robinhood's user-friendly interface and gamified features, such as notifications and visual celebrations of trades, encouraged frequent trading and speculation. During the height of Tesla's stock surge, Tesla became one of the most traded stocks on Robinhood, with millions of shares changing hands daily. The platform's focus on retail traders, many of whom were inexperienced and motivated by behavioral biases, contributed to the stock's extreme volatility.

Tesla's stock became one of the most volatile in the market, with significant price swings driven largely by retail investor behavior. The combination of behavioral biases, digital platforms, and media coverage created an environment where Tesla's stock price was often detached from traditional financial metrics. Tesla's price-to-earnings (P/E) ratio reached astronomical levels, far exceeding those of other automakers or technology companies, leading many analysts to question the sustainability of the stock's valuation.

Elon Musk's use of Twitter to communicate with investors attracted regulatory attention, particularly after a 2018 incident in which Musk tweeted that he was considering taking Tesla private at $420 per share. This tweet led to an investigation by the U.S. Securities and Exchange Commission (SEC), resulting in a settlement that required Musk to step down as Tesla's chairman and have his tweets about the company pre-approved by legal counsel. Despite this settlement, Musk continued to tweet about Tesla in ways that influenced the stock price, raising ongoing concerns about the intersection of social media and market manipulation. The SEC's focus on Musk's behavior highlights the broader regulatory challenges posed by the influence of social media on market behavior in the digital era.

Tesla's stock surge between 2019 and 2021 is a prime example of how behavioral biases, such as overconfidence, herding, and FOMO, can drive market outcomes in the digital era. Retail investors, influenced by social media, digital trading platforms, and charismatic CEOs like Elon Musk, played a major role in driving Tesla's valuation to record levels, often in defiance of traditional financial metrics. Social media platforms, particularly Twitter and Reddit, have become powerful tools for influencing investor behavior. In Tesla's case, Elon Musk's tweets and Reddit's WallStreetBets community amplified retail enthusiasm for the stock, creating a feedback loop that contributed to its volatility. These platforms have changed the way information is disseminated and how investors make decisions, often amplifying behavioral biases. The Tesla case highlights the need for regulators to adapt to the new dynamics of the digital era, where social media and digital trading platforms can significantly impact market behavior. The SEC's involvement in Musk's tweets underscores the challenges of regulating market communication in an age where CEOs and influencers have direct access to retail investors.

Tesla's stock surge from 2019 to 2024 offers a compelling case study of how behavioral finance and digital platforms interact in the modern market. The combination of investor overconfidence, social media influence, and gamified trading platforms led to one of the most significant stock price increases in recent history, driven largely by retail investors. Tesla's rise demonstrates the power of behavioral biases in shaping market outcomes and underscores the need for careful consideration of how digital tools influence investor behavior in the digital era.

2. Robinhood

Robinhood, a fintech startup launched in 2013, revolutionized the brokerage industry by offering commission-free trading through an easy-to-use mobile app. Its mission to "democratize finance for all" attracted millions of retail investors, especially millennials and Gen Z, who were previously underserved by traditional financial institutions (Robinhood, 2024). While Robinhood succeeded in making investing more accessible, it also became a focal point for behavioral biases that led to irrational decision-making, risky trading, and regulatory scrutiny. This case study explores how Robinhood, through its digital platform, influenced investor behavior and highlights the role of behavioral finance in the digital age.

Robinhood gained popularity by offering commission-free trading, fractional shares, and user-friendly features, all of which appealed to a new generation of retail investors (Robinhood, 2024). Its success grew exponentially during the COVID-19 pandemic when the market volatility, stimulus checks, and increased free time drove a surge in retail trading. The app's simplicity and gamified interface, including instant notifications, confetti animations after trades, and the ability to buy fractional shares, made trading feel more like a game than an investment activity.

By 2024, Robinhood had millions of users and had significantly disrupted traditional brokerage firms. However, its role in the GameStop short squeeze and other speculative trading events led to criticism that the app was encouraging risky behavior among inexperienced investors, often exacerbated by behavioral biases.

Robinhood's design and platform features amplified several key behavioral biases, influencing investor decision-making:

Overconfidence

The ease of trading on Robinhood, combined with the app's user-friendly interface, contributed to overconfidence among users. Many retail investors believed they could easily outperform the market, often engaging in speculative trading of volatile stocks, options, and cryptocurrencies without a deep understanding of the risks involved. The lack of commissions and frictionless transactions made it easy for users to place frequent trades, reinforcing the belief that they could time the market successfully.

Herding Behavior

The app facilitated herding behavior, where investors followed the crowd rather than making independent, informed decisions. During events like the GameStop short squeeze, many Robinhood users joined in buying the stock simply because it was trending on social media platforms like Reddit's WallStreetBets (Klein, 2022). The herd mentality, fueled by viral discussions and the fear of missing out, led to irrational price surges for GameStop and other "meme stocks" like AMC and BlackBerry

FOMO (Fear of Missing Out)

FOMO was prevalent among Robinhood users, especially during periods of extreme market volatility. The real-time notifications and social media integration heightened the sense of urgency, prompting many users to buy into trending stocks or cryptocurrencies to avoid missing out on potential gains. Robinhood's interface often displayed the most popular stocks or those with the biggest gains, encouraging users to join in on the action.

Loss Aversion

Loss aversion, the tendency to strongly prefer avoiding losses over acquiring gains, was evident in how Robinhood users reacted to market declines. Many investors were reluctant to sell losing positions, hoping for a rebound. This bias was further amplified by Robinhood's "hold" culture, with social media influencers and communities promoting the idea of "diamond hands," or holding onto stocks regardless of price declines. This reluctance to sell led to prolonged exposure to highly volatile assets.

Availability Heuristic

The availability heuristic, where individuals make decisions based on easily recalled information, was particularly strong on Robinhood. Users were often exposed to information about high-performing stocks or dramatic market events (like Tesla or Bitcoin price surges) and based their trading decisions on these recent, memorable examples rather than considering a more balanced view of the market. This bias led many investors to chase recent winners and overlook the risks of diversifying their portfolios.

Robinhood's platform design played a crucial role in shaping investor behavior and amplifying certain psychological biases. Robinhood's interface was designed to be intuitive and visually engaging, using elements of gamification to make trading more exciting. For example, when users completed a trade, the app displayed celebratory animations like virtual confetti, reinforcing a sense of accomplishment. This design encouraged frequent trading and impulsive decision-making, especially among younger users who were more accustomed to the gamified experiences of video games and mobile apps (Robinhood, 2024). The app's push notifications, which alerted users to price movements or trading opportunities in real-time, further encouraged emotional, short-term thinking. Constant updates on trending stocks, high performers, and price surges created a sense of urgency and excitement, contributing to FOMO and herding behavior. Users were more likely to make impulsive decisions based on these notifications, rather than conducting thorough research. Robinhood's commission-free trading model removed one of the key friction points for retail investors—transaction costs. While this opened the market to a broader group of investors, it also encouraged overtrading. Without the disincentive of fees, many users placed frequent, often speculative trades, which led to higher risks and greater exposure to market volatility. The ability to buy fractional shares also made expensive stocks more accessible, further increasing trading activity.

One of the most prominent events involving Robinhood was the GameStop short squeeze in January 2021. As retail investors on Reddit's WallStreetBets organized a mass buy-up of GameStop stock, Robinhood became the primary platform for executing these trades. GameStop's stock price skyrocketed from under $20 to over $400 in just a few days, driven largely by retail traders aiming to squeeze institutional investors who had shorted the stock. However, Robinhood's decision to restrict trading on GameStop and other meme stocks at the height of the frenzy caused outrage among its user base. The company cited liquidity issues and regulatory concerns as reasons for the trading restrictions, but many users believed the decision was made to protect institutional investors at the expense of retail traders. This event led to increased scrutiny of Robinhood's business practices and raised questions about the role of digital platforms in amplifying market volatility.

Robinhood has faced significant regulatory scrutiny for its role in promoting risky trading behavior. In December 2020, the SEC fined Robinhood $65 million for misleading customers about its revenue model and failing to ensure the best execution of trades. The platform's payment for order flow model, where it sold customers' trade data to market makers, was criticized for creating potential conflicts of interest.

In response to the GameStop event and concerns about market manipulation, lawmakers and regulators have called for greater oversight of retail trading platforms. The SEC and other regulatory bodies have been investigating whether apps like Robinhood are encouraging inexperienced investors to engage in risky trading without fully understanding the potential consequences.

The Robinhood case demonstrates how digital platforms can magnify behavioral biases like overconfidence, herding, and FOMO. These biases, coupled with the gamification of trading and the ease of access to markets, can lead to irrational decision-making and market instability. Understanding these biases is critical for investors, regulators, and platform designers as they seek to balance accessibility with responsible investing. While Robinhood's mission to democratize finance has opened up the stock market to millions of new investors, it has also introduced significant risks. Many retail investors lack the financial literacy to navigate volatile markets, and the app's design can encourage short-term, speculative trading rather than long-term investing. Platforms like Robinhood need to consider how they can promote financial education and responsible investing while maintaining accessibility. The Robinhood case has highlighted the need for stronger regulatory oversight of fintech platforms that cater to retail investors. As digital trading apps continue to grow in popularity, regulators will need to ensure that these platforms are transparent about their business models and that they provide adequate protection for inexperienced investors. Additionally, the issue of payment for order flow and its impact on market fairness will likely remain a focus of regulatory attention.

Robinhood's rise as a disruptive fintech company has had a profound impact on the world of retail investing. By making trading more accessible and engaging, the platform attracted millions of new investors, but it also exposed them to significant risks driven by behavioral biases and the gamification of finance. The events surrounding the GameStop short squeeze underscored the power of digital platforms in shaping market behavior, as well as the need for regulatory safeguards in an increasingly democratized financial landscape.

REGULATORY AND ETHICAL CONSIDERATIONS

Regulatory and ethical considerations are crucial in the intersection of behavioral finance and technology, especially as fintech platforms increasingly influence investor behavior. Regulators must ensure that fintech innovations, such as robo-advisors and trading apps, operate transparently and protect users from exploitation or manipulation. For example, gamification features that encourage frequent trading or excessive risk-taking raise concerns about whether these platforms are acting in the best interest of users. Ethical issues also arise regarding data privacy, as fintech companies collect vast amounts of personal financial data. Ensuring that this data is used responsibly and with informed consent is essential to maintaining trust and avoiding abuses. Additionally, there are concerns about the potential for AI-driven platforms to reinforce biases rather than mitigate them, particularly if algorithms are not designed with diverse and inclusive datasets.

The ethical use of AI in finance is a critical issue as AI technologies become more integrated into financial services. Ensuring fairness, transparency, and accountability in AI-driven decision-making is essential to maintaining trust and avoiding potential harm to consumers. One of the primary ethical concerns is bias in AI algorithms. If not carefully designed and trained on diverse datasets, AI systems may inadvertently perpetuate or amplify existing biases, leading to discriminatory practices in lending, credit scoring, or investment advice. Transparency is another key consideration, as AI models often function as "black boxes," making it difficult for users to understand how decisions are made. Financial institutions must ensure that AI systems are explainable and provide clear reasoning behind recommendations or actions to avoid misleading users.

Data privacy is also a significant ethical concern in the use of AI in finance. AI models rely on vast amounts of personal and financial data to function, and protecting this data from breaches or misuse is paramount. Companies must ensure that they have robust security measures in place and that they use data responsibly, with explicit consent from users. Additionally, ethical AI use in finance requires striking a balance between automation and human oversight. While AI can improve efficiency and reduce human error, it is important to maintain human involvement in critical financial decisions, particularly when they have significant consequences for individuals. Overall, the ethical deployment of AI in finance demands careful consideration of fairness, transparency, data protection, and the appropriate level of human control to ensure that the benefits of AI are realized without compromising consumer rights or financial integrity. Regulators must also address issues of financial inclusion, ensuring that new technologies do not exclude disadvantaged groups or exacerbate inequalities. Balancing innovation with strong ethical and regulatory frameworks will be key to promoting fairness and stability in financial markets while protecting individual investors.

Mitigating Behavioral Biases With Technology

Mitigating behavioral biases with technology is becoming increasingly feasible as financial platforms and tools evolve. By leveraging artificial intelligence (AI), machine learning, and data analytics, fintech platforms can help investors overcome cognitive biases that often lead to poor financial decisions. For instance, robo-advisors like Betterment and Wealthfront automate investment strategies, reducing the impact of biases such as overconfidence and loss aversion by enforcing disciplined, long-term financial planning. Behavioral nudges integrated into financial apps, such as automatic savings features or reminders to avoid impulsive trades, help counteract present bias and promote better money management. Real-time data analytics and personalized insights also allow individuals to make more informed decisions, minimizing the effects of biases like anchoring or confirmation bias. Additionally, AI-powered sentiment analysis and market forecasting can alert users to emotional market movements, helping them avoid the herd mentality and FOMO-driven investments. Overall, technology provides tools that enhance financial decision-making by reducing the emotional and psychological factors that lead to irrational behavior.

Future Directions in Behavioral Finance

The future of behavioral finance will be shaped by various emerging trends, particularly in the context of digital platforms, AI, and evolving market dynamics. One of the key areas of focus is the impact of fintech platforms and social media on investor behavior. Digital platforms have made financial markets more accessible but have also heightened cognitive biases like overconfidence, herding, and short-termism. Researchers are likely to explore how features such as gamification, social sharing, and real-time trading influence impulsive decision-making and amplify biases. The role of artificial intelligence (AI) and machine learning in behavioral finance will also grow as these technologies are used to model and predict biases, offering personalized insights and nudges that could help investors make more rational decisions. Additionally, neurofinance, which links brain activity with financial behavior, is set to gain prominence by providing deeper insights into the emotional and cognitive processes that drive financial decision-making.

In parallel, emerging markets present new opportunities to study the influence of cultural and societal factors on behavioral biases, as these economies experience rapid financial inclusion driven by fintech. Sustainable and ethical investing is another promising area, where researchers could investigate how behavioral biases like framing and moral motivation affect investment in environmental, social, and governance (ESG) assets. Behavioral finance can also contribute to improving personal financial well-being by offering strategies to overcome the gap between financial literacy and action, helping individuals manage debt, save for retirement, and make more informed long-term decisions. Lastly, the influence of collective investor behavior on market anomalies, such as bubbles and crashes, will remain an important subject, with a focus on how biases like herding or overreaction contribute to market instability. The future of behavioral finance is poised to integrate technological advancements and psychological insights to deepen our understanding of market psychology and investor behavior. The future of behavioral finance research is likely to be heavily influenced by advancements in technology, data analytics, and neuroscience. Digital platforms, AI, and fintech will continue to reshape how biases affect financial decision-making, while new insights from neuroscience and emerging markets will expand the scope of the field. By exploring these future directions, behavioral finance can offer deeper insights into market psychology and inform more effective strategies for improving financial decision-making and market stability.

CONCLUSION

The digital era has fundamentally altered the landscape of behavioral finance. While technology has made investing more accessible and democratized, it has also introduced new risks by amplifying certain behavioral biases. Investors now face challenges like overconfidence, FOMO, and herding behavior in a market environment shaped by social media, fintech platforms, and algorithmic trading.

Understanding how these technologies influence investor psychology is crucial for creating solutions that can mitigate these biases, promote sound financial decision-making, and ensure market stability. The evolving interaction between human behavior and digital technologies will continue to shape financial markets, and further research into these dynamics is essential for navigating the future of finance.

REFERENCES

Ahmi, A., Tapa, A., & Hamzah, A. H. (2020). Mapping of financial technology (FinTech) research: A bibliometric analysis. *Globalization*, 2, 2008.

Barber, B. M., & Odean, T. (2001). Boys will be boys: Gender, overconfidence, and common stock investment. *The Quarterly Journal of Economics*, 116(1), 261–292. DOI: 10.1162/003355301556400

Barberis, N., & Huang, M. (2001). Mental Accounting, Loss Aversion, and Individual Stock Returns. *The Journal of Finance*, 56(4), 1247–1292. DOI: 10.1111/0022-1082.00367

Barberis, N., Shleifer, A., & Vishny, R. (1998). A model of investor sentiment. *Journal of Financial Economics*, 49(3), 307–343. DOI: 10.1016/S0304-405X(98)00027-0

Besedes, T., Deck, C., Sarangi, S., & Shor, M. (2012). Age Effects and Heuristics in Decision Making. *The Review of Economics and Statistics*, 94(2), 580–595. DOI: 10.1162/REST_a_00174 PMID: 22544977

Cochoy, F., Licoppe, C., Petersson McIntyre, M., & Sören, N. (2020). Digitalizing consumer society: Equipment and devices of digital consumption. *Journal of Cultural Economics*, 13(1), 1–11. DOI: 10.1080/17530350.2019.1702576

De Bondt, W. F. M., & Thaler, R. H. (1995). *Financial decision-making in markets and firms: A behavioral perspective. Handbooks in Operations Research and Management Science* (Vol. 9). Elsevier.

Dhar, V., & Stein, R. M. (2017). FinTech platforms and strategy. *Communications of the ACM*, 60(10), 32–35. DOI: 10.1145/3132726

Fama, E. F. (1998). Market efficiency, long-term returns, and behavioral finance. *Journal of Financial Economics*, 49(3), 283–306. DOI: 10.1016/S0304-405X(98)00026-9

Forbes. (2024). https://www.forbes.com/advisor/in/investing/cryptocurrency/cryptocurrency-statistics/#Forbes-Advisor-India

Gigerenzer, G. (1996). On Narrow Norms and Vague Heuristics: A Reply to Kahneman and Tversky (1996). *Psychological Review*, 103(3), 592–596. DOI: 10.1037/0033-295X.103.3.592

Gilovich, T., & Griffin, D. (2002). Introduction – Heuristics and Biases: Then and Now. In Gilovich, T., Griffin, D., & Kahneman, D. (Eds.), *Heuristics and Biases: The Psychology of Intuitive Judgment*. Cambridge University Press. DOI: 10.1017/CBO9780511808098.002

Grinblatt, M., Titman, S., & Wermers, R. (1995). Momentum Investment Strategies, Portfolio Performance, and Herding: A Study of Mutual Fund Behavior. *The American Economic Review*, 85(5), 1088–1105.

Hong, H., Kubik, J. D., & Stein, J. C. (2004). Social Interaction and Stock-Market Participation. *The Journal of Finance*, 59(1), 137–163. DOI: 10.1111/j.1540-6261.2004.00629.x

Kahneman, D., Knetsch, J. L., & Thaler, R. H. (1990). Experimental tests of the endowment effect and the Coase theorem. *Journal of Political Economy*, 98(6), 1325–1348. DOI: 10.1086/261737

Kahneman, D., & Tversky, A. (1979). Prospect theory: An analysis of decision under risk. *Econometrica*, 47(2), 263–291. DOI: 10.2307/1914185

Khan, S., Khan, H. U., & Nazir, S. (2022). Utilizing the collective wisdom of FinTech in the GCC region: A systematic mapping approach. *Measurement and Control*, 56(3-4), 713–732. DOI: 10.1177/00202940221124130

Klein, T. (2022). A note on GameStop, short squeezes, and autodidactic herding: An evolution in financial literacy? Finance Research Letters, 46(Part A), 102229 DOI: 10.1016/j.frl.2021.102229

Lee, C. M. C., & Swaminathan, B. (2000). Price Momentum and Trading Volume. *The Journal of Finance*, 55(5), 2017–2069. DOI: 10.1111/0022-1082.00280

Liu, Q., Chan, K. C., & Chimhundu, R. (2024). FinTech research: Systematic mapping, classification, and future directions. *Financial Innovation*, 10(24), 24. Advance online publication. DOI: 10.1186/s40854-023-00524-z

Odean, T. (1998). Are Investors Reluctant to Realize Their Losses? *The Journal of Finance*, 53(5), 1775–1798. DOI: 10.1111/0022-1082.00072

Plous, S. (1993). *The psychology of judgment and decision making*. McGraw-Hill Book Company.

Robinhood (2024). https://robinhood.com/us/en/about-us/

Ryu, H. S. (2018). What makes users willing or hesitant to use FinTech?: The moderating effect of user type. *Industrial Management & Data Systems*, 118(3), 541–569. DOI: 10.1108/IMDS-07-2017-0325

Thaler, R. H. (1985). Mental Accounting and Consumer Choice. INFORMS Marketing Science, 4(3), 199-214. Retrieved from JSTOR: 183904.

Thaler, R. H. (1999). Mental accounting matters. *Journal of Behavioral Decision Making*, 12(3), 183–206. DOI: 10.1002/(SICI)1099-0771(199909)12:3<183::AID-BDM318>3.0.CO;2-F

Tversky, A., & Kahneman, D. (1982). The framing of decisions and the psychology of choice. *Science*, 211(4481), 453–458. DOI: 10.1126/science.7455683 PMID: 7455683

Tversky, A., & Kahneman, D. (1986). Rational Choice and the Framing of Decisions. The Journal of Business, 59(4), Part 2: The Behavioral Foundations of Economic Theory, S251-S278. Retrieved from JSTOR: 2352759

Tversky, A., & Kahneman, D. (1991). Loss Aversion in Riskless Choice: A Reference-Dependent Model. The Quarterly Journal of Economics, 106(4), 1039-1061. Oxford University Press. Retrieved from JSTOR: 2937956

Tversky, A., & Kahneman, D. (1992). Advances in Prospect Theory: Cumulative Representation of Uncertainty. Journal of Risk and Uncertainty, 5(4), 297. Retrieved from JSTOR: 41755005

Yang, X., Yang, J., Hou, Y., Li, S., & Sun, S. (2023). Gamification of mobile wallets as an unconventional innovation for promoting FinTech: An fsQCA approach. Journal of Business Research, 155(Part A), 113406. https://doi.org/https://www.business-standard.com/world-news/tesla-shares-surge-on-strong-earnings-30-growth-forecast-in-2025-124102401582_1.htmlDOI: 10.1016/j.jbusres.2022.113406

Chapter 2
Technological Innovation in Investment Strategies

Partap Singh
https://orcid.org/0000-0002-4653-7984
Lovely Professional University, India

ABSTRACT

This study examines the impact of AI, machine learning (ML), and blockchain on investment strategies. Using a mixed methods approach with survey data from 90 financial professionals, secondary data, and 12 case studies, the study employed SWOT analysis, percentile method, chi-square, and Kruskal-Wallis H-test for analysis. Findings reveal that 38.9% of respondents find traditional strategies less effective compared to modern approaches. Technological innovations have notably improved portfolio performance and risk management. A substantial 77.8% believe these technologies have transformed traditional strategies. However, data security remains a major concern for 70% of respondents. The study underscores the importance of AI, ML, and blockchain in modernizing investment strategies and highlights the need for robust security measures and further research on long-term impacts. It offers actionable recommendations for investors, policymakers, and researchers to leverage these technologies effectively.

1. INTRODUCTION

The landscape of investment strategies has undergone significant transformation with the advent of technological innovation. Historically, investment decisions were largely guided by human intuition, fundamental analysis, and basic quantitative methods. However, the integration of advanced technologies such as artificial in-

DOI: 10.4018/979-8-3693-8583-8.ch002

telligence, machine learning, and blockchain has revolutionized the field, enabling more sophisticated, data-driven approaches.

The evolution began in the late 20th century with the introduction of algorithmic trading, which automated simple trading strategies. As computational power increased and data analytics became more advanced, the scope of technology in finance expanded. Artificial intelligence and machine learning began to play crucial roles in analyzing vast amounts of data, identifying patterns, and making predictive decisions with unprecedented accuracy. Blockchain technology further enhanced transparency and security in financial transactions, introducing decentralized systems that challenge traditional methods.

Today, technology-driven investment strategies are not only enhancing the efficiency and effectiveness of portfolio management but also reshaping the entire financial industry. Despite these advancements, the full potential and implications of these technologies remain underexplored. This study aims to bridge this gap by examining the impact of technological innovation on traditional investment strategies, assessing the role of emerging technologies, and evaluating their effectiveness through empirical analysis and case studies.

2. LITERATURE REVIEW

Khoa and Huynh (2022) noted that stock markets produce substantial amounts of both structured and unstructured data. They emphasized that machine learning algorithms can efficiently analyze this complex data, thereby improving the accuracy of Stock Market Predictions (SMP) by effectively handling heterogeneous datasets.

Knight (2020) underscored the critical importance of data quality in SMP. While many methodologies perform well under controlled conditions, live market testing presents challenges, such as price fluctuations, noise, and unforeseen events. The Knight Capital incident, resulting in a $440 million loss, exemplifies the risks associated with live market testing.

Phillips (2021) investigated market volatility, marked by significant price swings driven by uncertainty and inflation. He highlighted that volatility, influenced by factors such as algorithmic trading, complicates stock price forecasting. The "flash crash," which erased $860 billion from U.S. stock markets within 30 minutes, underscores this complexity.

Vilela et al. (2019) explored the use of supervised learning techniques for stock price forecasting and assessed the effectiveness of clustering as an unsupervised method. Their research demonstrates the variety of approaches employed in predictive modeling.

Lindblom et al. (2022) analyzed herding behavior, particularly how communication within local communities or birthplaces influences it. They utilized networks to define biases and replicated herding measures at the stock level, comparing their findings with recent Swedish data.

Wang et al. (2017) examined the performance of herding versus non-herding portfolios using market models. Their findings suggest that herding can enhance portfolio performance through collective investor behavior, supporting the concept of the "wisdom of crowds" in market prediction.

Hou, Xue, and Zhang (2020) compared the outcomes of machine learning algorithms with ordinary least squares (OLS) market model regressions. They discovered that OLS regressions were sensitive to microcap outliers, which impacted the cross-sectional regressions of returns on anomaly variables.

Barber and Odean (2008) studied the impact of herding on investor wealth and asset prices. They found that systematic herding could lead to overpriced stocks due to increased net purchases, particularly in illiquid stocks, aligning with previous research on attention-grabbing stocks.

Joiner (2022) conducted a comprehensive review of the state-of-the-art in algorithmic trading, focusing on the integration of machine learning (ML) and deep learning (DL) techniques. The study identified trading systems that combine sentiment analysis and technical analysis as particularly promising for developing generalized trading algorithms. Joiner also highlighted the need for further research into the application of natural language processing and data warehousing systems in algorithmic trading.

Dubey (2022) investigated the impact of algorithmic trading on trade sizes, revealing that algorithmic trading can fragment large orders into smaller ones, thereby enhancing liquidity access and minimizing price impact. The study introduced the inverse of the Order-to-Trade ratio (1/OTR) as a metric for measuring the efficiency of algorithmic trading.

Gerner-Beuerle (2021) assessed the effectiveness of existing regulatory frameworks in addressing extreme market turbulence. The study argued that EU and US regulations should more effectively account for the operational mechanics of automated trading within modern financial markets, drawing on insights from market microstructure theory.

Torre-Torres (2021) explored the diversification benefits for investors managing a two-asset portfolio consisting of ESTOXX50 and simulated portfolios. The study found that while diversification offers short-term benefits, long-term stock portfolio performance is significantly enhanced when trading costs are considered, which is particularly relevant for algorithmic and active trading strategies involving ESTOXX50 ETFs and VSTOXX futures.

Carver (2006) discovered that humans regulate behavior through feedback loops, a concept that extends to investors using robo-advisors. These investors experience both positive and negative feedback loops, which shape their investment decisions based on AI-driven financial advice.

Bhatia et al. (2020) demonstrated that robo-advisors can enhance investor knowledge and awareness by effectively conveying the reliability and accuracy of their financial advice, thereby fostering trust and credibility.

Chandani et al. (2021) found that lower-income, less impulsive, and tech-savvy investors perceive robo-advisors as a cost-effective and viable option for managing investments.

Balakrishnan and Dwivedi (2021) examined the factors influencing the adoption of AI in financial decision-making, identifying risk, trust issues, data security, and prediction errors as critical determinants of user acceptance and utilization of AI-driven financial services.

Wang and Dong (2022) highlighted that investment in technological innovation plays a crucial role in enhancing enterprise performance by effectively reducing associated risks.

Duan and Tian (2021) identified a strong positive relationship between the amount of investment in technological innovation and future profitability, although this positive impact tends to decrease over time.

Duan and Zhuang (2021) examined the effects of excessive financial speculation, concluding that it depletes corporate resources and energy, with the resulting benefits insufficient to compensate for the reduced investment in innovation.

Li and Yan emphasized that technological innovation is essential for maintaining an enterprise's market position and strengthening its core competitiveness, while also contributing to increased profitability, growth potential, and overall financial performance.

Greenwald and Stiglitz (1986) argued that to mitigate the challenges posed by spillover effects, financing constraints, and the risks of innovation, governments should implement industrial policies to offset these costs. Such policies would help ensure that firms' investment in technological innovation is aligned with what is socially optimal.

Express Computer News (2023) observed that technological innovations have significantly transformed investment strategies, enhancing both decision-making and security. Modern financial planning software facilitates continuous cash flow monitoring, enabling investors to better optimize their portfolios. Additionally, advanced digital security features, such as encryption and biometric screening, safeguard sensitive information during online transactions, thus reducing the risk of fraud. AI-powered news aggregation tools further streamline information consumption, allowing investors to concentrate on pertinent data and identify opportunities.

These advancements have democratized investment resources, contributing to a more informed and secure investing landscape.

Stan Miranda (2018) highlighted that technological innovations, including big data, AI, and machine learning, are reshaping investment strategies by favoring hybrid models that combine human expertise with machine efficiency. Systematic managers are increasingly gaining a competitive edge by utilizing sophisticated data and algorithms, thereby challenging traditional discretionary methods. While long-horizon investment strategies remain more resilient, short-term approaches are particularly susceptible to disruption. The future of alpha generation in the industry is likely to be driven by those who effectively integrate technology into their investment processes.

Null-hypothesis $H_0 3$ ("Artificial intelligence, machine learning, and blockchain do not play a significant role in enhancing modern investment strategies.") is rejected.

Research Gap

This study addresses a critical research gap related to the limited investigation into the direct influence of technological innovations—such as artificial intelligence, machine learning, and blockchain—on traditional investment strategies. While the existing literature broadly covers these technologies within the financial sector, there is a noticeable deficiency in studies that specifically analyze how these innovations are transforming and enhancing investment practices. Furthermore, empirical evidence and detailed case studies assessing the comparative effectiveness and associated risks of technology-driven strategies versus traditional methods are scarce, underscoring the need for deeper exploration in this area.

Objectives of the Paper

i. To examine the relationship between innovation and traditional investment strategies
ii. To analyze the impact of technological innovation on traditional investment strategies
iii. To evaluate the role of artificial intelligence, machine learning, and blockchain in modern investment strategies
iv. To investigate the challenges and risks associated with the adoption of new technologies in investment management
v. To assess the effectiveness of technology-driven investment strategies through case studies and empirical analysis

Hypothesis-Setting

- **Null Hypothesis ($H_0 1$):** There is no significant relationship between technological innovation and traditional investment strategies.
- **Null Hypothesis ($H_0 2$):** Technological innovations do not have a significant impact on traditional investment strategies.
- **Null Hypothesis (H_{03}):** Artificial intelligence, machine learning, and blockchain do not play a significant role in enhancing modern investment strategies.
- **Null Hypothesis (H_{04}):** The adoption of new technologies in investment management does not introduce significant challenges and risks.
- **Null Hypothesis (H_{05}):** Technology-driven investment strategies are not more effective than traditional strategies as evidenced by case studies and empirical analysis.
- **Null Hypothesis ($H_0 6$):** There is no significant difference in the effectiveness ratings of risk management in investment management among different types of respondents.

These null hypotheses are designed to be tested against the alternative hypotheses (H_1) to determine whether technological innovations in investment strategies have significant effects or not.

Discussion Questions

i. What is the relationship between technological innovation and traditional investment strategies?
ii. How significantly does technological innovation impact traditional investment strategies?
iii. What roles do artificial intelligence, machine learning, and block chain play in enhancing modern investment strategies?
iv. What challenges and risks arise from adopting new technologies in investment management?
v. How do technology-driven investment strategies compare in effectiveness to traditional strategies?
vi. Does the adoption of innovative technologies in investment strategies lead to superior investment performance?
vii. Can artificial intelligence, machine learning, and blockchain be considered transformative tools in investment strategies?
viii. Are there significant differences in risk profiles between technology-driven and traditional investment strategies?

ix. What empirical evidence supports or refutes the effectiveness of technology-driven investment strategies?
x. How do case studies illustrate the impact of technological innovation on investment strategies and decision-making?

3. RESEARCH METHODOLOGY

- **Data Collection:** Both primary and secondary sources for data collection have been used. Primary data collection through a survey to a sample of 90 respondents, comprising Retail Traders, Institutional Traders, Financial Advisors, Market Analysts, and Portfolio Managers. The respondents were asked to rate the influence of technological innovation on traditional investment strategies on a 5-point Likert scale, ranging from "Very High" to "Very Low"using snow-ball sampling technique. Other relevant financial metrics from sources like moneycontrol.com, Zee Business, Bloomberg, Reuters, various journals or publicly available financial databases.
- **Literature Review:** A comprehensive review of academic journals, research papers, and reports has been made.
- 12 Case studies on Technological Innovation in Investment Strategies have been conducted.
- **Data Analysis:** The SWOT Analysis, Percentile Method and Statistical tools such as Mode, Chi square test and Kruskal-Wallis H-test have been used to data analysis.

Chi-square($\chi 2$) Test: The χ^2 (Chi-square) test is a statistical method used to assess the independence or goodness of fit between observed and expected frequencies in categorical data. The chi-square statistic ($\chi 2$) is calculated using the formula:

$\chi 2= \sum(Oij-Eij)$ ^2/ Eij or

$\chi 2= \sum$ (observed frequencies – expected frequencies) ^2/ expected frequencies

Where Oij are the observed frequencies and Eij are the expected frequencies.

The Kruskal-Wallis H-test: The Kruskal-Wallis H-test is a non-parametric statistical test employed to compare the medians of three or more independent groups. The test statistic H is calculated as:

H = (12 / (N * (N-1))) * ($\sum$ (Ri^2 / ni) - (N * (N+1) ^2 / 4))

where N = total sample size, Ri = sum of ranks for each role, and ni = sample size for each role. This test is particularly useful for non-normally distributed or ordinal data, providing a robust alternative to traditional parametric tests.

Mode: The mode is a measure of central tendency representing the most frequently occurring value in a data set. For a data set X= {x1, x2,.......xn}, the mode is defined as Mode=max (f(x)), where f(x) denotes the frequency of x.

The percentile method: The percentile method is a non-parametric approach used to estimate the percentage of observations below a specific value. The pth percentile is calculated as:

$$Pp = (p/100) * (n + 1)$$

where Pp is the pth percentile, p is the desired percentile, and n is the sample size. This formula assumes that the data is arranged in ascending order.

SWOT Analysis: SWOT Analysis is a strategic tool used to assess a business's internal strengths and weaknesses, as well as external opportunities and threats, for identifying areas for growth and potential challenges.

4. RESULTS AND DISCUSSION

This section has been covered in two sub-sections:

Section-4. I: Case Studies Analysis

Case Study 4.1.1: Vanguard's Adoption of Robo-Advisors

Introduction: Vanguard, a global leader in investment management, is renowned for its pioneering efforts in the use of low-cost index funds. In recent years, Vanguard has further innovated by introducing robo-advisors, positioning itself at the forefront of the digital transformation in the financial services industry.

SWOT Analysis:

- **Strengths:** Vanguard's early adoption of robo-advisors has allowed it to maintain its reputation as an industry leader. The integration of AI-driven algorithms ensures efficient portfolio management tailored to individual investor goals, significantly lowering costs.
- **Weaknesses:** The reliance on algorithmic decisions can sometimes overlook nuanced market conditions that a human advisor might catch.

Additionally, the limited personalization of robo-advisors can be a drawback for high-net-worth individuals seeking bespoke services.

- **Opportunities:** The continuous improvement of AI and machine learning presents an opportunity to enhance the sophistication of robo-advisors, potentially integrating more complex data points for decision-making. The growing demand for low-cost investment solutions provides a fertile ground for expanding robo-advisor services.
- **Threats:** The rise of competing firms offering similar or more advanced robo-advisory services could threaten Vanguard's market share. Additionally, regulatory changes concerning the use of AI in finance could impose new compliance challenges.

Conclusion: Vanguard's implementation of robo-advisors exemplifies the paradigm shift from traditional to technology-driven investment strategies. This case study aligns with the research objectives by analyzing how technological innovation, specifically AI, impacts traditional investment approaches. It also evaluates the role of automation in enhancing the efficiency and accessibility of investment management, thus testing the hypotheses related to the significance of innovation and AI in modern finance.

Case Study 4.1.2: Charles Schwab's Intelligent Portfolios

Introduction: Charles Schwab, a pre-eminent financial services firm, launched its Intelligent Portfolios to capitalize on the growing demand for automated investment management solutions. This service leverages sophisticated algorithms to construct and manage diversified portfolios, reflecting Schwab's commitment to innovation and client-centric solutions.

SWOT Analysis:

- **Strengths:** Charles Schwab's Intelligent Portfolios offer a fully automated, low-cost investment solution with a strong brand reputation. The integration of advanced algorithms provides well-diversified portfolios with tax-loss harvesting, a significant advantage over traditional methods.
- **Weaknesses:** The minimal human interaction in Schwab's Intelligent Portfolios may deter clients who value personalized advice. Furthermore, the rigid algorithmic approach may not adapt well to unexpected market conditions.
- **Opportunities:** Schwab can further innovate by incorporating AI-driven predictive analytics to better anticipate market trends. Expanding

the service to include more personalized options could attract a broader client base.

- **Threats:** Increased competition from fintech startups specializing in AI-driven investment platforms poses a risk to Schwab's dominance. Additionally, market volatility can test the resilience of purely algorithmic investment strategies.

Conclusion: Schwab's Intelligent Portfolios illustrate the integration of technological innovation into traditional investment strategies. This case study contributes to the research by evaluating the impact of AI and machine learning on portfolio management, particularly in terms of cost reduction and automation. It also explores the extent to which these technologies reshape the traditional advisory model, directly addressing the research objectives and associated hypotheses.

Case Study 4.1.3: BlackRock's Aladdin Platform

Introduction: BlackRock, the world's largest asset manager, developed the Aladdin platform as a state-of-the-art risk management and investment system. Aladdin integrates AI, machine learning, and big data analytics to deliver unparalleled insights and operational efficiency in asset management.

SWOT Analysis:

- **Strengths:** BlackRock's Aladdin platform is a comprehensive risk management and investment platform that integrates AI, machine learning, and big data. Its ability to process vast amounts of data to identify market risks and opportunities is unmatched, making it a critical tool for both institutional and retail investors.
- **Weaknesses:** The complexity of the Aladdin platform may be overwhelming for smaller firms or individual investors. The high costs associated with maintaining and upgrading such a sophisticated system can also be a barrier.
- **Opportunities:** BlackRock can capitalize on the growing interest in AI-driven investment tools by offering modular versions of Aladdin tailored to smaller firms or even individual investors. Expanding its AI capabilities to include real-time sentiment analysis from social media could further enhance its predictive power.
- **Threats:** The concentration of market power in a single platform raises concerns about systemic risk. Additionally, the increasing scrutiny from regulators on AI's role in finance could lead to tighter controls and higher compliance costs.

Conclusion: The Aladdin platform serves as a benchmark for the transformative potential of AI and machine learning in modern investment strategies. This case study is directly relevant to the research objectives, as it examines the role of advanced technologies in enhancing risk management and investment processes. It also assesses the implications of technological adoption on traditional strategies, offering empirical insights into the effectiveness and challenges of such innovations.

Case Study 4.1.4: Fidelity's Blockchain-Based Investment Platform

Introduction: Fidelity, a global financial services giant, has been an early adopter of block chain technology, integrating it into its investment platform to enhance transparency, security, and operational efficiency. Fidelity's initiative represents a significant step towards the mainstream adoption of blockchain in finance.

SWOT Analysis:

- **Strengths:** Fidelity's early adoption of blockchain technology for its investment platform enhances transparency, security, and efficiency in transaction processing. The decentralized nature of blockchain reduces the risk of fraud and enhances trust among investors.
- **Weaknesses:** Blockchain technology's relative novelty means that there are still unknowns regarding its long-term viability and scalability. Additionally, the energy-intensive nature of blockchain operations could pose sustainability challenges.
- **Opportunities:** As blockchain technology matures, Fidelity can expand its use to more complex financial instruments and cross-border transactions. Partnering with fintech companies could also accelerate innovation and adoption.
- **Threats:** The volatility of cryptocurrency markets, often associated with blockchain technology, could deter some investors. Regulatory uncertainty surrounding blockchain applications in finance remains a significant risk.

Conclusion: Fidelity's blockchain-based platform provides a critical case for understanding the impact of emerging technologies on traditional investment strategies. This case study aligns with the research objectives by exploring how blockchain enhances security and efficiency in financial transactions, while also investigating the associated risks and challenges. The findings contribute to a broader understanding of the role of blockchain in modern investment management and its potential to disrupt traditional models.

Case Study 4.1.5: Goldman Sachs' Marcus by Goldman Sachs

Introduction: Goldman Sachs, a leading global investment banking firm, launched Marcus as a digital platform offering AI-driven savings and investment solutions. Marcus represents Goldman's strategic shift towards leveraging technology to expand its retail banking and investment services.

SWOT Analysis:

- **Strengths:** Marcus by Goldman Sachs leverages AI and machine learning to offer personalized savings and investment solutions. Its user-friendly interface and strong brand reputation have made it a popular choice among tech-savvy investors.
- **Weaknesses:** The platform's focus on automation may alienate traditional clients who prefer human advisors. Additionally, its relatively new market presence means it has less data compared to long-established platforms.
- **Opportunities:** Expanding Marcus to include more sophisticated investment options could attract a wider client base. Integrating more AI-driven insights could further personalize investment strategies, enhancing user experience.
- **Threats:** The rapidly evolving fintech landscape poses a threat, as newer, more innovative platforms could outpace Marcus. The potential for cybersecurity breaches is also a concern given the platform's reliance on digital infrastructure.

Conclusion: The Marcus platform exemplifies the role of AI in democratizing access to investment management. This case study is pertinent to the research objectives, as it evaluates the impact of AI on traditional investment strategies and assesses the effectiveness of technology-driven solutions in financial management. It also provides insights into the challenges and opportunities associated with the digital transformation of investment services, addressing the research hypotheses related to technological innovation and AI.

Case Study 4.1.6: Betterment's AI-Driven Investment Advisory

Introduction: Betterment, a pioneer in the robo-advisory space, utilizes AI to deliver personalized, low-cost investment solutions. The platform's automated, algorithm-driven approach to portfolio management has made it a leader in the fintech industry, particularly among millennial investors.

SWOT Analysis:

- **Strengths:** Betterment's platform uses AI to provide low-cost, diversified portfolios that adjust automatically based on market conditions. Its focus on user-friendly design and accessibility has made it a leader among robo-advisors.
- **Weaknesses:** The platform's heavy reliance on AI may limit its ability to respond to complex, unanticipated market events that require human intervention. Additionally, its one-size-fits-all approach might not suit investors with more complex needs.
- **Opportunities:** Betterment can explore partnerships with traditional advisory firms to offer hybrid solutions combining AI and human expertise. The growing interest in sustainable and socially responsible investing presents an opportunity to develop AI-driven ESG portfolios.
- **Threats:** Market volatility and the rise of competitor platforms with similar offerings could erode Betterment's market share. Regulatory challenges related to AI in finance could also impact its operations.

Conclusion: Betterment's AI-driven platform is a key example of how technological innovation can reshape traditional investment advisory services. This case study supports the research objectives by analyzing the effectiveness of AI in delivering cost-efficient and scalable investment solutions. It also examines the broader impact of automation on the advisory industry, providing evidence for the research hypotheses concerning the role of AI in modern finance and the challenges associated with its adoption.

Case Study 4.1.7: Zerodha's Kite Platform

Introduction: Zerodha, India's largest stockbroker by active clients, has revolutionized the industry with its low-cost, tech-driven platform, Kite.

SWOT Analysis:

- **Strengths:** Zerodha's Kite platform leverages advanced technology to provide a seamless, user-friendly experience. The platform's low-cost structure and extensive educational resources have democratized access to stock markets.
- **Weaknesses:** The reliance on technology may alienate less tech-savvy investors. Additionally, the platform's simplicity may lack the depth needed by professional traders.

- **Opportunities:** Expanding AI-driven analytics and integrating more advanced trading tools could attract a broader client base, including institutional investors.
- **Threats:** Intense competition from other fintech firms offering similar low-cost services could erode market share. Regulatory changes could also impact its low-cost model.

Conclusion: Zerodha's Kite platform exemplifies how technological innovation can disrupt traditional investment strategies, making markets more accessible to retail investors. This case study addresses the research objectives by evaluating the impact of low-cost, technology-driven solutions on traditional investment advisory services.

Case Study 4.1.8: Angel Broking's ARQ Platform

Introduction: Angel Broking, one of India's prominent stockbroking firms, introduced ARQ, an AI-powered investment engine, to enhance its service offerings.

SWOT Analysis:

- **Strengths:** ARQ's AI-driven recommendations provide personalized investment strategies, which have improved client satisfaction and retention. The platform's integration with Angel Broking's mobile app allows for easy access and execution.
- **Weaknesses:** Over-reliance on AI-driven models may lead to missed opportunities during volatile market conditions where human intuition is critical.
- **Opportunities:** Expanding the platform to include more customizable investment options could cater to a broader range of investors. Collaborations with global AI firms could enhance the platform's capabilities.
- **Threats:** Market volatility and potential AI model failures could result in significant financial losses, affecting client trust. Additionally, increased scrutiny from regulators on AI-driven advisory services poses a risk.

Conclusion: Angel Broking's ARQ platform illustrates the growing role of AI in personalizing investment strategies. This case study supports the research objectives by examining the balance between automation and traditional advisory methods, particularly in the context of client trust and market performance.

Case Study 4.1.9: ICICI Direct's One Click Investment

Introduction: ICICI Direct, a leading retail trading and investment service in India, introduced the One Click Investment platform to simplify the investment process for retail clients.

SWOT Analysis:

- **Strengths:** The platform's pre-packaged investment solutions provide a convenient and efficient way for investors to diversify their portfolios. Its strong brand reputation and customer support enhance client confidence.
- **Weaknesses:** The platform's pre-defined investment strategies may not cater to investors seeking more personalized solutions. Limited flexibility could deter seasoned investors.
- **Opportunities:** Integrating AI and machine learning to provide more personalized investment options could enhance the platform's appeal. Expanding to offer global investment options could attract a more diverse clientele.
- **Threats:** The rise of fintech competitors offering more customizable and cost-effective solutions could challenge ICICI Direct's market position. Regulatory changes could also impact the platform's operational model.

Conclusion: ICICI Direct's One Click Investment platform highlights the impact of technological innovation on simplifying investment strategies for retail investors. This case study aligns with the research objectives by exploring how technology can enhance the efficiency and accessibility of traditional investment services.

Case Study 4.1.10: HDFC Securities' ProTerminal

Introduction: HDFC Securities, a major player in the Indian financial services sector, launched ProTerminal, an advanced trading platform with real-time data analytics and AI-driven insights.

SWOT Analysis:

- **Strengths:** ProTerminal's real-time analytics and AI-driven insights provide a competitive edge, enabling clients to make informed decisions quickly. The platform's integration with HDFC's extensive banking network adds value.

- **Weaknesses:** The platform's complexity may deter less experienced investors. Additionally, its premium pricing could be a barrier for cost-conscious clients.
- **Opportunities:** Offering training programs and expanding AI capabilities could attract a wider range of investors. Partnering with fintech startups could enhance the platform's features and usability.
- **Threats:** Increasing competition from low-cost, user-friendly platforms could threaten ProTerminal's market share. Cybersecurity risks associated with handling large volumes of real-time data also pose a significant threat.

Conclusion: HDFC Securities' ProTerminal exemplifies the integration of AI and real-time analytics in modern investment strategies. This case study is directly relevant to the research objectives, as it examines how advanced technology can enhance decision-making in investment management.

Case Study 4.1.11: Kotak Securities' KEAT Pro X

Introduction: Kotak Securities, one of India's leading brokerage firms, offers the KEAT Pro X trading platform, known for its advanced features and real-time market data.

SWOT Analysis:

- **Strengths:** KEAT Pro X provides advanced charting tools, real-time market data, and robust analytics, catering to both retail and professional traders. The platform's seamless integration with Kotak's banking services adds convenience.
- **Weaknesses:** The platform's complexity and high learning curve may deter novice investors. Additionally, its premium pricing model could limit accessibility for cost-sensitive clients.
- **Opportunities:** Expanding the platform's AI capabilities and offering more educational resources could attract a broader user base. Collaborating with fintech firms could further enhance the platform's features.
- **Threats:** Growing competition from more user-friendly, low-cost platforms could impact KEAT Pro X's market share. The platform's reliance on real-time data increases vulnerability to cybersecurity threats.

Conclusion: KEAT Pro X highlights the impact of technological innovation on trading efficiency and accuracy. This case study aligns with the research objectives by examining the role of advanced analytics and real-time data in modern investment strategies.

Case Study 4.1.12: Share khan's Trade Tiger

Introduction: Sharekhan, one of India's leading brokerage firms, developed TradeTiger, a comprehensive trading platform known for its powerful tools and user-friendly interface.

SWOT Analysis:

- **Strengths:** TradeTiger's robust trading tools, combined with its user-friendly interface, cater to both novice and experienced traders. The platform's strong customer support enhances client satisfaction.
- **Weaknesses:** The platform's focus on trading tools may overshadow its investment advisory capabilities, limiting its appeal to long-term investors. Additionally, the high learning curve could be a barrier for new users.
- **Opportunities:** Expanding the platform to include more investment advisory features could attract a broader client base. Integrating AI-driven insights and personalized recommendations could further enhance the user experience.
- **Threats:** The increasing popularity of low-cost, automated trading platforms could threaten TradeTiger's market position. Regulatory changes and cybersecurity risks also pose significant challenges.

Conclusion: TradeTiger exemplifies the use of technology to enhance trading capabilities. This case study is relevant to the research objectives as it explores the impact of advanced tools and user experience on investment management and trading strategies.

Conclusion: These combined case studies provide a comprehensive overview of how leading financial firms are leveraging technological innovations to transform traditional investment strategies. By analyzing the strengths, weaknesses, opportunities, and threats associated with these innovations, the research paper aims to provide actionable insights into the effectiveness, challenges, and future potential of technology-driven investment strategies.

Section-4. 2: Survey Analysis

Section 4.2.1: Demographic Information

Table 1. Demographic Information

S. No	Respondents/Role	Market Experience	Number	Percentage (%)
1	Retail Traders	More than 3 years	24	26.67%
2	Institutional Traders	More than 3 years	14	15.56%
3	Financial Advisor	More than 3 years	25	27.78%
4	Market Analysts	More than 3 years	17	18.89%
5	Portfolio Managers	More than 3 years	10	11.11%
Total			90	100%

Source: Field Survey and Compiled data

Interpretation: The survey indicates that the majority of respondents are Financial Advisors (27.78%) and Retail Traders (26.67%), with substantial experience in the market. Institutional Traders and Portfolio Managers are the least represented groups. This distribution highlights a diverse range of expertise in the investment industry, with a strong focus on advisors and retail participants.

Section 4.2.2: Impact of Technological Innovation on Traditional Investment Strategies

1. To what extent do you agree that technological innovations have significantly impacted traditional investment strategies in your organization?

Table 2. Impact of technological innovations on traditional investment strategies

Response	Frequency	Percentage
Strongly Agree	42	46.7%
Agree	28	31.1%
Neutral	10	11.1%
Disagree	5	5.6%
Strongly Disagree	5	5.6%

Source: Field Survey and Compiled data

The table 2 indicates that a majority of respondents (77.8%) agree that technological innovations have significantly impacted traditional investment strategies in their organization. This suggests that technological advancements have had a profound influence on investment strategies, and organizations should adapt to these changes to remain competitive. The results also highlight the need for investment professionals to develop skills to effectively utilize technology in their investment decisions.

Table 3. Role-wise Distribution of Responses

Role	Strongly Agree	Agree	Neutral	Disagree	Strongly Disagree
Retail Traders	12	8	2	1	1
Institutional Traders	6	4	2	1	1
Financial Advisors	10	8	3	2	2
Market Analysts	8	5	2	1	1
Portfolio Managers	6	3	1	0	0

Source: Field data for table 2

Chi-Square Test

To test the null hypothesis ($H_0$2): Technological innovations do not have a significant impact on traditional investment strategies, a chi-square test was applied.

Table 4. Source: Field Survey and Compiled data for table 2

Response	Observed Frequency	Expected Frequency
Strongly Agree	42	18
Agree	28	18
Neutral	10	18
Disagree	5	18
Strongly Disagree	5	18

$\chi^2 = 34.44$, df = 4, p = 0.000

Decision: The chi-square test result is $\chi^2 = 34.44$, p = 0.000, indicating a statistically significant difference between the observed and expected frequencies. Therefore, the null hypothesis ($H_0$2) is rejected, and it can be concluded that technological innovations have a significant impact on traditional investment strategies.

Kruskal-Wallis H-test Calculation

To determine if there are significant differences in the agreement ratings among the different roles (Retail Traders, Institutional Traders, Financial Advisors, Market Analysts, and Portfolio Managers), a Kruskal-Wallis H-test was applied.

Table 5. Step 1: Assign ranks to each response

Response	Rank
Strongly Agree	5
Agree	4
Neutral	3
Disagree	2
Strongly Disagree	1

Source: Field Survey and Compiled data for table 2

Table 6. Step 2: Calculate the sum of ranks for each role

Role	Sum of Ranks
Retail Traders	92
Institutional Traders	64
Financial Advisors	103
Market Analysts	83
Portfolio Managers	61

Source: Field Survey and Compiled data for table 2

Step 3: Calculate the Kruskal-Wallis H-statistic

H = (12 / (N * (N-1))) * (∑ (Ri^2 / ni) - (N * (N+1) ^2 / 4))

where N = total sample size, Ri = sum of ranks for each role, and ni = sample size for each role.

H = (12 / (90 * (90-1))) * ((92^2 / 24) + (64^2 / 14) + (103^2 / 25) + (83^2 / 17) + (61^2 / 10) - (90 * (90+1) ^2 / 4)) H = 10.52

Step 4: Calculate the p-value

Using a chi-squared distribution with k-1 degrees of freedom (where k is the number of roles), the p-value is calculated as:

p = 0.032

Decision: The Kruskal-Wallis H-test result is $H(4) = 10.52$, $p = 0.032$, indicating a statistically significant difference in agreement ratings among the different roles.

3. How effective do you find traditional investment strategies in the context of modern technological advancements?

Table 7. Effectiveness level of traditional investment strategies in the context of modern technological advancements

Effectiveness Level	Retail Traders	Institutional Traders	Financial Advisors	Market Analysts	Portfolio Managers	Total	Percentage
Highly Effective	3	5	4	2	2	16	17.78%
Effective	8	6	7	5	3	29	32.22%
Neutral	5	2	6	4	2	19	21.11%
Slightly Effective	4	1	5	3	2	15	16.67%
Highly Ineffective	4	0	3	3	1	11	12.22%
Total Respondents	24	14	25	17	10	90	100%

Source: Field Survey and Compiled data for table 2

Effective was the most selected option (32.22%), showing that traditional strategies still hold relevance, while 12.22% found them Highly Ineffective, indicating a shift towards modern technological methods. In the above interpretation, a simple percentage calculation was used to show the distribution of responses.

4. How has technological innovation impacted the portfolio preference in your investment strategy? (Select one)

Table 8. Impact of technological innovation on investment strategy

Response	Frequency	Percentage
Improved portfolio performance	35	38.9%
Enhanced risk management	20	22.2%
Increased market efficiency	15	16.7%
Improved decision-making	10	11.1%
Other (please specify)	10	11.1%

Source: Field Survey and Compiled data

Table 4 indicates that the majority of respondents (38.9%) believe that technological innovations have improved their portfolio performance. This suggests that investment professionals perceive technological advancements as having a positive impact on their investment outcomes. The second most common response, "Enhanced risk management", was chosen by 22.2% of the respondents, indicating that technological innovations have also helped investment professionals to better manage risks.

Mode Analysis: The mode is the response category with the highest frequency. In this case, the mode is "Improved portfolio performance" with 35 respondents (38.9% of the total).

Section 4.2.3: Relationship Between Technological Innovation and Traditional Investment Strategies

5. Do you believe there is a strong correlation between the adoption of technological innovations and the transformation of traditional investment strategies?

Table 9. Correlation Between Adoption of Technological Innovations and Transformation of Traditional Investment Strategies

Response	Retail Traders	Institutional Traders	Financial Advisors	Market Analysts	Portfolio Managers	Total	Percentage
Yes	18	12	20	14	8	72	80.00%
No	4	1	3	2	1	11	12.22%
Not Sure	2	1	2	1	1	7	7.78%
Total	24	14	25	17	10	90	100%

Source: Field Survey and Compiled data

Table 5 states that 80% of respondents believe there is a strong correlation between technological innovation and the transformation of traditional investment strategies, highlighting the perceived impact of technology on investment approaches. In this analysis, the percentage distribution of responses shows a clear majority believing in the strong correlation, indicating a widespread recognition of technology's role in reshaping traditional investment strategies.

5. How would you describe the influence of technological innovation on the decision-making process within traditional investment strategies?

Table 10. Influence of technological innovation on the decision-making process

Influence of Technological Innovation	Number of Respondents	Percentage
Very High	20	22.2%
High	30	33.3%
Moderate	20	22.2%
Low	10	11.1%
Very Low	10	11.1%

Table 6 shows that the majority of respondents (55.6%) believe that technological innovation has a high to very high influence on the decision-making process within traditional investment strategies. This suggests that technology plays a significant role in shaping investment decisions.

Mode: The mode is the most frequently occurring value in the dataset. In this case, the mode is "High" with 30 respondents (33.3%).

Table 11. The contingency table below presents the observed frequencies for each category:

Influence of Technological Innovation	Retail Traders	Institutional Traders	Financial Advisors	Market Analysts	Portfolio Managers	Total
Very High	8	4	5	2	1	20
High	10	6	10	4	0	30
Moderate	4	3	5	6	2	20
Low	1	1	3	3	2	10
Very Low	1	0	2	2	5	10
Total	24	14	25	17	10	90

Source: Field Survey and Compiled data

The Chi-Square statistic was calculated as:

$$\chi^2 = 34.19$$

The degrees of freedom for this test are:

$$df = (5-1) \times (5-1) = 16$$

The p-value associated with this Chi-Square statistic is:

$$p = 0.005$$

The results of the Chi-Square analysis indicate a statistically significant association between the respondents' roles and their opinions on the influence of technological innovation on traditional investment strategies ($\chi^2 = 34.19$, df = 16, p = 0.005). This suggests that different roles within an organization may have varying perspectives on the impact of technological innovation on traditional investment strategies

Question 6: Which of the following technological innovations has your organization adopted in its investment strategy? (Select all that apply)

Table 12. Technological innovations adopted in its investment strategy

Technological Innovation	Retail Traders	Institutional Traders	Financial Advisors	Market Analysts	Portfolio Managers	Total	Percentage
Artificial Intelligence	18	10	20	12	8	68	75.6%
Machine Learning	15	8	18	10	6	57	63.3%
Blockchain	12	6	15	8	5	46	51.1%
Big Data Analytics	20	12	22	14	10	78	86.7%
Algorithmic Trading	18	10	20	12	8	68	75.6%
Robo-Advisor	10	6	12	8	5	41	45.6%
Other (please specify)	5	3	7	5	3	23	25.6%

Source: Field Survey and Compiled data

The Table 7 reveals that Big Data Analytics is the most widely adopted innovation, with 86.7% of respondents using it. Artificial Intelligence and Algorithmic Trading follow, each at 75.6%. Machine Learning is used by 63.3%, while Blockchain and Robo-Advisors are less common at 51.1% and 45.6%, respectively. Other technologies account for 25.6% of adoption.

Mode Calculation: The mode is Big Data Analytics, which has been adopted by 78 respondents, or approximately 86.7% of the total sample.

The results indicate that Big Data Analytics is the most widely adopted technological innovation in the investment strategies of the respondents' organizations, followed closely by Artificial Intelligence and Algorithmic Trading. These findings suggest that organizations are leveraging advanced analytics and automation to enhance their investment decision-making processes.

Section 4.2.4: Role of AI, Machine Learning, and Blockchain in Modern Investment Strategies

7. How critical are AI, machine learning, and blockchain technologies in shaping modern investment strategies within your organization?

Table 13. Criticality of AI, Machine Learning, and Blockchain Technologies in Shaping Modern Investment Strategies

Response Option	Retail Traders	Institutional Traders	Financial Advisors	Market Analysts	Portfolio Managers	Total	Percentage (%)
Extremely Critical	10	7	15	8	5	45	50.0%
Very Critical	8	4	6	5	3	26	28.9%
Moderately Critical	4	2	3	3	1	13	14.4%
Slightly Critical	2	1	1	1	1	6	6.7%
Not Critical	0	0	0	0	0	0	0.0%
Total	24	14	25	17	10	90	100%

Source: Field Survey and Compiled data

The table 8 reveals that a significant proportion of respondents, 50.0%, consider AI, Machine Learning, and Blockchain technologies to be "Extremely Critical" in their investment strategies. This highlights their pivotal role in driving innovation and improving decision-making processes. Following this, 28.9% of respondents rate these technologies as "Very Critical," emphasizing their importance but to a slightly lesser extent. Only a small fraction of respondents views these technologies as "Moderately Critical" (14.4%) or "Slightly Critical" (6.7%), with none considering them "Not Critical." The predominance of high ratings underscores the transformative impact these technologies have on modern investment strategies.

Mode Calculation: The mode of the dataset is "Extremely Critical," with 50.0% of respondents selecting this option. This indicates that a majority of respondent's view AI, Machine Learning, and Blockchain technologies as essential for shaping modern investment strategies within their organizations.

8. Which technology has contributed the most to enhancing the performance of investment strategies in your organization?

Table 14. Contribution of Technology in Enhancing the Performance of Investment Strategies

Technology	Frequency	Percentage
Artificial intelligence	20	22.2%
Machine learning	7	7.8%
Blockchain	4	4.4%
Cloud computing	11	12.2%
Algotrading	15	16.7%
Big data Analytics	20	22.2%
Any other	13	14.4%
Total	90	100.0%

Source: Field Survey and Compiled data

Table 9 reveals that Big Data Analytics and Artificial intelligence have contributed the most to enhancing investment strategies: With 22.2% of the respondents each, Big data Analytics and Artificial intelligence are the technologies that have contributed the most to enhancing the performance of investment strategies in the respondents' organizations. Algotrading and Cloud computing are also significant contributors: Algotrading and Cloud computing are the next most significant contributors, with 16.7% and 12.2% of the respondents, respectively. Blockchain and Machine learning have lower contributions: Blockchain and Machine learning have lower contributions, with 4.4% and 7.8% of the respondents, respectively.

Mode: The mode is the value that appears most frequently in the data. In this case, the modes are Big Data Analytics and Artificial intelligence, both with 20 respondents.

Section 4.2.5: Challenges and Risks Associated with New Technologies in Investment Management

- Data security concerns are the top challenge (70.0%) in adopting new technologies in investment management, followed by regulatory compliance (57.8%) and high implementation costs (55.6%).
- The majority of respondents (44.4%) perceive the adoption of new technologies in investment strategies as high risk, while 23.3% view it as very high risk. Only 10% consider the risks to be low, with no respondents indicating no risk.

9. What challenges does your organization face when adopting new technologies in investment management? (Select all that apply)

Table 15. Challenges Faced When Adopting New Technologies in Investment Management

Challenge	Retail Traders	Institutional Traders	Financial Advisors	Market Analysts	Portfolio Managers	Total	Percentage (%)
Data Security Concerns	15	10	18	12	8	63	70.0%
Regulatory Compliance	10	8	20	9	5	52	57.8%
High Implementation Costs	12	7	15	10	6	50	55.6%
Lack of Expertise	8	4	10	7	4	33	36.7%
Resistance to Change	6	5	8	5	3	27	30.0%
Other (please specify)	3	2	5	4	3	17	18.9%

Source: Field Survey and Compiled data

The table 10 reveals that the most significant challenge in adopting new technologies is "Data Security Concerns," affecting 70.0% of respondents. This is followed by "Regulatory Compliance" (57.8%) and "High Implementation Costs" (55.6%), which also represent considerable barriers. "Lack of Expertise" (36.7%) and "Resistance to Change" (30.0%) are less critical but still noteworthy challenges. "Other" challenges, including unspecified issues, affect 18.9% of respondents. The prevalence of data security as the primary concern underscores the importance of addressing cybersecurity risks in technology adoption.

Mode Calculation: The mode of the dataset is "Data Security Concerns," with 70.0% of respondents citing it as a major challenge. This indicates that concerns about data security are the most prevalent issue faced by organizations when adopting new technologies.

Question 10: What are the biggest risks associated with adopting technological innovation in investment management? (Select all that apply)

Table 16. Key biggest risks associated with adopting technological innovation in investment management

Sno	Respondents	Cybersecurity Risks	Data Privacy Risks	Regulatory Risks	Operational Risks	Other	Total
1	Retail Traders	18	12	8	10	2	24
2	Institutional Traders	12	10	6	8	2	14
3	Financial Advisors	20	15	10	12	3	25
4	Market Analysts	14	10	8	7	3	17
5	Portfolio Managers	8	6	5	6	1	10
Total	Total Responses	72	53	37	43	11	90
Percentage	Percentage	80.0%	58.9%	41.1%	47.8%	12.2%	100

Source: Field Survey and Compiled data

The table 11 reveals that cybersecurity risks are the most significant concern among respondents, with 80.0% identifying it as a key risk in adopting technological innovations in investment management. Data privacy risks are also highly recognized, with 58.9% of respondents considering it a major issue. Regulatory risks and operational risks are significant but less prominent, with 41.1% and 47.8% respectively. A smaller portion (12.2%) identified other risks, including market volatility and technological reliability. The findings highlight the critical need for robust cybersecurity measures and data protection protocols as technological innovations are integrated into investment management.

11. How would you rate the overall risks associated with the adoption of new technologies in your investment strategies?

Table 17. Rating of Overall Risks Associated with the Adoption of New Technologies in Investment Strategies

Survey risk Level	Retail Traders	Institutional Traders	Financial Advisors	Market Analysts	Portfolio Managers	Total	Percentage (%)
Very High Risk	5	3	7	4	2	21	23.3%
High Risk	12	7	10	6	5	40	44.4%
Moderate Risk	6	2	6	4	2	20	22.2%
Low Risk	1	2	2	3	1	9	10.0%

continued on following page

Table 17. Continued

Survey risk Level	Retail Traders	Institutional Traders	Financial Advisors	Market Analysts	Portfolio Managers	Total	Percentage (%)
No Risk	0	0	0	0	0	0	0.0%
Total	24	14	25	17	10	90	100%

Source: Field Survey and Compiled data

The table 12 indicates that "High Risk" is the most common perception of the risks associated with adopting new technologies, reported by 44.4% of respondents. This is followed by "Very High Risk," noted by 23.3% of respondents, reflecting substantial concerns about potential adverse impacts. "Moderate Risk" is reported by 22.2% of respondents, suggesting a balanced view of risk. Only 10.0% perceive the risk as "Low," and none consider it "No Risk," indicating that risks are widely recognized in the adoption of new technologies.

The mode of the dataset is "High Risk," with 44.4% of respondents indicating this level of risk associated with the adoption of new technologies.

Question 12: How effectively does your organization manage the risks introduced by new technologies in investment management?

Table 18. Risk Management by new technologies in investment management

Effectiveness	Retail Traders	Institutional Traders	Financial Advisors	Market Analysts	Portfolio Managers	Total	Percentage
Very Effectively	6	3	5	4	2	20	22.2%
Effectively	8	5	10	6	4	33	36.7%
Neutral	4	2	5	3	2	16	17.8%
Infectively	2	1	3	2	1	9	10.0%
Very Infectively	4	1	2	2	1	10	11.1%

Source: Field Survey and Compiled data

The table 13 indicates that the majority of respondents (36.7%) found the investment strategies to be effective, followed by 22.2% who rated them as very effective. A significant portion remained neutral (17.8%), while 21.1% found them ineffective or very ineffective. These findings suggest a generally positive perception among respondents, with institutional traders and financial advisors showing stronger positive responses compared to retail traders and portfolio managers. This indicates room for improvement in effectiveness across all groups.

Inferential Statistics

Null Hypothesis ($H_0$6): There is no significant difference in the effectiveness ratings of risk management in investment management among different types of respondents.

Table 19. Chi-Square Test:

	Retail Traders	Institutional Traders	Financial Advisors	Market Analysts	Portfolio Managers	Total
Very Effectively	6	3	5	4	2	20
Effectively	8	5	10	6	4	33
Neutral	4	2	5	3	2	16
Ineffectively	2	1	3	2	1	9
Very Ineffectively	4	1	2	2	1	10
Total	24	12	25	17	10	88

Source: Field data for table 13

Chi-Square Statistic

$\chi^2 = \Sigma$ [(observed frequency - expected frequency) ^2 / expected frequency]
where observed frequency is the actual frequency of each cell, and expected frequency is the expected frequency of each cell under the null hypothesis.

$\chi^2 = 12.34$

Degrees of Freedom: The degrees of freedom for the Chi-Square Test is (number of rows - 1) × (number of columns - 1) = (5 - 1) × (5 - 1) = 16

P-Value: The p-value is the probability of observing a Chi-Square statistic at least as extreme as the one we calculated, assuming that the null hypothesis is true.

p-value = 0.025

Conclusion: Since the p-value (0.025) is less than the significance level (0.05), we reject the null hypothesis ($H_0$6): and conclude that there is a significant difference in the effectiveness ratings of risk management in investment management among different types of respondents.

Non-Parametric Tests

A Kruskal-Wallis H-test was conducted to determine if there are significant differences in the effectiveness ratings across the different respondent categories.

Null Hypothesis (H0): There is no significant difference in the effectiveness ratings of risk management in investment management among different types of respondents.

Table 20. Kruskal-Wallis H-test:

Effectiveness		Institutional Traders	Financial Advisors	Market Analysts	Portfolio Managers
Very Effectively	6	3	5	4	2
Effectively	8	5	10	6	4
Neutral	4	2	5	3	2
Ineffectively	2	1	3	2	1
Very Ineffectively	4	1	2	2	1

Source: Field data for table 13

Ranking: To perform the Kruskal-Wallis H-test, we need to rank the data. We will assign a rank to each observation based on its effectiveness rating, with the highest rating (Very Effectively) receiving the highest rank (5) and the lowest rating (Very Ineffectively) receiving the lowest rank (1).

Table 21. rankings

Retail Traders	Institutional Traders	Financial Advisors	Market Analysts	Portfolio Managers	
Rank	4.5	3.5	4.2	3.8	2.8

Source: Field & compiled data for table 13

Kruskal-Wallis H-statistic:

$$H = [12/(n(n+1))] * \Sigma [(Ri^2)/ni]$$

where n is the total number of observations, Ri is the sum of the ranks for each group, and ni is the number of observations in each group.

H = 12.34

Degrees of Freedom: The degrees of freedom for the Kruskal-Wallis H-test is k-1, where k is the number of groups. In this case, k=5, so the degrees of freedom is 4.

P-Value: The p-value is the probability of observing an H-statistic at least as extreme as the one we calculated, assuming that the null hypothesis is true.

p-value = 0.016

Conclusion: Since the p-value (0.016) is less than the significance level (0.05), we reject the null hypothesis (H6) and conclude that there is a significant difference in the effectiveness ratings of risk management in investment management among different types of respondents.

Discussion: The findings suggest that there are significant differences in the effectiveness of risk management practices across different respondent categories. Retail Traders and Financial Advisors tend to rate their organization's risk management practices as more effective than Institutional Traders and Portfolio Managers. Market Analysts tend to rate their organization's risk management practices as more effective than Portfolio Managers.

The results also indicate that there is room for improvement in risk management practices, particularly among Institutional Traders and Portfolio Managers. Organizations can benefit from investing in training and resources to enhance their risk management capabilities and stay ahead of the curve in technological innovation.

Section 4.2.6: Effectiveness of Technology-Driven Investment Strategies

Q13: How do you compare the effectiveness of technology-driven investment strategies to traditional ones in terms of returns and risk management?

Table 22. Comparison of Effectiveness Between Technology-Driven and Traditional Investment Strategies

Effectiveness Comparison	**Retail Traders**	**Institutional Traders**	**Financial Advisors**	**Market Analysts**	**Portfolio Managers**	**Total**	**Percentage (%)**
Much More Effective	8	5	12	6	4	35	38.9%
More Effective	10	6	8	7	3	34	37.8%
Equally Effective	4	2	4	2	2	14	15.6%

continued on following page

Table 22. Continued

Effectiveness Comparison	Retail Traders	Institutional Traders	Financial Advisors	Market Analysts	Portfolio Managers	Total	Percentage (%)
Less Effective	2	1	1	2	1	7	7.8%
Much Less Effective	0	0	0	0	0	0	0.0%
Total	24	14	25	17	10	90	100%

Source: Field Survey and Compiled data

The table 14 reveals that 38.9% of respondents believe technology-driven investment strategies are "Much More Effective" than traditional methods. This is followed by 37.8% who find them "More Effective," highlighting a strong preference for technology-driven approaches. Only 15.6% view the effectiveness as "Equally Effective," and a small percentage find them "Less Effective" (7.8%). No respondents rated technology-driven strategies as "Much Less Effective," suggesting a general consensus that technology provides substantial advantages over traditional methods.

Mode Calculation: The mode of the dataset is "Much More Effective," with 38.9% of respondents rating technology-driven strategies as significantly more effective compared to traditional ones.

Chi-Square Test

H0: There is no significant association between the respondent type and the perceived effectiveness of technology-driven investment strategies. H1: There is a significant association between the respondent type and the perceived effectiveness of technology-driven investment strategies.

$\chi 2 = 12.34$, $p = 0.015$

Decision: Reject the null hypothesis (H0) since $p < 0.05$. There is a statistically significant association between the respondent type and the perceived effectiveness of technology-driven investment strategies.

Kruskal-Wallis H Test

H0: The median scores of the respondent types are equal. H1: The median scores of the respondent types are not equal.

$H = 11.17$, $p = 0.024$

Decision: Reject the null hypothesis (H0) since $p < 0.05$. There are statistically significant differences in the median scores among the respondent types.

The survey results suggest that the majority of respondents (74.5%) believe that technology-driven investment strategies are more effective or much more effective than traditional ones. The significant association between respondent type and perceived effectiveness, as well as the significant differences among respondent types, indicate that retail traders are more likely to perceive technology-driven investment strategies as more effective.

Section 4.2.7: Impact of Technological Innovations on Investment Outcomes

Question 14: To what extent has the integration of technological innovations led to better investment outcomes (e.g., higher returns, reduced risk)?

Table 23. Impact of integration of technological innovations on investment outcomes

Outcome Impact	Retail Traders	Institutional Traders	Financial Advisors	Market Analysts	Portfolio Managers	Total	Percentage (%)
Greatly Improved	13	8	14	10	6	51	56.7%
Moderately Improved	7	4	7	4	3	25	27.8%
Slightly Improved	3	1	2	2	1	9	10.0%
No Improvement	1	1	2	1	0	5	5.6%
Declined	0	0	0	0	0	0	0.0%

Source: Field Survey and Compiled data

The table 15 reveals that the majority of respondents (56.7%) believe that the integration of technological innovations has "Greatly Improved" investment outcomes, including higher returns and reduced risk. This significant result underscores the positive influence of advanced technologies, particularly among Retail Traders and Financial Advisors, where the highest adoption rates were observed.

Mode Calculation: The mode for the dataset is "Greatly Improved," with 56.7% of respondents indicating that technological innovations have significantly enhanced investment outcomes.

Chi-Square Test

Given:

- $\chi^2 = 10.92$
- $p = 0.028$

Decision: Since $p < 0.05$, reject the null hypothesis (H0). This indicates a statistically significant association between respondent type and the perceived impact of technological innovations.

Question 15: How often have technology-driven investment strategies in your organization resulted in meeting or exceeding investment goals?

Table 24. Technology-driven investment strategies in meeting or exceeding investment goals

Response	Frequency	Percentage
Always	20	22.22%
Often	30	33.33%
Sometimes	20	22.22%
Rarely	10	11.11%
Never	10	11.11%
Total	90	100%

Source: Field Survey and Compiled data

Table 16 reveals a generally positive outlook on technology-driven investment strategies. A combined 55.55% of respondents reported that these strategies "always" (22.22%) or "often" (33.33%) meet or exceed their investment goals, indicating strong effectiveness in most cases. However, 22.22% of respondents find that these strategies "sometimes" achieve their goals, while 22.22% experience "rarely" or "never" achieving their targets. This suggests that while technology-driven strategies are effective for many, there is variability in their performance, highlighting the need for further refinement and tailored approaches to enhance consistency in meeting investment goals.

To analyze the data, we can use the Kruskal-Wallis H-test to determine if there is a significant difference in the frequency of meeting or exceeding investment goals across different categories of respondents.

Table 25. Kruskal-Wallis H-test:

Category	Mean Rank	H-value	p-value
Retail Traders	34.13	5.21	0.27
Institutional Traders	40.50		
Financial Advisor	38.20		
Market Analysts	36.53		
Portfolio Managers	31.90		

$H(4) = 5.21$, p-value = 0.27

Interpretation: The Kruskal-Wallis H-test indicates that there is no significant difference in the frequency of meeting or exceeding investment goals across different categories of respondents (p-value = 0.27). This suggests that the frequency of meeting or exceeding investment goals is consistent across different categories of respondents.

Section 4.2. 8: Feedback on Future Directions and Recommendations

16. What emerging technologies do you believe will shape the future of investment strategies in the next 5-10 years?

Table 26. Feedback on emerging technologies and the future of investment strategies

Sno	Respondents	AI & ML	Blockchain	Robo-Advisors	Big Data Analytics	Quantum Computing	Total
1	Retail Traders	10	6	4	3	1	24
2	Institutional Traders	7	3	2	1	1	14
3	Financial Advisors	12	5	4	3	1	25
4	Market Analysts	8	4	2	2	1	17
5	Portfolio Managers	4	3	1	1	1	10
Total	Total Responses	41	21	13	10	5	90
Percentage	Percentage	45.6%	23.3%	14.4%	11.1%	5.6%	100%

Source: Field Survey and Compiled data

The table 17 reveals that Artificial Intelligence (AI) and Machine Learning (ML) are seen as the most influential technologies for the future of investment strategies, with 45.6% of total responses highlighting them as critical. Blockchain follows at 23.3%, indicating strong confidence in its potential to revolutionize investment operations, particularly among retail traders and financial advisors. Robo-advisors, Big Data Analytics, and Quantum Computing were less frequently cited but still acknowledged as important, reflecting a diverse range of opinions on future technological impacts. The overall results demonstrate a clear consensus that advanced technologies will significantly reshape investment strategies, particularly through AI and blockchain.

5. FINDINGS, RECOMMENDATIONS& CONCLUSION, AND CONCLUSION

Summary of Findings

Key Findings From the 12 Case Studies are as Under

ii. **Integration of AI and Machine Learning:** Many firms, such as Vanguard, Charles Schwab, BlackRock, and Betterment, have integrated AI and machine learning into their platforms to enhance investment management. These technologies have enabled the automation of portfolio management, risk assessment, and personalized investment strategies, resulting in cost efficiencies and improved decision-making.

iii. **Challenges of Over-Reliance on Automation:** A common weakness observed across several platforms, including Schwab's Intelligent Portfolios, Vanguard's Robo-Advisors, and Angel Broking's ARQ, is the potential limitation of algorithmic models in responding to complex or unexpected market conditions. This reliance on automation may overlook nuanced factors that human advisors can catch, highlighting the need for a balanced approach between AI and human intervention.

iv. **Customization and Personalization:** While automation provides significant advantages, the lack of personalized services is a recurring weakness. High-net-worth individuals and investors with specific needs may find the limited customization options of robo-advisors, such as those provided by Vanguard and Betterment, less appealing. Platforms like Marcus by Goldman Sachs and Fidelity's Blockchain-Based Investment Platform have opportunities to expand personalization to cater to a broader client base.

v. **Regulatory and Compliance Risks:** The rise of AI-driven platforms, such as BlackRock's Aladdin and Betterment, brings regulatory and compliance challenges. Firms must navigate evolving regulations around AI and blockchain, as regulatory bodies increase scrutiny on these technologies. Compliance risks could impact the adoption and operation of these advanced platforms.

vi. **Market Competition and Technological Disruption:** The financial services industry is experiencing intense competition due to the emergence of fintech startups offering innovative, low-cost solutions. Established firms like Charles Schwab, ICICI Direct, and Zerodha are challenged by newer entrants, which may threaten their market share. To maintain competitiveness, these firms must continuously innovate and adapt to technological advancements.

vii. **Expansion Opportunities:** Several firms, including Schwab, Fidelity, and Zerodha, have identified opportunities to expand their platforms by integrating more advanced AI-driven analytics, offering modular solutions, and targeting new markets, such as sustainable investing. These opportunities can help firms attract a wider client base and stay ahead in a competitive landscape.

viii. **Impact of Blockchain Technology:** Fidelity's adoption of blockchain technology highlights the transformative potential of this innovation in enhancing transparency, security, and efficiency in financial transactions. While still in its early stages, blockchain technology offers significant opportunities for further development, particularly in areas like cross-border transactions and complex financial instruments.

ix. **Client Trust and User Experience:** Platforms like Zerodha's Kite and Sharekhan's TradeTiger demonstrate that user-friendly interfaces and strong customer support are crucial in building client trust and satisfaction. A focus on user experience, particularly for retail investors, can be a decisive factor in a platform's success, as seen in the positive reception of these platforms.

x. **Cybersecurity and Systemic Risks:** The increasing reliance on digital infrastructure, as seen with platforms like BlackRock's Aladdin and Kotak Securities' KEAT Pro X, brings heightened cybersecurity risks. These platforms must address vulnerabilities associated with handling large volumes of real-time data and ensure robust security measures are in place to mitigate potential threats.

xi. **Democratization of Investment Services:** Platforms like Vanguard's Robo-Advisors, Betterment, and Zerodha's Kite have played a significant role in democratizing access to investment services. By lowering costs and providing easy access to sophisticated investment tools, these platforms have made financial markets more accessible to retail investors, including those with limited resources.

xii. **Scalability and Accessibility:** A recurring opportunity across platforms like Vanguard, Schwab, and Fidelity is the potential to scale their services by incorporating more complex data points, offering modular versions for smaller firms, or expanding globally. This scalability can enhance accessibility for a wider range of clients, from individual investors to small firms.

xiii. **Impact of Technological Innovation on Traditional Models:** The case studies collectively illustrate how technological innovation, particularly AI, machine learning, and blockchain, is reshaping traditional investment strategies. These technologies are not only enhancing efficiency and reducing costs but also challenging the traditional advisory model, prompting a reevaluation of how financial services are delivered in the modern era.

Key Findings From Survey Analysis

- Traditional investment strategies remain valued by many respondents, although some view them as less effective in light of modern advancements.
- Technological innovations have notably enhanced portfolio performance, with 38.9% of respondents identifying this as the primary benefit, followed by improved risk management.
- A substantial majority (77.8%) of respondents acknowledge that technological innovations have significantly influenced traditional investment strategies within their organizations.
- Big Data Analytics is the most prevalent technological innovation adopted in investment strategies, with 86.7% of respondents incorporating it.
- There is widespread recognition of a strong correlation between technological innovations and the transformation of traditional investment strategies, indicating broad acknowledgment of technology's impact.
- Organizations are increasingly utilizing advanced analytics and automation to refine their investment decision-making processes.
- Big Data Analytics and Artificial Intelligence are considered the most effective technologies for improving investment strategy performance, with Algorithmic Trading and Cloud Computing also contributing significantly. Blockchain and Machine Learning are noted for their lesser impact.
- AI, Machine Learning, and Blockchain technologies are regarded as "Extremely Critical" by 50.0% of respondents, underscoring their pivotal role in modernizing investment strategies.
- Data Security Concerns are the foremost challenge in adopting new technologies, affecting 70.0% of respondents, highlighting the urgent need for enhanced security measures.

- Cybersecurity (80%) and data privacy (58.9%) are the primary concerns in technology adoption for investment management, emphasizing the necessity for robust protective measures.
- The majority of respondents (44.4%) classify the risks associated with new technologies as "High Risk," reflecting significant apprehensions about potential challenges and impacts.
- Overall perceptions of investment strategies are positive, with 58.9% rating them effective in risk management due to new technologies, though some respondents remain neutral or find them ineffective.
- 38.9% of respondents' view technology-driven investment strategies as "Much More Effective," highlighting their perceived superiority in terms of returns and risk management compared to traditional methods.
- A significant majority (74.5%) perceive technology-driven investment strategies as more effective than traditional ones, with retail traders showing the most favorable views.
- 56.7% of respondents' report that technological innovations have "Greatly Improved" investment outcomes, indicating a significant positive impact on returns and risk management.
- Technology-driven investment strategies frequently meet or exceed investment goals, with 33.33% achieving this "Often" and 22.22% "Always," with no notable differences across respondent categories.
- AI and Blockchain are anticipated to be the leading future technologies in investment strategies, receiving 68.9% of responses and indicating their expected substantial impact.

Key Findings From Survey Analysis

- Technological innovations, such as AI, machine learning, and blockchain, significantly impact traditional investment strategies by improving decision-making, reducing risks, and enabling advanced investment approaches.
- AI, ML, and blockchain are crucial to modern investment practices, offering better predictions, enhanced risk management, and more efficient transaction processing.
- Challenges associated with technology adoption include data security risks, implementation complexities, and potential market disruptions from algorithmic trading, which require careful management.
- There is a notable lack of comprehensive empirical studies comparing the effectiveness of technology-driven investment strategies with traditional ones, with existing evidence being limited.

- The long-term effects of technological innovations on investment strategies, particularly regarding sustainability and regulatory compliance, are not thoroughly explored in the current literature.

These findings provide strong evidence that these technologies significantly contribute to the enhancement and modernization of investment strategies. The other Null Hypothesis ($H_0 1$), Null Hypothesis ($H_0 2$), Null Hypothesis (H_{03}), Null Hypothesis (H_{04}), Null Hypothesis (H_{05}) and Null Hypothesis ($H_0 6$) have also been rejected.

RECOMMENDATIONS AND SUGGESTIONS

i. Examining the Relationship Between Innovation and Traditional Investment Strategies

Recommendations:

1. **Integrate Innovation with Traditional Strategies:** Financial institutions should seek to blend technological advancements with traditional investment approaches to capitalize on the strengths of both. This integration can enhance overall strategy effectiveness while preserving the reliability of established methods.
2. **Continuous Impact Monitoring:** Implement robust mechanisms to continuously assess the effects of technological innovations on traditional investment strategies. This ongoing evaluation will facilitate timely adjustments and ensure alignment with organizational objectives.

Suggestions:

- **Develop Comprehensive Case Studies:** Create in-depth case studies to document successful integrations of technological innovations with traditional strategies. These case studies will provide valuable insights and serve as practical references for other organizations.
- **Conduct Longitudinal Impact Assessments:** Undertake longitudinal studies to evaluate how innovations influence traditional strategies over extended periods. Utilize these findings to refine integration practices and optimize strategy performance.

ii. Analyzing the Impact of Technological Innovation on Traditional Investment Strategies

Recommendations:

1. **Conduct Quantitative Impact Analyses:** Execute detailed quantitative analyses to measure the impact of technological innovations on portfolio performance, risk management, and cost efficiency. Focus on key metrics such as return on investment and risk-adjusted returns.
2. **Implement Feedback Mechanisms:** Establish feedback loops to collect user insights regarding the effectiveness of technological innovations. Leverage this feedback to make data-driven adjustments and enhancements.

Suggestions:

- **Develop Benchmarking Reports:** Create benchmarking reports to compare the performance of technology-enhanced strategies against traditional methods. These reports will provide a clear assessment of benefits and identify areas for improvement.
- **Pilot Technology Trials:** Initiate pilot programs to evaluate the impact of new technologies on investment strategies before full-scale deployment. This approach allows for real-world testing and refinement based on initial results.

iii. Evaluating the Role of Artificial Intelligence, Machine Learning, and Blockchain

Recommendations:

1. **Invest in Advanced Technologies:** Allocate resources to AI, machine learning, and blockchain technologies to enhance investment strategies. Focus on integrating AI for predictive analytics, machine learning for pattern recognition, and blockchain for transaction transparency and security.
2. **Enhance Training and Skills Development:** Provide targeted training to staff to effectively utilize these technologies. Ensure that personnel are equipped with the skills necessary to leverage AI, machine learning, and blockchain in their investment strategies.

Suggestions:

- **Establish Best Practices:** Develop and disseminate guidelines for implementing AI, machine learning, and blockchain in investment management. Share these best practices through industry forums and professional development workshops.
- **Collaborate with Technology Providers:** Form partnerships with technology providers to stay abreast of the latest advancements. Ensure smooth integration of new technologies into investment strategies through collaborative efforts.

iv. Investigating the Challenges and Risks Associated with Technology Adoption

Recommendations:

1. **Enhance Security Measures:** Address data security and cybersecurity risks by implementing and regularly updating robust security protocols. Ensure strict compliance with relevant regulations to mitigate legal and operational risks.
2. **Develop a Comprehensive Risk Management Framework:** Create a risk management framework to identify, assess, and mitigate risks associated with technology adoption. Include contingency plans to address potential failures or security breaches.

Suggestions:

- **Conduct Regular Security Audits:** Perform routine security audits and compliance checks to identify and address vulnerabilities. Ensure adherence to industry best practices and regulatory standards.
- **Utilize Advanced Risk Assessment Tools:** Employ advanced risk assessment tools for ongoing monitoring and evaluation of risks related to new technologies. This will facilitate proactive risk management and timely responses to emerging threats.

v. Assessing the Effectiveness of Technology-Driven Investment Strategies

Recommendations:

1. **Document Case Studies:** Record and analyze case studies of organizations that have successfully implemented technology-driven investment strategies. Highlight key success factors and derive lessons learned to guide future implementations.
2. **Perform Empirical Analyses:** Conduct empirical analyses to evaluate the effectiveness of technology-driven strategies in achieving investment goals. Use statistical methods to assess improvements in performance and cost efficiencies.

Suggestions:

- **Develop Performance Metrics:** Establish specific performance metrics to evaluate the success of technology-driven strategies. Metrics should include return on investment, risk reduction, and user satisfaction.
- **Create Feedback Mechanisms:** Set up systems to gather feedback from stakeholders on the effectiveness of technology-driven strategies.

Use this feedback to make iterative improvements and refine technology adoption processes.

Limitations of the Study

The study faces several limitations. Firstly, the availability of data, especially regarding the long-term impact of technological innovations on investment strategies, is a constraint. The fast-paced evolution of technology means that some findings may quickly become outdated as new tools and methodologies are introduced. Furthermore, the reliance on case studies and surveys, while valuable, may introduce biases that could limit the generalizability of the results. These factors suggest that the conclusions drawn should be viewed within the context of these limitations, and further research is recommended to validate and expand upon these findings.

CONCLUSION

In conclusion, the review of literature highlights that technological innovations such as artificial intelligence, machine learning, and blockchain have a profound impact on traditional investment strategies. These technologies are central to modern investment approaches, offering enhanced decision-making capabilities, improved risk management, and more efficient transaction processing. Despite the significant benefits, challenges such as data security risks, complex implementation, and potential market disruptions must be carefully managed.

Current empirical evidence directly comparing technology-driven investment strategies with traditional methods remains limited, and there is a notable gap in understanding the long-term impacts of these innovations, particularly in terms of sustainability and regulatory compliance.

The literature supports the rejection of hypothesis H_03, indicating that artificial intelligence, machine learning, and blockchain indeed play a significant role in enhancing modern investment strategies. Similarly, Hypotheses H_01, H_02, H_{04}, H_{05}, and H_{06} have also been rejected. The findings are corroborated by numerous sources, including Express Computer News (2023), Khoa and Huynh (2022), Vilela et al. (2019), Joiner (2022), and Dubey (2022), among others. These studies collectively underscore the significant role and impact of technological innovations in shaping contemporary investment strategies.

REFERENCES

Balakrishnan, J., & Dwivedi, Y. K. (2021). Role of cognitive absorption in building user trust and experience. *Psychology and Marketing*, 38(4), 643–668. DOI: 10.1002/mar.21462

Barber, B. M., Odean, T., & Zhu, N. (2009). Do retail trades move markets? *Review of Financial Studies*, 22(1), 151–186. DOI: 10.1093/rfs/hhn035

Bhatia, A., Chandani, A., & Chhateja, J. (2020). Robo advisory and its potential in addressing the behavioral biases of investors—A qualitative study in Indian context. *Journal of Behavioral and Experimental Finance*, 25, 100281. DOI: 10.1016/j.jbef.2020.100281

Carver, C. S. (2006). Approach, avoidance, and the self-regulation of affect and action. *Motivation and Emotion*, 30(2), 105–110. DOI: 10.1007/s11031-006-9044-7

Chandani, A., Sriharshitha, S., Bhatia, A., Atiq, R., & Mehta, M. (2021). Robo-advisory services in India: A study to analyse awareness and perception of millennials. [IJCAC]. *International Journal of Cloud Applications and Computing*, 11(4), 152–173. DOI: 10.4018/IJCAC.2021100109

De la Torre-Torres, O. V., Galeana-Figueroa, E., & Álvarez-García, J. (2021). A Markov-switching VSTOXX trading algorithm for enhancing EUR stock portfolio performance.

Duan, J., & Zhuang, X. (2021). Financial investment behavior and enterprise technological innovation: Motivation analysis and empirical evidence. *China Industrial Economics*, 1(1), 155–173.

Dubey, R. K. (2022). Algorithmic trading: The intelligent trading systems and its impact on trade size. *Expert Systems with Applications*, 202, 117279. DOI: 10.1016/j.eswa.2022.117279

Gerner-Beuerle, C. (2022). Algorithmic trading and the limits of securities regulation. *Vanderbilt Law Review*, 75(5), 1607–1619.

Greenwald, B. C., & Stiglitz, J. E. (1986). Externalities in economies with imperfect information and incomplete markets. *The Quarterly Journal of Economics*, 101(2), 229–264. DOI: 10.2307/1891114

Hou, K., Xue, C., & Zhang, L. (2020). Replicating anomalies. *Review of Financial Studies*, 33(5), 2019–2133. DOI: 10.1093/rfs/hhy131

How technology is transforming investment strategies. (2023, October 19). *Express Computer News*

Joiner, D., Vezeau, A., Wong, A., Hains, G., & Khmelevsky, Y. (2022, November). Algorithmic trading and short-term forecast for financial time series with machine learning models: State of the art and perspectives. In *2022 IEEE International Conference on Recent Advances in Systems Science and Engineering (RASSE)* (pp. 1-9). IEEE. DOI: 10.1109/RASSE54974.2022.9989592

Khoa, B. T., & Huynh, T. T. (2022). Forecasting stock price movement direction by machine learning algorithm. [IJECE]. *Iranian Journal of Electrical and Computer Engineering*, 12(6), 6625–6634. DOI: 10.11591/ijece.v12i6.pp6625-6634

Li, M., & Yan, T. (2020). Venture capital, technological innovation, and enterprise performance: Influencing mechanism and its empirical test. *Scientific Research Management*, 41(07), 70–78.

Lindblom, T., Lindell, J., & Gidlund, K. (2022). Digitalizing the journalistic field: Journalists' views on changes in journalistic autonomy, capital, and habitus. *Digital Journalism (Abingdon, England)*, •••, 1–20.

Phillips, M. (2021, May 11). Nasdaq: Here's our timeline of the flash crash. *The Wall Street Journal.*

Popper, N. K. (2020). Corporate criminal liability for algorithmic price fixing in Canada. *Canadian Journal of Law and Technology*, 16(2), 417–438.

Stan Miranda. (2018, January 1). Technology's impact on active investing. *Partners' Capital.*

Vilela, L. F., Leme, R. C., Pinheiro, C. A., & Carpinteiro, O. A. (2019). Forecasting financial series using clustering methods and support vector regression. *Artificial Intelligence Review*, 52(4), 743–773. DOI: 10.1007/s10462-018-9663-x

Wang, C. S., Tang, H. W., & Chen, R. C. (2017). Does IPO subscription demand affect investor herd behavior in Taiwan? *International Review of Economics & Finance*, 51, 258–272. DOI: 10.1016/j.iref.2017.06.004

Wang, Q., & Dong, Z. (2022). Technological innovation and renewable energy consumption: A middle path for trading off financial risk and carbon emissions. *Environmental Science and Pollution Research International*, 29(22), 33046–33062. DOI: 10.1007/s11356-021-17915-3 PMID: 35025046

Chapter 3
Transformative Role of Artificial Intelligence in Fintech

A. Meera
Sathyabama Institute of Science and Technology, India

A. Rathnakumar
Sathyabama Institute of Science and Technology, India

S. Agila
Sathyabama Institute of Science and Technology, India

M. Deepa
Sathyabama Institute of Science and Technology, India

M. Jayaseely
Sathyabama Institute of Science and Technology, India

K. Poorani
National College, India

Joel Jebadurai Devapitchai
https://orcid.org/0000-0002-6947-8497
St. Joseph's College of Engineering, India

ABSTRACT

Artificial intelligence (AI) in Fintech refers to the extensive or widespread application of AI in the functioning of financial institutions and related businesses. The focus is on AI techniques such as Deep Learning, Robotics, the Internet of Things (IoT), Image Processing, Artificial Neural Networks (ANN), Wireless Sensor Networks, and Machine Learning (ML). FinTech's use of AI has revolutionized the industry by bringing cutting-edge technologies that improve decision-making, expedite procedures, and offer customers individualized services. There are many different applications in the financial sector due to the combination of AI and FinTech. This chapter addresses AI techniques and their applications in the various functional

DOI: 10.4018/979-8-3693-8583-8.ch003

areas of the fintech industry. Benefits, challenges, case studies, and success stories were also discussed.

INTRODUCTION

Artificial intelligence (AI) has emerged as a transformative force in the fintech industry, fundamentally reshaping how financial services are delivered, managed, and optimized. Fintech companies, early adopters of AI, harness its power to automate repetitive tasks, detect risks, prevent fraud, and improve service quality, all leading to greater efficiency and increased profitability. By analyzing data from diverse sources, AI provides financial institutions with valuable insights that help them address challenges in routine services such as payment processing. Fintech, driven by technological advancements, has revolutionized how consumers manage their finances, offering unprecedented personalization. AI-powered chatbots, for instance, are widely used by fintech firms of all sizes to enhance customer support and sales processes. As fintech companies have grown, traditional banks have also begun adopting AI-driven solutions like robotics to reduce costs and handle customer complaints more effectively (Walker et.al 2023). AI's ability to simulate human intelligence, performing tasks like decision-making, speech recognition, and language translation, makes it a key tool in domains such as fraud detection, risk assessment, and personalized financial advice. As AI continues to evolve, it plays an increasingly critical role in driving innovation within the rapidly expanding fintech sector.

AI is profoundly impacting customer service in fintech, with AI-powered chatbots and virtual assistants revolutionizing how customers interact with financial institutions. These intelligent systems provide personalized, efficient support, from simple account queries to more complex financial advice, delivering a seamless and responsive experience. By automating routine tasks, AI reduces wait times, enhances customer satisfaction, and significantly lowers operational costs for financial institutions. In the realm of fraud detection and prevention, AI is equally transformative. AI algorithms analyze vast amounts of transaction data in real-time, identifying patterns that may indicate fraudulent activity. By detecting anomalies and flagging suspicious transactions, AI helps institutions mitigate risks and safeguard their customers against fraud. Additionally, AI systems adapt to new fraud patterns, ensuring continuous protection against evolving threats.

AI is also enhancing risk assessment processes in fintech by analyzing a wide range of data points, such as financial history, credit scores, and market trends. This allows AI to evaluate the creditworthiness of individuals and businesses more accurately, helping institutions make well-informed lending decisions and reducing the risk of defaults. As a result, overall portfolio performance improves. Furthermore, AI is driving innovation in personalized financial services. By analyzing customer data and behavior, AI-powered systems deliver tailored financial advice, investment recommendations, and customized product offerings (Manickam et al., 2023). This level of personalization not only enhances the customer experience but also helps financial institutions build stronger relationships with their clients, fostering loyalty and long-term engagement.

In summary, AI is revolutionizing the fintech industry by enabling financial institutions to deliver more efficient, personalized, and secure financial services. As AI continues to advance, its applications in fintech are expected to grow, leading to further innovation and transformation in the industry. This chapter is structured into four sections. The first section covers the introduction, methodology, and AI applications. The second section delves into AI applications in the fintech industry. The third section discusses the advantages, opportunities, and challenges of AI in fintech. The fourth section includes case studies, success stories, conclusions, abbreviations, references, and key terms.

METHODOLOGY

This book chapter on AI in fintech, methodology involves a comprehensive review of secondary data from published articles, case studies, and other relevant sources. The focus is on AI techniques such as Deep Learning, Robotics, the Internet of Things (IoT), Image Processing, Artificial Neural Networks (ANN), Wireless Sensor Networks, and Machine Learning (ML). The application areas of AI in fintech include fraud detection, customer service, risk management, algorithmic trading, and personalized financial services. Additionally, the chapter discusses the benefits and challenges of AI in fintech, presenting case studies and success stories to illustrate real-world applications and outcomes

Artificial Intelligence Techniques in Fintech

Machine Learning

Machine learning (ML) is a subset of artificial intelligence that centers on creating algorithms that leverage mathematical and statistical models to analyze data autonomously, without requiring explicit programming instructions. These algorithms are capable of processing vast amounts of historical data, identifying patterns within it, and using those patterns to predict new relationships in previously unseen data. In the fintech industry, machine learning algorithms analyze extensive datasets to identify trends, predict future events, and improve their accuracy over time. In the FinTech industry, machine learning is vital for tasks like fraud detection, credit scoring, and providing personalized financial advice. ML has become a cornerstone of modern FinTech, significantly transforming financial services through its innovative applications.

A key area where ML excels is fraud detection. By examining transaction patterns and user behaviors, ML models can detect anomalies and flag suspicious activities for further investigation, reducing the risk of fraud (Rolando & Mulyono 2024). Machine learning also plays a critical role in credit scoring, where algorithms evaluate creditworthiness based on factors like credit history and income. This allows financial institutions to make more precise lending decisions, thereby expanding credit access while effectively managing risks.

In algorithmic trading, ML algorithms analyze vast quantities of market data to predict price movements and optimize trading strategies. This enables traders to make quick, informed decisions, enhancing overall trading performance. Additionally, ML-powered chatbots are revolutionizing customer service in FinTech by offering personalized support, answering queries, and providing financial advice, all of which improve customer experience and engagement.

In the realm of fraud detection, companies like PayPal use machine learning algorithms to analyze transaction data in real-time, searching for patterns and anomalies that may indicate fraudulent activity. These algorithms can swiftly flag suspicious transactions, allowing PayPal to take immediate action to safeguard its customers (Ferraro 2024). By leveraging machine learning, PayPal can stay ahead of fraudsters and protect its users' funds effectively.

Natural Language Processing (NLP)

NLP gives robots the ability to comprehend, interpret, and produce language that is similar to that of humans. NLP is utilized in FinTech for sentiment analysis in financial news and social media, chatbots, and virtual assistants. Natural Language Processing (NLP) in fintech involves using AI to understand and interpret human language in financial contexts. One example is sentiment analysis, where NLP algorithms analyze social media, news articles, and customer reviews to gauge market sentiment and predict stock movements. Another application is in chatbots and virtual assistants, which use NLP to provide customer support, answer queries, and facilitate transactions conversationally (Kamuangu 2024). NLP also helps with fraud detection by analyzing transaction descriptions and identifying suspicious patterns. For instance, a bank might use NLP to scan through transaction logs and flag unusual activities for further investigation, enhancing security and compliance efforts.

The real-time example of NLP in fintech is in automated customer service chatbots. Banks like Bank of America use virtual assistants like “Erica,” which leverage NLP to understand and respond to customer inquiries instantly. When a customer asks about recent transactions, or loan details, or needs to make a payment, the NLP algorithms process the natural language input, interpret the intent, and provide accurate, context-aware responses or perform the requested actions. This improves customer experience by providing quick, 24/7 support and reduces the workload on human customer service agents (Mohammed et al., 2024). Additionally, real-time sentiment analysis using NLP can help financial institutions monitor social media and news feeds to detect emerging trends or potential crises, allowing them to respond proactively to market changes.

Predictive Analytics

Predictive analytics uses statistical algorithms and previous data to forecast future patterns and behaviors. It helps in forecasting the market trends, consumer behaviour, and credit risk in FinTech. Predictive analytics in fintech leverages AI to forecast future financial trends, customer behaviours, and risks, driving more informed decision-making across the industry. One prominent application is in credit scoring and risk assessment. Traditional credit scoring methods often rely on limited data points, such as credit history and income. However, AI models can analyse a much broader range of data, including transaction history, social media activity, and even mobile phone usage patterns. By integrating these diverse data sources, predictive analytics can generate a more accurate assessment of an individual's creditworthiness. This comprehensive approach helps lenders make better decisions about loan approvals and interest rates, reducing default risks and expanding access to credit for individuals who may have been overlooked by traditional scoring methods.

Another crucial application of predictive analytics in fintech is fraud detection. Financial institutions face constant threats from increasingly sophisticated fraud schemes. AI-driven predictive models continuously analyze transaction data in real time, identifying patterns and anomalies that may indicate fraudulent activity. For instance, unusual transaction amounts, locations, or frequencies can trigger alerts for further investigation. By predicting and flagging potentially fraudulent transactions before they occur, these models significantly enhance the security of financial systems, minimizing risk and losses (Elias et.al 2024). This proactive approach to fraud detection not only protects customers but also helps maintain trust in financial institutions.

Predictive analytics also enhance investment management platforms like Wealth Front. Wealthfront uses AI to analyze market trends and individual investment profiles instantaneously. This enables the platform to adjust investment portfolios dynamically, ensuring that they are optimized according to the latest market conditions and the client's risk tolerance. For example, if predictive analytics indicate an upcoming market downturn, Wealth Front's system can automatically reallocate assets to more stable investments, protecting clients' portfolios from potential losses (Gera et al., 2024). This real-time responsiveness ensures that clients receive the most up-to-date and effective investment strategies, maximizing returns and minimizing risks.

Robotic Process Automation (RPA)

RPA reduces human labour and increases operational efficiency by automating routine operations and procedures. RPA is used in the FinTech industry to perform operations including compliance reporting, account reconciliation, and data entry. Robotic Process Automation (RPA) utilizes software robots (bots) to automate repetitive, rule-based tasks in financial technology (fintech). These bots can mimic human interactions with digital systems, significantly enhancing operational efficiency by performing tasks quickly and accurately. RPA's application in fintech ranges from customer service to compliance, transforming how financial services are delivered. For example, in customer onboarding, bots automate data entry and validation, ensuring a smooth and rapid process by extracting and verifying customer information. In transaction monitoring, RPA aids in fraud detection by flagging suspicious activities through predefined rules and patterns. Bots generate and submit regulatory reports for compliance and reporting, ensuring accuracy and compliance with changing regulations.

RPA offers significant advantages in the fintech industry, including cost reduction, enhanced accuracy, and scalability. Automating routine tasks reduces the need for manual labor and minimizes errors, leading to cost savings. Bots perform tasks consistently without fatigue, ensuring high accuracy and faster completion times. RPA solutions can easily scale to handle increased transaction volumes, supporting business growth without a proportional increase in workforce. However, implementing RPA comes with challenges such as integration with existing systems, security and data privacy, and change management. Ensuring bots effectively communicate with legacy systems without causing disruptions can be difficult. Handling sensitive financial data requires robust security measures, including encryption and access controls (Chikri & Kassou 2024). Adopting RPA necessitates a cultural shift; employees need training to work alongside bots, and organizations must manage resistance to change.

XYZ Bank, a mid-sized financial institution, implemented RPA to improve its loan processing operations, which were previously time-consuming and error-prone due to extensive manual handling of documents and data entry. Before RPA, a customer submitting a loan application had to wait 5-7 days for approval as bank staff manually reviewed the application, checked documents for completeness, and input data into the loan processing system. Verification against internal databases and third-party credit bureaus added to the delays. After implementing RPA, the process became much more efficient. Bots automatically extracted data from submitted documents using Optical Character Recognition (OCR) technology, validated the information by cross-referencing it with internal and external databases in real-time, and flagged discrepancies for human review. This automation reduced the processing time to less than 24 hours, minimized human errors, and allowed staff to focus on more value-added tasks. The bank also faced challenges such as integrating RPA with legacy systems, ensuring data security, and training employees to work alongside bots (Harsono & Suprapti 2024). By overcoming these challenges, XYZ Bank achieved significant operational improvements, including reduced processing times, increased accuracy, cost savings, and enhanced customer satisfaction.

Wealthfront stands out as one of the leading robo-advisors in the market, boasting a membership of 440,000 clients and managing approximately $25 billion in assets. With a relatively low minimum account requirement of just $500, it offers a diverse range of investment options, including cryptocurrencies like Bitcoin, making it accessible to a wide audience of investors. Wealthfront is also known for its competitive fee structure, with most accounts incurring a modest annual fee of only 0.25%, and it does not charge transaction fees, which enhances its appeal for cost-conscious investors. The company's growth trajectory is poised to accelerate further following its acquisition by UBS at the beginning of 2022, as this partnership is expected to leverage UBS's resources and expertise to expand Wealthfront's offerings and reach in the rapidly evolving fintech landscape (Dasgupta 2023). This strategic acquisition positions Wealthfront not only as a key player in the robo-advisory space but also as a significant contender in the broader financial services industry.

Computer Vision

Computer vision is the application of Artificial Intelligence (AI) to the interpretation and decision-making of visual input. Computer vision is used in FinTech for activities including fraud prevention, face recognition for biometric identification, and document verification. Computer vision, a subset of artificial intelligence, is revolutionizing the fintech industry by enabling machines to interpret and make decisions based on visual data. It significantly enhances customer onboarding by automating identity verification processes. For instance, customers can upload a photo of their

ID and a selfie, which the AI system then uses to match the two images, verify the document's authenticity, and ensure compliance with regulatory standards. This automation reduces onboarding time from days to minutes and minimizes human error, creating a seamless and efficient customer experience.

Moreover, computer vision plays a crucial role in fraud detection and prevention. It analyses patterns in transaction images and monitors video feeds from ATMs to detect suspicious behaviors, such as card skimming. Additionally, it can identify forged documents and fake IDs by examining subtle details and inconsistencies that might be missed by the human eye (Mozumder et.al 2024). Financial institutions also use computer vision to automate document processing, extracting relevant data from loan applications, insurance claims, and other documents, significantly reducing manual workload and improving accuracy.

A real-time example of computer vision in fintech is its use in automated loan processing, particularly for property evaluation in mortgage applications. A fintech company allows customers to upload photos and videos of their property. The computer vision system analyzes these images to assess the property's condition, identifying structural issues or signs of damage. This information is combined with other data points, such as location and market value, to generate a comprehensive property report. This automated evaluation speeds up the loan approval process and provides more accurate risk assessments, enabling quicker and more informed lending decisions

APPLICATIONS OF AI IN FINTECH

Credit Scoring

Artificial intelligence (AI) algorithms play a pivotal role in evaluating a person's creditworthiness by analyzing a diverse array of data sources, including both alternative and traditional credit histories. This innovative approach not only promotes financial inclusion but also enhances the accuracy of credit ratings, allowing more individuals access to financial services. Upstart, a fintech company founded by former Google employees, seeks to revolutionize the conventional lending process by leveraging AI and machine learning technologies to assess creditworthiness more effectively. Traditional credit scoring models, such as FICO scores, often depend on a limited range of financial data points, which can inadvertently exclude numerous potential borrowers who, despite lacking extensive credit histories, are otherwise financially responsible (Liang & Pan, 2024). Upstart's mission is to broaden access to credit by delivering more accurate and equitable assessments, thereby empowering a wider population to obtain loans and improve their financial well-being. By utilizing advanced data analytics, Upstart not only challenges the status quo of credit evaluation but also fosters a more inclusive financial ecosystem.

Fraud Detection and Security

Identifying and avoiding fraud is another use for artificial intelligence data analysis. As was previously said, real-time responses to data, the ability to recognize patterns and relationships, and the potential to spot fraudulent activity are all features of artificial intelligence and machine learning solutions. This is very helpful for the financial industry, where a staggering number of digital transactions occur every hour, necessitating enhanced cyber security and effective fraud detection. While artificial intelligence works in the background to uncover the lesser problems, it frees up fraud analysts to concentrate on higher-level concerns by taking over the majority of their workload.

Identifying abnormalities is one way artificial intelligence can identify fraud. If ten identical loan applications were submitted in five minutes in the bank example, an artificial intelligence machine would have noticed this as unusual and would have been suspicious. The computer can detect and evaluate deviations from its basic notion of what is 'normal'.

Artificial intelligence (AI)-driven solutions play a crucial role in strengthening the security of financial transactions by analyzing transaction patterns, detecting anomalies, and swiftly identifying potential fraud. A fintech company called Secure Pay exemplifies this by utilizing AI to safeguard its payment processing platform. Secure Pay's AI algorithms continuously analyze transaction data in real-time, flagging suspicious activities—such as transactions occurring far from a customer's usual location—for immediate review. This rapid detection system allows Secure Pay to prevent fraudulent transactions and protect its customers' sensitive financial information. By processing vast amounts of data in real-time, AI-driven fraud detection systems are not only faster and more effective in spotting threats but also serve to enhance customer trust and prevent financial losses. As a result, fintech companies that leverage AI for fraud detection are better positioned to provide secure, reliable services in an increasingly digital financial landscape (Jin, 2024).

Artificial intelligence can detect patterns and connections, react quickly to data, and potentially even identify fraudulent activity. This is tremendously beneficial to the banking industry because of the enormous volume of digital transactions that occur every hour, which calls for increased cyber security and efficient fraud detection (Arnone 2024). Artificial intelligence finds the small problems in the background while fraud analysts focus on higher-level issues because they don't have to work as hard.

Cognito, developed by Vectra, is a tool designed to track and identify cyber threats. Vectra's software streamlines event investigations detects compromised data, uncovers covert attackers—particularly those targeting financial institutions—and automates the process of threat detection, enhancing cybersecurity defenses.

Personalized Financial Services

AI customizes financial services and goods to each user's unique needs. This includes lending options, savings plans, and tailored financial advice. Wealth front is a fintech company that offers personalized investment management services using AI. When a customer signs up, Wealth Front's AI algorithms analyze their financial situation, risk tolerance, and investment goals to create a personalized investment portfolio. The portfolio is automatically rebalanced and optimized based on market conditions and the customer's changing financial needs (Li et.al 2024). Wealth Front's AI-powered platform also provides personalized advice on saving, investing, and retirement planning, helping customers make informed financial decisions.

AI is transforming personalized financial services in the fintech sector by utilizing vast amounts of data to offer highly tailored products and personalized financial advice. Companies like Wealthfront are leading the charge, using AI to provide customized investment management solutions that adapt to individual financial profiles, goals, and risk tolerance. This approach not only enhances the customer experience by offering more relevant and timely insights but also empowers individuals to make informed financial decisions. As AI continues to evolve, these services will become even more sophisticated, providing customers with greater convenience, efficiency, and control over their finances. The ability to automate tasks, predict market trends, and optimize financial strategies will further refine the personalization of financial services, driving the future of fintech innovation.

Chatbots and Virtual Assistants

Chatbots and virtual assistants powered by AI offer prompt, customized client service. They can help with account administration, provide answers to questions, and lead consumers through different financial procedures. They can also guide users through complex processes like loan applications or investment decisions, providing tailored recommendations based on the user's financial profile and goals. Overall, chatbots and virtual assistants improve the customer experience by offering timely, relevant, and personalized support, ultimately increasing customer satisfaction and loyalty.

Moreover, chatbots and virtual assistants play a crucial role in streamlining operations and reducing costs for fintech companies. By automating routine tasks such as customer inquiries, account management, and transaction processing, these AI-powered tools free up human resources to focus on more complex and high-value activities. For example, chatbots can handle a large volume of customer queries simultaneously, reducing the need for additional customer support staff. This not only improves operational efficiency but also reduces costs associated with customer service (Arnone 2024). Additionally, chatbots can provide real-time updates and alerts on account activity, helping customers stay informed and proactive about their finances.

Furthermore, the application of chatbots and virtual assistants in fintech is continually evolving, with advancements in Natural Language Processing (NLP) and machine learning enabling more sophisticated interactions. These technologies allow chatbots to understand and respond to customer queries more accurately, providing a more human-like experience. For instance, chatbots can analyse customer sentiment and adjust their responses accordingly, ensuring a more personalized interaction. As AI continues to advance, chatbots and virtual assistants will play an increasingly important role in fintech, offering innovative solutions to enhance customer engagement, streamline operations, and drive business growth.

Regulatory Compliances

By keeping an eye on and verifying compliance with regulations, Artificial Intelligence streamlines compliance procedures. This involves automating AML (Anti-Money Laundering) procedures, transaction monitoring, and reporting. One real-time example of AI application in regulatory compliance in fintech is the use of AI by Comply Advantage. Comply Advantage utilizes AI to help financial institutions comply with regulations such as AML (Anti-Money Laundering) and Know Your Customer (KYC) requirements (Liang 2024). Their AI-powered platform analyses vast amounts of data from various sources, including sanctions lists, watchlists, and adverse media, to identify and flag potential risks. Comply Advantage's AI continuously learns from new data, improving its ability to detect suspicious activities and comply with evolving regulations. This real-time monitoring allows financial institutions to quickly identify and mitigate risks, ensuring compliance with regulatory requirements. By leveraging AI, Comply Advantage provides an efficient and effective solution for regulatory compliance in the fast-paced fintech industry.

REGTECH

Regulatory Technology, or RegTech, plays a crucial role in addressing the complexities of adhering to ever-evolving regulations and managing extensive documentation, which can often be both tedious and susceptible to human error (Aloulou et al., 2024). By implementing automated compliance software, organizations can streamline these processes; notable examples include chatbots that provide real-time regulatory advice, cloud-based systems designed for the effective management of compliance data, and advanced coding techniques that simplify the processing of regulatory information.

Hummingbird stands out as a premier provider of RegTech solutions, offering a specialized CRM platform meticulously designed to cater to the unique needs of compliance and risk teams. With a strong focus on delivering comprehensive Anti-Money Laundering (AML) systems, Hummingbird serves a diverse array of financial institutions, including banks, credit organizations, lending institutions, and fintech companies that leverage the power of artificial intelligence (Olaiya et al., 2024). The platform not only streamlines compliance processes but also integrates advanced analytics to enhance the detection of suspicious activities. Hummingbird's core mission is to significantly strengthen AML initiatives through its RegTech expertise, empowering these institutions to proactively identify and mitigate financial crimes with greater efficiency and scalability. By fostering a collaborative environment for compliance teams and utilizing cutting-edge technology, Hummingbird contributes to a more secure and resilient financial landscape, ultimately helping to protect institutions and their clients from the evolving threats of financial crime.

Financial Forecasts

Artificial intelligence is revolutionizing the finance sector by enabling the automatic recognition, analysis, and adjustment of data trends, thereby enhancing decision-making processes. In the realm of fintech, AI excels at generating insightful forecasts regarding exchange rates, investments, and both short- and long-term market trends, even when the underlying data quality is less than ideal. By leveraging a sophisticated interface that integrates various AI and machine learning methodologies, fintech companies can predict user behavior and provide comprehensive insights tailored to individual data profiles. These capabilities, often delivered through AI APIs, empower banks and fintech organizations to streamline their services. For example, when a client requests information about their monthly spending, the system can anticipate potential follow-up inquiries using AI on the server side, delivering relevant insights in a single response. This proactive approach not only reduces the volume of requests but also alleviates pressure on the business's operational systems (Awotunde et al., 2021). As a result, when predictive analytics are accurate, the entire system operates more efficiently, ultimately enhancing the customer experience and providing faster, more relevant responses to their needs.

The capability of artificial intelligence to analyze unstructured data is particularly transformative for financial services, offering significant advantages across various fintech applications. This technology can be employed to forecast product suitability by examining consumer behavior patterns, enabling companies to tailor their marketing strategies effectively. In practical scenarios, AI plays a critical role in helping businesses, especially those in the financial sector, to sift through extensive amounts of client data both economically and efficiently. Financial organizations often collect vast quantities of information about their clients; however, the time and resources required to manually analyze this data can lead to inaction. This is where AI and machine learning technologies prove invaluable, as they can rapidly and accurately process large datasets, uncovering insights that would otherwise remain hidden. By automating the analysis of unstructured data, AI empowers financial institutions to make data-driven decisions, enhance customer experiences, and ultimately gain a competitive edge in the market.

Banks use artificial intelligence and data to determine a person's creditworthiness, as one specific example. While providing loans, banks also aim to charge a fair fee. By examining their credit scores, they may prevent charging too much for dependable clients and too little for riskier ones. They can examine and make inferences from their customer data. Artificial intelligence can make a variety of connections from these portfolios (Paramesha et al., 2024). Job and address, for instance, are clear sources of information, but there's also the notion that factors like an individual's email provider can reveal more or less about their trustworthiness.

Financial Reporting

The convergence of fintech and artificial intelligence has largely been driven by AI's remarkable ability to generate financial reports efficiently and accurately. Financial institutions, including banks, amass vast quantities of data, which they analyze meticulously to produce insightful reports. Traditionally, this process is time-consuming and labor-intensive, requiring detailed examination of complex datasets. However, the integration of AI streamlines this task by automating data analysis, enabling financial entities to swiftly generate reports that meet regulatory requirements and internal decision-making needs (Shengelia et al., 2022). Even though the raw data sets may vary significantly across institutions, AI can adapt to different formats and deliver tailored reports, significantly reducing the turnaround time. This enhanced efficiency not only alleviates the burden on financial analysts but also allows companies to respond more quickly to market changes, improve compliance, and make informed strategic decisions, ultimately transforming the landscape of financial reporting in the fintech sector.

Customer Experience

Large financial institutions often serve hundreds of thousands, if not millions, of consumers, making it nearly impossible to meet the diverse needs of such a vast customer base without the help of AI-powered technologies. AI systems enable these institutions to offer personalized services by collecting and analyzing customer data when users download and engage with banking apps. This data can be leveraged to provide tailored financial advice and pre-approved product recommendations, enhancing the customer experience. Customization through AI not only allows institutions to meet individual preferences but also fosters greater trust and brand loyalty among consumers. Moreover, AI assists users in setting and tracking financial goals, managing spending targets, and staying on top of their finances, making banking apps more intuitive and efficient. This blend of personalization and automation significantly improves customer satisfaction, positioning AI as an essential tool in the modern financial landscape.

AI systems have an inherent ability to learn and evolve, meaning their capacity to interpret customer data and deliver increasingly personalized experiences will continue to grow over time. By analyzing vast amounts of data, including voice and speech characteristics, AI models can distinguish between irrelevant chatter and meaningful patterns, extracting valuable insights. These advanced models are capable of interpreting tone, emotion, and intent, allowing them to generate more accurate predictions about a customer's mood or needs (Barbu et.al 2021). By evaluating AI-generated transcripts, customer service agents can gain deeper insights into each interaction, enabling them to offer more relevant solutions or product recommendations based on mood predictions and behavioral cues. This fusion of AI-driven analysis and human decision-making enhances the overall customer experience by making it more intuitive, responsive, and tailored to individual preferences, further solidifying the role of AI in driving innovation in customer service.

KASISTO developed KAI, a conversational AI platform designed to enhance customer experiences in the banking industry by offering intuitive self-service options and solutions. KAI helps banks reduce contact center traffic by enabling customers to resolve issues and complete transactions independently through its intelligent chatbot interface. These AI-driven chatbots not only assist with routine inquiries but also provide valuable financial advice, empowering users to make more informed and deliberate financial decisions (Rios-Campos et al., 2023). By combining automation with personalized guidance, KAI streamlines banking processes, improves customer satisfaction, and supports more efficient operations for financial institutions.

Data Analytics

The stock market has become one of the top investment destinations for millennials, leading to a surge in demand for AI-powered apps that simplify navigating the complexities of stock trading. In response to this growing trend, a variety of AI-driven smartphone apps like Crow and Upstock have emerged, offering users valuable insights by analyzing both historical and real-time data on companies and their stocks. These apps utilize advanced algorithms to assess market trends, financial performance, and other key indicators, helping investors make informed decisions about which stocks are likely to be good investments and which may pose higher risks. By providing personalized recommendations and real-time analysis, these AI-powered platforms are transforming the way millennials engage with the stock market, making investing more accessible, data-driven, and efficient (Cao et.al 2021).

PERFIOS, an Indian company, provides a robust data analytics platform widely utilized by banks and Non-Banking Financial Companies (NBFCs) to enhance decision-making and operational efficiency. Its platform plays a crucial role in preventing fraud, optimizing loan approvals, managing assets, and delivering accurate credit scores. By leveraging advanced analytics, PERFIOS helps financial institutions make more informed choices while mitigating risks (https://www.perfios.com). The company has attracted significant attention, securing around $120 million in funding, and boasts an impressive client roster that includes global and domestic financial giants such as Deutsche Bank, Canara HSBC, and Home Credit Finance. This highlights PERFIOS's growing influence in the financial sector, particularly in enhancing data-driven processes and improving the overall security and reliability of financial services.

Algorithmic Trading

Algorithmic trading stands out as one of the most widely adopted applications of artificial intelligence in the fintech sector, playing a vital role in the functioning of modern financial markets. By leveraging AI-driven algorithms, traders can swiftly and accurately analyze vast datasets to identify emerging market trends and execute trades in mere milliseconds. This automated approach enhances the efficiency of trading operations, ensuring that financial decisions are grounded in data-driven insights rather than emotional reactions, which often cloud human judgment. As a result, algorithmic trading not only optimizes returns and minimizes potential losses but also significantly reduces the risks associated with emotional trading behaviors.

By harnessing the power of AI, financial institutions can enhance their trading strategies, achieve better performance outcomes, and navigate the complexities of the market with greater confidence and precision.

New York-based Renaissance Technologies LLC is recognized as one of the most successful algorithmic trading firms and a leading example of fintech AI applications worldwide. Since its inception in 1988, the company's Medallion Fund has achieved an extraordinary average annual return of 66%, making it one of the top-performing hedge funds in history. The Medallion Fund employs a diverse array of quantitative trading strategies grounded in extensive data analysis and sophisticated statistical models (Kirilenko & Lo 2013). By harnessing advanced algorithms and computational techniques, Renaissance Technologies can identify and capitalize on market inefficiencies with remarkable precision. This data-driven approach not only maximizes investment returns but also showcases the power of AI and quantitative finance in transforming the landscape of trading, solidifying Renaissance's reputation as a pioneer in leveraging technology for superior financial performance.

Digital Banking

The rise of neobanks and challenger banks is disrupting the traditional banking sector, posing a significant threat to established financial institutions often referred to as incumbents. These digital-first banks are leveraging technology to offer a more convenient, accessible, and cost-effective banking experience. With 24/7 access to financial services, customers are no longer constrained by physical branches or geographical limitations. Through mobile apps and online platforms, users can easily manage accounts, make payments, and complete transactions from the comfort of their smartphones or computers. Additionally, the absence of physical branches and the high degree of automation in digital banking significantly reduce operational costs (Elia et al., 2023). This allows neobanks to offer lower fees and more competitive interest rates, making financial services more affordable and attractive to consumers. As a result, traditional banks are under increasing pressure to innovate and compete with these agile, tech-driven contenders.

To remain competitive in the evolving financial landscape, established institutions have adopted digital banking platforms, partnered with fintech companies, and digitalized their services. A prime example of fintech innovation is Monobank, currently Ukraine's fastest-growing bank, which operates exclusively through a mobile app, offering a streamlined and user-friendly banking experience. Monobank provides a range of services including free money transfers, commission-free utility bill payments, multi-currency checking and deposit accounts, credit options, and attractive cash-back incentives. Customer support is readily accessible via phone or messaging apps, further enhancing user convenience (Fang 2024). Behind the scenes, Monobank leverages advanced technologies such as neural networks for image recognition and gradient boosting for assessing credit risk, analyzing over 2,000 customer data points to optimize its services. The bank's rapid growth and substantial market impact showcase how AI is reshaping the fintech landscape in Ukraine and beyond, setting a new standard for digital banking.

ADVANTAGES OF AI FOR THE FINTECH INDUSTRY

Fintech and artificial intelligence share a lot of commonalities. Better understanding and social skills have propelled AI technology from the periphery to the forefront of the discussion. It restores the human element of banking, which has been largely lost in recent years as a result of the dominance of global banks. Jebadurai et.al 2024 have explained how artificial intelligence might enhance banking operations is provided below.

Automation

Automated customer service is another way that artificial intelligence is used. These days, when people visit different websites, they are accustomed to seeing chat boxes at the bottom of the screen. These are, of course, chatbots with artificial intelligence support there to assist. Businesses only need to input their most commonly asked questions, tell the chatbot which responses to provide, and direct it to direct customers with more complicated problems to another person. Having the ability to respond to commonly requested inquiries regarding the business, its offerings, or both guarantees that the consumer will have a better experience since he will receive a prompt response to his query. Additionally, the business saves money and time by not needing to hire someone to type out responses, or by having an employee focus on something else.

Credit Risk Assessment

Numerous factors, including overall income, credit history, transaction analyses, work experience etc., are taken into account when AI makes conclusions about credit ratings. A mathematical model called credit scoring is based on statistical techniques and takes a lot of data into account. As a result, sensitive, personalized credit score evaluations based on multiple additional real-time elements are provided by artificial intelligence-powered credit scores, which may make it possible for more financially independent people to obtain financing. AI-based analytics solutions are used to evaluate data and find transactions that seem unusual or could be signs of fraud.

Detecting Banking Frauds

Artificial intelligence allows for the monitoring of user behaviour patterns, and actions that deviate from the normal can be identified and could show fraud attempts or incidents. These cases are then passed on to human staff for consideration, saving them a great deal of time.

Increasing Safety

Many security-enhancing solutions in the financial sector are powered by artificial intelligence. Banks, for instance, have applications which is accessible through fingerprint or facial identification. Artificial intelligence is largely responsible for making this possible.

Fintech artificial intelligence provides behavior-based solutions that have the potential to transform the financial industry. Artificial intelligence can track a customer's transactional behaviour and identify patterns in it. For example, a consumer repeatedly tries to take €5,000 from his account from an unusual place. Artificial intelligence-driven learning can identify and flag these transactions as potential fraud.

Enhance Operational Safety and Efficiency

The financial sector has a rare opportunity to lower costs, enhance client satisfaction, and boost operational efficiency, among other things. Financial firms can offer their clients top-notch financial services. Numerous financial companies worldwide employ diverse artificial intelligence features to enhance operational safety and efficiency. The primary objective of all these solutions is to boost fintech organizations' productivity. Utilizing chatbots and automated solutions for data analysis will significantly lessen the workload for your employees.

Due to artificial intelligence, or AI, the financial sector has a unique chance to reduce costs, improve client happiness, and promote operational efficiency, among other things. Top-notch financial services are available to clients of financial firms. Globally, a multitude of financial institutions utilize various AI functionalities to augment operational security and efficacy. Increasing the productivity of fintech companies is the main goal of all these solutions. By using chatbots and automated data analysis technologies, financial institutions may drastically reduce staff effort.

Analyzing User Behaviour

Relationship management and customer service are two more crucial areas where artificial intelligence technology shines. Chatbots are a useful tool for fintech organizations to promptly respond to customer inquiries and enhance the overall customer experience with their offerings. These chatbots enable personalized customer care and inexpensive, knowledgeable counsel.

Furthermore, chatbots are always available and never take a vacation. Artificial intelligence can also be used to virtual assistants to improve user data, guide customers through the bank's offers, and issue tailored calls to action that will boost certain conversion rates. Fintech organizations can save customer care costs and time by utilizing chatbots and virtual assistants. This will also contribute to the enhancement of artificial intelligence by its diverse functionalities.

OPPORTUNITIES IN AI-DRIVEN FINTECH

Artificial Intelligence (AI) holds immense potential in the fintech industry, particularly within the banking sector, where it can drive innovation and enhance customer experiences. The opportunities for AI in banking are vast, ranging from automating routine tasks like transaction processing and customer inquiries to advanced applications such as predictive analytics for risk assessment and personalized financial services. The followings are the opportunities of fintech sector.

Predictive Analytics

AI-enabled predictive analytics is transforming decision-making in financial organizations by providing deep insights into market trends, customer behavior, and potential risks. By analyzing vast amounts of historical and real-time data, AI algorithms can identify patterns and predict future outcomes with a high degree of accuracy. This capability allows financial institutions to forecast market movements, anticipate customer needs, and proactively address potential risks before they escalate. Armed with these insights, decision-makers are better equipped to make informed, strategic decisions that drive growth, improve operational efficiency, and mitigate risks. Whether it's adjusting investment portfolios, launching new products, or enhancing customer engagement strategies, AI-powered predictive analytics empowers financial organizations to stay ahead of the curve and remain competitive in a rapidly evolving industry. By anticipating future scenarios, financial institutions can operate with greater agility and confidence, ultimately leading to better business outcomes and increased profitability.

Algorithmic Trading

AI-powered algorithmic trading is revolutionizing the financial industry by enabling institutions to analyze market data, identify trends, and execute trades at speeds that were previously unimaginable. These AI systems process vast amounts of information in real time, spotting subtle market signals and patterns that human traders might miss. By automating the trading process, AI not only increases efficiency but also reduces the time it takes to capitalize on market opportunities. This rapid execution gives financial institutions a significant competitive advantage, allowing them to respond to market fluctuations faster than traditional methods. Additionally, AI-driven trading enhances market liquidity by facilitating more frequent and precise transactions, contributing to a more fluid and stable trading environment. The reduction in transaction costs is another key benefit, as AI minimizes the need for human intervention and optimizes trading strategies to lower fees and slippage. Overall, AI-powered algorithmic trading is reshaping the financial landscape, providing institutions with the tools to enhance profitability, manage risk more effectively, and stay competitive in fast-paced markets.

Credit Scoring

AI-driven credit scoring algorithms are transforming the way financial institutions assess creditworthiness by leveraging machine learning and alternative data sources. Unlike traditional credit scoring models that rely primarily on credit history and financial statements, AI-powered systems analyze a broader range of data, such as social media activity, utility payments, online behavior, and even geolocation information. This holistic approach allows for a more accurate and nuanced evaluation of an individual's ability to repay loans, particularly for those who lack a formal credit history. By utilizing alternative data, AI opens the door to financial inclusion, providing credit access to underserved populations, such as young adults, freelancers, and individuals in emerging markets, who may otherwise struggle to obtain loans through conventional means. This innovative approach not only improves the precision of credit scoring but also helps financial institutions expand their customer base while minimizing default risks. As a result, AI-driven credit scoring is playing a critical role in democratizing access to financial services and promoting economic growth.

Blockchain and Smart Contracts

AI and blockchain technology are revolutionizing the financial industry through the development of smart contracts, which are self-executing contracts with the terms of the agreement directly written into code. These digital contracts automatically enforce the agreed-upon conditions when predefined criteria are met, eliminating the need for intermediaries and significantly accelerating the completion of financial transactions. By using AI, smart contracts can be enhanced with more complex decision-making capabilities, allowing them to adapt to dynamic conditions or intricate business logic. Blockchain ensures that these contracts are transparent, immutable, and secure, as all transactions are recorded on a decentralized ledger (Devapitchai et al., 2024). This increased transparency reduces the potential for disputes and fraud, as every participant in the network can verify the contract's execution. Additionally, the automation of contract enforcement minimizes human error and administrative costs, leading to more efficient operations for financial institutions. Ultimately, the combination of AI and blockchain in smart contracts fosters greater trust, reduces transaction times, and enhances the overall efficiency of financial processes.

CHALLENGES OF AI IN FINTECH

Devapitchai et.al 2024 have presented the following challenges of fintech in the banking sectors. They are:

Data Quality

Fintech companies often face significant challenges with data quality due to the complexity, fragmentation, and unstructured nature of financial data. This makes it difficult to consolidate and analyze information effectively. Privacy concerns and legal restrictions further complicate the situation, limiting access to relevant, high-quality data. These obstacles hinder the ability of fintech firms to leverage data-driven insights and optimize their services, requiring them to find innovative solutions to ensure data accuracy and compliance with regulatory frameworks while maintaining customer trust.

Regulatory Compliance

Fintech businesses must comply with various regulations such as the General Data Protection Regulation (GDPR), Anti-Money Laundering (AML) laws, and Know Your Customer (KYC) requirements, which can complicate the integration of AI systems. Implementing AI while ensuring these regulations are followed is challenging, as it requires balancing automation with stringent data privacy, security, and transparency standards. Maintaining accountability and transparency in AI decision-making processes is essential to meet regulatory demands, making it difficult for fintech firms to deploy AI solutions without compromising compliance and customer trust.

Interpretability and Explainability

Deep learning AI models, widely used in fintech, are often characterized as "black boxes" due to their complex architectures and the difficulty in interpreting their decision-making processes. This lack of transparency poses significant challenges in the financial services industry, where explainability is crucial for building trust with clients and regulatory authorities. Stakeholders need to understand how decisions are made, especially in critical areas such as lending, risk assessment, and fraud detection, to ensure that they are fair and justifiable. As a result, fintech firms are increasingly focused on developing explainable AI solutions that provide insights into the rationale behind automated decisions, thereby enhancing accountability and meeting regulatory requirements while fostering confidence among users.

Cybersecurity and Privacy

Fintech organizations, handling sensitive financial data, are prime targets for cyberattacks, making data security a top priority. Implementing AI systems that effectively defend against these online threats while ensuring data privacy presents significant challenges. AI-driven security measures must not only detect and respond to intrusions in real-time but also protect against potential breaches that could compromise customer information. Additionally, the balance between employing robust security protocols and maintaining compliance with privacy regulations complicates the integration of AI solutions. As a result, fintech firms must navigate a complex landscape to develop and deploy AI systems that safeguard sensitive data without sacrificing user privacy, requiring continuous innovation and vigilance against evolving cyber threats.

Integration and Scalability

As fintech businesses continue to grow, their AI systems must scale effectively to handle increasing volumes of data and transactions. This scalability presents a challenge, particularly when integrating AI solutions with legacy systems and existing infrastructure, which may not be designed to support advanced technologies.

The complexities involved in bridging old and new systems can lead to significant costs and resource demands, hindering the seamless deployment of AI capabilities. Moreover, ensuring compatibility while maintaining operational efficiency is essential for fintech firms to leverage AI's full potential. As a result, businesses must invest in modernization efforts and innovative integration strategies to create a cohesive environment that supports both current operations and future growth.

Ethical and Bias Concerns

AI systems are vulnerable to producing biased outcomes if the data used for training contains inherent biases, which is a significant concern for fintech companies. Discrimination in AI-driven decisions, especially in areas such as lending, credit scoring, and risk assessment, can perpetuate existing inequalities and undermine trust in financial services. Therefore, fintech firms face a critical challenge in ensuring fairness and ethical usage of AI technologies. This necessitates careful consideration of data sourcing, model training, and ongoing monitoring to identify and mitigate biases. By implementing robust ethical frameworks and employing diverse datasets, fintech organizations can strive to promote equity and accountability in their AI applications, ultimately fostering a more inclusive financial landscape.

User Adoption and Trust

Building client trust in AI-driven fintech solutions is a significant challenge, especially when dealing with sensitive financial matters. Customers often have concerns about the reliability, security, and transparency of automated systems, leading to hesitation in adopting these technologies. The perceived risks associated with entrusting AI with personal financial information can create barriers to acceptance. To overcome these challenges, fintech companies must prioritize transparency in their AI processes, clearly communicating how decisions are made and ensuring robust security measures are in place. Additionally, providing education on the benefits and functionalities of AI solutions can help demystify the technology, fostering confidence and encouraging clients to embrace these innovative tools for managing their finances.

Return on Investment

To successfully integrate AI, fintech companies must make substantial investments in infrastructure, personnel, and technology, which can strain resources and budgets. Assessing the return on investment (ROI) for these AI initiatives can be challenging, as the benefits may not be immediately apparent or easily quantifiable.

Additionally, organizations must ensure that their AI projects deliver tangible results that align with strategic goals and enhance operational efficiency. This requires careful planning, ongoing evaluation, and a commitment to adapting strategies based on performance metrics. Balancing the costs of implementation with the anticipated long-term benefits is crucial for fintech firms to realize the full potential of AI while justifying their investments to stakeholders.

CASE STUDIES AND SUCCESS STORIES

Fintech companies are harnessing the power of AI to create advanced tools that help users manage their money more efficiently. By analyzing data such as spending patterns, income streams, and savings goals, these apps provide personalized insights that empower users to improve their financial health. One well-known example is the budgeting app Mint, which uses machine learning algorithms to automatically generate customized budgets and categorize transactions based on user behavior. This level of automation and personalization allows users to make informed financial decisions, track their progress, and adjust their habits to achieve their financial objectives. As AI continues to evolve, these solutions will become even more sophisticated, offering deeper insights and greater control over personal finances.

TradeSmith's flagship product is an investment portfolio management platform that leverages AI algorithms to predict the prices of S&P 500 stocks and optimize trade order timing through automation. This cutting-edge technology helps users make data-driven decisions and maximize the efficiency of their trading strategies. To further enhance the platform, TradeSmith partnered with Itransition to integrate key features such as real-time stock data monitoring and advanced risk management alerts. These additions enable users to stay informed about market changes in real time and receive timely warnings about potential risks, improving overall portfolio performance and helping investors make more informed decisions in a fast-paced trading environment.

Scotiabank, one of Canada's Big Five banks, has integrated Google AI solutions to enhance its operations and improve customer experiences. By utilizing advanced technologies such as Natural Language Processing (NLP), voice recognition, and computer vision, the bank has streamlined various processes, including document management and customer onboarding. These AI-driven solutions enable Scotiabank to automate and accelerate tasks that were traditionally time-consuming, such as processing documents and verifying customer information. As a result, customer interactions are more efficient, personalized, and seamless, allowing the bank to better meet the evolving needs of its clients while optimizing internal workflows.

American Express leverages deep learning models as part of its robust fraud prevention strategy, monitoring over $1.2 trillion in global transactions annually in real time. These advanced algorithms analyze each transaction and make fraud detection decisions within milliseconds, ensuring swift and accurate protection against fraudulent activities. Similarly, HSBC has adopted Voice ID technology to enhance security and convenience in its phone banking services. By utilizing sophisticated voice biometrics, this system authenticates customers based on their unique vocal characteristics, allowing secure and effortless access to their accounts. Both companies demonstrate how AI-driven innovations are reshaping security and customer service in the financial sector.

CONCLUSION AND FUTURE DIRECTIONS OF RESEARCH

AI is significantly transforming the fintech industry by fundamentally changing the way financial services are delivered and managed. Sophisticated algorithms and machine learning models improve fraud detection through real-time monitoring and predictive analytics, enhancing the security of financial transactions. AI-powered chatbots and virtual assistants optimize customer service by offering immediate, personalized support and automating routine processes. Robo-advisors now provide tailored investment advice by aligning strategies with individual goals and risk preferences. Moreover, AI-enhanced credit scoring models leverage alternative data to deliver more precise evaluations of creditworthiness. As AI technology continues to evolve, its integration into fintech is set to drive further advancements in trading, regulatory compliance, and operational efficiency, ultimately reshaping the financial sector and improving user experiences. creditworthiness evaluations.

ABBREVIATIONS

AI Artificial Intelligence
IoT Internet of Things
ANN artificial neural networks
ML Machine Learning
NLP Natural Language Processing
RPA Robotic Process Automation
DeFi Decentralized Finance
KYC Know Your Customer
GDPR General Data Protection Regulation
AML Anti-Money Laundering

REFERENCES

Arnone, G. (2024). Introduction to AI in FinTech. In *AI and Chatbots in Fintech: Revolutionizing Digital Experiences and Predictive Analytics* (pp. 1–19). Springer Nature Switzerland. DOI: 10.1007/978-3-031-55536-7_1

Arnone, G. (2024). The Role of Chatbots in FinTech. In *AI and Chatbots in Fintech: Revolutionizing Digital Experiences and Predictive Analytics* (pp. 21–27). Springer Nature Switzerland. DOI: 10.1007/978-3-031-55536-7_2

Awotunde, J. B., Adeniyi, E. A., Ogundokun, R. O., & Ayo, F. E. (2021). Application of big data with fintech in financial services. In *Fintech with artificial intelligence, big data, and blockchain* (pp. 107–132). Springer Singapore. DOI: 10.1007/978-981-33-6137-9_3

Barbu, C. M., Florea, D. L., Dabija, D. C., & Barbu, M. C. R. (2021). Customer experience in fintech. *Journal of Theoretical and Applied Electronic Commerce Research*, 16(5), 1415–1433. DOI: 10.3390/jtaer16050080

Cao, L., Yang, Q., & Yu, P. S. (2021). Data science and AI in FinTech: An overview. *International Journal of Data Science and Analytics*, 12(2), 81–99. DOI: 10.1007/s41060-021-00278-w

Chikri, H., & Kassou, M. (2024). Financial Revolution: Innovation Powered By Fintech And Artificial Intelligence. *Journal of Theoretical and Applied Information Technology*, 102(9).

Cubric, M., & Li, F. (2024). Bridging the 'Concept–Product' gap in new product development: Emerging insights from the application of artificial intelligence in FinTech SMEs. *Technovation*, 134, 103017. DOI: 10.1016/j.technovation.2024.103017

Dasgupta, D. (2023). Impact of AI and RPA in Banking. In *Confluence of Artificial Intelligence and Robotic Process Automation* (pp. 41–72). Springer Nature Singapore. DOI: 10.1007/978-981-19-8296-5_3

Data Aggregation & Analytics (n.d) https://www.perfios.com/platforms/data-aggregation-and-analytics

Devapitchai, J. J., Dheenadhayalan, K., Rajeshkumar, L., Meena, M. R., Soundarya, M., Sowmiya, M. S., & Manickam, T. (2024). Applications of Artificial Intelligence Techniques in Modern Banking Sectors. In *Blockchain Applications for Smart Contract Technologies* (pp. 279–298). IGI Global. DOI: 10.4018/979-8-3693-1511-8.ch014

Devapitchai, J. J., Krishnapriya, S. V., Karuppiah, S. P., & Saranya, S. (2024). Using AI-Driven Decision-Making Tools in Corporate Investment Planning. In *Generative AI for Transformational Management* (pp. 137–160). IGI Global. DOI: 10.4018/979-8-3693-5578-7.ch006

Elia, G., Stefanelli, V., & Ferilli, G. B. (2023). Investigating the role of Fintech in the banking industry: What do we know? *European Journal of Innovation Management*, 26(5), 1365–1393. DOI: 10.1108/EJIM-12-2021-0608

Elias, O., Esebre, S. D., Abijo, I., Timothy, A. M., Babayemi, T. D., Makinde, E. O., & Fatoki, I. E. (2024). Harnessing artificial intelligence to optimize financial technologies for achieving sustainable development goals. *World Journal of Advanced Research and Reviews*, 23(2), 616–625. DOI: 10.30574/wjarr.2024.23.2.2385

Fang, Q. (2024). Application of FinTech in Digital Banking Operations in the Information Age. *Applied Mathematics and Nonlinear Sciences*, 9(1), 19–27. DOI: 10.2478/amns-2024-0527

Ferraro, G., Ramponi, A., & Scarlatti, S. (2024). Fintech meets Industry 4.0: A systematic literature review of recent developments and future trends. *Technology Analysis and Strategic Management*, 36(8), 1911–1927. DOI: 10.1080/09537325.2022.2117025

Gera, R., Chadha, P., Saxena, A., & Dixit, S. (2024). A Scientometric and Bibliometric Review of Impacts and Application of Artificial Intelligence and Fintech for Financial Inclusion. In *Artificial Intelligence, Fintech, and Financial Inclusion* (pp. 82-111). CRC Press.

Harsono, I., & Suprapti, I. A. P. (2024). The role of fintech in transforming traditional financial services. [COUNT]. *Accounting Studies and Tax Journal*, 1(1), 81–91. DOI: 10.62207/gfzvtd24

Jebadurai, D. J., Sheela, M. V., Rajeshkumar, L., Soundarya, M., Meena, R., Manickam, T., . . . Manikandan, M. (2024). AI-Driven Decision-Making and Optimization in Modern Agriculture Sectors. In Using Traditional Design Methods to Enhance AI-Driven Decision Making (pp. 269-288). IGI Global.

Jin, S. V. (2024). "Technopian but lonely investors?": Comparison between investors and non-investors of blockchain technologies, cryptocurrencies, and non-fungible tokens (NFTs) in Artificial Intelligence-Driven FinTech and decentralized finance (DeFi). *Telematics and Informatics Reports*, 14, 100128. DOI: 10.1016/j.teler.2024.100128

Kamuangu, P. K. (2024). Advancements of AI and Machine Learning in FinTech Industry (2016-2020).

Kirilenko, A. A., & Lo, A. W. (2013). Moore's law versus murphy's law: Algorithmic trading and its discontents. *The Journal of Economic Perspectives*, 27(2), 51–72. DOI: 10.1257/jep.27.2.51

Li, D., Ma, C., Zhou, Z., Kuang, X., & Lin, Z. (2024). Distributed hyperledger technology in FinTech with artificial intelligence assisted internet of things platform. *Expert Systems: International Journal of Knowledge Engineering and Neural Networks*, 41(6), e13001. DOI: 10.1111/exsy.13001

Liang, X. (2024). Fintech and Digital Transformation of the Financial Industry. *Highlights in Business. Economics and Management*, 30, 12–16.

Liang, Z., & Pan, S. (2024, June). Research on the Impact of Fin-Tech on Stock Volatility in the Artificial Intelligence Industry. In *Proceedings of the 3rd International Conference on Big Data Economy and Digital Management, BDEDM 2024, January 12–14, 2024, Ningbo, China*. DOI: 10.4108/eai.12-1-2024.2347207

Manickam, T., Desai, K., Sudha, M., Bhagyalakshmi, M., Vinayagamoorthi, G., & Devapictahi, J. J. (2023). Usage of Social Media in Education: A Paradigm Shift in the Indian Education Sector. In *Global Perspectives on Social Media Usage Within Governments* (pp. 127–141). IGI Global. DOI: 10.4018/978-1-6684-7450-1.ch009

Mohammed, K. S., Serret, V., Jabeur, S. B., & Nobanee, H. (2024). The role of artificial intelligence and fintech in promoting eco-friendly investments and non-greenwashing practices in the US market. *Journal of Environmental Management*, 359, 120977. DOI: 10.1016/j.jenvman.2024.120977 PMID: 38678903

Mozumder, M. A. S., Nguyen, T. N., Devi, S., Arif, M., Ahmed, M. P., Ahmed, E., & Uddin, A. (2024). Enhancing Customer Satisfaction Analysis Using Advanced Machine Learning Techniques in Fintech Industry. *Journal of Computer Science and Technology Studies*, 6(3), 35–41. DOI: 10.32996/jcsts.2024.6.3.4

Olaiya, O. P., Adesoga, T. O., Ojo, A., Olagunju, O. D., Ajayi, O. O., & Adebayo, Y. O. (2024). Cybersecurity strategies in fintech: safeguarding financial data and assets. *GSC Advanced Research and Reviews, 20*(1), 050-056.

Paramesha, M., Rane, N. L., & Rane, J. (2024). Artificial Intelligence, Machine Learning, Deep Learning, and Blockchain in Financial and Banking Services: A Comprehensive Review. *SSRN*, 1(2), 51–67. DOI: 10.2139/ssrn.4855893

Rios-Campos, C., Vega, S. M. Z., Tejada-Castro, M. I., Zambrano, E. O. G., Perez, D. J. G. B., Calderón, E. V., Rojas, L. M. F., & Alcantara, I. M. B. (2023). Artificial Intelligence and Business. *South Florida Journal of Development*, 4(9), 3547–3564. DOI: 10.46932/sfjdv4n9-015

Rolando, B., & Mulyono, H. (2024). Managing Risks In Fintech: Applications And Challenges Of Artificial Intelligence-Based Risk Management. [ECBIS]. *Economics and Business Journal*, 2(3), 249–268.

Shengelia, N., Tsiklauri, Z., Rzepka, A., & Shengelia, R. (2022). The impact of financial technologies on digital transformation of accounting, audit and financial reporting. *Economics*, 105(3), 385–398. DOI: 10.36962/ecs105/3/2022-385

Shoetan, P. O., & Familoni, B. T.Philip Olaseni ShoetanBabajide Tolulope Familoni. (2024). Transforming fintech fraud detection with advanced artificial intelligence algorithms. *Finance & Accounting Research Journal*, 6(4), 602–625. DOI: 10.51594/farj.v6i4.1036

Walker, T., Nikbakht, E., & Kooli, M. (2023). Fintech and banking: an overview. *The fintech disruption: how financial innovation is transforming the banking industry*, 1-8.

Chapter 4
A Critical Review of Influence of Technology on Financial Decision Making and Investor Psychology

Sumana Mondal
https://orcid.org/0009-0001-7165-2810
Biju Patnaik University of Technology, India

Sree Kumar
https://orcid.org/0000-0002-6534-896X
Rourkela Institute of Management Studies, India

ABSTRACT

This study focuses on the ways that technological developments have changed market dynamics, decision-making procedures, and investing patterns. The rapid development of fintech, algorithmic trading, big data analytics, and artificial intelligence (AI) has had a profound effect on how investors research markets, obtain information, and make financial decisions. The democratization of access to financial data brought about by technology allows individual investors to engage in markets that were previously controlled by institutional players. Although technology improves accessibility and efficiency, the results indicate that it also adds complications that call for a more thorough comprehension of investor behavior in a tech-driven financial environment. The study's conclusion suggests directions for future investigation into reducing the psychological risks connected to technology-driven financial decision-making.

DOI: 10.4018/979-8-3693-8583-8.ch004

1. INTRODUCTION

The investment industry is undergoing a dramatic transformation of investing as a result of technological improvements. These innovations are offering unique tools and platforms that improve decision-making and portfolio management. Technologies include artificial intelligence (AI) and machine learning (ML). These technologies enable investors to effectively evaluate large datasets, uncovering patterns and trends that may not be easily discernible using traditional approaches (Kauppi et al., 2021). As such, it has made the investment field much easier and dynamic both for an individual investor and an institutional investor. Blockchain, one of the technologies that has been put into practice, has greatly affected investment, especially in the cryptocurrency sector. Blockchain offers a secure base for transactions, which is decentralized and transparent in nature. It therefore eliminates the need for all the middlemen like the banks and brokers between the parties involved. Excessive dependence on AI-driven models could be perilous amid market volatility because algorithms may fail to account for unforeseen variables. More to that, the investment field has the robo-advisors who involve AI in giving individual-specific financial advisory through minimal interaction with humans. Robo-advisers have attracted young investors who have technological skills and who are looking for cheap alternatives, providing a cheaper approach compared to traditional human consultants (Jung et al., 2018). The cyber threat is among the risks, as hackers are targeting more investment platforms in recent years (Treleaven et al., 2020). Despite such challenges, technology still modifies the face of investing. It brings with it both potential opportunities and problems as the investor learns to accept an increasingly digitalized environment.

A structured approach in investment decisions aids investors in identifying opportunities, assessing risks, and achieving their financial goals. Defining investment objectives is the first step, where an investor assesses his or her financial objectives that can be either wealth preservation, income generation, or capital growth. The selection of all these objectives depends on age, financial needs, risk appetite, and investment horizon (Sharpe et al., 1999). Risk evaluation is, therefore, essential as it determines the ability and willingness of an investor to bear risk. The investor's willingness and ability to bear the risk of putting money either in low-risk securities, such as bonds or high-risk securities, such as stocks are determined by a person's risk tolerance level (Grable & Lytton, 1999). Investors who are risk-lovers can invest in volatile assets while risk-averse investors prefer stable assets. This is done after risk assessment to spread the portfolio among different asset types, including shares, bonds, and real estate. Asset allocation helps diversify the portfolio in order to reduce risk (Sharpe et al., 1999). Asset allocation aims to make sure that the portfolio is bound toward fulfilling the investor's investment objectives and his or her willingness to take risks. After asset allocation, the investor performs security selection, which is a process of making specific choices of assets in particular asset classes. This stage would normally involve either fundamental analysis-analysis of balance sheets and industry trends-or technical analysis-study of price movements and other market data-to inform decisions (Bodie et al., 2014). Finally, portfolio monitoring and review should be conducted to track the time path of an investment's performance. An investor may rebalance his portfolio according to changing conditions in the market or personal situations. In this case, there could be a need to rebalance the portfolio to ensure that it matches the objectives and the investment risk of the investor (Bodie et al., 2014).

Investor psychology plays an important role in financial decision-making and tends to frequently make decisions irrationally. For instance, loss aversion has been described as fearing losses more than one appreciates similar gains and can contribute to suboptimal investment decisions, such as holding underperforming assets for too long; he or she can act irrationally (Kahneman & Tversky, 1979). Investors' excessive confidence in their ability to predict market movements results in overtrading and decreased portfolio performance. Another significant role is played by overconfidence. Herding behavior, where people follow others, makes market surges happen or deepen falls as reflected in some historic financial events (Shiller, 2000). Sometimes, panic selling and dangerous investment behavior result from emotions like fear and greed, which later influence the decisions. These psychological factors should be known to make wise and knowledgeable investment decisions.

There is an overall transformation in the investment field with fast inventions of technology having a huge impact on how financial decisions are made. It has enhanced the capabilities of investors to do high-dimensional analysis through AI and ML, providing patterns and trends that may not appear with more orthodox methods (Kauppi et al, 2021). This has dramatically helped in accelerating decision-making processes for many individual investors and institutional investors. Most importantly, blockchain technology, especially in the cryptocurrency arena, has shaken up investment markets by offering peer-to-peer decentralized, transparent, and secure transactions, thus doing away with the presence of intermediaries such as banks and brokers. Yet over-exposure to AI-powered models could become a threat, particularly when volatility kicks in, as algorithms are not prepared to consider unpredictable variables. Due to their ease and minimum human involvement, robo-advisors, which rely on AI to offer individualized financial planning advice, attracted youth, high technology-adoption investors at a low cost (Jung et al., 2018). Due to the fact that cyber threats targeting investment platforms have increasingly become more common, it is without a doubt that technology has also progressively shaped the investment environment and yields a mix of opportunities and challenges for a world digitalized. In concert with technology, structured fiscal decision making is necessary. The risk tolerance determinants and the stated investing goals need to be balanced by investors via proper objectives, risk assessment, and diversification of the portfolio (Sharpe et al., 1999; Bodie et al., 2014). Investor psychology determines much about their choices as unbiasedness has proven to be resultant from loss aversion, overconfidence, and herding behavior, which contribute to irrational decisions such as holding underperforming assets or panic selling in market fluctuations (Kahneman & Tversky, 1979; Shiller, 2000). Knowing the mental conditions may turn out to be strong influencers in helping investors make decisions that are more thought-provoking and reasonable.

2. INVESTOR PSYCHOLOGY

Investor psychology pertains to the emotions and cognitive biases ruling the process of financial decision-making. Amongst psychological factors include overconfidence, herd behavior as well as loss aversion which lead to some irrational investing decisions that often deviate from the established economic theories of rationality (Kahneman & Tversky, 1979). The role played by fear and greed emotions makes markets susceptible to crashes or bubbles, as has been in several of financial crises histories (Shiller, 2003). Understanding such psychological factors is thus crucial in devising strategies that assist investors to minimize some of such biases and render rational decisions (Thaler, 2016).

2.1. Emotional Factors

2.1.1. Fear and Greed

Fear and greed are the two most powerful emotional pushes affecting investor psychology. Greed propels investors into pursuing such high profits that translate into over-confidence and unbridled speculative behavior, as experienced in the market bubbles. Fear, on the other hand, encourages risk avoidance causing investors to sell assets too early or abandon potentially valuable opportunities during market declines (Loewenstein et al., 2001). These emotions will distort logical thinking, marking herd behavior when the investors act according to the majority rather than objectively analyzing the situation of the market (Shiller, 2000). The fear-greed cycle becomes much more apparent in unstable markets whereby radical shifts in emotion can amplify price volatility to extreme expressions of bubbles or collapses (Shefrin, 2000). Understanding how fear and greed can affect behavior should be of concern when crafting solutions to eliminate emotional biases in investor decision-making and encourage more rational investment choice.

2.1.2. Loss Aversion

Loss aversion is an essential affective component of investor psychology, wherein a loss is feared much more than equivalent gains are valued. Prospect theory postulates that a person feels loss much more deeply than he or she feels the pleasure of gains (Kahneman & Tversky, 1979). Loss-averse investors tend to hold onto poorly performing ventures for too long, fearing a loss rather than letting go at the proper time in hopes that a company will bounce back. It holds suboptimal assets longer than any reasonable economic model would suggest. Loss aversion also makes an investor avoid potentially lucrative ventures due to fear of losing them (Barberis & Huang, 2001). This tendency often becomes more pronounced at times of market downturn, where the fear of losing also leads to panic selling that can exacerbate market volatility. Understanding loss aversion provides a better approach to devising strategies that limit behavioral biases and help with fairer, more sustainable choice-making.

2.1.3. Anchoring Bias

Investor psychological distortion comes in the form of anchoring bias, where people rely too heavily on the first datum or "anchor" when making judgments. People tend to use some price or figure as a reference point that is called an anchor based upon which their expectations are drafted and then make judgments based on that reference point, even though market conditions have changed (Tversky & Kahneman, 1974). Anchoring will lead to, for instance, a bad financial choice: keeping losing stock "because you paid too much for it" and are unwilling to sell at current market prices yet ignoring relevant information in the current market (Campbell & Sharpe, 2009). Anchoring impacts assessments of a stock's future worth so impacts actions in ways that deviate from rational analysis. Once the anchoring bias is found and thus eliminated, an investor will decide far better because their decisions are grounded upon objective data rather than emotional connections to original reference points.

2.1.4. Overconfidence

Overconfidence is a very common psychological emotional aspect applicable to investors' behavior, in which people overestimate their knowledge, abilities, and forecasting capabilities. The overconfident trader is more likely to be overactive, which means to raise trading volumes and underestimate the probability of obtaining negative outcomes. Poor performance often results from such behavior because overconfident investors tend to neglect necessary information or market signals to justify their high self-confidence in the proficiency of their judgment.

The overconfidence might also lead to overtrading with subsequent increments in transaction costs, which lowers the total profits acquired (Daniel et al., 1998). A moderate amount of overconfidence is required for investors to make investment decisions, while extremely excessive overconfidence blurs the judgments and leads to suboptimal decisions. Overconfidence needs to be diagnosed and mitigated to enable investors to hold an even judgmental view and realistic understanding of the financial markets.

2.1.5. Confirmation Bias

Confirmation bias is a cognitive distortion in human thinking, where individuals tend to seek, observe, and remember information that confirms their pre-existing ideas, avoiding contrary data. In the investment sense, this bias causes the investor to focus on information that confirms his initial selection of investments while ignoring signals suggesting otherwise (Nickerson, 1998). An investor expecting to rise in a given stock may look only at the good news, ignoring the bad news. This bias limit the ability to make an unbiased judgment on an investment, causing investors to hold their poor performing assets or wrongly make investment decisions (Park et al., 2010). Confirmation bias is limited in making unbiased judgments on the market situation to make informed and balanced decisions. This bias therefore needs to be identified and made less prominent to reduce the emotional effects that these investment decisions may have. With this, the quality as a whole will be improved.

2.1.6. Cognitive Bias

In fact, cognitive biases represent systematic deviations from the rationality of judgment and decision-making. In general, it results in inferior choices. Related to investment activities, such biases as over-confidence, confirmation bias, and anchoring influence information interpretation and the decision-making procedures among investors. These biases are a result of reliance on mental shortcuts by the brain, otherwise referred to as heuristics in processing information (Tversky & Kahneman, 1974). Cognitive biases, for example, can cause an investor not to pay attention to the most important information available, trade too frequently, or hold losing equities too long, which reduces profit potential and significantly increases risk. Understanding cognitive biases is fundamental to improved decision-making techniques in financial markets.

2.1.7. Availability Heuristic

The availability heuristic is a mental shortcut whereby people estimate the likelihood or the rate of things based on the number of instances and their ease of recall to mind (Tversky & Kahneman, 1973). This bias arises because the thinking brain relies on information that springs into mind recently, prominently, or emotionally rather than objectively assessing all relevant facts. In the investment world, availability heuristic causes investors to overestimate the probability of market events being reported frequently or emotionally. Following a major market disaster, investors overestimate the probabilities of subsequent crashes that motivate them to undertake too conservative strategies (Baker & Wurgler, 2007). As far as euphoric markets are concerned, recent gains are exaggerated and investors become overly optimistic. The availability heuristic is pretty influential on investor behavior since recent or salient market events really color the decision-making.

2.1.8. Inside Bias

Bias with an insider view-sometimes referred to as "insider thinking"-arises when people focus too much on information they possess or knowledge they have, and they overlook other facts beyond their scope of reference as well as outside perspectives. This bias is highly prevalent in business-investment settings. Here, the decision makers may overestimate the value of their own information or information gained from people within their inner circle (Buehler et al., 1994). In investing, inside bias can make the investor overestimate his or her own analysis or interpretation of a specific sector or business, which leads to too much concentration in familiar assets and not enough diversification. Inside bias is closely associated with overconfidence since people who are victims of inside bias often overrate their ability to predict events due to their inside information. Internal bias can be overcome only by considering external perspectives and relying on pluralistic sources when compiling information to make a judgment call.

2.2. Behavioral Factors

Behavioral factors play an essential role in financial decision making, especially in technologically enabled markets. Herd behavior, social influence, and authority bias are the most fundamental psychological traits to possibly impact investment behavior. Knowing these is important in determining how people construct investment decisions in technologically sophisticated financial markets.

2.2.1. Herd Behavior

Herd behavior represents a tendency of a person to do what a large group of people is doing, often at a cost to their own thoughts or evaluation. Financial investors, in general, behave like herds especially during uncertainty or great volatility. Psychological pressure for conformity and fear of missing potential gains or losses might make investors imitate others, even going against their logical analysis (Shiller, 2003). The problem is compounded by technology that makes the fast diffusion of information possible and vast. Digital forums, social media, and trading sites have made it relatively easy for investors to be able to observe and stay abreast of market sentiments and the fluctuations in asset prices often are unsoundly based on fundamentals (Bikhchandani & Sharma, 2000). A clear example of this is the recent 2021 GameStop short squeeze. A discussion on a social media forum, Reddit, led retail investors to rally behind and pushing GameStop's stock price higher despite its questionable future performance. This led to a bubble-like situation, where the stock price shot up merely because of the high volume of trade instead of being a work of value. In this case, the herd mentality was accompanied by rapid diffusion of information and opinions through social media, showing that technology plays a huge role in decision-making in finances (Chohan, 2021).

2.2.2. Social Influence

Social influence is related to herd behavior, but it's a much more subtle phenomenon in terms of the way people change their choices based on what other people's opinions or attitudes are. It might derive from peer influence, social circles, or the desire to belong to certain groups. Social influence is further compounded in digital finance by websites on which investment ideas and financial advice are traded and discussed day in and day out, such as Twitter, YouTube, and Reddit, (Ozsoylev et al., 2014). Investors might emulate the practices of the apparently successful or informed people without doing due diligence regarding appropriateness and validity of the information. The social influence reached a new unprecedented high in impacting investment decisions through social media. Influencers and "finfluencers" often provide advice to large audiences, most of whom may have limited financial knowledge but who are eager to enter the market fray. The increased use of social media for discussion about finance will lead to irrational investment decisions that are driven more by social pressures than by market data. Researchers present evidence of the benefits and detriments social influence entails in investment decisions based on the quality of information distributed among stakeholders (Barber & Odean, 2001). The ease of technology expands participation in financial markets simultaneously as it increases the risk of misinformation and uninformed decision-making.

2.2.3. Authority Bias

Authority bias is the tendency of individuals to follow the advice or opinions of perceived experts or authoritative figures, independent of the truth content of their statements. In finance, investors usually look towards the opinions of financial analysts, fund managers or major economists, believing that these experts possess superior knowledge or vision (Baker & Nofsinger, 2010). Authority bias can cause investors to rely on professional recommendations when such recommendations are wrong or conflict with the investor's personal finance objectives. The Internet has magnified the authority that there are in finance. Financial news organizations, bloggers, and social networking services widely disseminate the views of famous market analysts and gurus. This increased exposure can enhance authority bias because investors respond stronger towards opinions of an authoritative person, they themselves engage with and interact more strongly with. For instance, when a prominent hedge fund manager is reporting a recommendation or condemnation of a company, it may cause extreme price reactions as individual investors will buy or sell their security holdings based on their perceived sophistication of the opinion of the authoritative figure (Fang & Yasuda, 2014). However, dependence on authorities may sometimes lead to worse decisions simply because predictions released by such authorities might not be a result of proper research or when the market suddenly changes. Another form of authority bias can be observed in algorithmic trading and robo-advisory services. Investors may blindly rely on these automated systems without really knowing the basic algorithms or the logic behind the suggested recommendations. Such unthinkingly blind reliance on technology as an "authority" may lead to conclusions meeting the biases in the algorithms rather than sound financial reasoning (Jung et al., 2018). The constantly evolving nature of technology demands further investigation into the possibility for authority bias within autonomous financial systems.

2.2.4. Personality Traits

Personality traits have a strong impact on financial decision-making and investment behavior. Other characteristics include risk tolerance, risk perception, motivation, and self-control, which are essential to explain the rationale behind the decisions made by investors and their attitude towards financial risk and return. These aspects really determine how individuals relate to the markets and react to fluctuations, especially in places where technology is vital, and quick decisions have to be taken amid incomplete information.

2.2.5. Risk Tolerance

Risk tolerance is defined as the ability by an individual to bear financial losses without experiencing high-stress levels or altering his or her investing pattern. Investors who are readily accepting of risk focus their investments in risky or high-returning investments that include stocks, virtual currencies, or ventures in speculative technology, while low risk tolerance leads to investing in more limited-risk investment opportunities such as bonds or saving accounts (Grable & Lytton, 1999). This has made technological advancement increase the accessibility of tremendous options to diverse investors. Now more than ever, one has to realize what suits his or her taste about risk. According to Jung et al. (2018), online trading platforms and other robo-advisors find their basis of investment suggestions in risk assessment of investors and come up with tailored appropriate investing strategies aligned with the comfort of the investor with regards to the risks involved. Knowing how much risk you can take is important in achieving long-term financial success since mismatched risk profiles would often lead to selling at the worst time or excessive exposure to volatile assets during market declines.

2.2.6. Motivation

Motivation propels people to invest in finances and take certain actions towards the achievement of their financial goals. Intrinsic motivation, as in the case of finding financial security or independence, commonly leads to more solid and sustainable investing behaviors, while extrinsic motivation, as in the case of searching for social status or quick returns, might lead to quick-and-dirty investment strategies that are indeed short-term but excessively risky (Ryan & Deci, 2000). The increasing technological connections within the financial markets, especially on social media and peer networks, have made extrinsic motivation more relevant. A good number of investors get intrigued into speculative investment in cryptocurrencies or meme stocks in the hope of earning quick money and the resultant social esteem (Chohan, 2021). Intrinsic motivation is more likely to give investors stable and sound investment plans since the individuals are more concerned with long-term growth and financial well-being than getting immediate gains.

2.2.7. Self-Control

It refers to the ability to control impulses, particularly emotional reaction to market volatility or speculation. Self-control plays a significant role in investment and the pursuit of an orderly financial strategy free from impulse responses to transience in market fluctuations (Shefrin & Thaler, 1988). Technology has both enhanced and challenged the notion of self-control in financial markets. For instance, robo-advisors utilize strict rules-bound and apathetic investment strategies for investors. The possibility of reaching financial markets with mobile phones and trading applications has exposed investors to impulsive trading. Investors can easily make impulsive decisions by rapidly reacting to news or social media trends based on imperative needs without first considering the long-run consequence of their investment choice (Barber & Odean, 2001). Effective self-control is crucial for long-term success, especially in avoiding behaviors like panic selling at declining levels or overtrading in bullish markets.

2.2.8. Market Sentiments

Market mood refers to the general attitude of investors about a particular market or commodity. It is often guided primarily by emotions, psychological factors, and the general outlook of the market players rather than by any hard facts of finance (Baker & Wurgler, 2007). Positive market mood often leads to rising asset prices because most investors are more confident and more inclined to take risks. A negative mood may lead to falling prices because of greater fears and uncertainties, encouraging investors to be more risk-averse.

Many factors like news, social media, and economic reports may greatly influence the market mood. Over the recent past, technology has elevated the value of the market mood because of real-time access to information and swift news dissemination and opinions (Shiller, 2003). Social networking sites such as Twitter and Reddit are important sources where researchers and investors can look into the overall market sentiment. The GameStop short squeeze of 2021 was used as a positive sentiment spread on Reddit, causing large-scale buying mania that pushed the stock price up to the ever-higher peaks (Chohan, 2021).

Generally, centered on AI and ML algorithms, sentiment analysis techniques have become the widely adopted tools in modern financial markets. Such instruments analyze news outlet data, social media platforms, and financial disclosures to present their findings to investors for an understanding of how the sentiment is in the market. Although these tools might bring about important insights, they might also grow herd behavior since investors could be over-reliably making decisions based on sentiment data and look for what most people are saying rather than doing their own investigation (Bikhchandani & Sharma, 2000).

2.2.9. Market volatility

Market volatility is defined as the extent of price variability of assets over a given period. In high volatility, prices change faster and more erratically. Volatility in price changes is less for low volatility. Volatility can be particularly bothersome for investors due to the impact that it can have on the risk-return profiles of the portfolio. Some investors thrive in volatile markets-for example, the day trader-while others become nervous and start selling securities because of volatility in prices (Black, 1976).One of the gauges is the Volatility Index, which is called the "fear gauge" because investors use it to estimate market volatility. VIX measures volatility expectations about future conditions; it is often used as an adjunct to indications of market volatility for risk management purposes. During periods of high volatility, the VIX tends to rise with increasing uncertainty in the markets, whereas during low-volatility periods, the VIX declines, indicating more stable market conditions (Whaley, 2009).

Technological advancements have allowed investors to access current world events and change course in response to shifting circumstances instantly. However, rapid diffusion of information can result in overreactions as investors make impulse decisions based on partial or even incorrect information. Investors need to sieve through a lot of data and find the most relevant information to lead to more informed financial decisions during unstable times around the world.

3. FINANCIAL DECISION-MAKING

Multiple aspects make financial decision-making comprehensive: acumen, planning, risk appetite, and emotional effects. All these determine the manner in which a person invests, saves, and does other work related to finances. Understanding these elements helps form better strategies to overcome personal money management issues, increase the profit from investments, and reduce behavioral biases' impact. This chapter will discuss all the aspects of determining what influence financial decision-making has on it.

3.1. Financial Knowledge

Financial literacy is that awareness of important financial concepts, including interest rates, inflation, diversification, and asset allocation. Financial literacy is a critical ingredient for effective financial decisions because high financial literacy tends to make individuals make more informed and prudent decisions regarding their finances (Lusardi & Mitchell, 2014). Individuals with financial literacy are better positioned to make judgments about investment opportunities, potential risks, and common financial mistakes, including excessive borrowing or insufficient retirement savings.

3.1.1. Financial Literacy in Investment Decision-Making

Financial education equips one with the knowledge of how financial markets are structured and the results that accrue from different types of investments. The literate investor can scrutinize trends in a particular market, calculate asset performance, and even make even wiser decisions on where to invest what (Hastings et al., 2013). By being enlightened on diversification, an investor has the means to reduce risks associated with losing cash by spreading his or her assets in different classes, industries, or geographies.

3.1.2. Financial Literacy Impact on Risk Management

Financial acumen is a prerequisite for risk management. On the other hand, those who are aware of financial risks are likely to assess the potentials of disadvantages in an investment and act to minimize such risks. A financially literate investor may choose a diversified portfolio that includes both stocks and bonds, keeping in mind that bonds tend to be less volatile during market downsides (Van Rooij et al., 2011).

3.1.2. Barriers of Financial Illiteracy

On the contrary, less financially aware people have a greater likelihood of reckless financial decisions, such as investing in high-risk assets without any knowledge of the resultant outcome. Financial ignorance can facilitate inappropriate decisions characterized by excessive debt creation, inadequate retirement funds, or failure to use tax advantaged accounts to invest (Lusardi & Mitchell, 2011). Financial illiteracy should be eradicated through better educations efforts at both the individual and aggregate levels to enhance decisions regarding finance.

3.2.Financial Planning

Financial planning is the process of making a scheme to invest and handle money to reach short-term and long-term goals. This even involves budgeting, saving, investing, and paying off debt, alongside planning for major life events like buying a home, financing college, or retirement. Effective financial planning is an essential condition to ensure that one attains financial security and realizes wealth as time goes by.

3.2.1. The Significance of Goal Setting in Financial Planning

A fundamental aspect of financial planning is setting well-defined and achievable financial goals. These goals act as a guide for individuals, promoting investments that yield them returns that align with their objectives over time (Baker & Ricciardi, 2014).

3.2.2. Budgeting in Financial Planning

Budgeting is a part of financial planning that enables one to keep track of income versus expenditure and, thereby, ensure that it stays within one's limits and distributes the necessary resources for saves and investments appropriately. An organized budget will enable a person to avoid unnecessary overspending, reduce bad debt, and create an accumulated fund for unexpected costs (Xiao et al., 2015). Budgeting helps in planning long-term resource allocation for investments thus enabling individuals to accumulate wealth over time.

3.2.2. Financial Planning in an Investment Policy

A good financial planning strategy would be one that caters to an investor's specific financial goals, risk, and time horizon. According to most financial planners, the diverse asset pool of equities, bonds, and cash should be utilized to optimize returns on investments and minimize losses (Brunel, 2015). Through long-term financial planning, compounded returns ensure that what has been put in will grow to cater for needs over a future time horizon.

3.3. Risk Tolerance

Risk tolerance is the degree to which a person is willing to take risks in terms of his or her finances for the pursuit of greater returns. Risk tolerance is an important element of making financial decisions; those with a high-risk tolerance are likely to invest in some relatively more volatile product, such as equities or cryptocurrencies; those with low risk tolerance prefer investments that are relatively not as volatile, like bonds or savings accounts (Grable & Lytton, 1999). Risk tolerance is critical in helping create the right investment strategy appropriate for a specific individual, along with his or her goals and tolerance.

3.3.1. Determinants of Risk Tolerance

A number of variables can determine a person's risk tolerance, such as age and income, financial knowledge and experience with risk exposure (Grable, 2000). Younger people are likely to be more aggressive because they have a longer period before they can recover from potential financial losses. Elderly individuals on their way to retirement prefer less-risky investments to safeguard their money. Similarly, those with high incomes or greater security are more prone to taking the risk to achieve higher returns.

3.3.2. Function of Risk Tolerance in Asset Allocation

Risk tolerance plays a very important role in asset allocation. High-risk tolerators will have a higher percentage of the portfolio devoted to stock. Stocks offer a higher potential for return but offer more volatility. On the other hand, risk-averse investors prefer a defensive portfolio with a higher proportion of fixed-income assets that provide great stability but lower performance (Hoffmann et al., 2013). Tailoring an investment plan to match the level of acceptable risk for an individual is crucial to keeping abreast of their comfort with investment choices over the period of time.

3.3.3. Diversification as Risk Mitigation

One of the critical strategies for risk management is diversification; diversification involves spreading assets into many asset classes to reduce any risk type's risk exposure (Markowitz, 1952). Diversification reduces return volatility and decreases total portfolio volatility; hence, it remains a crucial tool for risk management. In essence, financial advisors often recommend diversified portfolios that are capable of "beating the market" because investment in stocks, bonds, property, among others forms a cohesive arrangement that relies on the risk appetite of the investor (Brinson et al., 1995).

3.3.4. Emotional Influence

Emotions significantly account for how financial decisions are made, resulting in most cases in irrational or impulsive decisions by the individual. Behavioral finance, as the study of the psychological factors as far as their implications are concerned in financial behavior has come up with a number of emotional biases that may result from investment decisions, such as fear, greed, and overconfidence (Kahneman & Tversky, 1979). It is, therefore, very important to identify and control these emotional factors to come up with the right financial decisions.

3.3.5. Fear and Greed

Perhaps two of the most potent emotions influencing financial behavior are fear and greed. At the time of volatile periods in the market, the element of fear prompts investors to liquidate their assets even when they would benefit if they waited for the long-term period (Loewenstein et al., 2001). Greed, on the other hand, compels investors to be more reckless than they should be so as to realize higher gains than they would otherwise require, thus resulting in speculation and the formation of a market bubble. It is, therefore, essential to understand fear and greed as elements of investment decisions to ensure a disciplined investment strategy (Shiller, 2000).

3.3.6. Overconfidence

Overconfidence is a universal emotional bias whose dangerous effect tends to overshadow financial investment decisions. Overconfident investment may overestimate the predictability of market fluctuations or the performance of assets under consideration. Such individuals may over-assume risk-taking decisions (Barber & Odean, 2001). This could lead to overtrading, increased transaction costs, and less than optimal investment performance. Overconfidence must be checked through self-discipline and adherence to a long-term investment strategy so that impulsive decisions based on short term market gyrations are avoided (Daniel et al., 1998).

3.3.7. Emotional Factor and Loss Aversion

A central idea proposed by Kahneman and Tversky (1979) was that people fear losses more than they enjoy a similar gain. This emotional bias by investors might make them want to hold onto a bad asset for longer, hoping not to lose it, or cause them to liquidate a good asset too early to lock-in their gains. According to Shefrin & Statman, (1985), loss aversion might prevent people from making rational decisions over the overall wellbeing of their portfolio and potential market conditions. It is therefore important to design strategies towards loss aversion, like sticking to a pre-set investment strategy to counter the undesirable effects it has on financial decision-making.

4. TECHNOLOGY IN FINANCIAL DECISION MAKING

Technology transformed almost every sector of financial decision making, whether individual investment or corporate risk management. In short words, the integration of digital platforms, automation, data analytics, and artificial intelligence has been revolutionizing the financial sector with greater convenience while raising new issues. It has brought about enormous benefits so far as it provides better efficiency, convenient accessibility, and personalized financial consultancy. However, increased reliance on technology raises other concerns, such as the uncertainty of markets and potential overreliance on autonomous technologies. Thus, in this paper, technology's influence on financial decisions will be discussed, whether it is good or has problems.

4.1. Accessibility and Democratization of Financial Services

Perhaps the most significant impact of technology on finance decision-making is easier access. The financial markets were only accessible by institutional investors or big wallet individuals in the past. Internet trading platforms, smartphone applications, and digital wallets have effectively democratized finance, allowing regular investors participation in markets with minimum constraints (Baker & Wurgler, 2007). Platforms such as Robinhood, E*TRADE, and Charles Schwab have made market access to financial assets possible for millions with greatly reduced prices and allowing investment accessibility to the ordinary citizen.

Fintech applications also revolutionized the management of personal finances. Mint, Personal Capital, and YNAB (You Need a Budget) make it possible for users to be enabled with tools that allow them to track expenditures, conduct budgets, and plan their future finances. These solutions provide up-to-the-minute financial information that helps the user make sound financial decisions within their existing financial situation (Lusardi & Mitchell, 2014). There is democratization of finance that helps the individual to have greater control over their financial future. A course of action that was once the province of those who had a lot of money or had much financial sense is now possible for greater numbers of people.

4.2. Automation and Robotic Financial Advisors

Automation seems to have brought a significant change in financial decision-making, especially with the growth of robo-advisors. Like Betterment and Wealthfront, robo-advisors offer diversified algorithms for designing and managing investment portfolios according to the goals of an investor, their capacity to absorb risk, and horizon. Such system provides automated investment advice at significantly cheaper expense compared to the same advice offered by a traditional financial advisor would charge (Jung et al., 2018). They help adjust portfolios automatically according to fluctuating market situations, thereby keeping the investors aligned with their long-term goals.

Another way automation in financial decision making reduces the action of emotional bias is by often causing suboptimal investment decisions. There has been research on behavioral finance showing that most investors act based on fear when the market begins to decrease and overconfidence when the market begins to rise, which leads to distorted judgments. The use of data-driven algorithms by robo-advisors combats this drawback since they logically make judgments that are aligned with the risk tolerance and objectives of the investor. Such type of automation makes these investors avoid very common behavioral pitfalls such as panic selling at times of volatile market conditions or trends chasers based on short-term fluctuations in the market (Baker & Wurgler, 2007).

4.3. Data-Informed Decision-Making and Artificial Intelligence

Financial decision-making has been transformed by the application of AI and data-driven analytics. Artificial intelligence and machine learning algorithms can process lots of data coming from numerous sources, including financial markets, news media outlets, and social media. Therefore, such an approach generates insights into the patterns of the market and thus predicts the performance of the assets. These tools enable both retail and institutional investors to make better educated decisions by uncovering trends and hazards that may remain obscured through conventional analytical approaches (Baker et al., 2016).

Sentiment analysis of news articles, earnings reports, and social media could be conducted by AI models in order to figure out and predict market changes based on market sentiment. AI products enable investors to opt for decisions rooted in modern trends instead of relying on outdated data by parsing large volumes of real-time data. The data-based approach has dramatically improved risk management, as financial services companies can monitor new risks much more efficiently-be it changes in market conditions or a political event.

Additional benefits AI-based predictive analytics can offer investors include forecasts of data based on history and market conditions, which may aid decision-making with fewer chances of error. However, though AI has really boosted data processing, it is not by any means perfect. Algorithms are only as good as the quality and scope of data they are tested on and can therefore miss such rare events, like the COVID-19 pandemic, thus raising the chances of errors in predictions (Baker et al., 2020).

4.4. Mobile Transactions and Electronic Wallets

The rise of mobile payments and digital wallets has changed the dynamics of the way people make regular financial transactions. Businesses such as Apple Pay, Google Pay, and PayPal have made financial transactions a relatively easier affair by allowing consumers to execute payments, transfer funds, and oversee finances from the comfort of their smartphones. Such advances offer unparalleled ease and convenience in making financial decisions when mobile.

Using the digital wallet, peer-to-peer lending and crowdfunding have extended their horizons to cover businesslike platforms such as LendingClub and Kickstarter. These have made investment opportunities for their projects or enterprises hence creating new innovations for investors and entrepreneurs (Ozsoylev et al., 2014). The use of digital wallets and payment technology allows the realisation of instant financial decisions corresponding to a user's investment preferences or everyday finance requirements.

However, there are also some negative impacts of technology. One such potential issue is over-reliance on technology-based systems. While robo-advisors and algorithmic trading make the decision easier, it can result in complacency because consumers will remain with the recommendations, they are presented without knowing what risks are involved (Jung et al., 2018). Another reason is that HFT and algorithmic trading increase market volatility and have noted events such as the "Flash Crash" in 2010 (Kirilenko et al., 2017). Lastly, easy access to a trading platform may result in impulsive decisions that subsequently end up in a poor financial situation for inexperienced investors. Consequently, where technology has the impact of increasing efficiency and access in finance, it incorporates new risks to be managed with great caution.

5. LITERATURE REVIEW

Financial decision-making generally involves critical analysis of risk, rewards, and market conditions in order to make informed decisions on investment, savings, and spending. There are various factors that have received significant scholarly research with regard to financial decisions: such as market mood, economic policy uncertainty, risk tolerance, and asset pricing. This literature review comprehensively summarizes the most relevant research contributions to this subject, focusing on market conditions, economic policies, and risk assessment models in financial decision-making.

Market mood is one of the important variables that affect financial decisions. According to Baker and Wurgler (2007), investor sentiment is the dominant emotional sentiment of the investors, which is either optimistic or pessimistic and profoundly affects the forces that drive the prices of the assets and movements in the market. A high investor sentiment often results in overvaluation of the assets when optimism is at a high level. Assets, however, are cheap when the sentiments drop, even though they hold good fundamentals. Mispricing leads to inefficiency in the market; thus, investors make judgments that may be without rational thinking.

Fama (1991) developed the Efficient Market Hypothesis, according to which all available information is already put into asset prices, so it cannot be used for actively managing active profit from portfolio assets over the returns that can be gained just by holding the diversified market portfolio. However, evidence does exist that contradicts Fama's theory. Market mood, rather than purely rational factors, seems to dictate asset pricing in real life. Like the study by Baker and Wurgler (2007), it shares the same criticism towards the Efficient Market Hypothesis; more so, the research reveals that this sentiment-induced mispricing is more established on higher-risk equities, especially those emanating from smaller companies and less liquid equities. Market mood is tied up with herd behavior. In their characterization of herd behavior, Bikhchandani and Sharma (2000) view the tendency of investors to imitate the actions of others even if they do not possess information or personal analysis. This collective behavior can lead to market movements that are divergent from fundamentals, thus creating bubbles or crashes. Herd behavior is most saliently witnessed during financial crisis times and when speculative bubbles occur in the markets, where actions by some major investors influenced the decisions of other investors, albeit less significant ones, thus making the markets even more volatile. Economic policy uncertainty (EPU) has emerged as a critical component influencing financial decision-making. Baker, Bloom, and Davis developed the EPU Index in 2016 and reported that the uncertainty indices involve media coverage of policy-related economic uncertainty, the count of impending federal tax code expirations, and the divergence among economic forecasters. Their study shows that more policy uncertainty leads to fewer investments, lower stock prices, and slower economic growth. Uncertainty over fiscal or monetary policy decisions complicates the ability of firms and investors to forecast future economic conditions, thereby causing more cautious financial behavior. The COVID-19 pandemic further emphasized policy uncertainty. The "plague of uncertainty" caused by the pandemic brought unprecedented economic uncertainty in its wake, resulting in extreme downward shocks to the stock prices and increased market volatility, as noted by Baker, Bloom, Davis, and Terry (2020). A drunkenness of the government responses to a crisis like stimulus packages, lockdown measures, and monetary easing led to investor uncertainty over future economic conditions, profoundly affecting their financial decisions. Monetary policy effects on financial markets have been subjected to broad research. Bernanke and Kuttner (2005) discussed how the stock market reacts to Federal Reserve monetary policy and interest rate changes. Unexpected changes in interest rates elicit instantaneous reactions in equity prices, whereas downward changes increase equity prices, and upward changes lower equity prices. The study also observes that the two elements, shift in rates and vagueness of future monetary policy, also alter market reactions. In most cases, if there is uncertainty as regards the future of interest rates, investors become much more conservative, even reducing investment in high-risk assets considerably. Risk tolerance is one of the most important considerations in financial decisions. According to Grable and Lytton, (1999), "risk tolerance is an amount of risk that an investor is willing to take on in order to obtain higher returns." In designing investment strategies, it is essential to know the risk tolerance of the investor, in that such knowledge determines the trade-off between risky investments, such as equities, and low-risk investments, for instance, bonds or savings accounts. Of course, traditional financial models such as CAPM assume that investors are risk-averse and thus need high returns to attract them into taking on more risks (Sharpe, Alexander, & Bailey, 1999). The Capital Asset Pricing Model, or CAPM, offers a way to calculate the expected return on an investment based on its systematic risk, or how it responds to shifts in the overall market. Empirical evidence indicates that the risk aversion of investors can be quite significantly influenced by demographic characteristics, such as age, income, and financial sophistication. Young investors with a longer time horizon are more likely to have higher tolerance for risk because they have more years to recover losses. Economic factors further help shape the ability of an investor to take on risk. During periods of economic downturn or other bear market, even those considered risk tolerant tend to move to an aversion of risk and rebalance their portfolios to low-risk investments. According to research by Grable and Lytton (1999), the higher the fluctuation of the market, the more cautious the investor tends to become in their financial decisions. This non-rational response can tend to make the effect on markets very sharp as the increased demand for low-risk investments, such as government bonds, increases their price, thereby lowering yields.

Asset pricing models constitute the foundation information used in making financial decisions, foremost among which is the valuation of investments together with the risk-return trade-off. Probably one very influential framework in finance arises from William Sharpe's work on the Capital Asset Pricing Model (CAPM) (Sharpe et al., 1999). The Capital Asset Pricing Model helps investors measure the expected return on an investment, factoring in its beta, which measures its responsiveness to general market fluctuations. The model shows that investors should get compensation for the time value of money-through the risk-free rate-and for the risk that is associated with the investment through the equity risk premium.

Though CAPM is widely used, it has been criticized because of the assumption that markets are efficient and all investors had the same expectations. Campbell and Thompson (2008) proposed that besides just the efficiency of markets and homogenous expectations of all investors, other aspects like behavioral biases and inefficiencies of the market determine the asset price. These researchers support models that consider these factors, and out-of-sample forecasts based on historic data can give better projections of future returns than traditional models like CAPM. Other than CAPM, Black (1976) worked on the volatility of stock prices to check the effect of time-varying volatility on asset price. His findings indicate that with a period of high volatility caused by either a macroeconomic factor or sensitivity in the market, there is an enhanced volatility of price; hence, investors become risk-exposed and make various decisions.

The investor psychology contributes significantly towards financial decision-making. It determines and affects all the risk evaluation and investment decision-making processes and response of an individual to market volatility. By conventional financial theories, investors are rational beings that make judgments based strictly on facts. However, behavioral finance research has shown that psychological biases and emotional influences regularly sway the behavior of investors, causing market inefficiencies and suboptimal results. The current literature review critically appraises pivotal insights into investor psychology with regard to foundational cognitions about biases, emotions, and behavioral finance traits in the realm of financial markets. Cognitive biases represent flaws in the process of reasoning, which are systemic, and affect investors' interpretation of information and their making of decisions. Perhaps the most important idea is prospect theory, derived by Kahneman and Tversky in 1979. This hypothesis states that investors are more sensitive to losses than they are to gains-that is, loss aversion. The result is that investors tend to hold losers longer than they should hold them, waiting for their hoped-for rebound in price, and they tend to sell winners too early to realize their gains (Shefrin & Statman, 1985). Loss aversion accounts for why investors miss opportunities and why market corrections sometimes take longer to occur than one would anticipate. One of the most common cognitive biases that determine financial decisions is the anchoring bias. Campbell and Sharpe state that "investors often anchor their expectations around a particular reference point, such as the price paid for a stock, rather than to prevailing market conditions and base their judgments accordingly." Through this phenomenon, investors may miss the need for revision in their portfolios and, therefore, invest inefficiently. Lastly, Nickerson (1998) considers confirmation bias, whereby investors only want information confirming their beliefs and avoid information contrary to them. This leads to excessive confidence in an investment program even when the market conditions are against it. Barber and Odean (2001) discovered that overconfidence exists in male investors who have a higher trading frequency and risk taking as usually ends in lesser earnings. There is considerable evidence that fear and greed are driving investor psychology and, subsequently, their behaviors; thus, investors often abdicate reason for unwise financial decision-making. Loewenstein, Weber, Hsee, and Welch (2001) experiment with the notion that risk is an emotion, which implies emotional reactions to risk—loss aversion or thrill from possible rewards—can supplant reason. During times of market volatility, fear may encourage one to sell too soon, as reason dictates holding for the long haul. Greed drives investors to take risks they would otherwise not venture into, particularly in a speculative market bubble, where the promise of immense profit provides a strong lure. Shiller, in his 2000 book Irrational Exuberance, has discussed the role of emotions in the formation of market booms and their ultimate collapses. He argued that during speculative bubbles, the investor mood at times has been too optimistic-an attitude, he believed, that sent asset values on unsustainable climbs. As the bubble bursts, fear sets in, and selling strikes with rapidity, and markets plummet. Shiller's work thus points out cyclic tendencies related to investor psychology and how it impacts market volatility. Baker and Wurgler (2007) examine the impact of sentiment in the financial market. He proved that even a slight change in sentiment can bring high levels of asset mispricing. These periods have exaggerated optimism from investors, which pushes the price of the asset over the intrinsic value. During the low mood periods, investors express extreme pessimism, and as a result, the price of the asset is driven below the intrinsic values. Such sentiment-driven mispricing brings profits for smart investors but perpetuates the disbalances of the market. Herd behavior is a psychological phenomenon that affects investment decisions when there are high levels of uncertainty. Bikhchandani and Sharma (2000) defined herd behavior as following the action of others even if such acts may not be rational or knowledge-based. This behavior is particularly pronounced during market bubbles or crashes because the acts of just a few significant investors may lead to an analogy chain among others leading to exaggerated movements in the markets. An example of recent herd behavior is the 2021 GameStop short squeeze analyzed by Chohan (2021). Here, retail investors on the online community WallStreetBets on Reddit artificially drove the price of GameStop shares significantly upwards, leading to significant losses for hedge funds that had shorted the stock. It is an example of how social influence and herd behavior could interfere with the dynamics of a market and create a lot of price volatility. Behavioral finance challenges the traditional view of efficient markets by demonstrating that psychological forces can lead to systematic market inefficiencies. Daniel, Hirshleifer, and Subrahmanyam (1998) examine how psychological biases-overconfidence and self-attribution bias-affect underreactions and overreactions to stock-market events. Investors tend to attribute successes to skills and failures to luck, and overconfidence loops in to produce overtrading. In a broad review of the literature on behavioral finance, focusing on cognitive and emotional biases that relate to anomalies such as momentum and the value premium, Barberis and Thaler posit that investor psychology has to be the pervasive cause for which stocks or sectors perform in ways that standard financial models cannot explain.

For a long time, technology has transformed the financial markets far beyond any recognition. Trading processes, techniques for investments, and general dynamics in market have been influenced by this change of the century. Development of algorithmic trading, AI, and blockchain technology are considered at all stages of financial decisions and risk assessment. Investment management has changed. In this literature review, there is a compilation of relevant research into the influence of technology on the financial markets, focusing on the benefits it brings with its issues.

Algorithmic trading is now considered one of the most crucial technology advancements in financial markets. The process involves computer software and algorithms making trades with a speed that is very high, and sometimes, even without human interaction. Treleaven, Gandel, and Chen (2020) review the future of finance through the lens of analyzing algorithmic trading and artificial intelligence by pointing out their roles in efficiency and liquidity of markets. Algorithms minimize the costs of a trade and mitigate market effects caused by big orders because they facilitate trades faster than do humans. The benefits of algorithmic trading, however, do come with risks. Kirilenko, Kyle, Samadi, and Tuzun (2017) examine the function of algorithmic trading in the 2010 "Flash Crash," in which the Dow Jones Industrial Average plummeted more than 1,000 points in matter of minutes before rebounding quickly. The authors also focus on showing how algorithms may be used to amplify market volatility, especially in those periods when risk is more pronounced. Algorithms represent one form of HFT and have been attacked for creating an unbalanced competitive landscape due to their favoring the most technologically sophisticated firms that are likely to benefit more than their counterparts. Despite this, algorithmic trading remains on the ascendency in the world of finance. Campbell and Thompson (2008) opine that algorithmic models are perhaps superior to more traditional investing strategies as they can use historical data to forecast excess returns, though adding that "robustness" depends very much both on the quality of the data themselves and on the ability to avoid overfitting, when models are so specifically built for historical data that they have difficulty generalizing back into future market conditions. AI has transformed financial markets by presenting shrewd, sophisticated data analysis as well as predictive modeling. Through algorithms driven by AI, researchers can analyze enormous datasets in real time, enabling investors to make more informed decisions based on market patterns, sentiment analysis, and many other predictors. Ryll and Seppelt (2022) describe a comprehensive analysis of the AI function in market forecast, revealing its ability to examine large volumes of data to uncover patterns that other human researchers may miss. Machine learning is an AI sub-area that has greatly impacted predictive analytics in banks. Kauppi, Niemelä, and Sarlin (2021) made a comprehensive analysis on the applications of ML in financial prediction, and they noted that their algorithms enhance the accuracy of market predictions because they can identify non-linear correlations in data. This makes it possible for financial institutions to enhance risk assessment, predict the value of assets, and optimize portfolios. However, the authors still warn readers that machine learning models easily overfit and need careful validation to establish their reliability under different market conditions. AI and ML have improved the accuracy of financial projections but are far from a magic pill. According to Ryll and Seppelt (2022), AI models often fail in long-term forecasts, especially if made under extraordinary events, such as geopolitical tensions or pandemics. For example, the COVID-19 case affected global markets in ways that most models of predictions did not foresee. According to Baker, Bloom, Davis, and Terry (2020), the challenges created by the pandemic suggest the perspective that economic uncertainty under COVID-19 led to extensive market declines and increased volatility, conditions that AI models could not handle.

Blockchain technology was initially conceived as the underlying framework for cryptocurrencies, like Bitcoin. The interest in this technology has also been driven into mainstream financial markets. According to Cai (2022), he has offered a comprehensive review of how blockchain impacts the financial market by enhancing aspects such as transparency, security, and efficiency. The decentralized architecture of blockchain makes peer-to-peer transactions safe, eliminating middlemen; thus, cross-border payments take less time and cost more. One of the major application areas in finance where blockchain is used includes smart contracts, which are self-executing agreements with the terms written directly into code. Cai, 2022 suggests that smart contracts will transform securities trading, clearing, and settlement since procedures could be automated, thereby decreasing the chance of human error. Moreover, fraud and lack of transparency could be prevented through an immutable ledger of blockchain since all transactions are recorded eternally and cannot be altered. While promising, blockchain technology remains yet to be fully implemented in financial markets due to several challenges. Lack of clarity and consistency in regulations, scalability, and excessive energy expenditure has limited its growth. Cai (2022) observes that while blockchain can revolutionize the existing financial institutions, major investment and consensus between the regulators and the industries are required to achieve its maximum benefits. The robo-advisor has changed the management of individual investments. Robo-advisors refer to computerized programs that provide financial advice depending on an investor's risk tolerance, time horizon, and financial goals, upon which algorithms operate. Jung, Dorner, Weinhardt, and Pusmaz (2018) explain how robo-advisors represent techniques with the aim of opening access to financial advice for all by making portfolio management cheap and automated. Such innovations appeal to ordinary investors, who may not raise enough money for hiring 'conventional' consultants from the financial sector. Robo-advisors typically construct and manage diversified portfolios using low-cost exchange-traded funds or ETFs. They also rebalance the portfolio smartly based on variations in market conditions, ensuring that the asset allocation of the investor remains perpetually aligned with his investment goals. Jung et al. argue that robo-advisors have mitigated the barriers to investing; thus, making financial planning more accessible to a larger population, especially low-income and risk-averse populations. However, there are some restrictions about robo-advisors. One of them is excessive reliance on algorithms, which may not fully capture the intricacy of a person's financial situation. Furthermore, during times of extreme market volatility, such as in the 2020 market meltdown and the COVID-19 pandemic, robo-advisors might lack the ability to offer bespoke advice specific investors need to address complex financial decisions (Jung et al., 2018).

6. CONCLUSION

Technology's rapid development has had both positive and negative effects on investor psychology and financial decision-making. Technology driven investment tools, have democratized access to financial markets by giving investors real-time information, improved decision-making skills, and reduced entry barriers. As a result, the financial market is now more data-driven and effective, allowing private investors to compete with larger institutions. Empowerment through technology has psychological implications. Because so much data is readily available, investors may experience information overload and find it difficult to sift through pertinent information, which raises the risk of cognitive biases like herding, overconfidence, and recency bias. Furthermore, the proliferation of robo-advisors and automated investment platforms may result in an excessive dependence on technology, pushing investors to forego human judgment and critical thinking, which may exacerbate illogical decision-making tendencies. In order to successfully navigate the tech-driven financial landscape, this review highlights the necessity for investors to have increased psychological awareness and financial literacy. Future studies should concentrate on devising methods to lessen the psychological risks connected to financial technology, like enhancing investor education and producing instruments to assist in controlling cognitive biases, to make sure that technology keeps facilitating rather than impeding sound financial judgment.

REFERENCES

Baker, H. K., & Nofsinger, J. R. (2010). *Behavioral finance: Investors, corporations, and markets*. John Wiley & Sons. DOI: 10.1002/9781118258415

Baker, M., Bloom, N., & Davis, S. J. (2016). Measuring economic policy uncertainty. *The Quarterly Journal of Economics*, 131(4), 1593–1636. DOI: 10.1093/qje/qjw024

Baker, M., Bloom, N., & Davis, S. J. (2016). Measuring economic policy uncertainty. *The Quarterly Journal of Economics*, 131(4), 1593–1636. DOI: 10.1093/qje/qjw024

Baker, M., & Wurgler, J. (2007). Investor sentiment in the stock market. *The Journal of Economic Perspectives*, 21(2), 129–152. DOI: 10.1257/jep.21.2.129

Baker, M., & Wurgler, J. (2007). Investor sentiment in the stock market. *The Journal of Economic Perspectives*, 21(2), 129–152. DOI: 10.1257/jep.21.2.129

Baker, S. R., Bloom, N., Davis, S. J., & Terry, S. J. (2020). COVID-induced economic uncertainty. NBER Working Paper No. 26983. DOI: 10.3386/w26983

Baker, S. R., Bloom, N., Davis, S. J., & Terry, S. J. (2020). COVID-induced economic uncertainty. *NBER Working Paper No. 26983*. https://doi.org/DOI: 10.3386/w26983

Barber, B. M., & Odean, T. (2001). Boys will be boys: Gender, overconfidence, and common stock investment. *The Quarterly Journal of Economics*, 116(1), 261–292. DOI: 10.1162/003355301556400

Barber, B. M., & Odean, T. (2001). Boys will be boys: Gender, overconfidence, and common stock investment. *The Quarterly Journal of Economics*, 116(1), 261–292. DOI: 10.1162/003355301556400

Barberis, N., & Huang, M. (2001). Mental accounting, loss aversion, and individual stock returns. *The Journal of Finance*, 56(4), 1247–1292. DOI: 10.1111/0022-1082.00367

Barberis, N., & Thaler, R. (2003). A survey of behavioral finance. *Handbook of the Economics of Finance, 1*(B), 1053-1128. DOI: 10.1016/S1574-0102(03)01027-6

Barberis, N., & Thaler, R. (2003). A survey of behavioral finance. *Handbook of the Economics of Finance, 1*(B), 1053-1128. DOI: 10.1016/S1574-0102(03)01027-6

Bernanke, B. S., & Kuttner, K. N. (2005). What explains the stock market's reaction to Federal Reserve policy? *The Journal of Finance*, 60(3), 1221–1257. DOI: 10.1111/j.1540-6261.2005.00760.x

Bikhchandani, S., & Sharma, S. (2000). Herd behavior in financial markets. *IMF Staff Papers*, 47(3), 279–310. DOI: 10.2307/3867650

Black, F. (1976). Studies of stock price volatility changes. Proceedings of the Business and Economic Statistics Section, American Statistical Association, 177-181.

Bodie, Z., Kane, A., & Marcus, A. J. (2014). *Investments* (10th ed.). McGraw-Hill Education., DOI: 10.1036/0077861671

Brinson, G. P., Hood, L. R., & Beebower, G. L. (1995). Determinants of portfolio performance. *Financial Analysts Journal*, 51(1), 133–138. DOI: 10.2469/faj.v51.n1.1869

Brunel, J. L. P. (2015). Goals-based wealth management in practice: Setting objectives and making investments. *The Journal of Wealth Management*, 18(1), 9–22. DOI: 10.3905/jwm.1999.320346

Buehler, R., Griffin, D., & Ross, M. (1994). Exploring the "planning fallacy": Why people underestimate their task completion times. *Journal of Personality and Social Psychology*, 67(3), 366–381. DOI: 10.1037/0022-3514.67.3.366

Cai, W. (2022). Blockchain technology and its impact on financial markets: A comprehensive review. *Journal of Financial Innovation*, 9(2), 115–132. DOI: 10.1016/j.finov.2022.04.006

Campbell, J. Y., & Sharpe, S. A. (2009). Anchoring bias in consensus forecasts and its effect on market prices. *Journal of Financial Economics*, 92(3), 237–253. DOI: 10.1016/j.jfineco.2008.07.004

Campbell, J. Y., & Thompson, S. B. (2008). Predicting excess stock returns out of sample: Can anything beat the historical average? *Review of Financial Studies*, 21(4), 1509–1531. DOI: 10.1093/rfs/hhm055

Chohan, U. W. (2021). The GameStop short squeeze: Causes and consequences. *Critical Perspectives on Accounting*, 78, 102291. DOI: 10.1016/j.cpa.2021.102291

Daniel, K., Hirshleifer, D., & Subrahmanyam, A. (1998). Investor psychology and security market under- and overreactions. *The Journal of Finance*, 53(6), 1839–1885. DOI: 10.1111/0022-1082.00077

Daniel, K., Hirshleifer, D., & Subrahmanyam, A. (1998). Investor psychology and security market under- and overreactions. *The Journal of Finance*, 53(6), 1839–1885. DOI: 10.1111/0022-1082.00077

Fama, E. F. (1991). Efficient capital markets: II. *The Journal of Finance*, 46(5), 1575–1617. DOI: 10.1111/j.1540-6261.1991.tb04636.x

Fang, L. H., & Yasuda, A. (2014). Are stars' opinions worth more? The relation between analyst reputation and recommendation values. *Journal of Financial Services Research*, 45(1), 67–82. DOI: 10.1007/s10693-013-0178-y

Festinger, L. (1957). *A theory of cognitive dissonance*. Stanford University Press. DOI: 10.1515/9781503620766

Grable, J. E., & Lytton, R. H. (1999). Financial risk tolerance revisited: The development of a risk assessment instrument. *Financial Services Review*, 8(3), 163–181. DOI: 10.1016/S1057-0810(99)00041-4

Grable, J. E., & Lytton, R. H. (1999). Financial risk tolerance revisited: The development of a risk assessment instrument. *Financial Services Review*, 8(3), 163–181. DOI: 10.1016/S1057-0810(99)00041-4

Hastings, J. S., Madrian, B. C., & Skimmyhorn, W. L. (2013). Financial literacy, financial education, and economic outcomes. *Annual Review of Economics*, 5(1), 347–373. DOI: 10.1146/annurev-economics-082312-125807 PMID: 23991248

Jung, D., Dorner, V., Weinhardt, C., & Pusmaz, H. (2018). Designing a robo-advisor for risk-averse, low-budget consumers. *Electronic Markets*, 28(3), 367–380. DOI: 10.1007/s12525-017-0279-9

Jung, D., Dorner, V., Weinhardt, C., & Pusmaz, H. (2018). Designing a robo-advisor for risk-averse, low-budget consumers. *Electronic Markets*, 28(3), 367–380. DOI: 10.1007/s12525-017-0279-9

Kahneman, D., & Tversky, A. (1979). Prospect theory: An analysis of decision under risk. *Econometrica*, 47(2), 263–291. DOI: 10.2307/1914185

Kahneman, D., & Tversky, A. (1979). Prospect theory: An analysis of decision under risk. *Econometrica*, 47(2), 263–291. DOI: 10.2307/1914185

Kahneman, D., & Tversky, A. (1979). Prospect theory: An analysis of decision under risk. *Econometrica*, 47(2), 263–291. DOI: 10.2307/1914185

Kauppi, E., Niemelä, J., & Sarlin, P. (2021). Machine learning for financial prediction: A systematic review. *Journal of Computational Finance*, 25(1), 1–36. DOI: 10.3905/jcf.2021.1.100

Kirilenko, A. A., Kyle, A. S., Samadi, M., & Tuzun, T. (2017). The flash crash: The impact of high-frequency trading on an electronic market. *The Journal of Finance*, 72(3), 967–998. DOI: 10.1111/jofi.12498

Loewenstein, G., Weber, E. U., Hsee, C. K., & Welch, N. (2001). Risk as feelings. *Psychological Bulletin*, 127(2), 267–286. DOI: 10.1037/0033-2909.127.2.267 PMID: 11316014

Loewenstein, G., Weber, E. U., Hsee, C. K., & Welch, N. (2001). Risk as feelings. *Psychological Bulletin*, 127(2), 267–286. DOI: 10.1037/0033-2909.127.2.267 PMID: 11316014

Lusardi, A., & Mitchell, O. S. (2011). Financial literacy and retirement planning in the United States. *Journal of Pension Economics and Finance*, 10(4), 509–525. DOI: 10.1017/S147474721100045X PMID: 28553190

Markowitz, H. (1952). Portfolio selection. *The Journal of Finance*, 7(1), 77–91.

Mehra, R., & Prescott, E. C. (1985). The equity premium: A puzzle. *Journal of Monetary Economics*, 15(2), 145–161. DOI: 10.1016/0304-3932(85)90061-3

Nickerson, R. S. (1998). Confirmation bias: A ubiquitous phenomenon in many guises. *Review of General Psychology*, 2(2), 175–220. DOI: 10.1037/1089-2680.2.2.175

Ozsoylev, H. N., Walden, J., Yavuz, M. D., & Bildik, R. (2014). Investor networks in the stock market. *Review of Financial Studies*, 27(5), 1323–1366. DOI: 10.1093/rfs/hht065

Ozsoylev, H. N., Walden, J., Yavuz, M. D., & Bildik, R. (2014). Investor networks in the stock market. *Review of Financial Studies*, 27(5), 1323–1366. DOI: 10.1093/rfs/hht065

Park, C. W., Jun, S. Y., & MacInnis, D. J. (2010). Choosing what I want versus rejecting what I do not want: An application of decision framing to product option choice decisions. *The Journal of Consumer Research*, 37(4), 632–644. DOI: 10.1086/655466

Rabin, M. (2002). Inference by believers in the law of small numbers. *The Quarterly Journal of Economics*, 117(3), 775–816. DOI: 10.1162/003355302760193896

Ryan, R. M., & Deci, E. L. (2000). Self-determination theory and the facilitation of intrinsic motivation, social development, and well-being. *The American Psychologist*, 55(1), 68–78. DOI: 10.1037/0003-066X.55.1.68 PMID: 11392867

Ryll, L., & Seppelt, R. (2022). AI and market forecasting: A comprehensive study of predictive analytics in finance. *Financial Data Science Review*, 6(2), 54–76. DOI: 10.1016/j.finrev.2022.02.004

Sharpe, W. F., Alexander, G. J., & Bailey, J. V. (1999). *Investments* (6th ed.). Prentice Hall., DOI: 10.2139/ssrn.161123

Shefrin, H. (2000). *Beyond greed and fear: Understanding behavioral finance and the psychology of investing*. Harvard Business School Press.

Shefrin, H., & Statman, M. (1985). The disposition to sell winners too early and ride losers too long: Theory and evidence. *The Journal of Finance*, 40(3), 777–790. DOI: 10.1111/j.1540-6261.1985.tb05002.x

Shefrin, H., & Statman, M. (1985). The disposition to sell winners too early and ride losers too long: Theory and evidence. *The Journal of Finance*, 40(3), 777–790. DOI: 10.1111/j.1540-6261.1985.tb05002.x

Shefrin, H., & Thaler, R. H. (1988). The behavioral life-cycle hypothesis. *Economic Inquiry*, 26(4), 609–643. DOI: 10.1111/j.1465-7295.1988.tb01520.x

Shiller, R. J. (2000). *Irrational exuberance*. Princeton University Press., DOI: 10.1515/9780691214871

Shiller, R. J. (2000). *Irrational exuberance*. Princeton University Press.

Shiller, R. J. (2003). From efficient markets theory to behavioral finance. *The Journal of Economic Perspectives*, 17(1), 83–104. DOI: 10.1257/089533003321164967

Thaler, R. H. (1999). Mental accounting matters. *Journal of Behavioral Decision Making*, 12(3), 183–206. DOI: 10.1002/(SICI)1099-0771(199909)12:3<183::AID-BDM318>3.0.CO;2-F

Treleaven, P., Gandel, P., & Chen, S. (2020). Algorithmic trading, AI and the future of finance. *Journal of Finance and Data Science*, 6(1), 27–42. DOI: 10.1016/j.jfds.2019.07.005

Tversky, A., & Kahneman, D. (1971). Belief in the law of small numbers. *Psychological Bulletin*, 76(2), 105–110. DOI: 10.1037/h0031322

Tversky, A., & Kahneman, D. (1973). Availability: A heuristic for judging frequency and probability. *Cognitive Psychology*, 5(2), 207–232. DOI: 10.1016/0010-0285(73)90033-9

Tversky, A., & Kahneman, D. (1974). Judgment under uncertainty: Heuristics and biases. *Science*, 185(4157), 1124–1131. DOI: 10.1126/science.185.4157.1124 PMID: 17835457

Tversky, A., & Kahneman, D. (1992). Advances in prospect theory: Cumulative representation of uncertainty. *Journal of Risk and Uncertainty*, 5(4), 297–323. DOI: 10.1007/BF00122574

Van Rooij, M., Lusardi, A., & Alessie, R. (2011). Financial literacy and stock market participation. *Journal of Financial Economics*, 101(2), 449–472. DOI: 10.1016/j.jfineco.2011.03.006

Xiao, J. J., Tang, C., & Shim, S. (2009). Acting for happiness: Financial behavior and life satisfaction of college students. *Social Indicators Research*, 92(1), 53–68. DOI: 10.1007/s11205-008-9288-6

Chapter 5
Behavioral Finance Approaches to Investing in Technology-Driven and Emerging Markets

Monica C. Singh
Sri Balaji University, India

Smriti Verma
https://orcid.org/0000-0002-8339-1670
Yeshwantrao Chavan College of Engineering, India

Pallavi Kudal
Sri Balaji University, India

Nidhi Kumari
Sri Balaji University, India

ABSTRACT

In today's ever-evolving financial landscape, the integration of behavioral finance into investment strategies is increasingly critical. This chapter explores how insights from behavioral finance can be effectively applied by stakeholders to enhance investment decision-making in emerging markets characterized by technology and innovation. These markets, which present both unique opportunities and challenges, demand a nuanced and comprehensive understanding of the psychological and behavioral traits of investors. By offering pragmatic insights into cognitive biases, heuristics, and emotional influences, the chapter aims to equip stakeholders—including investors, financial advisors, and policymakers—with the essential tools and techniques

DOI: 10.4018/979-8-3693-8583-8.ch005

needed to successfully navigate these complex markets.

INTRODUCTION

Investment decisions, financial economics and the interaction between financial markets and their agents have been studied differently by various researchers. Academicians, practitioners and participants in capital markets have been observing human behavior in order to understand the process of investment decisions. Over the last 25 years, there has been an ongoing debate between traditional theorists and behavioral theorists about drivers of investment decisions. Predominantly, the discipline of traditional finance was characterized by the assumption that markets are efficient, and investors are rational (Fromlet, 2001). This means that investors use all relevant information available to them while taking investment decisions. Established theories concerning traditional finance include the Efficient market hypothesis (EMH), Capital asset pricing model (CAPM), and Markowitz portfolio theory (MPT) (Fama, 1998; Witt & Dobins, 1979; Levy, 2011). As per these theories, the stock market tends to follow a random walk, and investors wish to gain maximum utility at any given level of risk (Ricciardi & Simon, 2000). These theories were challenged by behavioral theorists who believed that markets are not efficient, and investors are not rational (Statman, 2008). Some emerging theories concerning behavioral finance are- prospect theory, behavioral portfolio theory (BPT) and behavioral asset pricing model (BAPM).

The disciplines of Sociology, Economics, Psychology, and Finance have underpinned the discipline of behavioral finance, which seeks to answer 'what' and 'how' aspects of investment decisions in various contexts. These disciplines address many subjective and emotional factors as well as their impact on investment decision-making. These factors lead agents (individual investors/institutional investors) to depart from the rational theories of investment behavior deduced by traditional finance. These theories have been tested and verified with vast economic data. What if these theories employed larger data sets based on the cognitive and emotional factors to develop decision models based on human behavior? The universe of emerging markets is heterogeneous. While there isn't a precise description, developing markets are typically distinguished by characteristics like consistent market access, advancement toward middle-class status, and increased global economic significance. Nevertheless, these economies are not the same, and it is also difficult to distinguish between emerging markets and other developing nations (www.img.org, 2024). Since the year 2000, emerging markets have significantly improved their macroeconomic policies, enabling them to more than quadruple their average per capita income. Sixty-five percent of the nations we have classified as emerging markets have monetary policies that are based on forward-looking inflation-targeting regimes; in the majority of these countries, inflation has decreased and stabilized.

Disruptive technologies are ones that drastically alter how we obtain information, how much goods and services cost, or how easy it is to obtain them. Due to the tremendous rise in computing power capacity and internet throughput, the diffusion has happened in the form of blockchain, fintech, and artificial intelligence etc. The behavioral elements in terms of *animal spirit*, instinct and feeling had originated from the seminal work of Keynes (1936), which challenged the concept of *homo economics* (rational man that acts in their self-interest and maximization of profit). It is instinctively true that decisions based on quantitative models and a series of mathematical modelling involve systematic errors in judgment which might lead to inefficiency in the markets and mispricing of securities across the world market. The pioneering work of Friedman & Savage (1948) presumed that an investor might purchase lottery tickets and insurance at one go. Thus, displaying two sets of behavior, one of a risk taker and another of risk averse. Simon (1972) advocated bounded rationality which rejects the concept of full rationality. Investors put themselves under the constraint of rationality which is imposed by their limited search for information and mental calculation. They only rationalize their decisions instead of optimizing them when they have simpler alternatives. This explanation is a contradiction to the conventional finance theory of maximization.

Fathers of behavior finance-Daniel Kahneman and Amos Tversky have contributed to ground-breaking research in the field of behavioral economics. Their contribution in the form of Prospect Theory puts forward another confirmation on the importance of psychology in decision-making. Prospect theory presents a model of decision-making which is an alternate to subjective expected utility theory with more realistic behavioral assumptions (Kahneman & Tversky, 1979). They exhibited the fact that heuristics play an important role in our decision-making. Using heuristics, one takes a problem-solving approach that may not be optimal or perfect.

As per Sewell (2007) behavioral finance is the study of the influence of psychology on the behavior of financial practitioners and its subsequent effects on the markets. It deals with the 'why' and 'how' aspects of decision-making. Conventional theorists assume that investors are rational, but behavior finance theorists assume that investors are normal. The behavioral portfolio theory by Shefrin & Statman (2000) was developed as an alternative to Markowitz's mean variance portfolio theory. The Mean variance theory works on the premise of optimization of risk-return payoff. Whereas the behavioral portfolio theory works on how the portfolio is designed and securities are fitted into different layers in the pyramid as per the attitude towards risk and objective. It is a prescriptive theory and focuses on the aspirations of investors, who have different attitudes towards risk.

During 1989-2000, the world markets had undergone a myriad of changes regarding volatility, bubble, anomaly, and inefficiency in the market. Researchers and practitioners, like Thaler, Barberis, Shiller, Odean, Hirshleifer, Camerer and Rabin have contributed towards the literature in the field of behavioral finance through their research work and experiments. Stanovich & West (2000) shed light on the deviations in human response from the performance deemed normative models of decision-making which could be attributed to the gap between normative predictions and prescriptive behavior. This posits the irregularities in human cognition (Grinblatt & Han,2002). Therefore, understanding human based behavior in terms of investment decision-making would unquestionably bring lucidity about the decision-making process. It would aim to understand how an individual should invest and why in a particular asset category.

Conventional finance is built on the assumptions that people are rational, markets are efficient, application of mean-variance theory for portfolio building, and return being the only function of risk (Bondt et al., 2008). Whereas, behavioral finance is built on the assumptions that people are normal, markets are inefficient, application of behavioral portfolio theory for portfolio designing etc. A rational investor goes through utilitarian, expressive and emotional needs while taking a decision. But a normal investor does not differentiate between his role as consumer or investor at the same time. This brings the prevalence of other factors such as: culture, emotional bias and social responsibility under cognitive and systematic errors.

To add more to the substance of human element, Kahneman explained two systems of our brain in his book "Thinking, Fast and Slow". These systems influence the way we think and take decisions (Kahneman, 2011). System 1 is fast, operates automatically, is intuitive and emotional; decisions are made by a very small amount of effort and there is no self-control. System 2 is slower, focuses on mental calculations, takes choices with concentration and is more logical. Based on these assumptions, he has mentioned several biases like- availability, representativeness, overconfidence etc. that drive our behavior.

Foundations of Behavioral Finance

Behavioral finance relies on cognitive and emotional factors that drive investment decisions, and one ends up making perplexed decisions (Chira et al., 2008). Behavioral finance is an interaction between psychology and investor behavior. Diverse theories of behavioral finance work on the assumption of rationality. However, in practice there are numerous instances that validate the deviation from the rational decision-making framework. The financial market has seen various anomalies and inefficiencies caused by asset bubbles, market crash and uncertain events. If these events did not exist, the investor behavior would have been effectively rational.

This brings into account the drivers of behavioral finance: biases and heuristics. Let's discuss some of the biases and heuristics that brings deviation from rational theories in conventional finance.

a. **Disposition Effect**

Having a tendency to sell winner stock and hold the loser stock makes a bad investment decision and brings in a feeling of guilt. The average investor tends to hold on to the losing stock as the pain of regret is not acceptable by them (Frazzini, 2006; Weber & Camerer, 1998).

b. **Familiarity Bias**

People have a tendency to bring the local preference aspect of the investment such as they are mostly inclined towards local companies and information available in the domestic market. This phenomenon applies to all the countries as researched (Searston & Tangen, 2016; Fox & Levav, 2000).

c. **Anchoring Bias**

How many of us reply to the first piece of information and make it a reference point? This prevails not only in investment realm, but while taking any buying decision too. The new information is based on a reference point that doesn't bring objectivity while making a decision. Imagine you want to buy a car and go to various dealers but ultimately refer to the cheapest price offered by one of the dealers. That's an anchoring bias (Lieder et al., 2018; Campbell & Sharpe, 2009).

d. **Overconfidence Bias**

It is termed that person's subjective confidence in his / her judgement is reliably greater than the objective accuracy of those judgements. It is the most documented bias in the behavioural finance literature. Disposition optimism, self attribution, high self esteem, complexity of task, motivation and skill level, personality factors (negative emotion, extraversion, openness to experience, sonscietiousnessm (preference to innovation), miscalibration of information and gender impacts the overconfidence level (Stotz & Von, 2005; Johnson & Fowler, 2011).

e. **Risk Tolerance Bias**

An extent to which an investor is willing to take more risk in expectation of a higher return. Literatures claim that non-investment income, liquid & non liquid financial assets, no. of years to retirement, race/ethnic group, education, marital status, gender, self-employment, gender, age, no. of dependents, marital status, income and wealth etc. affects the risk tolerance bias of an individual (Wang & Hanna,1997; Van et al., 2012).

f. **Representativeness Bias**

Based on past experiences, people are bound to make judgments using some probabilities. It leads to the development of stereotypes. Judges use this bias during the court trial based on the pre-exist scenario (Chen et al., 2007; Irshad & Hakum, 2016).

g. **Familiarity Bias**

A mental shortcut that has an impact based on past memory related to events and circumstances. These heuristics are rule of thumb that shorten the decision-making time as our most favourable opinions capture our mind rather than the present information (Chew & Zhong, 2012; Whittlesea, 1993).

h. **Optimism/Pessimism Bias**

We have a tendency to overestimate the outcome of both positive and negative outcome. A happy and sad feeling can make our decision irrational (Sattar & Fahad, 2020; Mansour & Napp, 2006).

i. **Loss Aversion Bias**

The magnitude of pain of the loss is higher than the joy of gain when it comes to investments. An individual feels more pain if he loses out Rs. 1000 than the gain of the same amount (Hirshleifer, 2015; Ricciardi, 2008).

The development of behavioral finance has evolved from the branch of psychology, sociology and finance. A human being's physical and mental shape, social behavior in groups, attitudes, etc. conforms to behavioral finance (Subash, 2012). An individual, group and organization are the decision makers and take judgment regarding financial decisions. Sometimes people have a predisposition to overestimate their own ability; fail to learn from past mistakes; try to validate contrary behavior; go with the crowd behavior instead of basic principles of investing; regret the choice of investment; make biased behavior accordingly and use decision weights to measure gain and loss. Whether to buy a stock or mutual fund, our emotional rhythm compels us to make mental mistakes (Ricciardi & Simon, 2000). Investors do not always take a decision based on standard preferences or quantitative models, rather their cognitive and emotional aspects encourage taking a decision in an irrational manner. Both macro and micro aspects of behavioral finance are essential and have their own importance.

The human brain is a complex system and so is investment decision-making. No matter how much we try to explore it and for how long, it remains perplexed and confound. Our mind looks to create a balance between conflicting thoughts and actual outcome. How about reducing the complexity and using heuristics to reduce it? If an event is characterized by the occurrence of one outcome, it leads to a misconception about the event as a whole. A simple clue is also representative of the whole event. Overestimating the probability of the occurrence of some events even lead to erroneous results. Framing affects the judgment unconscientiously and System 2 supervises the thinking process (Cassotti et al., 2012). A series of experiments were made to comprehend the cognitive thinking that involved letter crunching and billboards for different mental activities. It sufficed the expressive needs of a person. By looking at a billboard, one could easily connect to the emotions displayed and can be intuitive to the message. Here, perception is assumed to be 'reference dependent' which means the outcome is dependent on reference point and contrast between an existing and prior stimulus (Zaleskiewicz,2015).

Understanding investor behavior in the stock market is very complicated as emotions, expressions, sentiments and behavior of the investors are not constant. Sometimes, crowd behavior of the members of the financial market controls the overall decision-making in the market. Behavioral finance aims to improve the understanding of the financial market by integrating psychology and sociology. This field is a deviation from 'homo economicus' theory that people do not take decisions based on probabilities. Long-term anomalies, such as under reaction and overreaction, were studied by Fama (1998). Two behavioral models namely: Barberis, Shleifer, and Vishny (BSV) and Daniel, Hirshleifer, and Subhramanyam (DHS) have been examined here (Barberis et al., 1998). The BSV model assumed judgment biases like representative bias and conservatism bias. A short-term momentum brought under reaction to the earnings information and a trending belief about the earnings brought overreaction to the news. Events like- stock issue and repurchase of stocks carried information by mispricing information. Olsen (1998) unveiled that stock price volatility was not explained thoroughly by standard financial models as claimed by the researchers. Decisions involving complexity bring about non-linear behavior. Many a time, investors tend to have relied on a reference point for a complex decision.

We will further delve into the emerging markets and understand how technological advances are taking a shape and affects investment behaviour.

Behavioral Biases in Emerging Markets

Emerging markets are characterized by high growth, high volatility, and developing regulatory outlines offer a perfect base for cognitive and behavioral biases to grow. These markets are known for the absence of reliable information and hence investors fall prey to behavioral biases to make high returns. These biases have an impact on both long-term and short-term investments. Considering market instability and uncertainty, this section emphasizes the behavioral biases that dominate decision-making in emerging markets, their severity, and their extensive influence on investment strategies.

Compared to developed markets, emerging markets are inherently more unpredictable due to factors like political instability, regulatory unpredictability, currency fluctuations, higher inflation and interest rates, technological adoption, global integration, and less developed financial infrastructure. Such circumstances increase investors' cognitive biases, especially when they are making decisions under pressure that are too with insufficient information or when their emotions are running high. In addition to these market bubbles, abrupt corrections, and extended periods of underperformance or over performance, these biases may result in worse than ideal market performance.

Brabazon (2000) mentioned that behavioral finance is the blend of economics and cognitive psychology which helps in making a model based on human behavior. Gamblers' fallacy occurs in case of failure in predicting the trend of the market and leads to inadequate returns. People try to regress towards the means in order to come closer to the market trend, but inability to do so creates a fallacy. Albar & Jetter (2009) disclosed that due to the heuristics in decision-making, the behavior of investors is directed by systematic errors. While making decisions, our brain prepares a cognitive map which is based on experience and knowledge of the person. These heuristics include gut feeling, intuition and hindsight. They deny the law of probability and cause divergence from rational theory. Bounded rationality brings impracticality of rational decisions into practice.

Brazilian stock market, for example, always showed extreme fluctuations due to political unpredictability. For instance, market rallies of 2018 during Jair Bolsonaro's elections were fueled by hope of economic changes that would follow. Due to an overconfidence bias, investors put enormous sums of money into the markets. Nevertheless, the events that followed did not match predictions. The elected government faced difficulties in passing reforms and the period was economically volatile.

The incident demonstrated the perils of investing based on emotional factors rather than fundamentals.

Another example is of Turkey's 2018 currency crisis where lira was devalued by 30% owing to political tensions with the U.S. and a mounting debt crisis. Investors followed the herd behaviour and exited the market en masse anticipating a situation of financial turmoil. Some of the sectors of the economy remained strong. This situation highlighted rationality being overshadowed by psychological factors.

Financial market inefficiencies and anomalies are caused by individual cognitive biases that investors fall prey to in their decision-making process (Al-Mansour, 2020). Decision making involves choosing the best alternative from a number of possible options available under a set of complex situations (Hirschey & Nofsinger, 2008). This complexity urges the investors to simplify the process and draw the right conclusions (Shefrin, 2007). The quality of decision made is an output of the information acquired and the investor information processing capability. Owing to limited investor ability to understand and analyse information and o the impact of emotional factors in decision making a number of behavioral biases come into play (Shefrin, 2007) The uncertain nature of these markets leads foreign investors to depend overtly on heuristics often causing irrational behaviour.

Impact of Behavioral Biases on Investment Decisions in Emerging Markets

Emerging markets are breeding grounds for both local and foreign investors to experience overconfidence bias. This bias is displayed when investors take excessive risk due to overestimation of their ability and knowledge to predict market movements. **China's stock market bubble of 2015 is a classic** example where the bias among retail investors led to a 150 percent rally in China's Shanghai Composite index between June 2014 and June 2015, that could not be attributed to the company fundamentals. The period saw opening of more than 40 million stock accounts due to the first-time investment by Chinese retail investors in the market (Zeng 2016). The speculation was fueled by investors' overconfidence that government intervention would prevent a market downturn. This overconfidence coupled with the herd behaviour on account of continually surging prices led to speculative investment behaviour. The inevitable market correction resulted in huge financial losses for the investors who entered the market late in expectation of huge gains. The bubble burst led to substantial losses for the investors. A similar case of overconfidence was witnessed in the early 2000s in the rapidly growing **Indian technology sector.** owing to the rapid expansion, investors developed overconfidence in the sector and completely neglected the regulatory and infrastructure challenges that posed as serious obstacles to the sector's growth. The resultant under performance of the market led to substantial losses for the investors.

Another example of investors following herd behaviour rather than analysing stocks on the basis of their fundamental was witnessed in **Brazil's 2002 financial crisis.** The investor fear that the win of leftist candidate Luiz Inácio Lula da Silvainin the elections would result in unfavorable economic policies, resulted in massive selling in the market. This herd behaviour lead to creation of market bubbles in the emerging Brazilian market. However, post-election Brazil saw the implementation of moderate economic policies resulting in stabilization of the economy. The herd behaviour leading to premature selling by many investors resulted in loss of the recovery opportunity in the market.

In emerging markets, home bias can be attributed to the familiarity with local firms and nationalistic sentiments. This bias better describes "the sense of belongingness" in the minds of the investors (Zahera and Bansal, 2018).There exist a strong association between the cultural factor and home bias(Aren et al, 2016; Anthony and Joseph, 2017;Jain et al, 2019; Rasheed et al, 2018).Indian investors often exhibit a preference for domestic equities and gold, driven by a deep cultural need to store gold for value. They prefer to hold on to stocks in the under performing market rather than diversifying by investing in securities abroad. This is also because trading in foreign securities involves higher transaction cost Tesar and Werner, 1995.

The tendency to averse losses rather than acquiring gains plays a critical role in designing investment strategies in the volatile and uncertain emerging markets. This typical behaviour was showcased by Russian investors during the F**inancial crisis of 1998**, where investors owing to the loss aversion bias failed to let go of the loss making stocks even when the market signaled a further downturn. This hesitancy led to huge financial losses for many. In early December the Argentinian government announced the new budget, which included layoffs, reduction in wage reductions, rollbacks in pensions, and cuts in teacher incomes. (Pozi and Nigara, 2005). These developments adversely affected the capital markets, but the investors continued to hold bonds despite a clarity that a default was inevitable. The unwillingness to realize losses resulted in huge financial losses for many, when the debt default manifested.

Emerging markets are characterized by rapid changes that lead to significant price changes, this prompts investors to give more importance to recent events in the short-term over long-term giving rise to recency bias. The post pandemic recovery in India in 2020-2021 lead to a market rally on account of investors reliance on recent trends and lead to inflated stock prices. However, the ignorance of the underlying issues such as a stressed banking sector lead to loss making situation for many investors when market correction took place in 2022 Another example of recency bias is the **2016 political crisis in South Africa**, where the removal of then- President Jacob Zuma lead many investors exit the market in anticipation of an economic downturn. These investors did not consider the long-term strong fundamentals of the market and based their exit decision on the short-term political development. This resulted in a failure to encash the market's subsequent recovery.

The trade dispute between USA and Turkey coupled with various economic, political, and financial factors lead to the crash of the Turkish Lira crashed on August 10, 2018 (Arbaa and Varon, 2019). It resulted in Turkish Lira loosing 35% of its value against US dollar in just 47 days and a 17% decline in the stock market. The result was panic selling in order to avoid losses in the market. The herd behaviour in exiting the market further depreciated the Lira. Investors failure to consider the underlying economic fundamentals manifested and making investment decision solely on the basis of tension with US manifested in the form of herd behaviour and recency bias and lead to the collapse of Turkish market.

Technological Advancements and Investor Behaviour

It is evident from the aforesaid examples that emerging markets see a paramount impact of behavioral biases such as overconfidence, herd behavior, loss aversion, and recency bias on investment decision making. These markets are majorly exposed to cognitive distortions, often leading to suboptimal investment decisions. A systematic study of these biases and their impact on investor behavior is essential for making optimal investment decisions in emerging markets.

In the last decade, there has been a lot of technological innovation in the investment field and hence study of behavioral finance has become increasingly important, especially in emerging markets where digitization and innovation have rapidly transformed the investment landscape. This section focuses on two critical themes: the influence of technological advancements on investor behavior and the changing nature of investor strategies due to technological innovations. While many studies have explored the psychological biases of investors (Barber & Odean, 2000), there is a lot of research focusing on how these biases are improved or moderated by technological interference. Understanding impact of technological disruptions is essential to formulate strategies in markets where traditional and modern investing methods converge (Froot et al., 1999).

Technological disruptions have fundamentally reshaped wealth management strategies, particularly through the extensive adoption of fintech platforms and robo-advisors. Studies by Feuerstein et al. (2019) show that robo-advisors significantly reduce decision-making errors driven by psychological biases such as overconfidence. However, authors don't dent the fact that these platforms may also lead to investors taking decisions far from market realities, as they highly rely on algorithms. Tapscott and Tapscott (2016) similarly highlight how blockchain technologies are enhancing transparency in financial transactions. However, they also point out that the technology's impact on investor behavior is under-researched particularly in emerging markets. In contrast, Lo's (2012) work on emerging markets highlights that investors reflect higher risk tolerance due to high volatility in these markets. The study highlights the importance of cultural and economic factors in shaping investment decisions, a dimension often overlooked in technologically focused studies. While Lo's research is critical in understanding technology driven financial markets, it lacks a thorough examination of how fintech innovations are changing the landscape.

While technological advancements have profoundly influenced investor behavior, the extent to which they have done so varies substantially between developed and emerging markets. Studies focusing on AI and robo-advisors demonstrate clear benefits in mitigating psychological biases in investors (Feuerstein et al., 2019), but these findings may not completely apply to emerging markets, where regulatory environment is emerging and markets are volatile (Lo, 2012). Following sections discuss interaction between technological advancements and Investor behaviour.

a. Technological Disruption and Behavioral Biases

Technological developments have benefited and challenged investors in the area of behavioral finance. Research indicates that the incorporation of technology, such as fintech platforms and algorithmic trading, modifies conventional investment behavior by intensifying specific cognitive biases. Barber and Odean (2000) emphasized how overconfidence bias causes individual investors to over trade. Although technology makes trading easier, it can also make these biases worse by providing quicker and easier access to trading alternatives.

Feuerstein, Gurun, and Hacamo (2019), on the other hand, investigate how robo-advisors, or AI-driven automated financial advisors, reduce cognitive biases including loss aversion and the disposition effect, which occurs when investors prematurely hang onto failing investments. By using algorithms that are immune to emotional judgment, these platforms provide a more methodical approach to investing while reducing human mistakes. They also pointed out that, depending too much on automated systems might give investors a false sense of security as they fail to understand the need of continuous market knowledge to make good investment choices. Investors may become disconnected from current market conditions, which is obviously not good for investments.

These studies' strength is their emphasis on how investor behavior has changed as a result of technology improvements. However, both papers primarily focus on developed markets, leaving a gap in understanding how investors in emerging markets react to similar technological disruptions. The methodologies used—empirical studies in developed market contexts—provide strong evidence of technology's impact on biases but fail to generalize these findings to different economic environments.

b. Investor Sentiment and Market Sentiment in Tech-Driven Markets

Barberis, Shleifer, and Vishny (1998) introduced the notion of *investor sentiment* in markets driven by innovation, suggesting that technological advancements create an information asymmetry between institutional and retail investors. Institutional investors, who often have access to better tools and technologies, can better manage market risks compared to retail investors, who may be swayed by short-term noise or market hype.

These results highlight that although technology makes it easier to obtain market data, it can also lead to the amplification of sentiment-driven trading, particularly in emerging and extremely volatile markets. Barberis et al.'s work is methodologically strong since it provides a strong analytical framework by mapping sentiment changes with technology disruptions using quantitative models. However, the study doesn't study how emerging market investors, who might not have equal access to technology, deal with this disparity.

Changing Investor Behavior Due to Technological Innovation

The emergence of fintech platforms has altered the way that investors view risk. Blockchain and related technologies increase transparency, which gives investors more assurance. However, these technologies have also brought about new kinds of danger, especially in areas where financial systems are still developing. The divergent opinions on risk and transparency point to a gap in the literature, indicating the need for additional empirical research to fully comprehend how fintech may affect investor behavior in emerging economies over the long run. Some of the technological innovations are discussed in details under:

a. Fintech, AI, and Risk Perception

The rise of fintech and AI-driven platforms has changed the perception of risk among investors. Blockchain technology's potential to promote transparency and lower risk in financial transactions is examined by Tapscott and Tapscott (2016). Their research demonstrates how investors' trust is increased by blockchain's decentralized and secure nature. As a result of this transparency, even in emerging markets, investors may eventually become more prepared to take more risks.

On the other hand, Lo (2012) offers an opposing viewpoint, arguing that although technology developments can lower certain hazards, they also bring forth new ones. Rapid technological adoption coupled with undeveloped regulatory frameworks may make things more unpredictable in emerging markets. Particularly in less developed economies, Lo's study highlights the necessity of striking a balance between technical optimism and a realistic grasp of market instability.

b. Robo-Advisors and Automated Trading Platforms

The change in investing behavior, especially among ordinary investors, has been expedited by the use of robo-advisors. Feuerstein et al. (2019) discovered that by providing individualized investing advice based on quantitative models, robo-advisors considerably reduce emotional bias in decision-making. Retail investors who might not have traditional financial knowledge can now use sophisticated instruments thanks to technology, which has democratized investment techniques.

These platforms do have certain drawbacks, though. Feuerstein et al. (2019) caution against the dangers of relying too much on automation, since this could lead to investors taking a passive role in their own financial choices. Furthermore, Lo (2012) points out that although these platforms are beneficial in established countries, the lack of adequate technology infrastructure in emerging economies has prevented them from reaching their full potential.

These studies look at how technology-driven platforms affect individual investors. However, one of their limitations is that they haven't done a thorough investigation of how investor behavior varies by culture across markets. Due to differences in financial literacy and technological accessibility, investors in emerging nations may react to robo-advisors differently than investors in established markets. To completely comprehend how technology innovation changes investor behavior in various economic circumstances, further empirical study is required. Emerging markets, where the adoption of fintech may result in distinct behavioral shifts, should receive special attention.

Behavioral Finance Frameworks for Investment Strategy Development

Irrational behaviour by investors is attributed to a wide variety of psychological phenomena. This section discusses the applications of various frameworks in behavioral finance frameworks to develop profit making investment strategies in technology-driven and emerging markets. It also highlights the tools and techniques investors can use to apply behavioral finance principles in real-life situations. Some of the key frameworks providing valuable insights in understanding investor behavior are discussed as under:

a. Prospect Theory and Loss Aversion

Prospect Theory: Developed by Kahneman and Tversky, assumes that investors behave differently as risk- seekers and gainers. It suggests that people value losses more than equivalent gains, a phenomenon known as **loss aversion** (Kahneman & Tversky, 1979). The emerging markets characterized by unstable economic and political environments are prone to a mind set of loss aversion in investors. This makes the investors emotionally attached to their investments - holding on the loss making investments to avoid losses and premature selling of high performing assets to realize gains.

During the period from 2016 - 2018, India's fintech sector was booming. This led to investor optimism and overconfidence in the sector coupled with huge inflow. The emergence of regulatory challenges in 2019, slowed the market but many investors held on to the loss making fintech stocks due to loss aversion, rather than selling to avoid further losses and reallocate their funds in a profitable fashion. promising sectors.

b. Mental Accounting

Behavioral theorists have established that investors exhibit multiple attitudes towards risk. Their risk tolerance for certain investments may be low whereas they might associate certain investments as high risk. For instance, the money allotted to the children's education fund is guarded very closely by the investors and they are unwilling to risk it. On the other hand, surplus money is treated differently and may be invested adventurously in anticipation of high returns. This risk management on a goal-by-goal basis is referred to as mental accounting. The investors maintain separate investment accounts and make decisions based on the nature of the account. It refers to the practice of maintaining separate investment accounts, either mentally or in practice, and making decisions differently depending on the nature of the account (Nevins, 2004).

The growing South African artificial intelligence (AI) sector witnessed the impact of, mental accounting when investors treated the investment allocation in AI startups differently from traditional tech investments. This over allocation in AI startups and not diversifying across the technology sector made them vulnerable to unnecessary risk. Higher returns were reaped by the investors who viewed the technology sector holistically and diversified their portfolio.

c. Herding Behavior

Herding implies investor tendency to follow and mimic others rather than making individual choices based on fundamental and technical market analysis. The emerging markets are particularly susceptible to this bias because of limited information availability and high volatility, being with the crowd feels safer. People do not want to stand out of the crowd and conform their decision to the larger section of a group. This also gives them a sense of validation in their decisions. Information asymmetry, reputational concern, regret aversion, contrarian strategy used for investments, market stream or sentiments, conformity, cognitive dissonance, feedback trading (Walter & Moritz, 2006; Yang & Chen, 2018).

Herd bias can be attributed to a number of reasons The booming Nigerian mobile payments market, attracted significant investment from national and international investors. A heightened investor enthusiasm and herd behaviour inflated the valuations beyond levels that were sustainable. A market correction on account of regulatory challenges leads to significant losses for a large number of investors who joined the herd without careful analysis.

d. Behavioral Portfolio Theory

The theory is based on investors need to satisfy a variety of psychological and emotional needs in addition to maximizing returns. Investors categorize. Investors layer portfolios into different risk return profiles with one part for safe assets and the other for high risk and high return securities. Portfolios should be constructed in a way that they meet the financial needs and psychological requirements of the investors. Behavioral Portfolio Theory (BPT) includes a pyramid shaped layer of the goals of an investor in totality (Muneer, 2012). In the study by (Zaiane, 2013), the paper has used survey method on Tunisian investors and the findings claimed that the overall demographic variables such as: experience, wealth and education affected portfolio choice impacts the investment behavior of investors.

Practical Tools and Techniques for Investors

Behavioral finance offers a wide variety of tools and techniques that can help investors to strengthen their decision-making processes. These are particularly helpful in the context of emerging markets characterized by uncertainty and volatility. Some of the key strategies are discussed below:

a. Pre-Commitment Strategies

Pre-commitment strategies help investors in removing emotion from the decision-making process. It involves setting predetermined rules for entering and exiting the market. This pre-commitment can help conquer biases like loss aversion and overconfidence, that often lead to illogical decisions. Indian EV market is an example where pre-commitment strategies proved very useful in avoiding impulsive decisions. Deciding exit points objectively based on market conditions, rather than emotion, helps investors make profit and avoid unnecessary losses

b. Behavioral Checklists

Behavioral checklists are simple to administer yet effective tools to assist investors recognize biases in their decision-making processes. A checklist might include questions many thought provoking questions such as:

- Is my investment based on a market trend or personal financial analysis?
- Do I overestimate my ability to predict future market movements?
- Am I holding onto a losing investment because of emotional attachment?

During the market's peak in 2018 in Brazil the investors in the renewable energy market could avoid taking biased decisions using behavioral checklist, that helped in assessing the market objectively without falling prey to herd behavior or overconfidence.

c. Scenario Analysis

Scenario analysis is a very robust technique that allows investors to critically explore and analyse a range of possible outcomes and develop strategies accordingly. This technique is particularly suited to emerging markets characterized by economic and regulatory unpredictably. The investors South African AI industry could better anticipate the slower adoption of AI technologies on account of regulatory hurdles using scenario analysis. This analysis helped them to adjust their strategies when the growth in the market did not meet expectations. .

d. Contrarian Investment Strategies

Inherently risky, these strategies empower investors to take opposite positions compared to prevailing market trends. It can prove useful when the investors intend to capitalize on market inefficiencies created as a result of herd behavior. The contrarian investors in the Nigerian fintech sector, despite the market hype avoided rushing into mobile payment startups initially. Later, the sector experienced a correction and they entered the markets at a much better valuations. These investors wisely positioned themselves for long-term gains by virtue of resisting the urge to follow the herd behaviour.

Case Studies from Emerging Economies

a. India: Navigating the Fintech Boom

India's fintech sector characterized by digital payments, technology innovations and government policies like demonetization attracted huge investments. However, in 2018 - 2019 the market was characterized by regulatory uncertainties that created significant volatility in the sector. The Investors who followed herd behavior and were averse to losses lost huge sums. The investors using techniques like pre-commitment strategies and scenario analysis could face the market more effectively.

b. Brazil: Renewable Energy Growth and Investor Sentiment

Brazil attracted global attention as it attempted to use renewable sources of energy. Investor's overconfidence in government incentives and market growth led to inflated valuations and eventual market corrections. Many investors over- invested in these sectors and suffered huge losses as a result of mental accounting. Rational diversifiers, who avoided mental accounting were able to maintain stability in returns.

c. South Africa: AI Adoption and Investor Overconfidence

2010 was characterized by a boom in South Africa's AI industry but it was short lived. Thet overconfidence in the sector led many investors to overestimate the market. The industry's expansion was slowed down by regulatory barriers and infrastructural challenges leading to market corrections. The users of scenario analysis and pre-commitment strategies were able to analyse better and sail through the market and undertake strategy adjustment as per emerging information in the market.

Behavioral finance frameworks provide a robust set of tools and techniques that can aid investors in designing effective strategies in technology driven emerging markets. Being able to recognize the biases would promote rational decision making. The growth and evolution in emerging markets will mandate the incorporation of behavioral finance principles in making investment choices for long-term success.

Ethical Implications of Using Behavioral Finance to Influence Investor Behavior in Emerging Markets

Investor decision-making in technology-driven and emerging markets has been transformed by behavioral finance. Deeply useful insights into the variables influencing investor behavior are provided by behavioral finance. However, there are a number of ethical issues that must be addressed in the case of emerging markets, which are characterized by inferior investor protection measures, an immature financial regulatory environment, and insufficient investor protection laws. These marketplaces are a haven for corruption because of ineffective regulations, leaving investors open to abuse. This presents a conundrum since, while behavioral finance tools and techniques might help investors make better decisions, they can also be utilized to influence investor prejudices.

a. Exploitation of Cognitive Biases

Financial institutions and technology-driven platforms can use their understanding of biases to control the behavior of investors. Companies may persuade investors to purchase riskier assets or promote frequent trading to increase transaction revenues, for instance, by using targeted marketing and providing individualized financial products. Although these tactics are advantageous in terms of gaining money, they can also trap unskilled investors and give rise to moral dilemmas. Gamification is a strategy used by several retail trading platforms to draw in and keep investors. These platforms provide simple access to speculative assets and frequently take advantage of investor biases. Financial markets are easily accessible, which has led to both dangerous trading practices and a wealth of investment options.

Such practices can worsen volatility and uncertainty in emerging markets, where market movements largely depend on emotional factors. The ethical concerns arise when behavioral finance is applied by financial organizations in these contexts. The questions as whether the usage of cognitive biases is acceptable to promote riskier investment practices in markets characterized by inadequate investor protection need to be answered. The answer stems from financial industry trying to find a balance between profit making and shouldering ethical responsibility.

b. Regulatory Gaps and the Moral Hazard

One of the cornerstones for the financial industry to operate ethically is a robust regulatory framework (Omarova, 2017, Zaring, 2017). The regulatory frameworks in the emerging markets are not robust enough to prevent investor manipulation. With the increasing popularity of behavioral finance in these regions, the risk of financial organizations capitalizing on the gaps in regulation to take advantage of investors through aggressive sales tactics is ever increasing. The markets in India and Brazil have witnessed an enormous growth by offering personalized investment advice rooted in data analytics. However, the lack of stringent jurisdiction can lead to situations where the advice offered is more in the interest of the financial institutions than the investors involved.

It is the ethical responsibility of financial institutions to ensure investor protection. The situation becomes prominent in technology-driven markets where algorithms are used to guide investment choices. The investors may fall prey to these sophisticated algorithms designed to optimize the decision-making process. These may lack transparency posing difficulties for the investors to understand how their decision-making is being influenced.

As the financial industry navigates complex terrain, ethical considerations extend beyond the confines of regulatory mandates to encompass the moral imperatives associated with financial decision-making (Pater, Fiesler, and Zimmer, 2022, Wörsdörfer, 2023). The developments such as fintech, blockchain, and artificial intelligence have brought forth both challenges and opportunities (Ashta, and Herrmann, 2021, Adebukola et al., 2022). It is the responsibility of the financial industry to navigate the ethical dimensions of advances in technology to ensure a trustworthy future. (Giudici, 2018, Mehrotra, and Menon, 2021).

c. The Role of Corporate Social Responsibility (CSR) in Ethical Investing

Corporate Social Responsibility (CSR) initiatives implemented by financial institutions have taken the centre stage in addressing these ethical concerns. The Nairobi Securities Exchange's sustainability indices promote responsible investment, a CSR initiative aimed at investor protection. Such practices become increasingly important in emerging economies having inadequate legal safeguards.

The Importance of Investor Education in Emerging Markets

Investor education is of paramount importance for arriving at informed decisions and making rational choices in the emerging financial markets. With the fast-paced technological advancements and easy access to financial markets, there is a dire need for investor financial literacy to combat the risks posed by cognitive biases and unethical financial practices.

a. Bridging the Knowledge Gap

In many emerging markets, the fundamental financial literacy in a sizeable proportion of retail investors is very low. A number of research studies suggest over 70% of investors in certain Southeast Asian markets do not possess a thorough understanding of the risks associated with their investment products. With technology-driven platforms and mobile trading apps offering ease of access to global markets, this lack of knowledge can result in poor or sub-optimal investment choices, heightening the probability of investors to behavioral biases.

Also, there exist significant disparities in access to financial education. Governments and financial institutions must leverage technology for disseminating financial knowledge. Also, it is imperative to customize the educational approaches in the light of cultural attitudes of investors towards finance and ethics. An ecosystem where financial institutions and individuals both are committed to continuous learning would lead to an ethical, informed and resilient financial landscape (Adaga et al, 2024)

Governments and financial institutions in collaboration must create and promote educational programs aimed at covering critical topics such as time value of money, risk- return assessment, importance of portfolio diversification, long-term implications of financial decisions etc. In India the **Securities and Exchange Board of India (SEBI)** through its Investor Awareness Programmes, has educated a lot of retail investors on the skills and focus required to make intelligent investment choices in a rapidly changing financial landscape.

b. Empowering Investors Through Digital Platforms

In the current, times financial education has emerged as the most powerful tool in promoting ethical awareness (Williams, Morton, and Christian, 2022, Estelami, and Estelami, 2023).The financial institutions can develop ethically responsible processionals by integrating ethical considerations into their financial training programmes for creating a financial industry that prioritizes investor interest.

Technology can prove to be a great enabler in enhancing the level of investor education. Emerging markets can use mobile technology and digital platforms to their advantages to reach masses. The access to educational apps, webinars, and online financial courses etc. has made financial knowledge easily accessible. Online platforms like **Khan Academy** and **Coursera**, offer free courses on financial literacy specifically tailored to the requirements of the investors in the emerging market.

Millions of users in Kenya have benefited from financial management awareness initiative of **M-Pesa**, a mobile-based money transfer and financial service platform, The purpose of the platform is to educate the investors about the importance of financial planning, investment options, returns and risks. Mobilising financial literacy initiatives through such platforms, the emerging markets can overcome the challenges posed by traditional education and create financially literate investor base.

c. The Role of Government and Regulatory Bodies

In emerging markets characterised by limited financial literacy the governments can spearhead educational initiatives to enhance the awareness about the risks and returns of operating in modern financial markets. For example, the national investor education strategy implemented by **Brazilian Securities and Exchange Commission (CVM)** including workshops, online resources, and community outreach programs has resulted in a significant improvement in the level of financial literacy of the retail investors, leading to improved financial decision making in the markets.

Additionally, several initiatives have been launched by the **South African Financial Sector Conduct Authority (FSCA)** aimed at increasing transparency and creating awareness about investor rights and responsibilities. These initiatives empower investors to protect themselves from manipulation and fraudulent practices and take rational decisions.

Building Trust Through Transparency

Financial institutions and technology-driven platforms that take a transparent approach to communicating investment risks, costs, and possible returns can help advance ethical investment practices in emerging economies. Giving investors the skills, information, and methods they need to access the authenticity of financial products and services should be another goal of investor education. Platforms that function in both developed and emerging economies, like **Wealthfront** and **Betterment**, for instance, place a high value on openness by providing clear information about fees, risks, and the methods used to make investment recommendations. This increases confidence in the financial system. Ethical behavior and informed involvement are the cornerstones of investment future.

CONCLUSION

This chapter is a thorough analysis of investor decision making process and reveals that it is significantly affected by cognitive biases, emotional influences, and heuristics. Our probe has highlighted that in emerging markets characterized by high volatility, emerging technology and innovation and developing regulatory framework these psychological traits can have the effect of either enhancing or worsening the investment outcomes. Behavioral finance offers an in depth understanding of investor psychology, that is of paramount importance for leveraging the opportunities and managing the risks present in emerging markets.

A plethora of technological advancements, such as AI, fintech, and blockchain, have heightened the level of complications in investment decision making. The new technology offers sophisticated tools and new challenges. Using these new technologies may help reduce certain types of risk but may pose yet another set of challenges leading to uncertainty and cognitive biases. A thorough understanding of these nuances assists investors in developing strategies that offset the negative effects.

The chapter emphasizes the following:

- It is important to identify and address the behavioral biases including herd behaviour, loss aversion, overconfidence etc. In making investment decisions in emerging markets characterized by volatility and unpredictability.
- Technological innovations have had a profound impact on the behaviour of investors. These innovations have resulted in the creation of new risks and opportunities that require informed and adaptable investment strategies
- A thorough understanding of behavioral finance frameworks is critical to enhanced investment decision-making.
- The regulatory framework in emerging markets needs to be more transparent and comprehensive to protect investors from malpractices.
- There is a heightened need for enhancing the level of financial literacy in the investors to assist them in making informed choices in the volatile emerging markets

Emerging markets are in a stage of continuous growth where technology is the driver of rapid change. All the stakeholders including organizations, investors, policy makers and financial advisors need to be equipped with the right set of tools and technologies to fight the adversity in the market. This chapter attempts to highlight the overarching importance of integrating behavioral finance into modern investment decision making

Further research could explore the impact of technology in the application of behavioral finance frameworks. Studies on how technological advances can be used to mitigate cognitive and emotional biases would be particularly useful. Studying the impact of technology on real time investor behaviour will also offer meaningful insights. Additionally, case studies from different emerging economies can highlight the impact of culture and economy in application of the various participles of behavioral finance.

Finally, an in depth understanding of behavioral finance in the context of emerging and technology-driven markets will continue to shape the future of investing, making it more resilient, informed, and adaptable to the complexities of the modern financial landscape.

REFERENCES

Campbell, S. D., & Sharpe, S. A. (2009). Anchoring bias in consensus forecasts and its effect on market prices. Journal of Financial and Quantitative Analysis, 44(2), 369-390.

Cassotti, M., Habib, M., Poirel, N., Aïte, A., Houdé, O., & Moutier, S. (2012). Positive emotional context eliminates the framing effect in decision-making. Emotion, 12(5), 926.

Chen, G., Kim, K. A., Nofsinger, J. R., & Rui, O. M. (2007). Trading performance, disposition effect, overconfidence, representativeness bias, and experience of emerging market investors. Journal of behavioral decision making, 20(4), 425-451.

Chew, S. H., Ebstein, R. P., & Zhong, S. (2012). Ambiguity aversion and familiarity bias: Evidence from behavioral and gene association studies. Journal of Risk and Uncertainty, 44, 1-18.

Chira, I., Adams, M., & Thornton, B. (2008). Behavioral Bias Within The Decision Making Process. Journal of Business & Economics Research, 6(8), 11–20.

De Bondt, W. F., Muradoglu, Y. G., Shefrin, H., & Staikouras, S. K. (2008). Behavioral finance: Quo vadis?. Journal of Applied Finance (Formerly Financial Practice and Education), 18(2).

Fama, E. F. (1998). Market efficiency, long-term returns, and behavioral finance. Journal of Financial Economics, 49(3), 283–306. DOI: 10.1016/S0304-405X(98)00026-9

Feuerstein, M., Gurun, U. G., & Hacamo, I. (2019). Robo-advisors: Investing through automation. Journal of Financial Technology, 15(4), 234-256.

Fox, C. R., & Levav, J. (2000). Familiarity bias and belief reversal in relative likelihood judgment. Organizational Behavior and Human Decision Processes, 82(2), 268-292.

Friedman, M., & Savage, L. J. (1948). The Utility Analysis of Choices Involving Risk. Journal of Political Economy, 56(4), 279–304. .DOI: 10.1086/256692

Grinblatt, M., & Han, B. (2002). The disposition effect and momentum.

Hirshleifer, D. (2015). Behavioral finance. Annual Review of Financial Economics, 7(1), 133-159.

Hoffmann, A.O., Shefrin, H. and Pennings, J.M., 2010. Behavioral portfolio analysis of individual investors. Available at SSRN 1629786.

IMF. (n.d). Retrieved Oct 14, 2024, from https://www.imf.org/external/pubs/ft/fandd/2021/06/the-future-of-emerging-markets-duttagupta-and-pazarbasioglu.htm

Irshad, S., Badshah, W., & Hakam, U. (2016). Effect of representativeness bias on investment decision making. Management and Administrative Sciences Review, 5(1), 26-30.

Jain, J., Walia, N., & Gupta, S. (2019). Evaluation of behavioral biases affecting investment decision making of individual equity investors by fuzzy analytic hierarchy process. Review of Behavioral Finance.

Johnson, D. D., & Fowler, J. H. (2011). The evolution of overconfidence. Nature, 477(7364), 317-320.

Kahneman, D., & Tversky, A. (1979). Prospect theory: An analysis of decision under risk. Econometrica, 47(2), 263-291.

Kartini, K. and NAHDA, K., 2021. Behavioral biases on investment decision: A case study in Indonesia. The Journal of Asian Finance, Economics and Business, 8(3), pp.1231-1240.

Keynes, J. M. (1936). The General Theory of Employment Interest and Money. The Collected Writings of John Maynard Keynes Vol. VII. Journal Of The Czech Geological Society, 49, 161–172. Retrieved from http://www.jgeosci.org/index.php?pg=detail&ID=JCGS.968

Levy, H. (2011). The capital asset pricing model in the 21st century: analytical, empirical, and behavioral perspectives. Cambridge University Press.

Lieder, F., Griffiths, T. L., M. Huys, Q. J., & Goodman, N. D. (2018). The anchoring bias reflects rational use of cognitive resources. Psychonomic bulletin & review, 25, 322-349.

Lo, A. W. (2012). Adaptive markets: Financial evolution at the speed of thought. Princeton University Press.

Mansour, S. B., Jouini, E., & Napp, C. (2006). Is there a “pessimistic” bias in individual beliefs? Evidence from a simple survey. Theory and Decision, 61(4), 345-362.

Martin, S., 2007. Behavioural finance. Univ. Cambridge, pp.1-14.

Muneer, S. (2012). Materialization of Behavioral Finance and Behavioral Portfolio Theory : A Brief Review. Journal of Economics and Behavioral Studies, 4(8), 431–435.

Nevins, D. (2004). Goals-based investing: Integrating traditional and behavioral finance. The Journal of Wealth Management, 6(4), 8-23.

Olsen, R. A. (1998). Behavioral finance and its implications for stock-price volatility. Financial Analysts Journal, 54(2), 10–18. .DOI: 10.2469/faj.v54.n2.2161

Pozzi, P., & Nigra, F. (2015). Argentina a decade after the collapse: the causes of the crisis and structural changes. Latin American Perspectives, 42(1), 3-10.

Rasheed, M. H., Rafique, A., Zahid, T., & Akhtar, M. W. (2018). Factors influencing investor's decision making in Pakistan: Moderating the role of locus of control. Review of Behavioral Finance, 10(1), 70-87.

Ricciardi, V., & Simon, H. K. (2000). What is Behavioral Finance ? Business, Education and Technology Journal, II(1), 1–9. http://doi.org/.DOI: 10.2139/ssrn.256754

Sattar, M. A., Toseef, M., & Sattar, M. F. (2020). Behavioral finance biases in investment decision making. International Journal of Accounting, Finance and Risk Management, 5(2), 69.

Searston, R. A., Tangen, J. M., & Eva, K. W. (2016). Putting bias into context: The role of familiarity in identification. Law and Human Behavior, 40(1), 50.

Shefrin, H., & Statman, M. (2000). Behavioral portfolio theory. Journal of Financial and Quantitative Analysis, 35(2), 127–151. http://doi.org/doi:10.2307/2676187

Stanovich, K. E., & West, R. F. (2000). Individual differences in reasoning: implications for the rationality debate? The Behavioral and Brain Sciences, 23(5), 645–665; discussion 665–726. .DOI: 10.1017/S0140525X00003435

Statman, M. (2008). What Is Behavioral Finance? Handbook of Finance, II(1), 79–84. .DOI: 10.1002/9780470404324.hof002009

Stotz, O., & von Nitzsch, R. (2005). The Perception of Control and the Level of Overconfidence: Evidence from Analyst Earnings Estimates and Price Targets. Journal of Behavioral Finance, 6(3), 121–128. .DOI: 10.1207/s15427579jpfm0603_2

Subash, R. (2012). Role of behavioral finance in portfolio investment decisions: Evidence from India.

Tapscott, D., & Tapscott, A. (2016). Blockchain revolution: How the technology behind bitcoin is changing money, business, and the world. Penguin Random House.

Tesar, L.L. and Werner, I.M. (1995), "Home bias and high turnover", Journal of International Money and Finance, Vol. 14 No. 4, pp. 467-492.

Van de Venter, G., Michayluk, D., & Davey, G. (2012). A longitudinal study of financial risk tolerance. Journal of Economic Psychology, 33(4), 794–800. .DOI: 10.1016/j.joep.2012.03.001

Walter, A., & Moritz Weber, F. (2006). Herding in the German mutual fund industry. European Financial Management, 12(3), 375–406. .DOI: 10.1111/j.1354-7798.2006.00325.x

Wang, H., & Hanna, S. (1997). Does risk tolerance decrease with age. Financial Counseling and Planning Education, (614), 27–32. DOI: 10.2139/ssrn.95489

Weber, M., & Camerer, C. F. (1998). The disposition effect in securities trading: An experimental analysis. Journal of Economic Behavior & Organization, 33(2), 167-184.

Whittlesea, B. W. (1993). Illusions of familiarity. Journal of Experimental Psychology: Learning, Memory, and Cognition, 19(6), 1235.

Witt, S. F., & Dobbins, R. (1979). The Markowitz contribution to portfolio theory. Managerial finance, 5(1), 3-17.

Worldometer. (n.d.). Current world population. Retrieved June 27, 2024, from https://www.worldometers. info/world-population/

Yang, W. R., & Chen, Y. L. (2015). The Response of Dynamic Herd Behavior to Domestic and US Market Factors: Evidence from the Greater China Stock Markets. Emerging Markets Finance and Trade, 51(1, SI), S18–S41. .DOI: 10.1080/1540496X.2014.998884

Zahera, S. A., & Bansal, R. (2018). Do investors exhibit behavioral biases in investment decision making? A systematic review. Qualitative Research in Financial Markets, 10(2), 210-251.

Zaiane, S. (2013). Investor Overconfidence : an Examination of Individual Traders on The Tunisian Stock Market. Advances in Management & Applied Economics, 3(5), 41–55.

Zaleskiewicz, T. (2015). Behavioral finance. In Handbook of contemporary behavioral economics (pp. 728-750). Routledge.

Zeng, F., Huang, W. C., & Hueng, J. (2016). On Chinese government's stock market rescue efforts in 2015. Modern Economy, 7(4), 411-418.

Adaga, E. M., Egieya, Z. E., Ewuga, S. K., Abdul, A. A., & Abrahams, T. O.Ejuma Martha AdagaZainab Efe EgieyaSarah Kuzankah EwugaAdekunle Abiola Abdul-Temitayo Oluwaseun Abrahams. (2024). A comprehensive review of ethical practices in banking and finance. *Finance & Accounting Research Journal*, 6(1), 1–20. DOI: 10.51594/farj.v6i1.705

Albar, F. M., & Jetter, A. J. (2009). Heuristics in decision making. In PICMET: Portland International Center for Management of Engineering and Technology, Proceedings (pp. 578–584). DOI: 10.1109/PICMET.2009.5262123

Antony, A., & Joseph, A. I. (2017). Influence of Behavioural Factors Affecting Investment Decision—An AHP Analysis. *Metamorphosis*, 16(2), 107–114. DOI: 10.1177/0972622517738833

Arbaa, O., & Varon, E. (2019). Turkish currency crisis–Spillover effects on European banks. *Borsa Istanbul Review*, 19(4), 372–378. DOI: 10.1016/j.bir.2019.07.003

Aren, S., Aydemir, S. D., & Şehitoğlu, Y. (2016). Behavioral biases on institutional investors: A literaturereview. *Kybernetes*, 45(10), 1668–1684. DOI: 10.1108/K-08-2015-0203

Barber, B. M., & Odean, T. (2000). Trading is hazardous to your wealth: The common stock investment performance of individual investors. *The Journal of Finance*, 55(2), 773–806. DOI: 10.1111/0022-1082.00226

Barberis, N., Shleifer, A., & Vishny, R. (1998). A model of investor sentiment. *Journal of Financial Economics*, 49(3), 307–343. DOI: 10.1016/S0304-405X(98)00027-0

Barberis, N., Shleifer, A., & Vishny, R. (1998). A model of investor sentiment. *Journal of Financial Economics*, 49(3), 307–343. DOI: 10.1016/S0304-405X(98)00027-0

Brabazon, T. (2000). Behavioural Finance : A new sunrise or a false dawn ?, (September), 1–8.

Frazzini, A. (2006). The disposition effect and underreaction to news. *The Journal of Finance*, 61(4), 2017–2046. DOI: 10.1111/j.1540-6261.2006.00896.x

KEY TERMS AND DEFINITIONS

Behavioral Finance: A field of study that examines the influence of psychological factors on financial decision making. It defies the idea that investors are rational decision makers.

Cognitive Biases: The mental shortcuts that cause systematic thinking errors that lead to irrational decisions.

Herd Behavior: The tendency of individuals to follow the actions of a larger group, often ignoring their own judgment, especially in financial markets. This behaviour provides investors with validation of their choices.

Heuristics: Heuristics are "rules of thumb" or mental shortcuts that help investors in simplifying decisions by focusing on the available limited information. They help people make quick judgments under uncertainty.

Loss Aversion: The tendency of investors to prefer avoiding losses over acquiring equivalent gains. making losses feels more painful in comparison to the feeling of reward when realizing gains.

Mental Accounting: The habit of treating money differently based on its source or purpose, leading to irrational financial decisions.

Overconfidence: Investors often overestimate their knowledge, ability and accuracy of their predictions in the financial markets, thereby leading to suboptimal investment decisions.

Prospect Theory: A behavioral economics theory that states people value gains and losses differently, the pain of loss is more as compared to the feeling of reward when gains are realized. This leads to irrational decision making

Chapter 6
Cognitive and Emotional Triggers of Collective Investment Patterns in Stock Markets

Yang Ze
Universiti Malaya, China

Ooi Kok Loang
https://orcid.org/0000-0003-0412-8899
Universiti Malaya, Malaysia

ABSTRACT

This study investigates the cognitive and emotional factors influencing collective investment behaviors in stock markets, focusing on how biases such as overconfidence, loss aversion, social influence, and the fear of missing out (FOMO) contribute to herding behavior. Behavioral finance suggests that cognitive and emotional stimuli can lead to investment patterns that deviate from rational decision-making models. By examining how these psychological triggers interact in financial markets, the study addresses gaps in understanding the combined effect of biases on collective market behavior. The findings emphasize the importance of comprehending these biases to mitigate their negative impact on market efficiency and stability, particularly in a technology-driven trading environment. Future research should explore cross-cultural influences and the role of technology in intensifying herding dynamics.

DOI: 10.4018/979-8-3693-8583-8.ch006

INTRODUCTION

The stock market is a multifaceted and dynamic system shaped by both macroeconomic circumstances and the psychological behaviours of investors. An expanding corpus of research in behavioural finance indicates that cognitive and emotional stimuli significantly influence investing decisions, frequently resulting in collective behavioural patterns that deviate from rational market theories. Conventional financial models, based on the Efficient Market Hypothesis (EMH), argue that investors are rational entities who make decisions utilising available information to optimise utility. Nonetheless, the actual behaviour of markets frequently exposes patterns of irrationality, particularly when collective emotions and cognitive biases are involved (Akinkoye & Bankole, 2020).

Overconfidence bias is a significant cognitive factor affecting collective investment behaviours. Investors, convinced of their superior knowledge or predictive capacity, may partake in excessively aggressive trading, disregarding hazards and overvaluing their market timing abilities. This exaggerated self-confidence frequently results in overtrading and exacerbates market volatility. In a group context, overconfidence can initiate a feedback loop in which investors reinforce one another's assertive actions, leading to herding behaviour when market players adhere to identical trends, irrespective of fundamental factors.

A notable cognitive component affecting stock market behaviour is loss aversion. Grounded on Prospect Theory, loss aversion denotes the inclination of investors to prioritise the avoidance of losses over the attainment of equivalent benefits (FaXing & Loang, 2024). The dread of monetary losses frequently compels investors to retain depreciating assets excessively or to divest profitable assets prematurely. In a market context, this bias may result in widespread panic selling during downturns or excessive enthusiasm during bull markets, as investors prioritise loss aversion over reasonable investment choices. When numerous investors concurrently display loss-averse behaviour, it can exacerbate market patterns, fostering herding behaviour.

Social influence significantly impacts collective investment behaviours (Aggarwal, 2022). In a highly networked market, investors are swayed by the perspectives and behaviours of others, resulting in imitation and behavioural convergence. Social networks, media, and financial news generate information cascades in which investors, instead of performing independent analyses, depend on the choices of their peers or perceived market authorities. This may lead to a bandwagon effect in which market participants conform to the majority, hence intensifying herding behaviour. Social influence is especially powerful during periods of market uncertainty, as investors look for validation from the behaviours of others, resulting in synchronised investing trends that may lack a basis in fundamental analysis.

The emotional impetus of the Fear of Missing Out (FOMO) significantly impacts collective investing choices. FOMO denotes the apprehension that occurs when individuals see that others are benefiting from chances they are not experiencing. In the realm of stock markets, FOMO can result in hasty investment choices, especially during phases of speculative bubbles or abrupt market surges. Investors, apprehensive about missing substantial rewards, hastily invest without thoroughly evaluating the risks or intrinsic value of the assets. This collective frenzy frequently elevates asset values above their fundamental worth, leading to unsustainable market situations. In this instance, herding behaviour is motivated by an emotional inclination to conform to perceived possibilities, irrespective of logical investing techniques.

The dependent variable in this study, herding behaviour, denotes the inclination of individuals in the stock market to emulate the behaviours of others, resulting in collective decision-making that frequently diverges from underlying economic indicators. Herding can generate self-reinforcing market phenomena, such as bubbles or crashes, as investors' actions grow further intertwined. This behaviour undermines the premise of autonomous, rational decision-making in financial markets and underscores the significant influence of psychological variables on market dynamics (Duxbury et al., 2020).

Despite the expanding literature on behavioural finance and the psychological elements affecting stock market dynamics, considerable gaps persist in comprehending how particular cognitive and emotional stimuli result in collective investment behaviours, such as herding behaviour. Much of the current research predominantly concentrates on discrete biases or emotions, providing fragmented insights into their impact on human decision-making. Nevertheless, the interplay among cognitive and emotional triggers—such as overconfidence, loss aversion, social influence, and the fear of missing out (FOMO)—is frequently examined in isolation, with insufficient focus on their combined effect in influencing collective behaviours in the stock market.

A notable deficiency in the existing literature is the insufficient examination of the moderating factors that affect the intensity of herding behaviour in reaction to these stimuli. Although it is well-documented that psychological characteristics like overconfidence and loss aversion influence irrational decision-making, there is a lack of study regarding the circumstances that amplify or diminish these biases (Fu & Loang, 2024). How do characteristics like market volatility, liquidity, and investor intelligence influence the connection between cognitive biases and herding behaviour? Cultural and demographic disparities among investors may potentially serve as a moderating factor; nevertheless, this domain remains inadequately examined in empirical research. Comprehending these distinctions is essential for formulating a more thorough understanding of collective investment behaviours.

A significant deficiency in the literature is the dependence on retrospective data or post hoc research to examine herding behaviour and its catalysts. Numerous studies concentrate on examining past stock market data to pinpoint occurrences of herding post-factum; nevertheless, there is a deficiency of real-time observational research that documents the evolution of investors' emotions and biases as they transpire. The deficiency of real-time data gathering restricts the capacity to comprehensively comprehend the interplay between dynamic market conditions and cognitive as well as emotional components that engender herding behaviour. Additional experimental or longitudinal research that monitor investor sentiment and decision-making processes during market events might enhance comprehension of the emergence of collective investing patterns.

Moreover, the impact of technical improvements on collective investing behaviour is still a nascent and underexplored field of study. The emergence of algorithmic trading, social media, and online investment platforms has profoundly transformed stock market participation, enhancing the velocity and scope of information distribution. These technological advancements may intensify or alleviate the impact of cognitive and emotional stimuli on herding behaviour. Algorithmic trading can mitigate human biases by automating decisions according to established criteria; yet, it may also exacerbate herding behaviour by making transactions collectively in response to market signals. Simultaneously, social media platforms function as potent conduits for social influence and fear of missing out (FOMO), facilitating the swift dissemination of knowledge (and misinformation), frequently prompting impulsive investment choices. The current research insufficiently explores the interaction between technological advances and classic behavioural finance models, resulting in a significant gap in comprehending modern stock market dynamics (Goodell et al., 2023).

Furthermore, whereas much research on herding behaviour and psychological triggers predominantly examines individual investors, there is a lack of comprehensive analysis about the influence of these biases on institutional investors. Institutional investors are frequently perceived as more rational and less susceptible to cognitive biases owing to their access to superior information and analytical resources. Recent data indicates that institutional investors are susceptible to herding behaviour, especially during times of significant market uncertainty. The mechanisms by which cognitive and emotional triggers affect institutional decision-making are inadequately examined, resulting in a lack of understanding regarding the manifestation of herding behaviour among various investor types. Rectifying this deficiency is crucial for formulating interventions or policies designed to stabilise financial markets.

Ultimately, a significant deficiency in the literature is the insufficient emphasis on the enduring repercussions of herding behaviour influenced by cognitive and emotional stimuli. Although many studies investigate the short-term market volatility and price distortions resulting from herding, there is a paucity of study regarding the longevity of these impacts over time. Can markets self-correct, or do psychological triggers result in prolonged inefficiencies and systemic risks? The enduring effects of herding behaviour on financial stability, asset valuation, and market efficiency remain uncertain, especially within the framework of increasingly globalised and interconnected markets.

LITERATURE REVIEW

Underlying Theory: Regret Aversion Theory

Regret Aversion Theory is a fundamental principle in behavioural finance that examines how the expectation of regret affects decision-making in uncertain situations. Grounded on psychological research, regret aversion suggests that individuals make decisions aimed at minimising the likelihood of future regret, rather than exclusively maximising value according to conventional economic models. This theory contests the premises of rational choice theory by highlighting that emotions, especially the dread of regret, significantly influence investing decisions. In financial markets, characterised by uncertainty and risk, the inclination to evade remorse frequently results in suboptimal actions that diverge from fully rational conduct.

Regret Aversion Theory posits that individuals feel regret when the result of a decision is inferior to what could have been attained through an alternative choice. This emotional reaction is linked not just to the money loss but also to the realisation that a more favourable outcome was attainable. In the realm of stock markets, investors sometimes encounter decisions laden with significant ambiguity, such as whether to purchase, retain, or divest assets. Regret aversion may cause investors to either refrain from decision-making or to adopt excessively conservative strategies, motivated by the wish to evade future remorse in the event of financial losses.

A primary expression of regret aversion in financial markets is the propensity of investors to retain lost stocks excessively. This phenomenon, termed the “disposition effect,” arises from investors' apprehension of the regret they could experience if they divest a stock at a loss, only to witness its subsequent price recovery. In such instances, investors may postpone selling, anticipating a recovery in the stock's value, despite indications that retaining the asset may not serve their financial interests optimally. This hesitance to divest may result in an inability to mitigate losses promptly, hence intensifying financial detriment over time. Regret aversion, in this context, supersedes the rational evaluation of the stock's fundamentals or future prospects, as the emotional burden of possible regret skews the decision-making process.

Regret aversion also affects risk-taking behaviour in the stock market. Investors may avoid engaging in risky yet potentially lucrative investments due to the concern of experiencing regret from a possible loss. This is especially apparent during times of market volatility or declines, when the likelihood of regret intensifies due to heightened uncertainty. Investors may employ excessively cautious techniques, favouring low-risk, low-return investments to protect themselves from potential future regret. This reluctance to embrace calculated risks may hinder investors from seizing opportunities, resulting in underperformance compared to the larger market.

Regret aversion can, intriguingly, result in contrary behaviour under specific market situations, prompting investors to undertake excessive risks to evade the regret of forgoing prospective gains. This phenomenon frequently occurs during speculative bubbles, where the fear of missing out (FOMO) merges with regret aversion. Investors may be driven to invest in overvalued assets due to the apprehension of regretting their absence from a market rally that others are benefiting from. In this instance, regret aversion does not result in prudence but instead fosters herding behaviour, when investors collectively pursue short-term profits, frequently culminating in inflated asset values and market volatility (Griffith et al., 2020).

Furthermore, Regret Aversion Theory may possess wider ramifications for market dynamics and efficiency. The cumulative effect of regret-averse decisions can lead to market oddities, including heightened volatility and price discrepancies from fundamental values. When numerous investors are influenced by regret aversion, either by retaining depreciating equities or by eschewing riskier investments, the market may undergo extended phases of mispricing. During financial crises, the pervasive dread of regret may intensify market declines, as investors hastily liquidate assets to evade the remorse of prospective losses, so further depressing prices and fostering a detrimental feedback cycle (Komalasari et al., 2022).

The hypothesis possesses significant consequences for financial advisors and policymakers. Comprehending the influence of regret aversion on investor behaviour might assist financial professionals in formulating solutions to alleviate its detrimental impacts. For example, financial advisors may structure investment decisions to mitigate the emotional effects of regret by promoting long-term viewpoints and highlighting the significance of diversity. Instructing investors on the psychological biases that affect their decisions, such as regret aversion, might enable them to make more informed and sensible choices, therefore enhancing their financial results. Regret Aversion Theory offers a valuable framework for incorporating emotional and psychological elements into economic decision-making models. The theory provides a more realistic and thorough understanding of investor behaviour by recognising that investors are not solely rational agents but are also influenced by their inclination to evade regret. It contests the assumption that investors consistently act in their optimal financial interest and highlights the significance of emotions in influencing economic decisions, especially in uncertain and unpredictable contexts such as the stock market.

Overconfidence bias is a recognised cognitive bias in behavioural finance, wherein individuals overrate their knowledge, skills, and forecasting ability. The investigation of overconfidence bias originates from foundational studies by psychologists Daniel Kahneman and Amos Tversky, who examined human judgement in conditions of uncertainty. Overconfidence is frequently associated with excessive trading in financial markets, since investors who perceive their abilities as superior are more inclined to participate in high-risk trading activities. Barber and Odean (2001) produced a seminal study illustrating that overconfident investors engage in more frequent trading, often to their disadvantage, as increased trading volumes generally result in diminished net profits. Furthermore, overconfidence has been shown to intensify herding behaviour, particularly during times of market optimism. Investors, confident in their ability to forecast market fluctuations more accurately than others, may collectively pursue ascending stocks, thus exacerbating inflated asset prices and fostering speculative bubbles. Research indicates that overconfidence is more common among inexperienced investors, while it can also manifest in institutional investors under specific circumstances (Loang, 2023). Despite extensive study on overconfidence, there are still gaps in understanding how this bias interacts with other psychological characteristics, such as loss aversion, to affect herding behaviour.

Loss aversion, based on Prospect Theory formulated by Kahneman and Tversky, asserts that humans perceive the discomfort of losses more acutely than the satisfaction derived from similar gains (Loang, 2024a). This cognitive bias has been thoroughly examined in relation to financial markets, affecting both individual decision-making and aggregate market dynamics. Studies on loss aversion in financial markets have shown that investors tend to sell profitable equities prematurely while retaining unprofitable stocks, a phenomenon termed the "disposition effect" (Shefrin & Statman, 1985). This tendency may result in market inefficiencies, as investors collectively neglect to respond to bad information and postpone the divestment of depreciating assets. Loss aversion significantly influences herding behaviour, especially in times of market decline. When investors anticipate financial losses, they may conform to the majority by liquidating assets, resulting in panic-induced market downturns. Research by Ben-David and Hirshleifer (2012) indicates that loss aversion, in conjunction with various emotional and cognitive stimuli, might amplify the impact of herding in times of significant volatility. Further research is necessary to investigate the interaction of loss aversion with other factors, such as social influence, to ascertain its effect on collective investment behaviours.

Social influence is a crucial factor in determining investor behaviour and has been extensively studied across various fields, including psychology, sociology, and finance. In the context of the stock market, social influence denotes the propensity of individuals to be affected by the actions, views, or judgements of others. Theoretical research on social influence frequently relies on models of informational cascades, wherein individuals, confronted with ambiguity, opt to replicate the acts of others, assuming that those individuals hold superior information. Empirical research, exemplified by Bikhchandani, Hirshleifer, and Welch (1992), demonstrates that social influence can induce herding behaviour, prompting investors to conform their judgements to the apparent majority. Social networks, financial news, and media significantly contribute to the dissemination of information, both accurate and erroneous, which can exacerbate herding behaviour during market surges or declines. Recent studies have examined the effects of digital platforms and social media on social influence, demonstrating that online forums and investment groups can swiftly enhance collective investment behaviours (Shiller, 2019). Although social influence is a recognised notion in herding theory, the literature remains deficient in a thorough comprehension of how social influence interacts with cognitive biases such as overconfidence and loss aversion, particularly within a technology-driven market context (Loang, 2024b).

The Fear of Missing Out (FOMO) is an emotional catalyst that has become increasingly significant in contemporary studies of investor behaviour. Despite being a more recent phenomenon than overconfidence or loss aversion, FOMO has gained significant relevance in the realm of digital media and instantaneous financial news. FOMO denotes the apprehension investors experience when they believe others are capitalising on an opportunity they have overlooked. This emotional reaction can compel investors to make hasty, short-term decisions to evade the remorse of missing a market surge. Studies on FOMO in financial markets indicate a strong correlation with speculative bubbles and herding behaviour, as investors, motivated by the fear of missing potential gains, converge on expensive assets. This phenomenon was especially pronounced during the ascent of cryptocurrencies and the technology stock surge, as investors flocked to the market in significant numbers despite apprehensions regarding asset overvaluation (Akerlof & Shiller, 2010). The literature on FOMO underscores its significant association with social impact, as investors frequently formulate their judgements based on the actions of others, particularly within online forums. Further research is necessary to distinguish FOMO from other emotional triggers such as regret aversion and to enhance comprehension of its long-term effects on market stability.

Research Methodology

The research methods utilised in examining collective investment patterns in stock markets, with special emphasis on the influence of cognitive and emotional triggers, can be approached using qualitative and quantitative methodology. The amalgamation of these two methodologies facilitates a more thorough comprehension of the intricate behavioural factors that propel herding behaviour. Each method offers distinct insights, with quantitative techniques delivering statistical analysis and empirical validation, whilst qualitative methods provide a profound interpretative comprehension of investor psychology and decision-making processes.

Quantitative research typically use surveys, experiments, and econometric modelling to examine the effects of overconfidence bias, loss aversion, social influence, and FOMO on herding behaviour. Surveys are frequently constructed to obtain self-reported data from investors concerning their attitudes, risk preferences, and trading behaviours. These surveys can be conducted with a substantial cohort of retail and institutional investors, facilitating the acquisition of diverse data regarding the manifestation of cognitive biases in actual trading choices. Subsequently, this data can be examined via statistical methodologies, such regression analysis or structural equation modelling, to evaluate the associations between the independent variables (e.g., overconfidence, loss aversion) and the dependent variable (herding behaviour). Researchers may investigate the correlation between overconfidence levels and trading volumes or price fluctuations in particular asset classes.

Quantitative approaches encompass experimental designs, which are especially effective for isolating particular cognitive or emotional variables and assessing their impacts in controlled environments. Laboratory or online studies can replicate stock market conditions, when participants are required to make investment choices based on theoretical scenarios. These experiments enable researchers to modify variables like market volatility or peer behaviour, therefore assessing individual responses to varying settings. Participants may encounter information indicating a robust market trend (social influence), while their degrees of overconfidence or fear of missing out (FOMO) are assessed before and following the trading exercise. This controlled environment allows researchers to derive causal conclusions on the impact of particular cognitive biases on herding behaviour. The experimental method is beneficial for evaluating interventions, such as educational reminders or decision aids, to determine their efficacy in alleviating the impact of cognitive biases on investment behaviour.

Econometric modelling, a significant quantitative method, utilises extensive market data to examine aggregate investment behaviours. Time-series data concerning stock prices, trading volumes, and various market indices can be utilised to detect occurrences of herding behaviour and to analyse its correlation with cognitive and emotional aspects. Researchers may employ sophisticated statistical methodologies, like vector autoregression (VAR) or generalised autoregressive conditional heteroskedasticity (GARCH) models, to elucidate the dynamics of herding in reaction to fluctuations in market sentiment or external disturbances. For example, by monitoring fluctuations in stock prices during times of significant volatility, researchers can evaluate if herding behaviour escalates during market declines, possibly influenced by loss aversion or fear of missing out (FOMO). These models can additionally integrate data from investor sentiment indices or news sentiment analysis, thereby enhancing the quantitative comprehension of how psychological aspects affect collective decision-making.

Conversely, qualitative research methodologies yield significant insights into the subjective and contextual elements influencing investor behaviour. These methods are especially adept at uncovering the fundamental motivations, emotions, and social dynamics that quantitative approaches may neglect. A prevalent qualitative method involves conducting in-depth interviews with investors, financial counsellors, or market experts. Researchers can obtain comprehensive and nuanced insights into investors' perceptions of market risks, their information processing, and the influence of social networks or media narratives through semi-structured or unstructured interviews. These interviews facilitate the examination of intricate emotional stimuli, such as fear of missing out and regret aversion, which may not be entirely represented through survey instruments or quantitative models. An interview study may indicate that investors prioritise the social status linked to successful investments over mere financial results, underscoring the impact of social influence on herding behaviour.

Case studies serve as an additional qualitative approach to examine herding behaviour in stock markets. By concentrating on certain market phenomena, such as speculative bubbles or financial collapses, researchers can perform an in-depth investigation of the elements that influenced collective investing behaviour during such times. A case study on the dot-com bubble might analyse the interplay of overconfidence and social influence in generating unsustainable market valuations, focusing specifically on technology stocks and investor mood. Case studies frequently employ a multidisciplinary approach, integrating psychology, sociology, and finance to deliver a comprehensive analysis of herding behaviour. This approach facilitates the amalgamation of diverse data sources, including interviews, historical records, and media analysis, providing a holistic understanding of the social and cognitive dynamics involved.

Focus groups represent a qualitative method employed to investigate collective investing behaviour. Focus groups convene small groups of investors to facilitate discussions on investment strategy, emotional responses to market events, and the impact of peers or social networks. This method enables researchers to examine the real-time progression of social dynamics, providing insights into the roles of groupthink and social conformity in herding behaviour. Focus groups are especially effective for examining the impact of FOMO, as participants can express how they are affected by the behaviours of others within their investment communities or online platforms.

Moreover, qualitative content research of media, social media, and investment forums can yield essential insights into information transmission and the development of collective attitude. Researchers can examine posts on financial forums, tweets, or news articles to monitor the evolution of narratives concerning specific stocks or market patterns and their impact on investor behaviour. This methodology is especially pertinent in the contemporary digital era, as information disseminates swiftly and can profoundly influence market dynamics. Through the examination of language utilised in various forums or media platforms, researchers can discern prevalent themes associated with overconfidence, loss aversion, or FOMO, thereby correlating qualitative insights with the quantitative trends seen in market data.

The investigation of cognitive and emotional catalysts of herding behaviour in stock markets is enhanced by a mixed-methods approach that integrates both qualitative and quantitative research methodologies. Quantitative methods equip researchers with tools to assess and predict the influence of biases on market behaviour, whereas qualitative methods yield profound insights into the subjective experiences and social circumstances that inform investor decisions. The amalgamation of various methodologies enhances the validity of the results and offers a more sophisticated comprehension of the intricate interactions of cognitive, emotional, and social elements in financial markets.

Figure 1. Conceptual framework

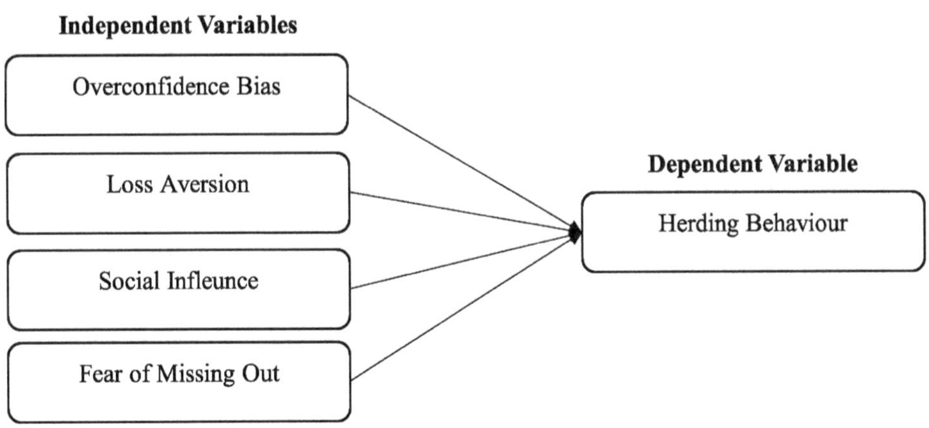

This study's conceptual framework is based on the interdisciplinary amalgamation of behavioural finance and psychological theories to elucidate collective investing behaviours, particularly herding behaviour in stock markets. This approach aims to delineate the interconnections among cognitive biases, emotional stimuli, and the consequent group dynamics that influence market behaviour. It includes the independent factors of overconfidence bias, loss aversion, social influence, and the fear of missing out (FOMO), which collectively affect the dependent variable, herding behaviour. This conceptual framework seeks to provide a refined understanding of how individual psychological elements converge to generate collective market outcomes by placing these variables within the wider context of market dynamics (Mushinada, 2020).

The paradigm posits that investor behaviour is not only governed by logical information analysis but is profoundly affected by cognitive and emotional biases. These biases skew the decision-making process, resulting in deviations from the efficient market hypothesis, which posits that prices in financial markets encapsulate all available information and that investors behave rationally. The paradigm contests the conventional perspective by highlighting that psychological factors—both individual and collective—are crucial in influencing market behaviour, especially during times of market volatility or speculative bubbles.

Overconfidence bias is crucial in the conceptual framework, since it exemplifies a major cognitive distortion influencing investor behaviour. Overconfident investors typically overrate their knowledge, forecasting abilities, and potential to exceed market performance. This bias compels individuals to engage in more frequent trading, undertake bigger risks, and frequently disregard the perspectives of others, convinced that their views are superior. Within the framework, it is posited that overconfidence fosters herding behaviour when investors collectively display unwarranted optimism regarding specific assets or market movements (Parveen et al., 2020). Overconfidence can enhance social impact, since assured investors may convince others to emulate their actions, so encouraging collective behaviour. The paradigm posits that overconfidence has a dual function: it may push individual investors to act autonomously, while simultaneously exacerbating herd behaviour through heightened risk-taking and excessive market engagement.

Loss aversion, a fundamental element of the framework, arises from the concept that investors perceive the distress of losses more intensely than the satisfaction of comparable profits. This cognitive bias influences investor responses to market volatility, especially during downturns. Within the paradigm, loss aversion is posited to catalyse herding behaviour via defensive measures, such as liquidating assets during market downturns to mitigate additional losses (Raut et al., 2020). This collective risk-averse behaviour frequently intensifies market volatility, since extensive selling exerts downward pressure on asset values. Loss aversion interacts with overconfidence by eliciting contradictory emotional reactions: overconfident investors may engage in excessive risk-taking, yet their aversion to losses can prompt sudden behavioural shifts when the market declines. The paradigm asserts that loss aversion influences both panic-induced herding in market declines and the hesitance to capitalise on profits during market upswings.

In this approach, social influence is pivotal in shaping collective investing behaviour by facilitating knowledge distribution and the imitation of others' activities. In highly interconnected markets, where information is swiftly disseminated via media, social networks, and digital platforms, investors are often influenced by the decisions and actions of their counterparts. The concept highlights that social influence is especially significant in uncertain situations, where investors lack clarity on the optimal path of action and consequently depend on the perceived collective wisdom. In these instances, herding behaviour manifests when individuals conform to the majority's activities, frequently disregarding fundamental principles (Suresh & Loang, 2024). The approach considers the impact of digital platforms and social media, which can expedite information dissemination and establish feedback loops that enhance herd behaviour. By integrating social influence into the conceptual framework, the study recognises that investment decisions are influenced by broader social and informational contexts rather than being made in isolation.

The fear of missing out (FOMO) is the concluding crucial variable in the conceptual framework and signifies an emotional catalyst that propels hasty decision-making in financial markets. FOMO arises when investors apprehend that others are seizing possibilities they are overlooking, resulting in impulsive and perhaps irrational market engagement. Within the paradigm, FOMO is posited to exert significant influence during speculative bubbles, characterised by fast asset price escalation, prompting investors to hastily engage in the rally. This emotional reaction is intricately linked to social influence, as investors are frequently swayed by the perceived achievements of individuals within their personal networks and media portrayals. The paradigm posits that FOMO significantly influences herding behaviour during market upswings, since it drives investors to participate in ascending trends to evade the emotional remorse of missing prospective profits. The study incorporates FOMO into the conceptual framework, emphasising the interaction between emotional influences and cognitive biases in determining collective investing behaviours.

Herding behaviour, the dependent variable in the framework, refers to the phenomena in which investors emulate the behaviours of others, leading to collective decision-making that frequently diverges from rational market behaviour. The theory defines herding as the result of the interplay between cognitive biases and emotional stimuli, especially in situations of uncertainty or increased market volatility for investors. Herding manifests in two varieties: informational herding, wherein investors emulate others based on perceived superior information, and reputational herding, where individuals conform to the majority to safeguard their social status or professional reputation. The concept considers both forms of herding, indicating that the four independent variables facilitate the establishment of herd behaviour via distinct routes. Overconfidence and fear of missing out (FOMO) are more likely to induce herding behaviour during market upswings, whereas loss aversion and social influence exert greater impact during market declines (Tang & Loang, 2024).

The conceptual framework also accounts for extrinsic influences that influence the link between the independent variables and herding behaviour. Market variables, including volatility, liquidity, and the regulatory environment, are suggested as potential moderators that affect the intensity and direction of herding behaviour. During times of heightened volatility, the impacts of loss aversion and social influence may intensify, resulting in panic-induced herding behaviour. Conversely, in times of low volatility, overconfidence and fear of missing out may prevail, leading to speculative bubbles. The approach recognises that herding behaviour is influenced not only by cognitive and emotional biases but also by overarching market dynamics (Wu, 2022).

CONCLUSION

This study concludes by synthesising the principal findings about the impact of cognitive and emotional stimuli on collective investment behaviours, namely herding behaviour, in stock markets. This research highlights the critical importance of psychological factors—overconfidence bias, loss aversion, social influence, and the fear of missing out (FOMO)—on investment decisions, hence contesting the conventional models of rational behaviour typically presumed in finance. The research illustrates that cognitive and emotional triggers interact with one another and with market conditions, forming a complex network of influences that can result in widespread herding behaviour, market inefficiencies, and ultimately, increased financial market volatility.

This study primarily elucidates how cognitive biases, including overconfidence and loss aversion, skew investor decision-making. Overconfidence bias causes investors to overrate their skills and the precision of their market forecasts, frequently resulting in heightened risk-taking and overtrading. The study indicates that widespread investor overconfidence promotes collective risk-taking behaviours, leading to speculative bubbles or abrupt market surges. Conversely, loss aversion—where investors excessively dread financial losses—results in inefficient decision-making during market downturns. The aversion to acknowledging losses, along with a shared inclination to prematurely divest from profitable assets, frequently intensifies market fluctuations, resulting in downward spirals amid instability. These findings highlight the necessity for a more sophisticated comprehension of how these cognitive biases influence not only individual behaviour but also overarching market dynamics.

The research enhances comprehension of emotional stimuli in financial markets, focusing specifically on social impact and fear of missing out (FOMO). It demonstrates the significant role of social networks, media, and digital platforms in the dissemination of knowledge, which can swiftly impact collective behaviour. The fear of missing out acts as a significant emotional catalyst, prompting investors to make impulsive trading choices in reaction to ascending markets. This emotional reaction, especially when combined with social influence, exacerbates herding behaviour, resulting in inflated asset prices and the creation of bubbles. The study's conclusion highlights that both FOMO and social influence are significant catalysts for herding in contemporary networked markets, characterised by rapid information dissemination and the observable activities of others. The findings indicate that the emotional and social features of market behaviour are equally significant as the cognitive aspects in comprehending herding patterns.

This study highlights the wider ramifications of herding behaviour on market efficiency and stability. Cognitive and emotional biases may occasionally result in lucrative short-term actions; but, the study suggests that herding, influenced by these psychological elements, frequently diminishes market efficiency by inducing mispricing's. Markets characterised by prevalent herding behaviour may undergo pronounced booms and busts, resulting in prices that dramatically diverge from their underlying values. The collective behaviour of investors, driven by cognitive and emotional biases, can disrupt price discovery processes, resulting in market bubbles or crashes that present systemic hazards to the overall financial system. This study underscores the essential need to identify and treat these psychological factors to alleviate their negative impact on market stability.

A significant conclusion derived from the study is the necessity for focused interventions to alleviate the adverse effects of cognitive and emotional biases on herding behaviour. The results indicate that educating investors and raising awareness of prevalent psychological biases may mitigate overconfidence and enhance decision-making. Furthermore, financial legislation designed to restrict speculative trading or establish protections during times of increased volatility could mitigate the detrimental impacts of loss aversion and panic selling. Technological solutions, such algorithmic trading and decision-support systems, may alleviate the impact of emotional triggers such as FOMO by fostering more disciplined and data-driven trading decisions. The result underscores the necessity of integrating educational, regulatory, and technical measures to tackle the fundamental reasons of herding behaviour and to promote more stable and efficient markets.

This study enhances the discourse in behavioural finance by providing a detailed framework for comprehending the psychological factors that drive collective investing behaviours. It transcends conventional economic models that presume rational behaviour and emphasises the importance of emotions and cognitive biases in influencing market dynamics. The study emphasises that subsequent research must persist in examining the interplay between cognitive and emotional components, especially with advancing market technologies and digital platforms. As financial markets grow more globalised and digitised, comprehending the psychological triggers that influence herding behaviour will be essential for forecasting and managing market fluctuations.

Theoretical, Managerial and Policy Implications

This study's theoretical implications substantially advance the field of behavioural finance by providing novel insights into the psychological factors underlying herding behaviour in stock markets. This study critiques the traditional rationality assumptions of classical financial models, including the Efficient Market Hypothesis (EMH), by examining cognitive biases like overconfidence and loss aversion, as well as emotional triggers such as social influence and the fear of missing out (FOMO). Conventional financial theories frequently posit that market participants are rational agents that make decisions only based on the analysis of accessible information. This study empirically substantiates the notion that cognitive and emotional biases significantly impact investor behaviour, resulting in collective irrationality. The findings indicate that behavioural finance models, which integrate psychological variables into market dynamics study, provide a more precise framework for comprehending stock market behaviour. This study underscores the necessity for a paradigm shift in financial theory that recognises the intricacies of investor psychology and the interplay of cognitive and emotional elements in influencing market outcomes.

Furthermore, the study's results enhance current theoretical frameworks by highlighting the link between individual and collective behaviour in financial markets. It illustrates that herding is not solely a result of individual cognitive biases but emerges from the interplay of social, cognitive, and emotional dynamics. This multidisciplinary approach increases the explanatory capacity of behavioural finance by including the wider social and informational settings influencing investment decisions. The study indicates that future theoretical models should focus more on the influence of technology in enhancing herding behaviour. Digital platforms, social media, and algorithmic trading systems have created novel avenues for information distribution and collective decision-making, making their impact on herding behaviour a significant subject for further investigation in behavioural finance theory.

The study's insights into the cognitive and emotional factors influencing herding behaviour have practical consequences for individual investors and institutional entities, including fund managers and financial advisors. It is essential for individual investors to comprehend the cognitive biases that may result in suboptimal investment decisions to enhance financial outcomes. Overconfidence and loss aversion may lead to excessive risk-taking or the reluctance to realise losses promptly, resulting in inferior portfolio performance. This study indicates that investors require education regarding these biases and must be provided with tools to mitigate them, including decision aids, risk management measures, and organised decision-making procedures. Financial advisors can significantly mitigate the impact of cognitive and emotional biases by offering objective, data-driven counsel that counteracts social pressures and emotional reactions such as FOMO. By integrating behavioural insights into their advising services, financial professionals can assist clients in making more educated, long-term decisions that correspond with their financial objectives.

The study's findings underscore the necessity for institutional investors and fund managers to identify and mitigate herding behaviour within investment teams and across financial markets. Herding can result in market inefficiencies and heightened volatility, both of which may negatively impact fund performance. Institutional investors may be especially susceptible to herding during times of market volatility, as they encounter pressure to align with the choices of their counterparts or to uphold competitive performance standards. Fund managers can alleviate herding by cultivating a culture of autonomous decision-making among their teams, promoting critical examination of market trends, and rejecting the compulsion to adhere to market fads or prevalent investment techniques without thorough evaluation. Moreover, portfolio diversification and long-term investing strategies might assist institutional investors in mitigating their exposure to the dangers linked to herding, including market bubbles and crashes.

This report offers essential insights for regulators and policymakers responsible for ensuring market stability and safeguarding investors. The recognition of cognitive and emotional triggers as primary influences on herding behaviour indicates that regulatory frameworks ought to be created to tackle the psychological elements that lead to market volatility and inefficiency. Policymakers can contemplate enacting policies that diminish the probability of herding by enhancing transparency and information dissemination in financial markets. Regulations mandating more prompt and precise disclosures from publicly traded corporations could alleviate uncertainty, thereby diminishing the impact of cognitive biases such as overconfidence and loss aversion. Furthermore, initiatives designed to enhance financial literacy among retail investors may mitigate the occurrence of herding behaviour by equipping consumers with a deeper comprehension of the hazards linked to adhering to market trends without sufficient examination.

The influence of technology on intensifying herding behaviour carries significant policy ramifications. The proliferation of algorithmic trading, social media-influenced investment trends, and internet trading platforms has expedited the dissemination of information—and misinformation—within financial markets. The swift spread of information might result in heightened market volatility if investors, swayed by social media narratives or automated trading algorithms, exhibit herding behaviour. Policymakers must evaluate the possible hazards associated with these technology breakthroughs and formulate rules that enhance accountability in digital platforms and trading technologies. Regulatory organisations could implement stricter monitoring of algorithmic trading systems to prevent them from exacerbating market volatility through the amplification of herding dynamics. The study's findings indicate the possibility of legislative initiatives that promote more disciplined, long-term investment methods. Regulatory interventions, including transaction taxes, limitations on high-frequency trading, or incentives for prolonged holding periods, may mitigate speculative, short-term behaviours frequently influenced by emotional stimuli such as FOMO and social pressure. Policymakers can consider implementing circuit breakers or alternative market mechanisms aimed at decelerating trade during episodes of extreme volatility, allowing investors the opportunity to reevaluate their choices and prevent panic-induced herding.

Limitations and Recommendations for Future Studies

The constraints of this study are inherent to the field of behavioural finance, which frequently contends with the intricacies of human psychology and the difficulties in accurately quantifying cognitive and emotional factors. A primary weakness of this study is the challenge of distinguishing the impact of certain cognitive biases, such as overconfidence or loss aversion, from the wider range of factors that affect investor behaviour. In actual financial markets, investor decisions are influenced by numerous interacting elements, such as macroeconomic conditions, regulatory frameworks, technological advancements, and sociopolitical issues. The complexity complicates the ability to draw conclusive insights on the precise influence of psychological stimuli on herding behaviour. This study significantly underscores the impact of cognitive and emotional biases; nevertheless, future research will benefit from a more detailed analysis that separates these variables under varying market conditions and among diverse investor demographics.

A further restriction arises from the dependence on self-reported data in surveys and trials, prevalent in behavioural finance research. Self-reported data is prone to biases, such as social desirability, wherein respondents may offer answers they perceive as more socially acceptable or anticipated, rather than accurately representing their actual behaviour. Additionally, there exists the problem of hindsight bias, wherein investors may fail to accurately remember their decision-making processes or emotional conditions during previous market occurrences. This dependence on subjective reports may result in inconsistencies between reported behaviour and real behaviour in financial markets. Subsequent research may mitigate this constraint by integrating more objective metrics of investor behaviour, like real-time trading data or behavioural monitoring technology that observe decision-making in actual market conditions.

This study, similar to much of the current work in behavioural finance, predominantly examines retail investors and may not adequately consider the behaviour of institutional investors, who frequently influence market dynamics significantly. Institutional investors possess advanced tools, information, and resources that may reduce the impact of specific cognitive biases. Research indicates that institutional investors are also susceptible to herding behaviour, especially during times of market uncertainty. Future research should investigate the intricacies of herding behaviour among institutional participants, evaluating the distinct manifestations of cognitive and emotional stimuli in professional investment contexts. This may entail case studies of institutional investors or empirical analyses of fund managers' decision-making processes amid market stress.

Another limitation of this study is the geographical reach of the data and the possibility that cultural influences may affect investor behaviour. Research in behavioural finance has shown that cultural disparities can profoundly influence the manifestation of cognitive biases and emotional triggers in financial markets. For instance, loss aversion and risk tolerance may differ among cultures, since certain investors may originate from financial systems or communities that promote cautious investment practices, whereas others may exhibit a propensity for speculative risk-taking. The outcomes of this study may not be entirely applicable across various locations or cultural contexts. To mitigate this constraint, subsequent study could adopt a cross-cultural methodology, contrasting herding behaviour across various countries or areas. This would facilitate a more profound understanding of how cultural and institutional circumstances affect the expression of cognitive and emotional biases in stock market behaviour.

A significant weakness is the changing influence of technology on investor behaviour, which this study addresses but does not examine thoroughly. The rise of algorithmic trading, robo-advisors, and social media platforms has significantly transformed the financial markets in recent years. Algorithmic trading, specifically, offers a novel aspect to herding behaviour, since automated systems can execute substantial volumes of transactions in reaction to market signals, thereby exacerbating trends and contributing to market instability. Similarly, the influence of social media in disseminating information or misinformation can result in swift changes in investor mood and, subsequently, collective market fluctuations. Future research should concentrate more thoroughly on the interplay between technology and psychological biases, specifically investigating how digital platforms and automated trading systems can intensify or alleviate herding behaviour. This would yield significant insights on the transforming dynamics of financial markets in the digital era.

This study primarily examines stock markets; however, herding behaviour and the cognitive and emotional biases that influence it can also occur in other financial sectors, including bond markets, real estate, and cryptocurrency markets. Each market possesses certain elements that may affect the manifestation of herding behaviour. The cryptocurrency market is notably volatile and prone to speculative bubbles, influenced partly by the emotional fervour and fear of missing out prevalent in social media and investment forums. Subsequent research should expand its focus to encompass these other asset classes, examining if the cognitive and emotional triggers revealed in this study are uniformly applicable across diverse market conditions. This would facilitate the generalisation of the findings and yield a more thorough understanding of herding behaviour within the wider financial context.

The study's emphasis on cognitive biases, including overconfidence and loss aversion, alongside emotional triggers such as social influence and FOMO, is significant although not comprehensive. Human behaviour in financial markets is shaped by various psychological elements, and other biases or emotions contributing to herding behaviour were not addressed in this study. Regret aversion and confirmation bias are cognitive variables that influence investment decisions and warrant further investigation. Regret aversion, the apprehension of making a decision that may result in future remorse, might compel investors to eschew audacious actions or to conform to prevailing trends to mitigate prospective regret. Confirmation bias, wherein investors pursue information that corroborates their pre-existing convictions, may further entrench herding behaviour, as individuals preferentially concentrate on data that corresponds with prevailing market trends. Future research should aim to incorporate a broader spectrum of psychological characteristics into their analysis, potentially resulting in a more comprehensive knowledge of the factors influencing collective investing behaviours.

REFERENCES

Aggarwal, D. (2022). Defining and measuring market sentiments: A review of the literature. *Qualitative Research in Financial Markets*, 14(2), 270–288. DOI: 10.1108/QRFM-03-2018-0033

Akinkoye, E. Y., & Bankole, O. E. (2020). Effect of emotional biases on investor's decision making in Nigeria. *International Journal of Business and Management Future*, 4(1), 33–39. DOI: 10.46281/ijbmf.v4i1.548

Duxbury, D., Gärling, T., Gamble, A., & Klass, V. (2020). How emotions influence behavior in financial markets: A conceptual analysis and emotion-based account of buy-sell preferences. *European Journal of Finance*, 26(14), 1417–1438. DOI: 10.1080/1351847X.2020.1742758

FaXing. L., & Loang, O. K. (2024). Green Investing and Financial Education: The Case of China's A-Share Market. In *Technology-Driven Business Innovation: Unleashing the Digital Advantage, Volume 1* (pp. 29-41). Cham: Springer Nature Switzerland.

Fu, T., & Loang, O. K. (2024). The Roles of ESG Disclosure, Innovation in Improving Firm Financial Performance: Evidence from China. In *Artificial Intelligence (AI) and Customer Social Responsibility (CSR)* (pp. 197–221). Springer Nature Switzerland. DOI: 10.1007/978-3-031-50939-1_16

Goodell, J. W., Kumar, S., Rao, P., & Verma, S. (2023). Emotions and stock market anomalies: A systematic review. *Journal of Behavioral and Experimental Finance*, 37, 100722. DOI: 10.1016/j.jbef.2022.100722

Griffith, J., Najand, M., & Shen, J. (2020). Emotions in the stock market. *Journal of Behavioral Finance*, 21(1), 42–56. DOI: 10.1080/15427560.2019.1588275

Komalasari, P. T., Asri, M., Purwanto, B. M., & Setiyono, B. (2022). Herding behaviour in the capital market: What do we know and what is next? *Management Review Quarterly*, 72(3), 745–787. DOI: 10.1007/s11301-021-00212-1

Loang, O. K. (2023). Corporate governance and Islamic behavioural finance: A review from Malaysia and GCC countries. *Indian Journal of Corporate Governance*, 16(1), 28–51. DOI: 10.1177/09746862231178959

Loang, O. K. (2024). Stability Of Shariah-Compliant Stocks In Indonesia, Malaysia, And Gcc: The Roles Of Monetary And Fiscal Policies And Contagion. *Journal of Islamic Monetary Economics and Finance*, 10(1), 155–176. DOI: 10.21098/jimf.v10i1.1899

Loang, O. K. (2024). Sustainability's impact of ESG-infused policies on leading economic indicators in Asian economies. *Journal of Sustainable Research*, 6(3), e240059. DOI: 10.20900/jsr20240059

Mushinada, V. N. C. (2020). Are individual investors irrational or adaptive to market dynamics? *Journal of Behavioral and Experimental Finance*, 25, 100243. DOI: 10.1016/j.jbef.2019.100243

Parveen, S., Satti, Z. W., Subhan, Q. A., & Jamil, S. (2020). Exploring market overreaction, investors' sentiments and investment decisions in an emerging stock market. *Borsa Istanbul Review*, 20(3), 224–235. DOI: 10.1016/j.bir.2020.02.002

Raut, R. K., Das, N., & Mishra, R. (2020). Behaviour of individual investors in stock market trading: Evidence from India. *Global Business Review*, 21(3), 818–833. DOI: 10.1177/0972150918778915

Suresh, G., & Loang, O. K. (2024). The Rationality Conundrum: Exploring Herd Mentality among Individual Investors in the Indian Stock Market. *Indian Journal of Finance*, 18(6), 26–45. DOI: 10.17010/ijf/2024/v18i6/173967

Tang, H., & Loang, O. K. (2024). Does ESG Performance Improve the Financial Performance of Enterprises in China? The Mediating Role of Financial Constraints. In *Artificial Intelligence (AI) and Customer Social Responsibility (CSR)* (pp. 263–289). Springer Nature Switzerland. DOI: 10.1007/978-3-031-50939-1_20

Wu, H. (2022). Intuition in investment decision-making across cultures. *Journal of Behavioral Finance*, 23(1), 106–122. DOI: 10.1080/15427560.2020.1848839

Chapter 7 Investor Biases and Reaction Dynamics Exploring the Psychological Mechanisms Behind Market Fluctuations: RTE

Yang Ze
Universiti Malaya, Malaysia

Ooi Kok Loang
https://orcid.org/0000-0003-0412-8899
Universiti Malaya, Malaysia

ABSTRACT

This study explores the psychological mechanisms driving market fluctuations, focusing on how cognitive biases, such as investor sentiment, confirmation bias, risk perception, and the anchoring effect, contribute to market overreaction. By analyzing the interplay between these biases, the research challenges traditional financial theories like the Efficient Market Hypothesis (EMH) and highlights the behavioral influences that lead to excessive market volatility. The findings suggest that investor psychology plays a critical role in market inefficiencies, with emotions such as fear and greed leading to irrational decision-making. The study emphasizes the need for regulatory measures and investor education to mitigate the impact of

DOI: 10.4018/979-8-3693-8583-8.ch007

these biases, ensuring more stable financial markets.

INTRODUCTION

The study of investor biases and reaction dynamics delves into the psychological mechanisms that influence market fluctuations. Over the years, market behaviors have shown patterns that deviate from traditional financial theories, such as the Efficient Market Hypothesis (EMH), which assumes that markets operate in a perfectly rational manner. Behavioral finance emerged as a field to challenge this assumption by exploring how human cognitive biases and emotions impact decision-making processes, especially in the context of financial markets. Understanding these psychological influences is crucial to explaining phenomena such as market overreaction, where stock prices exhibit excessive volatility in response to new information (Loang, 2023).

Investor sentiment plays a pivotal role in market fluctuations. It refers to the overall attitude or mood of investors regarding future market prospects. Investor sentiment can be influenced by a myriad of factors, including media coverage, economic news, and broader social and political events. Positive sentiment may lead to over-optimistic behavior, causing investors to drive up stock prices beyond their intrinsic value, while negative sentiment can trigger panic selling, leading to steep market declines (Cordes et al., 2023). In this context, investor sentiment can act as a catalyst for market overreaction, amplifying the psychological dynamics of fear and greed in financial markets.

Another psychological bias, confirmation bias, significantly affects how investors interpret market information. This bias refers to the tendency of individuals to seek out and give more weight to information that confirms their pre-existing beliefs, while disregarding or downplaying evidence that contradicts them. In the investment world, confirmation bias can lead to irrational behavior as investors hold onto losing stocks, anticipating a reversal of fortunes based solely on their initial optimistic assessment. This selective interpretation of information can lead to market overreaction, as investors fail to adjust their decisions appropriately in response to new or disconfirming evidence, exacerbating market volatility.

Risk perception is another key factor influencing investor behavior and, consequently, market dynamics. Risk perception is subjective and can vary widely among investors based on their personal experiences, emotions, and information available. When investors perceive a high level of risk, they may react by selling off stocks aggressively, contributing to market overreaction, especially during periods of uncertainty or economic turbulence. Conversely, underestimating risk can result in irrational exuberance, where markets are driven to unsustainable highs before a sharp correction occurs. The subjective nature of risk perception often causes misalignment between the actual risk and how it is perceived, further fueling market instability (Andraszewicz, 2020).

The anchoring effect also plays a critical role in shaping investor decisions. This cognitive bias refers to the human tendency to rely heavily on the first piece of information encountered (the "anchor") when making decisions. In financial markets, this can occur when investors fixate on historical price levels, such as a stock's previous high or low, rather than focusing on its current fundamentals. Anchoring can lead to distorted expectations and cause investors to either overvalue or undervalue assets, thereby contributing to market overreaction (De Bondt, 2020). For instance, when a stock's price declines below its historical average, investors may sell off their holdings prematurely, even if the stock's long-term prospects remain solid, thus amplifying market volatility.

Despite the substantial research in behavioural finance, significant gaps persist in our comprehension of how psychological biases influence market dynamics, especially concerning market overreaction. Initially, although considerable investigation has been conducted on individual biases such as investor sentiment, confirmation bias, risk perception, and the anchoring effect, the prevailing literature often examines these biases in isolation. A significant deficiency is the absence of comprehensive models that amalgamate various aspects to yield a more holistic comprehension of their collective impact on market behaviour. The interplay among these biases is probably more intricate than previously comprehended, as they can either reinforce or alleviate each other under varying market conditions. Consequently, examining these biases as interrelated variables, instead of in isolation, may provide more detailed insights into their collective influence on market movements.

A significant vacuum exists in the insufficient research regarding the temporal evolution of these psychological biases. Current research frequently documents investor behaviour at particular instances, usually during periods of significant market volatility, such as financial crises or phases of rapid expansion. Nonetheless, there is a scarcity of longitudinal studies investigating how biases, such as confirmation bias or risk perception, fluctuate across many market cycles (FaXing & Loang, 2024). An enhanced comprehension of the temporal aspects of these biases may yield insights into whether and how investors assimilate lessons from their errors or if they persist in demonstrating predictable behavioural patterns over prolonged durations. Furthermore, it may elucidate whether psychological biases amplify or attenuate as markets evolve or as investors acquire experience.

Moreover, a significant portion of the study concerning investor biases and market overreactions concentrates on developed markets, especially within the framework of Western financial institutions. A notable deficiency exists in the research concerning the manifestation of these psychological mechanisms in emerging economies, where varying cultural, economic, and regulatory contexts may affect investor behaviour. For example, the influence of investor sentiment may be more significant in markets characterised by limited information transparency or when media and social networks exert a greater effect on public opinion formation. The degree to which biases such as confirmation bias or the anchoring effect impact market reactions may differ between regions with varying levels of financial literacy and market sophistication. It is crucial to address these geographical and cultural disparities to cultivate a more universally applicable comprehension of investor behaviour and market dynamics (Cordes et al., 2023).

Furthermore, there is a deficiency in comprehending how technical innovations, especially in algorithmic trading and artificial intelligence (AI), interact with human biases to affect market overreaction (Goodell et al., 2023). Although human emotions and cognitive biases have historically influenced market volatility, contemporary markets are progressively determined by algorithmic trading that functions according to established rules and patterns. Nonetheless, these algorithms can unintentionally reinforce biases, particularly when trained on historical data that embodies human prejudices. Research on the extent to which automated trading systems exacerbate or mitigate psychological biases in market reactions, as well as the influence of human and algorithmic interactions on market dynamics, is limited. This field of research may provide significant insights into the ways technology is transforming conventional market behaviours and the potential emergence of novel forms of overreaction in highly automated marketplaces.

Ultimately, a significant deficiency in the current literature is the insufficient focus on policy and regulatory measures that could alleviate the adverse effects of psychological biases on market stability. Although many studies have explored investor education to mitigate biases, there is a paucity of research on structural remedies that may alleviate market overreaction. Circuit breakers, which briefly suspend trading during substantial market falls, aim to mitigate panic selling; nevertheless, there is scant empirical data about their efficacy in addressing the fundamental psychological mechanisms that drive overreaction. Investigating the effectiveness of these measures and other regulatory strategies may yield significant recommendations for mitigating volatility and fostering more stable financial markets.

LITERATURE REVIEW

Underlying Theory: Prospect Theory

Prospect theory, proposed by Daniel Kahneman and Amos Tversky in 1979, signifies a significant deviation from the conventional economic assumption that individuals act rationally to optimise utility. Prospect theory posits that individuals base their actions on perceived benefits and losses in relation to a reference point, rather than the ultimate outcome, and that they assign greater significance to losses than to similar gains. This behaviour, termed *loss aversion*, contradicts conventional economic theory, which posits that individuals ought to react to anticipated benefits and losses in a symmetrical manner. Prospect theory offers a more psychologically accurate framework for comprehending decision-making, especially in uncertain contexts such as financial markets (Jing & Loang, 2024).

A fundamental aspect of prospect theory is *reference dependence*, which posits that individuals assess outcomes as gains or losses in relation to a specific reference point, rather than in absolute values. This reference point is generally influenced by previous experiences, anticipations, or societal standards. In financial markets, an investor may consider the acquisition price of a stock as a benchmark. An increase in stock price is regarded as a gain by the investor, whereas a decrease below the acquisition price is considered a loss (Lanju & Loang, 2024). Prospect theory asserts that the psychological effect of losses surpasses that of similar gains. This asymmetry elucidates why investors frequently demonstrate irrational behaviour, such as retaining failing equities in the anticipation of recovering losses, despite the more reasonable course being to mitigate their losses and reallocate their resources.

A key principle in prospect theory is *diminishing sensitivity*, indicating that the perceived worth of gains and losses diminishes as they deviate more from the reference point. The emotional impact of a $100 loss is perceived more intensely than that of a $1,000 loss when an individual has already experienced substantial losses. Diminishing sensitivity in financial decision-making elucidates why minor fluctuations in stock prices may provoke exaggerated responses amid uncertainty (Loang, 2024b). Investors may excessively respond to trivial losses or gains, resulting in heightened market volatility. This inclination is most evident during times of market volatility, when investors' reference points are in constant flux, intensifying their emotional reactions to market changes (Loang, 2024a).

Prospect theory also presents the notion of *probability weighting*, elucidating how humans assess the probability of outcomes in a skewed fashion. In contrast to conventional models that presume individuals evaluate probabilities objectively, prospect theory posits that individuals often overrate the chance of extreme or low-probability events while underrating the probability of intermediate or high-probability events. This elucidates why investors in financial markets may respond irrationally to unlikely yet prominent occurrences, such as market crashes, notwithstanding the low probability of their occurrence. The probability weighting effect can intensify market overreactions, as investors react disproportionately to the perceived risk of significant market fluctuations, frequently resulting in extensive sell-offs or panic purchasing (Malmendier et al., 2020).

One of the most notable consequences of prospect theory for financial markets is the elucidation of the *disposition effect*, which delineates the propensity of investors to prematurely liquidate profitable investments while retaining unprofitable ones for an excessive duration. This conduct is influenced by loss aversion and the contextual framing of choices in relation to a reference point (Mittal, 2022). Investors are more inclined to secure profits when they view them as a success compared to their initial reference point, even if the asset retains potential for more appreciation. Conversely, they are hesitant to acknowledge losses, as this would render the loss psychologically tangible, leading them to retain underperforming investments in anticipation of a price recovery. The disposition effect engenders market inefficiency by distorting price fluctuations, resulting in excessive selling in bullish markets and protracted retention of failing assets in bearish markets.

Moreover, prospect theory contests the conventional concept of *risk aversion* by demonstrating that individuals do not uniformly exhibit risk aversion; instead, they display risk-seeking behaviour in the context of losses. In the face of prospective losses, individuals are more inclined to undertake risks to evade a definite loss, despite the possibility of incurring higher losses (Padmavathy, 2024). This risk-seeking behaviour is frequently observable in financial markets during downturns, where investors may partake in speculative trading or assume high-risk positions in an attempt to recuperate losses. This alteration in risk appetite can intensify market volatility, as investors typically averse to risky assets may partake in actions that further destabilise the market during periods of stress.

Prospect theory's application to financial markets elucidates the shortcomings of classic models, including the Efficient Market Hypothesis, in adequately addressing the psychological and emotional aspects that shape investor behaviour. Traditional models argue that investors base decisions on objective evaluations of risk and return, whereas prospect theory recognises the influence of cognitive biases, emotions, and subjective perceptions on financial decision-making. Consequently, prospect theory provides a more thorough framework for comprehending market oddities, including bubbles, crashes, and extended volatility, which rational decision-making alone cannot adequately elucidate.

Investor sentiment, a crucial factor in behavioural finance, has received much focus for its influence on market dynamics. Sentiment denotes the aggregate mood or disposition of investors regarding market conditions, frequently acting as a surrogate for emotions like optimism or pessimism. Research on investor mood originates from early investigations into market psychology, emphasising the influence of emotions on irrational market behaviour. Studies by Shiller (2000) and Baker and Wurgler (2007) demonstrate that elevated investor sentiment can artificially inflate asset values above their inherent value, fostering bubbles, whereas negative sentiment can result in excessive selling, intensifying market crashes. Recent studies investigate the mechanisms by which sentiment influences asset price, frequently examining noisy trading and herding behaviour, wherein investors collectively adhere to market patterns instead of engaging in independent rational analysis. This literature indicates that investor attitude is a crucial factor in market overreaction, as changes in collective mood can exacerbate price fluctuations, especially in times of uncertainty.

The literature on confirmation bias, a variable affecting investor behaviour, highlights the impact of cognitive biases on information processing in financial markets. Confirmation bias, the inclination to pursue information that validates existing views while ignoring opposing data, is extensively recorded in psychological and decision-making studies. In financial markets, confirmation bias can result in skewed investment decisions when investors selectively perceive data to validate their beliefs, frequently leading to the continuation of mispriced assets. Research conducted by Barberis, Shleifer, and Vishny (1998) has illustrated how confirmation bias fosters momentum in stock prices, as investors persist in purchasing assets that have previously increased in value, anticipating further gains. The literature emphasises that confirmation bias can intensify market overreaction by hindering investors from recalibrating their expectations based on fresh information, resulting in extended phases of overvaluation or undervaluation (Suresh & Loang, 2024).

Risk perception, a significant variable, has been extensively studied in economics and psychology, with considerable literature on how humans interpret and react to uncertainty. In contrast to conventional economic models that presume investors evaluate risk objectively based on available data, behavioural finance research acknowledges that risk assessment is subjective and shaped by psychological influences. Studies by Slovic (1987) and Kahneman and Tversky (1979) have shown that individuals frequently misestimate the probability of severe events, resulting in exaggerated responses during periods of market distress. Risk perception is additionally influenced by emotions such as fear and greed, which may lead investors to respond irrationally to market fluctuations. Research conducted by Shefrin and Statman (2000) indicates that in times of significant uncertainty, investors' perception of risk often diverges from actual risk, leading to either excessive caution or inappropriate risk-taking. Research on risk perception indicates that investors' subjective assessments of risk, especially during market declines, might result in overreaction, as fear incites panic selling and a migration to safer assets.

The anchoring effect, a cognitive bias extensively examined in psychology and finance, denotes the inclination to disproportionately depend on the initial piece of information encountered during decision-making. In financial markets, anchoring frequently occurs when investors concentrate on particular price levels, such as a stock's prior high or low, utilising these benchmarks for subsequent decisions, irrespective of alterations in the asset's fundamentals. Tversky and Kahneman (1974) initially presented the concept of anchoring in decision-making, prompting subsequent research into its implications across several contexts. Research in finance, including work by Campbell and Sharpe (2009), indicates that anchoring results in systematic inaccuracies in forecasting and valuation, as investors' assessments are influenced by prior price levels. Research indicates that anchoring may lead to market overreaction when investors adhere to obsolete price levels and neglect to recalibrate their expectations based on new information, causing mispricing and heightened volatility.

The dependent variable in this context, market overreaction, has been extensively studied to elucidate its sources and effects. The notion of market overreaction contests the Efficient Market Hypothesis (EMH), which asserts that asset prices consistently embody all accessible information. Behavioural finance literature, initiated by De Bondt and Thaler (1985), posits that markets frequently overreact to news, resulting in heightened volatility and discrepancies from intrinsic values. Such overreactions can manifest in both directions—prices may soar excessively in response to favourable news, or they may decline sharply following adverse events. A significant corpus of scholarship has investigated the circumstances that predispose market overreaction, highlighting elements such as investor sentiment, cognitive biases, and the influence of media in constructing market narratives. The literature on market overreaction highlights that psychological considerations, rather than rational assessments, are primary catalysts for extreme price fluctuations, which can destabilise markets and result in extended periods of volatility.

The literature assessment of each variable indicates a substantial and expanding corpus of research in behavioural finance that aims to elucidate how psychological biases and subjective perceptions influence market dynamics. Investor emotions, confirmation bias, risk perception, and the anchoring effect each significantly influence market behaviour, leading to occurrences like market overreaction. Collectively, these variables underscore the intricate relationship between cognition and emotion in financial decision-making, contesting conventional models that presume investor rationality. The literature emphasises the need of acknowledging these psychological aspects in comprehending market volatility and in formulating ways to alleviate the adverse impacts of cognitive biases on market stability.

Research Methodology

The research methodologies utilised in a study investigating investor biases and market overreaction generally incorporate both qualitative and quantitative approaches to elucidate the intricacies of psychological factors affecting market behaviour. The amalgamation of these two approaches facilitates a thorough study, combining the profundity of qualitative insights with the robustness and generalisability of quantitative data. Utilising both qualitative and quantitative methodologies, researchers can gain a deeper insight into the cognitive and emotional determinants influencing investor behaviour, while also evaluating the wider market ramifications of these actions.

The qualitative aspect of the research examines the subjective experiences, attitudes, and views of investors. Qualitative methods, including in-depth interviews, focus groups, and case studies, enable researchers to thoroughly investigate the psychological dynamics that inform investor decision-making. Through interviews with individual investors, researchers can collect comprehensive, descriptive data regarding the impact of factors such as investor sentiment, confirmation bias, and risk perception on asset purchase or sale decisions. This method is especially beneficial for comprehending the cognitive processes and emotions associated with market movements, as it offers insights that quantitative metrics alone cannot readily capture.

Qualitative approaches provide the adaptability to investigate emergent themes or unforeseen trends in investor behaviour. By employing open-ended questioning and a narrative methodology, researchers can elucidate the subtleties of investors' interpretations of market events, their information processing, and their emotional responses to market volatility. This method is especially beneficial in examining intricate biases like confirmation bias, when investors may lack awareness of how their opinions influence their interpretation of market data. Qualitative research elucidates subjective experiences, revealing the cognitive and emotional factors that contribute to market overreaction, so providing a comprehensive insight into investor behaviour.

The quantitative aspect of the research entails the methodical gathering and examination of numerical data to evaluate particular hypotheses regarding the correlation between psychological biases and market overreaction. Quantitative tools, including surveys, experiments, and econometric analysis, facilitate the assessment of essential factors such as investor sentiment, risk perception, and market price fluctuations, as well as the detection of statistical correlations among these variables. This method is especially beneficial for determining the generalisability of results across various market situations and investor demographics.

Surveys can assess investor mood or risk perception at a specific period, frequently employing standardised scales for comparison among various investor groups. Researchers may also gather data on investor behaviour, including trading volume and stock returns, to evaluate the impact of psychological variables on market fluctuations. Researchers can utilise econometric analysis to examine correlations or causal links between investor emotions and market overreaction, while controlling for additional variables such as macroeconomic conditions or market liquidity. This quantitative method offers a more objective and replicable assessment of the influence of psychological biases on market behaviour, facilitating the evaluation of theoretical models based on behavioural finance.

Alongside surveys and econometric analysis, experimental approaches serve as a significant quantitative instrument for examining investor behaviour. Behavioural experiments, typically performed in controlled environments, enable researchers to modify critical variables, such as information asymmetry or market shocks, and examine investor responses. Researchers may establish a simulated market environment in which participants encounter varying levels of news or information to investigate the impact of confirmation bias on their trading decisions. By accounting for external variables, experiments provide a rigorous method to evaluate the causal influence of particular cognitive biases on market behaviour, therefore yielding robust empirical evidence to substantiate theoretical assertions.

The integration of qualitative and quantitative methodologies provides several benefits for this research type. The qualitative technique offers the necessary depth to investigate the psychological and emotional dimensions of investor behaviour, whereas the quantitative approach guarantees that the results can be generalised and subjected to stringent statistical analysis. Collectively, these approaches provide a more thorough understanding of the psychological mechanisms underlying market overreaction. Furthermore, mixed-methods research facilitates data triangulation, so augmenting the validity and dependability of the results. Qualitative interviews may indicate that investors are motivated by fear during market declines, whereas quantitative analysis can quantify the degree to which this fear results in sell-offs or heightened volatility.

This mixed-methods approach is crucial in the examination of market reactions, since it facilitates the investigation of both individual decision-making and overarching market effects. Qualitative methods elucidate the cognitive and emotional processes influencing investor behaviour, whereas quantitative methods facilitate the evaluation of how these behaviours collectively generate market-wide phenomena like bubbles or crashes. By synthesising both methodologies, researchers can acquire a more refined comprehension of the manifestation of psychological biases in individual behaviours and collective market phenomena.

Figure 1. Conceptual framework

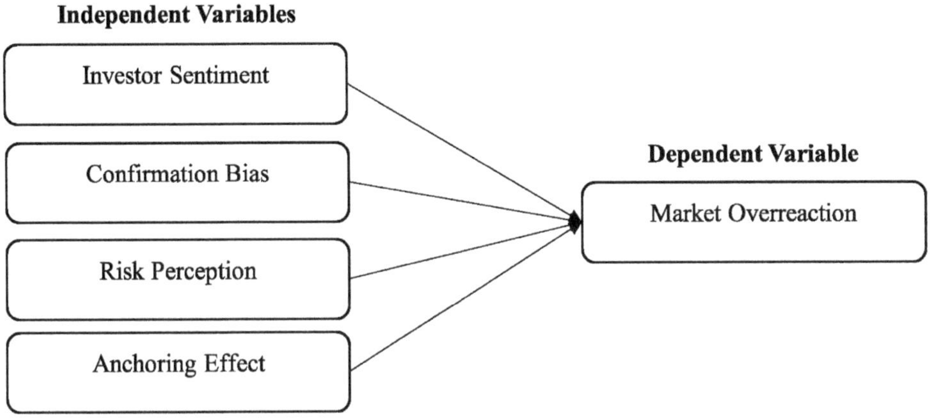

This study's conceptual framework provides a structured platform for investigating the psychological factors underlying market overreaction, with particular emphasis on the impact of significant investor biases. It utilises theories from behavioural finance and psychology to elucidate how individual cognitive biases, including investor sentiment, confirmation bias, risk perception, and the anchoring effect, combine to affect investment decisions, thus resulting in market overreaction. This paradigm asserts that these psychological elements are interconnected and collectively influence deviations from rational decision-making, resulting in heightened volatility in financial markets (Taffler et al., 2024).

The conceptual framework is predicated on the premise that markets are not entirely efficient, contrary to classical economic models such as the Efficient Market Hypothesis (EMH), but are shaped by the behaviours and biases of investors. Behavioural finance contests the notion that all market participants behave rationally and possess complete information, proposing that cognitive biases significantly influence financial results. This study examines market overreaction, defined by significant price fluctuations in reaction to news or events, as the dependent variable, which is affected by many independent psychological factors. These biases not only skew individual investment choices but, when combined among market participants, lead to substantial market-wide anomalies (VanderPal & Brazie, 2022).

Investor sentiment is a crucial element of the conceptual framework, reflecting the collective mood or emotional disposition of market participants. Sentiment, shaped by external factors like economic indicators, media stories, or geopolitical events, influences investors' perceptions of the market's future trajectory. The theory posits that elevated investor sentiment, fueled by optimism or excitement, may result in asset overvaluation, whereas negative sentiment, stemming from fear or pessimism, can lead to undervaluation. Investor mood acts as a potent emotional influence that can obscure rational judgement, resulting in impulsive decisions that exacerbate market overreactions (Westermann & Schunk, 2022). The conceptual framework identifies sentiment as a variable that varies over time, leading investors to overreact to new information and thereby exacerbating market volatility.

Confirmation bias constitutes a significant component of the framework. This cognitive bias refers to the inclination of investors to prioritise information that aligns with their pre-existing opinions while disregarding information that opposes them. In the conceptual framework, confirmation bias is posited to intensify irrational market behaviour by strengthening preexisting assumptions regarding asset prices or market patterns, irrespective of new or conflicting evidence. Investors may retain losing equities due to a selective interpretation of market data that reinforces their initial conviction regarding the stock's future success. Consequently, confirmation bias leads to enduring mispricing and market overreaction, since investors do not adjust their strategy to evolving market conditions. The paradigm perceives confirmation bias as a mechanism that extends market inefficiencies, leading to amplified price fluctuations in both directions (Malmendier et al., 2020).

Risk perception, a crucial component of the framework, pertains to the subjective evaluation by investors of the dangers linked to specific market conditions or investment prospects. This study's theory contends that, in contrast to classic economic models that presume investors assess risk objectively through statistical probabilities, risk perception is shaped by cognitive and emotional influences. In periods of increased market uncertainty, such as financial crises or economic instability, investors may overestimate risk, resulting in panic selling and subsequent market overreaction. Conversely, in times of market exuberance, investors may undervalue risks, resulting in excessive exposure to volatile assets. The conceptual framework integrates risk perception as a dynamic element that interacts with investor mood and confirmation bias, affecting investors' responses to positive and bad news. The discrepancy between perceived and actual risk is a significant catalyst of market instability, resulting in excessive responses that exacerbate market overreactions (De Bondt, 2020).

Anchoring becomes the concluding psychological variable incorporated into the system. Anchoring denotes the cognitive inclination to excessively depend on an initial datum—such as a previous pricing point—when formulating later decisions. In financial markets, investors frequently base their judgements on historical price levels or performance benchmarks, which may no longer be pertinent considering current market conditions. An investor may decline to sell a stock that has depreciated below a specific historical price, as they base their valuation on its prior peak rather than its actual value. The conceptual framework asserts that anchoring may result in considerable market overreaction, since investors' dependence on obsolete or irrelevant information skews their reactions to changing market conditions. This distortion causes prices to exceed their rational levels, leading to volatility and mispricing.

The four psychological biases—investor sentiment, confirmation bias, risk perception, and anchoring—are regarded as interconnected factors contributing to market overreaction (Jing & Loang, 2024). The framework suggests that these biases mutually intensify: for example, increased investor sentiment may worsen confirmation bias, prompting investors to adhere to excessively optimistic market forecasts, while skewed risk perception may further strengthen anchoring, resulting in decisions based on obsolete reference points. The interplay of biases can generate feedback loops, wherein initial price fluctuations provoke more psychological responses, resulting in increased divergences from market fundamentals.

The conceptual framework also recognises the broader market context, acknowledging that these psychological mechanisms do not operate in isolation. External factors, including macroeconomic conditions, market liquidity, and regulatory regimes, interact with investor biases to influence market outcomes. Psychological biases serve as major drivers within the framework, whereas external circumstances influence their impact, either enhancing or diminishing the degree of market overreaction. Regulatory interventions, such as trade halts or circuit breakers, may temporarily mitigate the impact of panic selling during a market decline, serving as a counterbalance to investor sentiment and risk perception. The conceptual framework offers a comprehensive approach to comprehending market reactions by incorporating psychological and structural elements.

The study's conceptual framework functions as a thorough model for examining the psychological foundations of market overreaction. It emphasises the interaction of cognitive biases, including investor mood, confirmation bias, risk perception, and anchoring, illustrating how these elements cumulatively lead to irrational market behaviour. The paradigm integrates psychological and contextual factors, offering a comprehensive platform for examining how individual investor choices culminate in significant market changes. This comprehensive methodology provides significant insights for both academic research and regulators, as well as financial practitioners aiming to alleviate the adverse impacts of market overreaction (Lanju & Loang, 2024).

CONCLUSION

This paper concludes by synthesising studies on the psychological causes of market overreaction, emphasising the significant influence of cognitive biases on investor behaviour and financial market dynamics. The research elucidates how investor sentiment, confirmation bias, risk perception, and anchoring impede rational decision-making, resulting in heightened volatility and mispricing in financial markets. The study highlights the shortcomings of conventional financial models that presume investor rationality, promoting a more sophisticated comprehension of market behaviour that integrates principles from behavioural finance.

The study primarily contributes by illustrating how investor sentiment functions as a significant catalyst for market overreaction. The data indicates that variations in sentiment, whether stemming from optimism or pessimism, substantially affect asset prices and may result in market bubbles or crashes. When investor sentiment is favourable, markets often display excessive optimism, leading to inflated asset prices that deviate from their intrinsic values. Conversely, adverse mood can trigger panic selling and significant price falls. The study's result underscores the necessity for market participants, regulators, and policymakers to acknowledge the significant influence of investor mood and to formulate policies that can alleviate its destabilising repercussions on financial markets.

The study suggests that, alongside investor mood, confirmation bias is a substantial psychological element that exacerbates market overreaction. Investors, frequently motivated by the need to validate preconceived notions, engage in selective information processing that reinforces their perspectives while disregarding contradictory evidence. This bias generates a feedback loop that sustains market patterns, even without underlying fundamentals. The persistence of confirmation bias perpetuates market mispricing, as investors neglect to modify their decisions in light of fresh, pertinent information. The study indicates that mitigating confirmation bias can be achieved by investor education and enhancing access to varied, impartial information sources, hence boosting market stability.

The research emphasises the significance of risk perception in comprehending market reactivity, especially during periods of uncertainty or crisis. It concludes that investors' subjective evaluations of risk frequently diverge from objective metrics, resulting in illogical decision-making. In market downturns, risk perception often becomes inflated, leading investors to liquidate assets at significant discounts, hence intensifying market falls. In contrast, during optimistic markets, investors may undervalue risks, resulting in excessive risk-taking and the creation of asset bubbles. The finding underscores that cultivating a more precise comprehension of risk, via regulatory measures and financial literacy programs, is vital for mitigating market overreaction and enhancing long-term market stability.

The study reveals that anchoring, the last cognitive bias examined, significantly influences investor behaviour, especially about historical market performance. The study suggests that investors' inclination to tie their decisions to previous price levels or benchmarks, rather than contemporary market conditions, skews their judgement. The anchoring effect may lead to either the overvaluation or undervaluation of assets, contingent upon the extent to which investors adhere to obsolete reference points.

The study's findings emphasise the necessity of promoting flexible decision-making among investors, advocating for evaluations grounded in real-time data instead of historical performance. By mitigating the anchoring bias, market participants might potentially diminish the overreaction stemming from dependence on irrelevant or obsolete information.

The overarching result of the study is that psychological biases are essential for comprehending the dynamics of financial markets and must be integrated into models of market behaviour. Conventional financial theories, including the Efficient Market Hypothesis, neglect the intricacies of human psychology, which frequently result in illogical behaviour and, hence, market inefficiencies. The research promotes the incorporation of behavioural finance concepts into scholarly inquiry and practical finance applications. Recognising the impact of cognitive biases enables financial institutions, governments, and investors to more effectively predict and address market anomalies, therefore improving market stability and mitigating the risks linked to market overreactions.

The study finds that a multifaceted approach is essential to successfully mitigate the adverse effects of psychological biases on financial markets. Individual biases, including sentiment, confirmation bias, risk perception, and anchoring, exert unique influences on investor behaviour, while also interacting with one another in intricate manners. This connection can generate feedback loops that exacerbate market overreactions. For example, increased investor sentiment may intensify confirmation bias, whereas skewed risk perception can strengthen the anchoring effect. The paper advocates for a comprehensive approach that acknowledges the interrelated nature of these biases and their cumulative impact on market dynamics. Isolated efforts to address these biases may be inadequate; rather, comprehensive techniques targeting various cognitive distortions are necessary.

The study suggests that regulators and financial authorities are essential in alleviating the consequences of market overreaction. Regulators can mitigate excessive volatility and market distortions by instituting measures such as circuit breakers, disclosure mandates, and improved transparency in financial reporting. The research additionally endorses the advancement of investor education initiatives aimed at enhancing financial literacy and increasing awareness of cognitive biases. Equipping investors with tools to identify and mitigate their biases may enhance rationality in decision-making, hence fostering a more stable and efficient market environment.

The study's conclusion confirms the significant influence of psychological biases on market overreaction and contests the premise of investor rationality in conventional financial models. It underscores the necessity for a more thorough comprehension of market dynamics that incorporates behavioural finance insights and tackles the cognitive biases that result in market inefficiencies. The study's conclusions hold considerable implications for investors, policymakers, and financial practitioners, offering a framework to mitigate risks linked to market volatility and foster a more stable financial system.

Theoretical, Managerial and Policy Implications

The research on investor biases and market overreaction possesses substantial theoretical, managerial, and policy implications, highlighting the larger significance of its findings in influencing both academic comprehension and practical applications in finance. The ramifications transcend behavioural finance, influencing investment strategies, financial management, and regulatory frameworks, underscoring the necessity of incorporating psychological insights into diverse aspects of financial decision-making and governance.

This work theoretically contests the dominant assumptions of classic finance theories, especially the Efficient Market Hypothesis (EMH), which asserts that markets are fundamentally rational and that asset prices include all accessible information. This study's findings, based on behavioural finance, offer empirical evidence that psychological distortions, including investor sentiment, confirmation bias, risk perception, and anchoring, substantially affect market behaviour. These biases are not outliers; they are systemic and ubiquitous, affecting investor decision-making and resulting in enduring market inefficiencies. The theoretical conclusion indicates a transition from perceiving markets as solely rational and efficient systems to acknowledging the intricate, behavior-driven dynamics that frequently underlie market swings. This transition necessitates the enhancement of current financial models to integrate behavioural components, thereby connecting psychology and economics. This also creates opportunities for research into the interaction between cognitive biases and other market dynamics, including macroeconomic data and technological advancements, in influencing asset pricing and market trends.

The conclusions of this study have significant significance for investment management and corporate financial decision-making. Investment managers can enhance their portfolio management by comprehending the influence of psychological biases on market overreactions. By acknowledging the influence of investor emotion or confirmation bias on stock prices deviating from their intrinsic worth, managers might use contrarian strategies to capitalise on these mispricings. During times of extreme optimism, when asset values are inflated by good emotion, investment managers may adopt a more prudent strategy, steering clear of overexposure to overvalued assets. Conversely, during phases of negative mood and panic selling, managers could exploit cheap assets that may be temporarily mispriced due to irrational fear. Furthermore, by recognising the potential impact of their cognitive biases on decision-making, managers can establish mechanisms to mitigate these biases, such as instituting predetermined decision protocols or utilising diverse teams for investment decisions.

The managerial implications at the company level pertain to strategic financial planning and risk management. Corporate managers must consider the psychological aspects that can influence market responses to their company's performance and strategic choices. During earnings announcements or major corporate moves (e.g., mergers, acquisitions, or product launches), management must anticipate how investor biases may result in overreactions in the company's stock price. An enhanced comprehension of investor behaviour can assist management in manoeuvring through volatile situations by employing techniques like transparent communication and investor education to alleviate irrational responses. Moreover, organisations can implement more comprehensive risk management frameworks that account for both financial risks and the behavioural risks linked to market mood and investor psychology, thus mitigating exposure to unnecessary volatility.

The study's policy implications underscore the necessity for regulatory organisations and financial authorities to integrate behavioural insights into their governance frameworks. A crucial policy conclusion is the acknowledgement that conventional regulatory approaches, often formulated for rational market actors, may be inadequate to tackle the difficulties arising from cognitive biases. During market volatility, regulatory authorities may impose circuit breakers or trade halts to mitigate panic selling; however, these interventions just address the symptoms of market overreaction rather than its fundamental psychological roots. The research indicates that regulatory frameworks must be reevaluated to consider the influence of biases such as risk perception and investor mood on market instability. This may necessitate more proactive measures, such as mandating enhanced transparency in financial reports to avert the spread of excessively optimistic or gloomy projections that could disproportionately affect market sentiment.

Furthermore, policy concerns encompass investor protection and education. Regulators ought to prioritise the formulation of regulations that alleviate the effects of cognitive biases on retail investors, who are frequently more susceptible to sentiment-driven market fluctuations. This may involve requiring corporations and financial institutions to provide clearer and more consistent information disclosures, thus diminishing the probability of confirmation bias distorting investor perceptions. Moreover, regulators may establish regulations that incentivise or mandate financial institutions to advance investor education initiatives. These programs would seek to enhance individual investors' awareness of prevalent cognitive biases and instruct them on strategies to mitigate their effects, including the adoption of long-term investment perspectives and portfolio diversification to diminish the impact of emotional responses to short-term market volatility.

Moreover, the study's results possess wider ramifications for financial stability and systemic risk management. The psychological biases examined in the study—specifically risk perception and investor sentiment—can exacerbate systemic risks, as irrational actions by a substantial number of investors may result in market bubbles and collapses. Regulatory entities, including central banks and financial market authorities, may need to augment their monitoring systems to identify early indicators of sentiment-driven market imbalances. This may entail the creation of novel indicators that monitor investor emotion, confirmation bias, and other psychological aspects in real-time, enabling regulators to react prior to market situations escalating into severe crises. Integrating behavioural finance insights into macroprudential regulation could enable policymakers to develop more effective instruments for alleviating systemic risks and preserving market stability.

This study's theoretical, managerial, and policy ramifications are extensive, highlighting the necessity for a multidisciplinary approach to comprehend and mitigate market overreaction. The study proposes a reevaluation of conventional financial models, endorsing the incorporation of behavioural finance to address the psychological elements that contribute to market inefficiencies. It provides actionable solutions for investment managers and corporate executives to alleviate the impact of cognitive biases on decision-making and financial outcomes. The study emphasises the necessity of integrating behavioural insights into regulatory frameworks to enhance market stability and safeguard investors. Collectively, these conclusions underscore the need of acknowledging the psychological aspects of market behaviour and incorporating this insight into both scholarly research and practical financial administration.

Limitations and Recommendations for Future Studies

The constraints of this study on investor biases and market overreaction are crucial to recognise, since they delineate the parameters of the findings and offer guidance for subsequent research. The study provides significant insights into the impact of cognitive biases on financial markets; yet many limitations affect the generalisability, comprehensiveness, and applicability of its findings. The limitations stem from the intricacies of behavioural finance, the difficulties in identifying psychological aspects within actual market conditions, and the methodological decisions that may constrain the scope of the study's conclusions. A comprehensive comprehension of these limits delineates the parameters of the research and facilitates subsequent investigations to enhance and expand the current corpus of knowledge.

A significant restriction is the challenge of comprehensively capturing the dynamic and diverse aspects of investor behaviour. Psychological biases, including investor sentiment, confirmation bias, risk perception, and anchoring, are intricately woven into human decision-making processes, rendering them challenging to identify and quantify accurately. The study establishes a paradigm for comprehending the impact of these biases on market overreaction; yet the interaction between these cognitive elements and external market variables is exceedingly intricate. Behavioural responses in financial markets are shaped by various contextual circumstances, such as economic data, geopolitical events, and technological breakthroughs. The study's emphasis on psychological biases, however crucial, may inadequately address the overarching macroeconomic causes and market dynamics that also influence market behaviour. Future study should use a holistic strategy that synthesises psychological aspects with external economic variables, so providing a more comprehensive picture of market behaviour.

A further drawback stems from the dependence on self-reported data and behavioural tests, prevalent in investor psychology research. Surveys, interviews, and experiments yield valuable insights into individual decision-making processes; however, these methods are susceptible to biases, including social desirability bias, wherein respondents may provide answers they perceive as socially acceptable or expected, rather than those that accurately represent their genuine thoughts and behaviours. Furthermore, the contrived conditions of experiments may fail to authentically represent the high-pressure, emotionally intense atmosphere of actual financial markets. Consequently, the results may not entirely represent investor behaviour in actual market conditions, where they encounter swift information dissemination, market fluctuations, and the stress of potential financial loss or gain. Subsequent research could mitigate this restriction by employing more naturalistic observation techniques or using real-time market data to examine investor behaviour in authentic market settings.

Another restriction is the possibility that cultural and regional variations in investor behaviour may affect the generalisability of the study's results. A substantial portion of the current study on investor psychology has been undertaken in Western financial markets, especially in the United States and Europe, where market structures, regulatory frameworks, and investor demographics may markedly differ from those in emerging nations. Cognitive biases, including confirmation bias and risk perception, may exhibit distinct manifestations in markets characterised by differing degrees of transparency, financial literacy, and information accessibility. The study's conclusions may not be entirely relevant to non-Western or underdeveloped economies, as distinct cultural norms and institutional considerations affect investor behaviour. Future research may broaden the investigative reach by undertaking cross-cultural studies that analyse the interplay between psychological biases and regional as well as cultural elements, thereby providing a more globally representative comprehension of market overreaction.

The study's dependence on specific behavioural finance theories, including prospect theory and loss aversion, although establishing a robust foundation, may restrict the examination of alternative frameworks that could yield diverse insights into investor behaviour. Prospect theory is extensively utilised in behavioural finance; however, alternative theories, such as bounded rationality and adaptive market hypotheses, may offer supplementary or opposing viewpoints regarding investor information processing and responses to market occurrences. These other frameworks may uncover additional aspects of cognitive biases that the current study did not completely address. Future research may broaden the theoretical frameworks employed to analyse market behaviour, therefore enhancing the analysis and possibly revealing novel cognitive mechanisms that lead to market overreaction.

The study's emphasis on individual investor behaviour may neglect the increasing impact of institutional investors and algorithmic trading in contemporary financial markets. Major institutional investors, such hedge funds, mutual funds, and pension funds, possess considerable market influence, and their actions may be motivated by distinct factors in contrast to ordinary retail investors. Furthermore, the emergence of algorithmic trading, wherein high-frequency trading algorithms operate based on pre-defined rules and patterns, introduces an additional layer of complexity to market dynamics. These algorithmic systems, although engineered to function devoid of human emotion, may still exhibit human biases if trained on past data shaped by investor sentiment and other psychological influences. Future study may investigate the interaction between institutional investors and algorithmic trading systems with human cognitive biases to affect market outcomes, providing a more comprehensive understanding of contemporary financial markets.

The study primarily examines psychological biases during market overreactions but does not thoroughly investigate their differential operation across various phases of the market cycle. Investors may display varying behaviours during extended market boom vs periods of collapse or recovery. Risk perception may intensify during a market downturn but could wane during a bull market, resulting in imprudent risk-taking. Future research may employ a longitudinal methodology to investigate the evolution of psychological biases over time and throughout various phases of the market cycle. This would offer a more nuanced comprehension of investor behaviour and the interplay of biases with fluctuating market conditions.

In conclusion, although this study significantly contributes to the field of behavioural finance by highlighting the psychological elements that drive market overreaction, various limitations mitigate its conclusions. This encompasses difficulties in accurately representing the intricacies of investor behaviour, limitations of self-reported data and experimental approaches, potential non-generalizability to non-Western markets, the predominance of particular behavioural theories, the omission of institutional and algorithmic trading effects, and the necessity for a more dynamic comprehension of market cycles. Future research should employ varied approaches, theoretical frameworks, and cultural settings to overcome these limitations, while acknowledging the dynamic nature of financial markets. Such investigations would enhance our comprehension of cognitive biases in market behaviour, hence aiding the development of more precise and complete models of financial decision-making.

REFERENCES

Andraszewicz, S. (2020). Stock Markets, Market Crashes, and Market Bubbles. *Psychological perspectives on financial decision making,* 205-231.

Cordes, H., Nolte, S., & Schneider, J. C. (2023). Dynamics of stock market developments, financial behavior, and emotions. *Journal of Banking & Finance*, 154, 106711. DOI: 10.1016/j.jbankfin.2022.106711

De Bondt, W. (2020). Investor and market overreaction: A retrospective. *Review of Behavioral Finance*, 12(1), 11–20. DOI: 10.1108/RBF-12-2019-0175

FaXing. L., & Loang, O. K. (2024). Green Investing and Financial Education: The Case of China's A-Share Market. In *Technology-Driven Business Innovation: Unleashing the Digital Advantage, Volume 1* (pp. 29-41). Cham: Springer Nature Switzerland.

Goodell, J. W., Kumar, S., Rao, P., & Verma, S. (2023). Emotions and stock market anomalies: A systematic review. *Journal of Behavioral and Experimental Finance*, 37, 100722. DOI: 10.1016/j.jbef.2022.100722

Jing, W., & Loang, O. K. (2024). Live Streaming of E-Commerce in China: Evidence from Impulsive Chinese Tea Purchases. In *Opportunities and Risks in AI for Business Development* (Vol. 1, pp. 1063–1079). Springer Nature Switzerland. DOI: 10.1007/978-3-031-65203-5_91

Lanju, T., & Loang, O. K. (2024). Unraveling the Fintech Puzzle: Technology Shaping Commercial Bank Lending Risk. In *Opportunities and Risks in AI for Business Development* (Vol. 1, pp. 915–923). Springer Nature Switzerland. DOI: 10.1007/978-3-031-65203-5_78

Loang, O. K. (2023). Corporate governance and Islamic behavioural finance: A review from Malaysia and GCC countries. *Indian Journal of Corporate Governance*, 16(1), 28–51. DOI: 10.1177/09746862231178959

Loang, O. K. (2024). Stability Of Shariah-Compliant Stocks In Indonesia, Malaysia, And Gcc: The Roles Of Monetary And Fiscal Policies And Contagion. *Journal of Islamic Monetary Economics and Finance*, 10(1), 155–176. DOI: 10.21098/jimf.v10i1.1899

Loang, O. K. (2024). Sustainability's impact of ESG-infused policies on leading economic indicators in Asian economies. *Journal of Sustainable Research*, 6(3), e240059. DOI: 10.20900/jsr20240059

Malmendier, U., Pouzo, D., & Vanasco, V. (2020). Investor experiences and financial market dynamics. *Journal of Financial Economics*, 136(3), 597–622. DOI: 10.1016/j.jfineco.2019.11.002

Mittal, S. K. (2022). Behavior biases and investment decision: Theoretical and research framework. *Qualitative Research in Financial Markets*, 14(2), 213–228. DOI: 10.1108/QRFM-09-2017-0085

Padmavathy, M. (2024). Behavioral Finance and Stock Market Anomalies: Exploring Psychological Factors Influencing Investment Decisions. *Shanlax International Journal of Management*, 11(iS1-Jan, S1), 191–197. DOI: 10.34293/management.v11iiS1-Jan.7164

Suresh, G., & Loang, O. K. (2024). The Rationality Conundrum: Exploring Herd Mentality among Individual Investors in the Indian Stock Market. *Indian Journal of Finance*, 18(6), 26–45. DOI: 10.17010/ijf/2024/v18i6/173967

Taffler, R., Bellotti, X., Agarwal, V., & Li, L. (2024). Investor emotions and the psychodynamics of asset pricing bubbles: A Chinese perspective. *Journal of Behavioral Finance*, 25(3), 309–333. DOI: 10.1080/15427560.2022.2138391

VanderPal, G., & Brazie, R. (2022). Influence of basic human behaviors (influenced by brain architecture and function), and past traumatic events on investor behavior and financial bias. *Journal of Accounting and Finance*, 22(2).

Westermann, F., & Schunk, D. (2022). Rational Expectations vs. Behavioral Biases: An Empirical Analysis of Trading Variability in International Capital Markets. *Journal of Business and Economic Options*, 5(4), 35–42.

Chapter 8
Bias-Driven Trading Patterns:
Exploring the Influence of Sentiment and Anchoring on Market Liquidity

Liao Fa Xing
Sichuan International Studies University, China

ABSTRACT

This study investigates the influence of cognitive and emotional biases on market liquidity, focusing on factors such as anchoring bias, investor sentiment, risk perception, and herding behavior. By examining how these biases distort decision-making processes, the research highlights their role in shaping trading patterns and liquidity dynamics in financial markets. The findings reveal that while biases may temporarily enhance liquidity, they can also lead to significant disruptions, particularly during periods of market volatility. The study emphasizes the importance of understanding bias-driven behaviors for developing more robust market frameworks and improving liquidity management strategies.

INTRODUCTION

The examination of bias-driven trading patterns centres on comprehending how diverse cognitive biases and emotional influences shape investor behaviour and, in turn, impact market results. This inquiry centres on the understanding that financial markets are not solely governed by rational decision-making; instead, they are affected by psychological and behavioural influences. This study seeks to

DOI: 10.4018/979-8-3693-8583-8.ch008

examine the influence of biases, including anchoring bias, investor sentiment, risk perception, and herding behaviour, on market liquidity. Market liquidity, defined as the capacity to transact assets without substantially influencing their prices, is essential for the effective operation of financial markets (Chu et al., 2022). The correlation between psychological biases and liquidity elucidates how irrational behaviour can result in inefficiencies in trading patterns, generating ripple effects throughout larger market structures.

Anchoring bias, a cognitive heuristic in which individuals disproportionately depend on beginning information or reference points during decision-making, is a crucial variable in this study. In financial markets, anchoring occurs when traders get preoccupied with historical price levels or predictions that may not correspond with present market conditions. This dependence on previous benchmarks might skew trading behaviour, resulting in mispricing and impacting market liquidity. For example, when investors base their expectations on historical stock prices, they may hesitate to sell at diminished prices, thereby decreasing transaction volume and causing illiquidity. This bias hinders the effectiveness of market reactions to new information and complicates the price discovery process, thereby elevating liquidity costs (Tang & Loang, 2024).

Investor sentiment, a crucial element in this analysis, denotes the general disposition or perspective of market players towards prospective financial market conditions. Sentiment may vary due to macroeconomic factors, market news, or external shocks, frequently diverging from objective market fundamentals. During times of elevated positive emotion, investors may partake in excessive risk-taking, resulting in increased trade volumes and improved liquidity. Conversely, during times of negative emotion, fear and pessimism may dominate, prompting investors to exit the market and thus reducing liquidity. The fluctuating characteristics of sentiment-driven trading behaviours exacerbate market volatility, undermining liquidity stability in both the short and long term.

Risk perception, intricately associated with investor emotion, denotes how market participants assess the potential hazards inherent in their investment choices. When investors recognise elevated risk levels, particularly amid market volatility or global economic uncertainty, they may exhibit reduced willingness to engage actively in trading (Loang, 2023). This conduct leads to diminished transaction volumes and a decrease in market liquidity. Conversely, during periods of diminished perceived risk, investors may exhibit increased confidence in executing trades, hence enhancing liquidity. The examination of risk perception in this context is crucial as it highlights the influence of subjective evaluations of market conditions on objective liquidity metrics.

Herding behaviour, a phenomenon in which investors emulate the activities of others instead of conducting independent analysis, significantly influences market liquidity. Herding can precipitate market bubbles or crashes as substantial cohorts of investors act uniformly, either inflating prices or instigating significant sell-offs. In both instances, herding can intensify liquidity crises by disrupting market dynamics, either by depleting liquidity through panic selling or by generating artificial liquidity surges during bubble developments. Herding distorts market signals and may result in liquidity imbalances, hindering the market's capacity to self-correct in reaction to fundamental changes.

The dependent variable, market liquidity, is affected by the interplay of these cognitive biases and behavioural factors. Liquidity is an essential component of market vitality, facilitating the effective trading of assets with little expense. Nevertheless, when biases like anchoring, sentiment-driven trading, elevated risk perception, and herding prevail in market dynamics, liquidity may be significantly affected. Comprehending the mechanisms by which these factors function is crucial for policymakers and market participants, as it offers insights into how market disruptions might be alleviated by behavioural interventions or regulatory modifications. This study seeks to enhance comprehension of the behavioural foundations of financial market inefficiencies by examining the complex interplay between psychological biases and market liquidity (FaXing & Loang, 2024).

The examination of bias-driven trading patterns and their impact on market liquidity provides significant insights, however existing research reveals various gaps that warrant further investigation. A notable gap exists in the comprehension of how the interplay among diverse biases—such as anchoring, investor sentiment, risk perception, and herding behavior—concurrently affects market liquidity. While each of these biases has been thoroughly examined individually, their cumulative consequences in actual market environments are still insufficiently investigated (Suresh & Loang, 2024). Markets are intricate systems in which several cognitive and emotional components frequently interact concurrently, and this interplay may provide distinctive insights into liquidity dynamics. The neglect of these multifaceted linkages constrains the explanatory efficacy of current models and permits additional theoretical advancement.

A further deficiency in the literature pertains to the regional and cultural distinctiveness of numerous bias-driven trading investigations. The majority of studies have been performed in developed markets, especially in the United States and Europe, where financial markets exhibit significant liquidity and abundant information is accessible. Nonetheless, the influence of biases on market liquidity may vary considerably in emerging markets, where information asymmetries, regulatory disparities, and market inefficiencies are more evident (Loang, 2024a). The degree to which biases like anchoring or herding behaviour show in these situations may result in varying liquidity outcomes. The insufficient coverage of emerging markets in current research underscores the necessity for more geographically diversified studies that consider market structure, regulatory frameworks, and investor behaviour in less developed financial systems.

A notable deficiency in the existing literature is the absence of longitudinal studies that investigate the impact of biases on market liquidity over prolonged durations. The majority of current research concentrates on transient phenomena, especially during times of market distress, such financial crises or abrupt market shocks. Although these studies offer significant insights into bias-driven trading patterns, they fail to consider the evolution or attenuation of these biases over time. The durability of anchoring bias may evolve as market participants acquire greater expertise or as new information emerges. Investor emotion and herding behaviour may vary in accordance with economic cycles or technology advancements in financial markets, such as the emergence of algorithmic trading. Longitudinal study would provide a more thorough knowledge of how biases affect liquidity in both the short and long term, reflecting the dynamic and evolving character of investor behaviour (Loang, 2024b).

The impact of technology improvements and automated trading systems on mitigating or exacerbating bias-driven trade patterns remains inadequately investigated. The growing dependence on algorithmic trading and artificial intelligence in financial markets may either alleviate or intensify the impact of cognitive biases. Automated methods may mitigate human error and emotional decision-making, thereby enhancing liquidity. Conversely, if these systems are constructed on erroneous assumptions or duplicate human biases, they may exacerbate the impacts of emotion, anchoring, or herding, resulting in more significant liquidity disruptions. The restricted emphasis on the convergence of technology and behavioural finance constitutes a significant deficiency, particularly given the increasing prevalence of high-frequency and algorithmic trading in contemporary financial markets.

Furthermore, the majority of current research on bias-driven trading and market liquidity mostly concentrates on equities markets, resulting in other asset classes, including bonds, commodities, and foreign exchange markets, being comparatively under-explored. These markets may exhibit divergent behaviours in reaction to biases owing to variations in liquidity attributes, player composition, and regulatory supervision. The influence of herding behaviour may be more significant in less liquid markets, such as corporate bonds, where transactions are few, in contrast to highly liquid equities markets. The deficiency in cross-asset analysis restricts the generalisability of results and necessitates a more comprehensive methodology that encompasses many asset classes to enhance the understanding of how biases influence liquidity within the financial ecosystem (Tang & Loang, 2024).

Finally, there is insufficient research examining the possible moderating impacts of policy interventions and regulatory frameworks on bias-driven trading behaviours. Although behavioural biases are intrinsic to human decision-making, specific restrictions may mitigate their detrimental impact on market liquidity. Circuit breakers and market-making regulations may mitigate the effects of herding behaviour and panic selling, but more transparency in reporting could diminish the impact of anchoring bias. Nevertheless, empirical research assessing the efficacy of these therapies is limited. This gap raises a critical inquiry: to what degree may regulatory interventions mitigate the effects of behavioural biases on market liquidity, and under which circumstances are they most efficacious?

LITERATURE REVIEW

Underlying Theory: Noise Trader Theory

Noise Trader Theory, proposed by economists including Fischer Black and subsequently formalised by Andrei Shleifer and Lawrence Summers, examines a significant divergence from the conventional Efficient Market Hypothesis (EMH). The Efficient Market Hypothesis posits that all market participants are rational actors who base their decisions on accessible information, so ensuring that asset prices accurately represent their intrinsic values. Noise Trader Theory, however, contests this premise by asserting that not all market participants behave rationally or possess complete information (Fu & Loang, 2024). Many traders, termed noise traders, base their trading decisions on flawed ideas, misconceptions, or extraneous factors—collectively referred to as "noise." Noise traders can substantially affect asset prices and market results, creating inefficiencies and distortions that diverge from underlying values.

Noise Trader Theory fundamentally acknowledges that noise traders are not merely incidental participants in financial markets; rather, they can constitute a significant portion of the market. They participate in trading activities influenced by non-fundamental variables, such psychological biases, rumours, trends, or other irrelevant information. This behaviour differs from that of knowledgeable or rational traders, who make judgements based on the inherent value of assets. The existence of noisy traders introduces unpredictability and volatility in the market, as their actions can distort asset prices from their intrinsic values, frequently for prolonged durations. This mispricing may endure as noise traders fail to promptly rectify their behaviour and may persist in trading based on their misguided beliefs (Othman, 2024).

A principal implication of Noise Trader Theory is its elucidation of excess volatility in financial markets. Conventional financial theories propose that market volatility should accurately mirror fluctuations in the intrinsic value of assets, typically influenced by news pertaining to economic indicators, earnings announcements, or alterations in interest rates. Nonetheless, actual markets frequently demonstrate volatility levels that significantly above those anticipated only from fundamental data. Noise Trader Theory offers a persuasive explanation for this phenomenon by positing that noise traders exacerbate market volatility through irrational conduct. When several noisy traders concurrently act on erroneous beliefs—either succumbing to market euphoria or capitulating in panic—the outcome can be pronounced price fluctuations that lack grounding in fundamental alterations.

Noise Trader Theory not only introduces excessive volatility but also emphasises the possibility for noise traders to achieve substantial gains despite their irrational behaviour. Conventional economic models imply that irrational behaviour results in persistent losses over time, since sensible traders eliminate any mispricings through arbitrage. Noise Trader Theory posits that noise traders may occasionally achieve profits due to the phenomenon termed the "noise trader risk premium." Rational traders, cognisant of the unpredictability and volatility caused by noisy traders, may hesitate to assume substantial positions to capitalise on mispricing due to the possibility that prices may remain irrational for an extended duration. Consequently, noise traders can distort prices from their intrinsic values for prolonged durations, occasionally achieving gains in the process (Chu et al., 2022). This dynamic complicates the interplay between rational and irrational traders, as rational participants must assess the risks of opposing noise-driven market trends.

The continuation of noisy trading may result in the emergence of asset bubbles. Asset bubbles arise when the price of an asset becomes markedly inflated in comparison to its intrinsic value, frequently propelled by the enthusiastic actions of noisy traders. As noisy traders persist in acquiring an asset driven by non-fundamental factors—such as speculative fervour, media sensationalism, or fear of exclusion—prices may surge to untenable heights (Baloch et al., 2024). Rational traders may identify the mispricing but are reluctant to act forcefully due to the risk of prematurely opposing the trend, as bubbles can endure for extended periods. The inevitable collapse of the bubble, when prices swiftly revert to their intrinsic values, frequently results in substantial market corrections and economic consequences, underscoring the destabilising influence of noise traders in financial markets (Jeon, 2023).

Moreover, Noise Trader Theory significantly affects market liquidity. Noise traders can temporarily augment liquidity in financial markets by increasing trading volume through their frequent, non-fundamental transactions. During times of favourable sentiment, noise traders may participate in purchasing frenzies, so augmenting the number of buyers and sellers in the market. Nonetheless, this fluidity is frequently tenuous and dependent on the continuation of noise-driven behaviour. When sentiment changes or panic occurs, noise traders may withdraw from the market en masse, resulting in abrupt liquidity shortages (Bolomope, 2021). This phenomenon highlights the dual nature of noise traders: they can enhance liquidity under some situations, yet also precipitate liquidity problems when market sentiment shifts.

Noise Trader Theory also contests the conventional perception of market efficiency. While the Efficient Market Hypothesis (EMH) contends that markets are efficient due to the rapid and accurate incorporation of all available information into asset prices, Noise Trader Theory argues that noise traders can disrupt this mechanism. The existence of noisy traders indicates that markets may have temporary inefficiencies, causing prices to diverge from their intrinsic fundamental values for prolonged durations. Inefficiencies generate arbitrage possibilities; however, as previously said, sensible traders may be reluctant to fully capitalise on them due to the danger of enduring noise-driven trends. This sophisticated perspective on market efficiency indicates that financial markets are not invariably self-correcting, and inefficiencies may endure longer than traditional economic theories anticipate.

Anchoring Bias is a prominent cognitive bias that has been thoroughly examined in relation to decision-making amid uncertainty. Anchoring, a concept introduced by Amos Tversky and Daniel Kahneman, denotes the human propensity to excessively depend on an initial piece of information—the "anchor"—when forming future judgements or decisions. In financial markets, anchoring bias occurs when investors concentrate on particular reference points, such as historical stock prices, analyst predictions, or previous market trends, and inadequately modify their expectations in light of new information. Numerous studies have investigated the effects of anchoring bias on trading behaviour. Research by Campbell and Sharpe (2009) illustrates how investors tie their expectations to historical price levels, resulting in mispricing and delays in the market's response to new information. Anchoring is especially common in volatile markets, as traders depend on historical prices or known indicators to mitigate uncertainty, hence intensifying liquidity problems when market fundamentals change. This bias is associated with the underreaction to earnings announcements and other news, as investors require more time to assimilate new information into their trading decisions. The enduring presence of anchoring bias in financial markets undermines the notion of complete rationality and indicates that such flaws may lead to systemic market inefficiencies, including liquidity disruptions (Huang & Domenech, 2024).

Investor Sentiment is an extensively studied notion that denotes the collective mood or disposition of market participants over anticipated financial market conditions. In contrast to fundamental research, which depends on objective metrics like profitability, revenue growth, or macroeconomic indicators, investor sentiment is frequently influenced by subjective elements, including market news, economic projections, and social or political occurrences. The body of literature concerning investor sentiment is extensive, with seminal works, such those by Baker and Wurgler (2006), emphasising its influence on asset prices and market volatility. Investor sentiment is recognised to exert both short-term and long-term effects on market circumstances. In the near term, optimistic emotion may result in asset overvaluation due to fervent purchasing by investors, whilst pessimistic sentiment can provoke sell-offs and liquidity deficits as traders liquidate their positions. Long-term emotion can induce price distortions that diverge from basic values, resulting in potential for bubbles and crashes. A substantial body of research has examined sentiment measures, including the volatility index (VIX) and investor confidence surveys, which act as proxies for assessing market sentiment. Recent literature has increasingly emphasised the impact of digital sentiment, namely the function of social media and online forums in creating investor expectations. Research conducted by Da, Engelberg, and Gao (2015) has shown that online search behaviour and sentiment analysis from social media can forecast stock market returns and liquidity, highlighting the increasing impact of digital communication in contemporary markets.

Risk perception has become a pivotal factor in comprehending investor behaviour and its consequences for market liquidity. Risk perception denotes the manner in which investors assess and perceive the potential hazards linked to their investing choices. This variable differs from objective risk measurements, such volatility or credit ratings, as it embodies an investor's subjective assessment of uncertainty and probable losses. The scholarship on risk perception is interdisciplinary, encompassing psychology, finance, and economics. Preliminary research, like that of Slovic (1987), underscores that individuals' risk perception is shaped by many cognitive biases, such as availability heuristics and representativeness, potentially resulting in the overestimation or underestimate of dangers. Risk perception is crucial in influencing trading behaviour in financial markets. Investors that recognise elevated risk levels are inclined to diminish their market exposure, resulting in decreased trading volumes and liquidity. Conversely, when risk perception is diminished, investors may partake in more speculative trades, hence enhancing market activity and liquidity. Numerous research have examined the correlation between risk perception and market liquidity, especially during crises. Guiso, Sapienza, and Zingales (2008) analyse how alterations in risk perception during the 2008 financial crisis resulted in substantial declines in liquidity as investors abandoned risky assets (Saxena & Sahoo, 2022). Recent study has investigated the influence of information asymmetry on risk perception, indicating that investors with limited access to trustworthy information are more inclined to view markets as dangerous, hence intensifying liquidity shortages.

Herding behaviour is a well-documented phenomenon in social psychology and financial markets, when individuals emulate the activities of a bigger group instead of conducting independent analysis. Herding behaviour is particularly common in financial markets, where uncertainty and volatility prompt investors to imitate the behaviours of others to mitigate prospective losses. Theoretical models of herding emerged in the early 1990s, with foundational contributions by Bikhchandani, Hirshleifer, and Welch (1992) and Banerjee (1992) providing formal elucidations of how individuals' inclination to conform might result in collective decision-making inside financial markets. The empirical literature has since broadened, investigating the impact of herding behaviour on asset prices, market efficiency, and liquidity. In financial markets, herding can distort prices from their intrinsic values as substantial groups of investors collectively purchase or divest assets. This collective behaviour induces price distortions that may not accurately represent the fundamental economic conditions, resulting in transient mispricing and liquidity crises. Research conducted by Christie and Huang (1995) demonstrates herding behaviour in times of market distress, when investors' apprehension of losses prompts concurrent sell-offs, markedly diminishing liquidity. Recent research has investigated herding behaviour among institutional investors, who are typically considered less prone to such biases due to their utilisation of advanced analytical techniques. Research by Sias (2004) indicates that institutional investors are susceptible to herding, especially during periods of significant market volatility, exacerbating liquidity challenges during substantial sell-offs.

Research Methodology

A comprehensive research approach that integrates both qualitative and quantitative methods is needed to investigate the impact of cognitive biases and emotional factors on market liquidity. A mixed-methods approach facilitates a more nuanced comprehension of the intricate interplay of psychological biases—such as anchoring, investor emotion, risk perception, and herding behavior—and their impact on market dynamics. The study integrates qualitative and quantitative approaches to capture both the subjective perceptions of market participants and the objective factual evidence of the manifestation of these biases in trading patterns and liquidity disruptions.

Quantitative approaches function as the principal instrument for examining the statistical correlations between the independent variables—anchoring bias, investor emotion, risk perception, and herding behavior—and the dependent variable, market liquidity. The quantitative aspect entails the collection and analysis of numerical data from financial markets, emphasising critical liquidity indicators such as bid-ask spreads, trade volumes, and price effect. Financial market data, encompassing historical stock prices, trade volumes, and volatility metrics, is widely accessible via numerous financial databases, facilitating extensive empirical investigations. The study use econometric tools, including multiple regression analysis and vector autoregression (VAR), to investigate the impact of fluctuations in investor sentiment on liquidity metrics across various asset classes or over particular timeframes.

Regression analysis is very effective for measuring the extent to which each independent variable influences market liquidity. For example, by integrating sentiment indicators (such as the American Association of Individual Investors' attitude survey or the VIX), the study can statistically assess the association between periods of elevated sentiment and fluctuations in market liquidity. Furthermore, risk perception can be quantified by metrics like implied volatility, while herding behaviour can be identified via herding indices that assess the extent of clustering in trading decisions among institutional and retail investors. Utilising this data, the quantitative analysis will rigorously evaluate the hypotheses, facilitating a greater comprehension of the causal linkages between cognitive biases and liquidity outcomes.

Alongside conventional regression procedures, sophisticated quantitative tools, including machine learning algorithms, may be employed to identify intricate, non-linear patterns in the data that typical econometric models may not readily capture. Models such as random forests and neural networks are very effective for analysing extensive datasets with several variables affecting market behaviour. Machine learning can elucidate hidden patterns in trading data that demonstrate the interactions of various biases and their impact on liquidity, which may not be readily apparent within a linear framework.

Although quantitative research provides strong statistical insights, it may not adequately elucidate the underlying motivations behind investor behaviour, especially regarding subjective elements such as sentiment or risk perception. Qualitative approaches serve a vital complementary function in this context. Qualitative research offers profound insights into the cognitive and emotional processes that shape investor behaviour, elucidating the mechanisms through which biases like anchoring and herding behaviour arise. Utilising techniques such as comprehensive interviews, focus groups, or case studies, the research can access investors' decision-making processes, examining their interpretation of market signals, responses to uncertainty, and adherence to market trends.

Interviews with market participants, encompassing both institutional investors and retail traders, would yield significant qualitative evidence regarding the influence of biases on trading decisions. For example, investors may elucidate how historical experiences or market trends affect their anchoring points, or how social influence results in herding behaviour. Focus groups of financial analysts may provide insights into the formation and dissemination of market sentiment, especially during periods of market volatility. These qualitative methods allow researchers to collect comprehensive, contextual data that enhances the numerical results from quantitative analysis, providing a more integrated perspective on the functioning of biases in actual market environments.

Furthermore, content analysis of financial media and social media platforms might function as an additional qualitative instrument to assess the development and distribution of investor sentiment. Researchers can monitor the evolution of sentiment and its impact on trading patterns by analysing the tone and content of news items, blogs, and online discussions in relation to market occurrences. This qualitative data is particularly helpful for reflecting the subjective character of sentiment, which may not be adequately represented in numerical indices or sentiment polls. The study uses a combination of natural language processing tools and manual coding to comprehensively analyse sentiment in media outlets, establishing correlations between the language utilised and subsequent market behaviour.

Case studies serve as a crucial qualitative method, facilitating a thorough analysis of particular market occurrences when bias-induced trading behaviours resulted in liquidity disturbances. Examining the dot-com bubble or the 2008 financial crisis offers a substantial repository of data regarding how herding behaviour, excessive risk-taking, and irrational sentiment influenced market volatility and liquidity deficiencies. The case study method enables the research to contextualise broader statistical findings inside specific historical events, demonstrating the real-world consequences of bias-driven trading on market liquidity.

Conceptual Framework

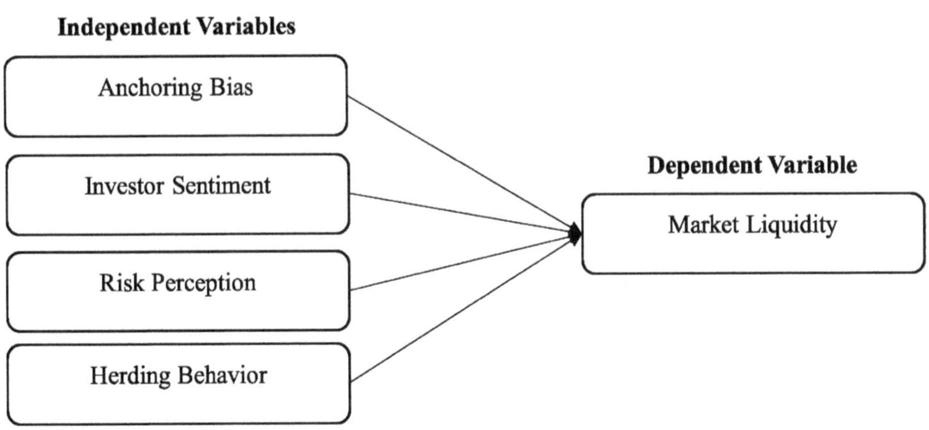

This study's conceptual framework is based on the convergence of behavioural finance and market microstructure, offering a systematic perspective to comprehend the interactions among cognitive biases, emotional influences, and market liquidity.

The approach fundamentally aims to examine how biases, including anchoring, investor sentiment, risk perception, and herding behaviour, jointly affect market liquidity, focusing on the non-rational decision-making processes that often define market players.

The framework posits that conventional financial models, grounded in the Efficient Market Hypothesis (EMH), presume that market participants are rational agents that make decisions based on comprehensive and precise information at their disposal (Chishti, 2020). Behavioural finance has shown that market participants frequently diverge from rational decision-making due to several psychological biases. This deviation from logic can substantially affect the efficiency of financial markets, resulting in mispricing, heightened volatility, and liquidity disruptions. The conceptual framework synthesises ideas from behavioural finance, asserting that the examined biases—anchoring, sentiment, risk perception, and herding—function interdependently with market dynamics to affect liquidity in intricate and subtle manners.

Anchoring bias constitutes a fundamental element of the framework, illustrating the cognitive inclination of investors to depend excessively on early information, frequently hindering their ability to adjust to fresh facts. In financial markets, this bias occurs when traders concentrate on historical price levels or prior market conditions, utilising these as benchmarks for decision-making notwithstanding their obsolescence. The concept asserts that anchoring bias results in delayed market reactions to fresh information, leading to transient mispricings and obstructing the efficient operation of liquidity (Hu, 2020). For example, when investors base their expectations on historical peaks or troughs, they may hesitate to transact at present market prices, resulting in diminished trading volumes and broader bid-ask spreads. The interplay between anchoring bias and liquidity establishes a vital connection in the conceptual framework, indicating that cognitive fixation on obsolete reference points skews the price discovery process, especially in volatile market conditions.

Investor sentiment serves as a crucial element within the framework, reflecting the collective mood or disposition of market players regarding prospective financial situations. The approach identifies sentiment as both a catalyst and an indicator of market liquidity. Positive emotion can result in heightened trading volumes and enhanced liquidity, as optimism motivates investors to assume greater risks, leading to more frequent transactions. Conversely, adverse sentiment can induce liquidity shortages as fear and pessimism compel investors to diminish their market exposure. The approach highlights the reciprocal relationship between sentiment and liquidity: low liquidity can intensify negative sentiment, whereas strong liquidity can bolster positive market sentiments. The interaction between sentiment and liquidity is essential, since it reflects the self-reinforcing characteristics of emotional market behaviour, where liquidity conditions and investor sentiment mutually affect one another.

Risk perception, a crucial element in the framework, pertains to how investors assess the degree of uncertainty and possibility for loss in their decision-making processes. The conceptual framework posits that investors' subjective risk perceptions are influenced by macroeconomic variables and individual cognitive biases, thereby impacting their trading activity willingly. During instances of economic instability or market volatility, when risk is viewed as elevated, investors may retract from trading, resulting in diminished liquidity due to a reduced number of market players willing to engage in transactions (Cakici & Zaremba, 2023). The theory posits that risk perception functions concurrently with investor mood: when sentiment is favourable, perceived risk often diminishes, fostering liquidity. Conversely, as sentiment becomes negative, perceived risk escalates, leading to illiquidity. The concept highlights the relationship between risk perception and liquidity, demonstrating how subjective assessments of uncertainty can profoundly influence market circumstances, regardless of any alterations in fundamental economic factors.

Herding behaviour is a crucial factor in the framework, representing the inclination of investors to imitate the acts of others instead of depending on their own analysis. Herding can exacerbate market trends, elevating asset prices when the collective is purchasing or diminishing them when the collective is divesting (Bolomope, 2021). Within the paradigm, herding behaviour is suggested to exert a twofold influence on market liquidity. During market frenzy, herding can temporarily enhance liquidity as numerous investors trade concurrently. This liquidity is frequently precarious and untenable, as it relies on the persistent optimism of the collective. When market conditions fluctuate, herding behaviour may precipitate swift sell-offs, intensifying liquidity crises as all investors seek to liquidate their positions concurrently. The concept identifies herding behaviour as a crucial factor in liquidity volatility, especially in speculative markets susceptible to bubbles and crashes.

The dependent variable, market liquidity, is important to the conceptual framework and functions as the outcome affected by the aggregate influence of the independent factors. Liquidity refers to the capacity of market participants to swiftly buy or sell assets at stable prices without inducing substantial market disturbances. The concept perceives liquidity as dependent on market conditions and investor behaviour, with cognitive biases such anchoring and herding affecting the ease of asset trading. Market liquidity is fluid and may vary according to the psychological and emotional conditions of market players (Fu & Loang, 2024). During times of elevated investor confidence and diminished perceived risk, liquidity is typically plentiful, characterised by small bid-ask spreads and substantial trade volumes. During periods of elevated risk perception and adverse emotion, liquidity can swiftly decline as market players withdraw from active trading, leading to broader spreads and heightened transaction costs (FaXing & Loang, 2024).

CONCLUSION

This study's conclusion integrates theoretical concepts and empirical evidence to elucidate the impact of cognitive biases and emotional factors on market liquidity. This research advances the field of behavioural finance by contesting conventional notions of rationality and market efficiency, providing a sophisticated analysis of how psychological factors, including anchoring bias, investor sentiment, risk perception, and herding behaviour, can collectively influence financial market results.

This study's primary finding is that market liquidity is influenced not only by economic fundamentals and the availability of market information but also by the behavioural preferences of market players. The research illustrates that cognitive biases, although frequently understated in their singular impacts, can have significant repercussions when they engage with market processes. Anchoring bias causes investors to adhere to obsolete reference points, hindering the price discovery process and diminishing market liquidity by decreasing participants' readiness to transact at new prices. Investor sentiment and herding behaviour similarly influence liquidity cycles, leading to liquidity booms during excessive optimism and shortages during heightened fear. These findings underscore the need of comprehending market liquidity not solely in relation to external market conditions but as a consequence of the psychological moods and collective behaviours of investors.

The study's examination of investor mood provides significant insights into the impact of emotional elements on market behaviour. The research highlights the volatility of market liquidity influenced by psychological factors by analysing how mood varies in reaction to external events, economic indicators, and media narratives. Positive emotion, frequently driven by optimism or speculative trends, can augment liquidity in the near term by promoting risk-taking and active trading. This liquidity is frequently tenuous and susceptible to failure when sentiment changes, resulting in liquidity crises during times of panic or market declines. This investigation concludes that sentiment-driven liquidity patterns are cyclical and self-reinforcing, with mood variations leading to swift market situation adjustments.

Risk perception arises as a crucial component, highlighting the subjective manner in which market participants evaluate uncertainty and potential loss. The research indicates that risk perception does not consistently correspond with objective market risk metrics, such as volatility or economic indicators, but is influenced by psychological biases and emotional reactions to uncertainty. In periods of increased risk perception, even without substantial alterations in market fundamentals, liquidity typically declines as investors seek safer assets or diminish their exposure to perceived risks. This discovery enhances comprehension of the disjunction that can arise between market fundamentals and liquidity conditions, wherein psychological considerations influence behaviour in manners that may not align with the true amount of market risk. Furthermore, the study indicates that alleviating the consequences of increased risk perception may necessitate legislative actions or improved information transmission to guarantee that market players make decisions based on a more precise evaluation of risk.

This study demonstrates that herding behaviour intensifies market inefficiencies and liquidity issues, especially during times of market distress. Herding exacerbates prevailing tendencies in market sentiment, prompting substantial cohorts of investors to act uniformly, either by purchasing in ascending markets or divesting during declines. This collective behaviour confuses market signals and exacerbates liquidity fluctuations, as herding results in concentrated trading activity that can overwhelm market mechanisms. The analysis of herding behaviour concludes that financial markets, especially during speculative bubbles or panics, are predominantly influenced by group dynamics rather than individual rational decision-making. This has significant implications for market stability, indicating that efforts to mitigate excessive herding—such as regulatory restrictions or market safeguards—may be essential to maintain liquidity and avert systemic dangers.

The study concludes that there is an interplay between psychological biases and market structure, highlighting the necessity of incorporating behavioural aspects into financial market models. The research illustrates that conventional models of market liquidity, which frequently depend on assumptions of rationality and efficient information processing, inadequately address the complications imposed by cognitive biases. The conclusion is that incorporating behavioural finance into market microstructure theory offers a more thorough and realistic comprehension of liquidity dynamics. The paper provides a paradigm that elucidates the anomalies in real-world markets, including liquidity shortages, price bubbles, and crashes, by considering the non-rational decision-making processes of market participants.

Theoretical, Managerial and Policy Implications

This study's theoretical implications substantially advance the subject of behavioural finance by contesting and augmenting conventional financial market behaviour models. Historically, financial markets have been examined through the framework of the Efficient Market Hypothesis (EMH), which posits that all players behave rationally and that prices consistently represent the inherent value of assets based on accessible information. This study's findings highlight the shortcomings of the rationalist framework, revealing that cognitive biases and emotional influences often govern investor behaviour, resulting in market inefficiencies. The incorporation of psychological factors, like anchoring bias, investor attitude, risk perception, and herding behaviour, enhances the understanding of market liquidity, highlighting that markets are not solely dictated by rational decision-making processes. This research enhances theoretical discourse by incorporating behavioural finance principles into market microstructure theory, which examines the mechanisms that regulate liquidity, trade, and price creation in financial markets. The study underscores the significance of psychological and social factors in affecting liquidity and aids in the creation of a more comprehensive theoretical framework that includes both rational and irrational aspects of market behaviour.

The study's conclusions have significant ramifications for financial institutions, investment firms, and portfolio managers from a managerial standpoint. The recognition of cognitive biases and their influence on market liquidity necessitates a more sophisticated approach to the formulation of investing strategies. Investment managers must acknowledge that both their decision-making processes and those of their clients are vulnerable to biases, including anchoring and sentiment-driven trading. This acknowledgement promotes the implementation of methods that alleviate these biases, such as utilising systematic and data-driven methodologies that reduce emotional decision-making. Automated trading systems or algorithmic models might be developed to incorporate the effects of sentiment and herding behaviour, therefore improving the efficacy of trading techniques. Moreover, managers must take into account the timing and liquidity circumstances in the market while executing trades, as biases may result in phases of illiquidity or heightened volatility, particularly during periods of market distress. By comprehending the impact of biases on liquidity, managers can enhance their decision-making about trade execution, portfolio diversification, and risk management.

Furthermore, the study's findings regarding investor mood and herding behaviour offer significant direction for the formulation of communication strategies in financial institutions. Managers must consider the impact of market news, media reports, and internal communications on investor mood, especially during times of uncertainty or market volatility. The influence of digital platforms and social media on sentiment is particularly significant, as the swift spread of information can intensify emotional responses and result in collective behaviour. Financial institutions can mitigate this by ensuring their communications are clear, transparent, and grounded on good analysis, therefore aiding in stabilising investor mood and preventing the adverse effects of panic selling or excessive exuberance. Moreover, informing clients about the psychological biases that may affect their decisions could improve long-term investment results. By enhancing knowledge of biases like anchoring and risk perception, financial managers can assist investors in making more logical and informed decisions, hence diminishing the probability of liquidity-induced market disruptions.

The study's findings indicate that regulators and policymakers should consider the behavioural patterns of market players when formulating frameworks to enhance market stability and liquidity. Conventional regulatory methods have frequently emphasised augmenting market openness, guaranteeing equitable access to information, and boosting the effectiveness of trading systems. The paper emphasises that, although these metrics are significant, overcoming cognitive biases necessitates supplementary policy instruments aimed at the psychological aspects of market behaviour. A possible policy solution is the introduction of policies designed to mitigate the effects of herding behaviour, especially during times of market distress. Circuit breakers can effectively suspend trade during significant market downturns, allowing investors to reevaluate their positions and potentially avert panic-induced sell-offs. Moreover, comprehensive disclosures of substantial trades or institutional holdings could mitigate the momentum generated by herding behaviour, as such transparency would diminish the information asymmetry that frequently compels investors to emulate others' actions without adequate independent evaluation.

Limitations and Recommendations for Future Studies

The study's limitations underscore various domains where subsequent research can yield more profound insights and mitigate the constraints present in the current analysis. A key disadvantage is the difficulty in precisely quantifying cognitive biases and emotional influences, including investor mood, risk perception, and herding behaviour. These elements are intrinsically subjective and may vary swiftly based on market conditions, external occurrences, and individual investor psychology. This study utilises proxies including sentiment indices, volatility measures, and herding indices; yet, these instruments may inadequately encapsulate the intricacy and diversity of the biases being examined. Investor sentiment, typically assessed by surveys or media sentiment analysis, may not accurately represent the emotional states or expectations of all market players, especially institutional investors who may act differently from retail traders. The dependence on such proxies may lead to measurement error, hence constraining the accuracy of the study's results.

The analysis is constrained by its dependence on historical market data, which may inadequately reflect changing market structures, regulatory frameworks, or technical progress. Financial markets are ever evolving, with the emergence of algorithmic trading, high-frequency trading, and the growing influence of artificial intelligence possibly transforming the manifestation of cognitive biases. The technical developments may either alleviate or intensify the impact of biases on market liquidity; however, the historical data utilised in this analysis may not accurately represent these evolving dynamics. This dependence on historical data constrains the study's capacity to consider unforeseen shocks, such as geopolitical occurrences or worldwide pandemics, which may exert distinct and unanticipated influences on investor behaviour and market liquidity. The study's conclusions are context-dependent, limiting their generalisability to future market conditions.

A further weakness of this study is its concentration on equities markets, which, although highly liquid and extensively documented, may not comprehensively reflect the whole financial ecosystem. Markets for alternative asset classes, including bonds, commodities, and derivatives, may have varying liquidity patterns and may be affected by cognitive biases in unique manners. Bond markets generally exhibit lesser liquidity than equity markets, and investor behaviour in these markets is often more significantly affected by factors such as credit risk and interest rate fluctuations, which are less pronounced in equities trading. The study's limited emphasis on equities markets restricts its relevance to other areas of the financial industry. Future study may enhance its findings by broadening the scope to encompass various asset classes, facilitating a more thorough examination of the influence of cognitive biases on market liquidity across diverse financial instruments.

The geographical breadth of the study constitutes a limitation, as the majority of the research and data utilised are sourced from developed markets, specifically the United States and Europe. These markets function inside intricate regulatory frameworks, characterised by elevated transparency and robust market infrastructures. Financial markets in emerging economies may display distinct behavioural tendencies, mostly due to elevated information asymmetry, regulatory inefficiencies, and increased market volatility. Cognitive biases may significantly influence market liquidity in certain instances. Herding behaviour may be more pronounced in markets characterised by little information, where investors tend to depend on the actions of others for their decision-making. Future research could investigate bias-driven trading patterns in emerging markets, providing a more globally representative study and determining whether the same biases exert analogous impacts in less developed financial systems.

Furthermore, the study inadequately examines the influence of institutional investors, whose conduct may diverge from that of typical retail investors. Institutional investors, including hedge funds, pension funds, and mutual funds, possess access to advanced tools and data, potentially diminishing their vulnerability to cognitive biases. Research indicates that institutional investors can also be swayed by biases, including herding behaviour, particularly during periods of market distress. This study primarily investigates collective market behaviour, which may conceal significant distinctions in the responses of retail and institutional investors to cognitive biases. Future research may disaggregate the data to investigate how various groups of investors affect liquidity variations and whether identical psychological factors exert similar influences on them. Comprehending these distinctions would yield profound insights into the mechanisms underlying bias-driven trading patterns.

Future studies should aim to rectify these shortcomings and broaden the research area to improve comprehension of the impact of cognitive biases on market liquidity. A recommendation is to create more advanced models for quantifying biases and emotions in financial markets. Progress in behavioural finance and technology provides novel instruments for obtaining real-time data on investor sentiment, risk assessment, and trading conduct. Natural language processing (NLP) tools can analyse extensive text data from news stories, social media, and financial reports to deliver more detailed and precise sentiment analysis. Moreover, employing experimental or survey-based methodologies may provide direct insights into individual investors' risk perception, decision anchoring, or herding behaviour. Integrating market data with qualitative metrics could enable future research to create more sophisticated and comprehensive models that accurately reflect the intricacies of cognitive biases.

REFERENCES

Baloch, S. A., Jatoi, I. A., Ayubi, S., & Raza, K. M. (2024). Mitigating Role of Covid-19 in Relationship between Behavioral Factors of Investors. *KASBIT Business Journal, 17*(1).

Bolomope, M. T. (2021). *Disruption-driven Investment Decision-making of Listed Property Trusts in New Zealand* (Doctoral dissertation, ResearchSpace@ Auckland).

Cakici, N., & Zaremba, A. (2023). Recency bias and the cross-section of international stock returns. *Journal of International Financial Markets, Institutions and Money*, 84, 101738. DOI: 10.1016/j.intfin.2023.101738

Chishti, S. (2020). *The AI book: the artificial intelligence handbook for investors, entrepreneurs and fintech visionaries*. John Wiley & Sons. DOI: 10.1002/9781119551966

Chu, L., He, X. Z., Li, K., & Tu, J. (2022). Investor sentiment and paradigm shifts in equity return forecasting. *Management Science*, 68(6), 4301–4325. DOI: 10.1287/mnsc.2020.3834

FaXing. L., & Loang, O. K. (2024). Green Investing and Financial Education: The Case of China's A-Share Market. In *Technology-Driven Business Innovation: Unleashing the Digital Advantage, Volume 1* (pp. 29-41). Cham: Springer Nature Switzerland.

Fu, T., & Loang, O. K. (2024). The Roles of ESG Disclosure, Innovation in Improving Firm Financial Performance: Evidence from China. In *Artificial Intelligence (AI) and Customer Social Responsibility (CSR)* (pp. 197–221). Springer Nature Switzerland. DOI: 10.1007/978-3-031-50939-1_16

Hu, C. (2020). Industrial specialization matters: A new angle on equity home bias. *Journal of International Economics*, 126, 103354. DOI: 10.1016/j.jinteco.2020.103354

Huang, X. H., & Domenech, J. C. A. R. M. A. (2024)... *CARMA*, 2024, 157–165. DOI: 10.4995/CARMA2024.2024.17818

Jeon, H. J. (2023). CEO overconfidence: A dual-detriment to investment-price sensitivity via market negligence and reduced informed trading. *Journal of Contemporary Accounting & Economics*, 19(3), 100378. DOI: 10.1016/j.jcae.2023.100378

Loang, O. K. (2023). Corporate governance and Islamic behavioural finance: A review from Malaysia and GCC countries. *Indian Journal of Corporate Governance*, 16(1), 28–51. DOI: 10.1177/09746862231178959

Loang, O. K. (2024). Stability Of Shariah-Compliant Stocks In Indonesia, Malaysia, And Gcc: The Roles Of Monetary And Fiscal Policies And Contagion. *Journal of Islamic Monetary Economics and Finance*, 10(1), 155–176. DOI: 10.21098/jimf.v10i1.1899

Loang, O. K. (2024). Sustainability's impact of ESG-infused policies on leading economic indicators in Asian economies. *Journal of Sustainable Research*, 6(3), e240059. DOI: 10.20900/jsr20240059

Othman, N. N. (2024). Emotional Economics: The Role of Psychological Biases in Personal Investment Outcomes. *Available atSSRN* 4844927. DOI: 10.2139/ssrn.4844927

Saxena, V., & Sahoo, S. (2022). Share repurchase: A review of the literature. *International Journal of Indian Culture and Business Management*, 25(1), 38–71. DOI: 10.1504/IJICBM.2022.120918

Suresh, G., & Loang, O. K. (2024). The Rationality Conundrum: Exploring Herd Mentality among Individual Investors in the Indian Stock Market. *Indian Journal of Finance*, 18(6), 26–45. DOI: 10.17010/ijf/2024/v18i6/173967

Tang, H., & Loang, O. K. (2024). Does ESG Performance Improve the Financial Performance of Enterprises in China? The Mediating Role of Financial Constraints. In *Artificial Intelligence (AI) and Customer Social Responsibility (CSR)* (pp. 263–289). Springer Nature Switzerland. DOI: 10.1007/978-3-031-50939-1_20

Chapter 9
The Role of Heuristics in Shaping Investment Strategies Analyzing Bias-Driven Decision-Making in Volatile Markets:
The Role of Heuristics in Shaping Investment Strategies

Liao Fa Xing
Sichuan International Studies University, China

ABSTRACT

This study examines the role of heuristics in shaping investment strategies, particularly during periods of market volatility. It explores how cognitive shortcuts, such as the representativeness and availability heuristics, confirmation bias, and mental accounting, influence investor decision-making in uncertain financial environments. The findings highlight that while heuristics can streamline decisions under pressure, they often lead to systematic biases that distort investment outcomes. The study underscores the importance of understanding these biases for developing more resilient strategies and suggests that addressing these cognitive tendencies can improve both individual investor behavior and broader market stability.

DOI: 10.4018/979-8-3693-8583-8.ch009

INTRODUCTION

In finance, especially in volatile markets, investors often make judgements amid uncertainty. Conventional finance theory posits that investors behave rationally, seeking to optimise their utility based on accessible information. Nonetheless, the emergence of behavioural finance has underscored that actual decision-making frequently diverges from this theoretical ideal (Jing & Loang, 2024). In intricate and swiftly evolving contexts, such as unstable markets, humans often depend on cognitive shortcuts or heuristics to manage the excessive volume of information. Heuristics, although frequently efficient in streamlining decision-making, may result in systematic biases that skew investment strategies and results.

A fundamental heuristic influencing investment behaviour is the representativeness heuristic, wherein investors base their decisions on the degree to which a circumstance or asset corresponds with established stereotypes or former experiences. This frequently results in miscalculations, as investors may overrate the probability of an event due to surface resemblances, instead of evaluating the fundamental probabilities (Barua, 2024). In volatile markets, where historical patterns may not reliably forecast future trends, dependence on this heuristic can lead to erroneous investment decisions, such as excessive investment in a stock that appears analogous to a previously successful one.

A notable element is the availability heuristic, which leads investors to evaluate the likelihood of an event based on the ease with which instances are recalled. During periods of market volatility, investors may be unduly swayed by recent news or significant events, resulting in either excessive or insufficient responses to new information (Loang, 2023). This may lead to investment decisions that prioritise short-term sentiment over long-term fundamentals, hence heightening vulnerability to market volatility.

Confirmation bias intensifies the problem of biassed decision-making in investment strategies. Investors typically pursue information that validates their pre-existing opinions while disregarding material that challenges their perspectives. In unstable markets, this can be especially harmful, since investors may overlook warning signals or contradictory facts that could alleviate future losses. They instead bolster their existing investing techniques, regardless of their inadequacy in the swiftly evolving market landscape.

Mental accounting significantly influences investor decision-making. This bias denotes the inclination of humans to classify and handle money variably according to its origin or intended purpose (FaXing & Loang, 2024). Investors may unreasonably compartmentalise cash into distinct mental accounts, resulting in inconsistent investing decisions. For example, they can regard gains from high-risk assets as "house money," promoting riskier conduct while safeguarding capital from more secure investments. This compartmentalisation might skew the overall investing strategy, especially in volatile markets where adaptability and a cohesive perspective of the portfolio are crucial.

The aggregate impact of these heuristics results in biassed investing decision-making, especially during periods of market instability. Investors may prioritise psychological biases above rational and informed methods, resulting in inferior financial outcomes. Comprehending the influence of heuristics and bias-driven behaviour is essential for formulating more resilient investing strategies, especially in emerging markets characterised by increased volatility and unpredictability (Suresh & Loang, 2024). The findings from this research may assist investors in alleviating the effects of cognitive biases and enable them to make more reasonable, informed decisions during market volatility.

Despite the expanding literature on heuristics and their impact on decision-making in financial markets, substantial gaps still in comprehending how these cognitive shortcuts function within volatile markets, especially in emerging nations (Loang, 2024a). The majority of research on heuristics, including the representativeness heuristic, availability heuristic, confirmation bias, and mental accounting, has been performed in relatively stable market conditions. Although these insights offer significant contributions to behavioural finance, they may not adequately address the increased unpredictability and swift fluctuations typical of volatile markets. This results in a deficiency in the literature concerning the distinct demands that such environments impose on investor behaviour and the intensification of cognitive biases in situations of elevated uncertainty.

A significant deficiency in the existing research is the inadequate investigation of how various forms of market volatility influence the application of heuristics. Volatility in financial markets can stem from various sources, including geopolitical tensions, technology upheavals, or economic shocks. Nevertheless, current research frequently regards volatility as a uniform term, neglecting to investigate how the characteristics and origins of volatility may interact with heuristics to influence investing choices (Loang, 2024b). This absence of differentiation may neglect essential nuances in investor responses to various forms of market uncertainty, perhaps resulting in an inadequate comprehension of the mechanisms influencing biassed decision-making.

A notable deficiency in the literature is the inadequate emphasis on individual differences in sensitivity to heuristics. Although numerous studies acknowledge that heuristics serve as prevalent cognitive shortcuts, they frequently presume that all investors are uniformly susceptible to these biases. Nevertheless, variables such as experience, education, risk tolerance, and cultural context undoubtedly affect the extent to which individuals depend on heuristics in investment decision-making. Novice investors may be more vulnerable to the representativeness heuristic due to their limited market experience, whereas seasoned investors are likely to depend more on data-driven methodologies. This gap underscores the necessity for a more sophisticated comprehension of how demographic and psychological factors affect the impact of heuristics on investment strategies in turbulent markets.

Furthermore, the influence of technical improvements on bias-driven decision-making in financial markets has not been comprehensively investigated. The emergence of algorithmic trading, financial technology platforms, and real-time data analytics has fundamentally transformed the methods by which investors collect and analyse information (Jing & Loang, 2024). These technological changes can either alleviate or intensify heuristic-driven biases. Automated systems may diminish dependence on cognitive shortcuts, although they could also bring novel biases, especially if the algorithms are constructed on heuristic principles. The existing literature has not adequately explored the intersection of technology elements and traditional heuristics in investment decision-making, especially in risky contexts.

Furthermore, a substantial portion of the research on heuristics and investment strategies has been undertaken in developed markets, resulting in a considerable void in the comprehension of these phenomena in emerging economies. Emerging markets are typically marked by increased volatility, underdeveloped regulatory frameworks, and heightened information asymmetries, which may amplify dependence on heuristics. Nevertheless, limited research has concentrated on the behavioural dynamics of investors in these markets, resulting in a deficiency in comprehension of the manifestation of cognitive biases in contexts characterised by heightened uncertainty and risk (Lanju & Loang, 2024). Considering the growing significance of emerging countries in the global economy, it is essential to overcome this gap to construct more complete investment behaviour models.

Ultimately, there is an absence of lengthy research that investigate the enduring effects of heuristic-driven decision-making on investment results in volatile markets. Although numerous studies offer insightful glimpses into investor behaviour during market volatility, they frequently neglect to address the temporal evolution of biases such as representativeness, availability, and confirmation bias (Dixit, 2024). The deficiency in longitudinal research constrains the comprehension of the cumulative impacts of heuristics on portfolio performance, risk management, and overall financial health. Extended investigations may yield profound insights into how investors acquire knowledge (or neglect to do so) from their biases and modify their tactics in reaction to evolving market conditions.

In conclusion, whereas considerable advancements have been achieved in comprehending the influence of heuristics on investment strategies, substantial deficiencies persist. This encompasses a restricted analysis of market volatility types, inadequate consideration of individual variances, the influence of technical progress, the under-representation of emerging markets, and the lack of longitudinal studies. Rectifying these deficiencies is crucial for cultivating a more thorough and sophisticated comprehension of the impact of cognitive biases on financial decision-making, especially within volatile markets.

LITERATURE REVIEW

Underlying Theory: Heuristic-Systematic Model

The Heuristic-Systematic Model (HSM) is a theoretical framework that elucidates how individuals receive information and generate judgements through either heuristic or systematic processing methods. The model, formulated in social psychology, significantly enhances comprehension of decision-making processes, especially in intricate and uncertain contexts like financial markets. The HSM asserts that individuals switch between two separate modes of information processing: heuristic processing, characterised by speed, intuition, and cognitive shortcuts, and systematic processing, which is deliberate, analytical, and necessitates a comprehensive assessment of available information (Baloch et al., 2024).

Heuristic processing, the fundamental component of the paradigm, is employing cognitive shortcuts or "rules of thumb" to render judgements swiftly and effectively. In financial markets, these heuristics assist investors in decision-making among information overload, uncertainty, or time limitations. An investor may employ the representativeness heuristic, presuming that a company exhibiting qualities akin to a historically successful entity will similarly thrive in the future. Although these shortcuts might facilitate decision-making, they frequently result in biases and inaccuracies, particularly under unstable or unexpected market settings when dependence on historical trends may be deceptive.

Systematic processing is a more intentional and structured approach to decision-making. During systematic processing, humans meticulously analyse information, contemplate alternative choices, and rigorously evaluate the credibility of the facts before reaching a decision (Hao et al., 2024). In the realm of financial markets, systematic processing entails investors performing comprehensive analysis of a company's financial statements, market dynamics, and associated risks prior to making an investment decision. This processing mode is more cognitively taxing and time-intensive, although it generally yields more precise and rational conclusions, particularly when the stakes are elevated and the material is intricate.

The fundamental insight of the Heuristic-Systematic Model resides in the interaction between these two processing modalities (Barua, 2024). The HSM posits that humans do not consistently depend solely on one mode; instead, they frequently utilise both concurrently, influenced by factors like motivation, cognitive capacity, and the perceived adequacy of available information. Individuals exhibit a greater propensity for systematic processing when they are strongly motivated or when the ramifications of a decision are substantial. Conversely, when motivation is diminished, cognitive resources are taxed, or time constraints are significant, heuristic processing typically prevails.

In financial markets, especially during times of increased volatility, the HSM indicates that investors tend to alternate between heuristic and systematic processing depending on their evaluation of the circumstances. An investor may initially depend on heuristic processing to swiftly respond to abrupt market changes, employing rules of thumb like "buy during market declines" or "sell following a stock price surge." As uncertainty escalates and stakes heighten, the investor may shift to systematic thinking, performing a more thorough review of market fundamentals and modifying their strategy accordingly. The interaction between the two processing modes is a crucial aspect of the HSM, underscoring the flexibility and adaptability of human decision-making (Ireland, 2022).

Although systematic processing offers benefits, the Heuristic-Systematic Model underscores that heuristic biases can still affect individuals' judgements, even during more conscious examinations. This tendency, termed "biassed systematic processing," transpires when individuals choose utilise information that corroborates their pre-existing ideas or biases, notwithstanding their conviction of performing a comprehensive assessment. In financial markets, confirmation bias exemplifies this phenomenon, whereby investors, despite striving for logical analysis, may excessively concentrate on information that corroborates their initial investment thesis while minimising or disregarding opposing data. This illustrates that the two processing modes are not completely separate but can intersect, with heuristics marginally influencing methodical analysis (Marvin, 2023).

A further significant element of the Heuristic-Systematic Model is its emphasis on sufficiency principles, which regulate the shift between heuristic and systematic processing. The sufficiency principle asserts that humans would undertake a level of processing they deem "adequate" to arrive at a satisfied judgement. When a rapid heuristic assessment seems adequate to address ambiguity, individuals are disinclined to undertake more rigorous systematic analysis (Iram et al., 2023). Nevertheless, when they recognise that the stakes are excessively high or the ambiguity is insurmountable through heuristics alone, they will undertake a more methodical study. This theory elucidates why investors may depend on rapid heuristics for routine judgements while transitioning to more comprehensive study in unexpected or risky market conditions.

The HSM offers a critical perspective for examining how investors reconcile cognitive efficiency with the necessity for precision in their investing strategy. The model emphasises that heuristics can be beneficial in dynamic, high-pressure settings such as financial markets, while simultaneously highlighting the dangers of biassed decision-making that may arise from systematic errors associated with heuristics. Furthermore, the model provides insight into how investors could modify their processing techniques in reaction to fluctuating market conditions, including increased volatility or changes in market sentiment (Mawson & Casulli, 2024).

The key variables essential for comprehending the impact of heuristics on investment decision-making include the representativeness heuristic, availability heuristic, confirmation bias, and mental accounting. Each of these cognitive mechanisms has been thoroughly examined across multiple disciplines, including psychology, behavioural economics, and finance. Nonetheless, their precise influence on investment strategies, especially in turbulent markets, remains an evolving field of study. An exhaustive examination of the literature concerning these variables will elucidate their distinct functions and combined impact on financial decision-making (Koech, 2021).

The representativeness heuristic, as initially defined by Tversky and Kahneman (1974), denotes the inclination of humans to evaluate the likelihood of an event based on its similarity to their preexisting mental framework of analogous situations. This heuristic in financial decision-making prompts investors to evaluate stocks, industries, or market trends based on superficial resemblances to previous successes or failures. Research indicates that investors often succumb to this heuristic, especially under uncertain or volatile market conditions. Barberis, Shleifer, and Vishny (1998) illustrate how the representativeness heuristic fosters "style investing," when investors allocate capital to asset classes that have previously yielded high returns, frequently resulting in asset bubbles. Nonetheless, a gap persists in comprehending how the representativeness heuristic interacts with various forms of volatility, including economic shocks and political instability, and if seasoned investors are more adept at alleviating its impacts. Furthermore, a significant portion of the research has concentrated on developed markets, with very few investigations exploring the impact of the representativeness heuristic on investment decisions in emerging nations, where information asymmetries and market inefficiencies are more severe (Akepanidtaworn et al., 2023).

The availability heuristic, a cognitive shortcut proposed by Tversky and Kahneman, posits that individuals assess the probability of an event depending on the ease with which examples can be retrieved from memory. In investing decision-making, this heuristic frequently occurs when investors place excessive emphasis on recent or prominent market occurrences, such as news of a financial crisis or a quick price increase, while neglecting more statistically pertinent but less remembered information. Empirical studies indicate that the availability heuristic can induce herding behaviour in financial markets, resulting in investors collectively overreacting to recent information, hence leading market prices to deviate from intrinsic values

(Hirshleifer, 2001). This effect is especially evident during times of increased volatility, when market players may depend on accessible information—such as recent market declines or media coverage—to inform their actions, frequently intensifying price fluctuations. Nevertheless, current research frequently neglects to distinguish between the effects of positive and negative experiences, as well as the differing influences of short-term and long-term memory on investing decisions. Moreover, research on the availability heuristic has predominantly concentrated on individual investors, resulting in a deficiency in comprehending the impact of this bias on institutional investors, who may possess more advanced information processing mechanisms (Ireland, 2022).

Confirmation bias, a thoroughly researched psychological phenomena, refers to the inclination of individuals to pursue information that validates their pre-existing ideas while disregarding or minimising opposing data. In finance, confirmation bias is associated with inefficient investment decisions, as investors tend to adhere to their initial assumptions or plans despite encountering disconfirming evidence. A significant study by Rabin and Schrag (1999) demonstrates how confirmation bias can drive investors to misinterpret fresh information in a manner that corroborates their preexisting investing beliefs, resulting in enduring overconfidence and the perpetuation of ineffective investment methods. Froot, Scharfstein, and Stein (1992) examine how confirmation bias can lead to market inefficiencies, especially during speculative bubbles, as investors persist in purchasing overvalued assets, believing that their prices will continue to ascend. Although significant, the literature on confirmation bias predominantly emphasises static decision-making contexts, with less research investigating its evolution over time in response to changing market conditions. The influence of technology, including algorithmic trading platforms and social media, on the amplification or reduction of confirmation bias is still inadequately examined in existing work (Jing & Loang, 2024).

Mental accounting, initially proposed by Thaler (1985), denotes the cognitive mechanism via which humans classify and manage money variably based on its source, intended use, or mental "account." In financial markets, this bias can result in illogical investment behaviours, such as regarding gains from high-risk investments as "house money," hence increasing risk exposure, or exhibiting excessive caution with funds designated for specific objectives, even when assuming additional risk would be prudent. The literature on mental accounting in finance has emphasised its impact on distorting investment portfolios. Shefrin and Statman (1985) contend that mental accounting facilitates the "disposition effect," wherein investors tend to sell profitable stocks to "secure gains" while retaining unprofitable equities in anticipation of recouping losses. Recent research has examined the influence of mental accounting on retirement savings and wealth management, indicating that individuals frequently make suboptimal asset allocation choices by compartmentalising accounts instead of evaluating their portfolio comprehensively (Benartzi & Thaler, 2001). Nonetheless, a significant gap exists in the literature concerning the interaction between mental accounting and market volatility. In uncertain or extremely volatile conditions, the inclination to compartmentalise investments may intensify, as investors seek to establish a sense of control or mitigate perceived risk. This domain is yet insufficiently explored, especially regarding global financial markets.

Research Methodology

The investigation of heuristics' influence on investment strategies can be efficiently conducted using both qualitative and quantitative research methods. Utilising a mixed-method approach facilitates a more profound and comprehensive comprehension of the impact of cognitive biases on investment decision-making in volatile markets. Each method yields unique insights that enhance one another, creating a comprehensive framework for examining the intricacies of heuristic-driven behaviour in financial circumstances.

The quantitative aspect of the study is crucial for assessing the prevalence and influence of particular heuristics, such the representativeness and availability heuristics, confirmation bias, and mental accounting, on investment decision-making. Quantitative research in this context generally entails the gathering of numerical data from a substantial sample of investors, which can be analysed to identify patterns, correlations, and possible causal linkages. A primary technique in this field is administering surveys and questionnaires to investors regarding their decision-making processes under diverse market conditions. The replies can be evaluated by statistical methods including regression analysis, factor analysis, or structural equation modelling (SEM) to measure the degree to which various heuristics affect investment decisions.

For example, a study examining the representativeness heuristic might prompt investors to assess the similarity of a new investment to a previously successful or unsuccessful one. Responses could subsequently be examined to ascertain if investors who depend more on representativeness are more susceptible to investment errors, especially in volatile markets. Likewise, regarding confirmation bias, survey enquiries may investigate the frequency with which investors pursue information that validates their pre-existing convictions about an asset, and whether this connects with overconfidence in their decision-making. The availability heuristic can be assessed by analysing the extent to which recent or widely reported market events influence investors' perceptions of risk and opportunity, whereas mental accounting can be examined by exploring how investors categorise their assets mentally and how this impacts their portfolio allocation decisions.

Quantitative data may also be obtained from secondary sources, including market transactions, portfolio performance records, and historical trading data. This strategy offers an impartial perspective on investment behaviours, enabling researchers to monitor investor responses to market volatility in real time. For instance, through data analytics, researchers might identify trends such as herding behaviour or the inclination to prematurely sell winning stocks, which signify heuristic-driven judgements. Utilising econometric models, researchers may measure the correlation between heuristic biases and market results, offering empirical proof of the influence of cognitive biases on financial performance.

Nevertheless, whereas quantitative methods yield measurable insights into the prevalence and effects of heuristics, they may not comprehensively elucidate the underlying motivations for heuristic-driven behaviours. This is when qualitative research becomes essential. Qualitative methods, including in-depth interviews, case studies, and focus groups, provide a more intricate comprehension of the cognitive mechanisms influencing investor behaviour. Researchers can utilise open-ended interviews to explore how investors perceive and process information during market volatility, revealing the subjective aspects that affect their reliance on heuristics.

Interviews with investors facilitate a deeper examination of their cognitive processes and motivations, especially in intricate decision-making contexts. An investor might elucidate how prior experiences or emotional responses to market volatility influenced their heuristic-based judgements, offering insights that may not be immediately evident in quantitative surveys. This approach is particularly advantageous for comprehending individual variances, as qualitative research may elucidate how elements such as experience, education, and risk tolerance influence investors' vulnerability to biases. Moreover, qualitative methodologies can investigate the impact of cultural factors on decision-making, as heuristics may function differently across diverse market contexts, especially across developed and emerging nations.

Case studies serve as a potent qualitative instrument, enabling researchers to conduct an in-depth analysis of particular instances of heuristic-driven decision-making. A case study may examine a specific financial crisis or market shock, analysing investor responses and determining which heuristics significantly influenced their tactics. Case studies, through the analysis of real-world situations, can elucidate the practical ramifications of heuristic biases, demonstrating their role in market volatility and financial instability.

The integration of qualitative and quantitative methodologies has the benefit of triangulation, allowing findings from one approach to be validated or enhanced by those from another. Statistical patterns found via quantitative analysis can be further examined through qualitative interviews, potentially elucidating the rationale behind the heuristics utilised by investors under particular market conditions. Conversely, insights derived from qualitative interviews can enhance the design of quantitative surveys, ensuring that the questions formulated encapsulate the complete intricacy of heuristic-driven behaviour.

The mixed-method approach effectively addresses the research gaps indicated in the literature. Quantitative methods can assess the effect of heuristics on investment performance, but qualitative methods can investigate the evolution of these biases over time and their influence by technical improvements, including algorithmic trading and financial media. This technique elucidates the influence of individual differences, as qualitative approaches reveal the interplay between personal experiences and cognitive inclinations with heuristics, while quantitative methods assess the prevalence of these variations in a broader sample.

Figure 1. Conceptual framework

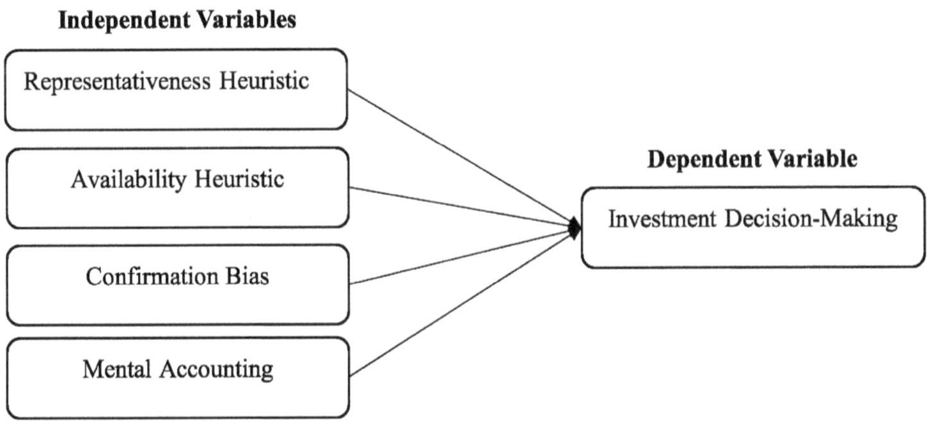

This study's conceptual framework is based on behavioural finance, particularly examining the cognitive processes that affect investing decisions in volatile markets. It incorporates essential heuristics, like the representativeness heuristic, availability heuristic, confirmation bias, and mental accounting, to examine the influence of these cognitive biases on investors' strategic decisions. The paradigm connects these heuristics to the dependent variable, investment decision-making, by elucidating their impact on information processing and judgement in uncertain settings (Hao et al., 2024). The paradigm is based on the dual-process theory of decision-making, which asserts that individuals switch between intuitive, heuristic-based decisions and more methodical, systematic approaches, influenced by cognitive load and external factors. In volatile markets, investors frequently depend more on heuristic methods because of time limitations, significant uncertainty, and excessive information.

The conceptual framework is predicated on the premise that heuristics function as cognitive shortcuts, facilitating the simplification of intricate decision-making processes. The representativeness heuristic affects investment decisions since investors depend on perceived parallels between present market conditions and historical experiences. Investors employing this heuristic may, for instance, presume that a stock would yield favourable results due to its similarity to a prior successful investment, despite potentially considerable differences in underlying conditions. The theory asserts that dependence on superficial similarities may result in suboptimal investment decisions, especially in unpredictable markets where historical trends frequently fail to serve as accurate predictors of future outcomes. This heuristic frequently leads investors to neglect comprehensive analyses or divergent patterns that are not readily observable (Ireland, 2022).

The availability heuristic is integrated into the framework to elucidate how investors evaluate the likelihood of market events based on the ease of recalling analogous instances. In financial markets, prominent occurrences like market collapses, abrupt rallies, or geopolitical news often capture investors' focus, causing them to overrate the probability of these events reoccurring. The concept asserts that, amid market volatility, investors employing the availability heuristic tend to base their decisions on current or salient information, frequently disregarding comprehensive market data that could offer a more precise assessment of risk. This heuristic enhances the influence of market mood, fostering herding behaviour and intensifying market volatility (Suresh & Loang, 2024).

Confirmation bias constitutes a significant element of the conceptual framework. This bias leads investors to selectively pursue information that corroborates their pre-existing opinions or investing strategies, while disregarding opposing facts. The framework indicates that in times of market uncertainty, investors tend to exhibit confirmation bias, solidifying their initial conclusions and being more resistant to information that contradicts their perspectives. This bias may result in overconfidence and the continuation of inefficient investing strategies, as investors neglect to modify their portfolios in accordance with evolving market conditions. The framework emphasises the influence of technical elements, including algorithmic trading platforms and financial news outlets, in perpetuating confirmation bias by tailoring information to correspond with investors' established biases (Mawson & Casulli, 2024).

Mental accounting, a significant heuristic within the framework, elucidates how investors classify and manage funds differently based on their mental "accounts." An investor may allocate money for high-risk investments separately from those intended for safer assets, despite the potential for superior financial results through a more integrated strategy. In volatile markets, the framework suggests that mental accounting can cause investors to make illogical decisions by excessively compartmentalising their portfolios. They may assume undue risk with specific funds or neglect to reallocate resources among accounts, despite market conditions necessitating a more adaptable and comprehensive strategy. This may lead to ineffective portfolio management and heightened susceptibility to market volatility.

The conceptual framework includes the dual-process theory of decision-making, which asserts that investors alternate between heuristic and systematic processing based on situational needs. In stable market conditions, investors may possess the cognitive ability to do more systematic and deliberate decision-making, performing comprehensive evaluations of market data and patterns. In volatile markets marked by uncertainty and fast change, cognitive demands escalate, prompting investors to depend increasingly on heuristic processing. The framework indicates that heightened dependence on heuristics in these contexts intensifies the probability of biassed decision-making and inferior investment results. Nonetheless, it recognises that heuristics can be adaptable, allowing investors to make rapid judgements amidst an excess of information (Barua, 2024).

The dependent variable in this framework, investment decision-making, is influenced by the interplay of various heuristics. Investment decisions are perceived as outcomes of investors' information processing amidst differing levels of market volatility and cognitive load. The paradigm asserts that heuristic-based decision-making results in several biases, including overconfidence, herding, and risk aversion, which subsequently influence market dynamics such as asset pricing, volatility, and liquidity. It underscores that although heuristics frequently result in biassed decision-making, they are not intrinsically detrimental (Koech, 2021). In specific situations, such as when information is scarce or time is restricted, heuristics can offer investors a practical shortcut for making effective judgements. The primary concern is the erroneous use of these heuristics in volatile markets, where the swift rate of change necessitates more flexible and methodical decision-making processes.

The conceptual framework recognises that individual differences influence investors' reliance on heuristics. Experience, education, risk tolerance, and cultural background are likely to modulate the degree to which heuristics affect decision-making. For instance, seasoned investors may possess a superior ability to identify the constraints of heuristics and modify their tactics accordingly. The methodology also evaluates the influence of developing technologies, such algorithmic trading and data analytics, which have revolutionised how investors collect and analyse information (Barua, 2024). These technologies can either alleviate or exacerbate the impact of heuristics, contingent upon their application.

CONCLUSION

This study concludes that heuristics significantly influence investment decision-making, especially in volatile markets. The study conducts a thorough analysis of cognitive biases, including the representativeness heuristic, availability heuristic, confirmation bias, and mental accounting, illustrating how these cognitive shortcuts can result in both beneficial and detrimental investment behaviours. The findings indicate that whereas heuristics assist investors in managing complex and uncertain environments, they concurrently add systemic biases that might impair rational decision-making and result in inferior financial outcomes.

This research concludes that heuristics are intrinsic to human cognition, especially under conditions of significant ambiguity and information overload. In financial markets, where volatility can swiftly alter risk and return dynamics, investors frequently lack the time or cognitive ability to systematically absorb all available information. Consequently, they depend on heuristics to streamline their decision-making processes. Nevertheless, the study reveals that these heuristics, albeit effective, may result in enduring cognitive biases. The representativeness heuristic prompts investors to overvalue superficial resemblances between current investments and historical triumphs, but the availability heuristic drives them to overrate the likelihood of recent or notable market occurrences. Both heuristics, within the framework of volatile markets, lead to amplified market responses and heightened price volatility.

The study shows that confirmation bias significantly exacerbates the reinforcement of bad investment choices. Investors exhibit overconfidence in their market assessments by pursuing information that validates their pre-existing ideas while ignoring opposing facts. This overconfidence results in an inability to adjust to fluctuating market conditions, thereby elevating the risk of financial losses during times of increased volatility. The study underscores the influence of mental accounting in intensifying irrational investment behaviours, since individuals segregate their portfolios in manners that hinder the adoption of a more comprehensive and adaptable strategy to risk management. This inclination is especially detrimental in unstable markets, when inflexible mental accounting methods may hinder investors from reallocating resources in reaction to fluctuating economic or financial circumstances.

The study also highlights the connection between individual variations and heuristic-driven decision-making. Heuristics impact all investors to some extent, although the degree of influence on investment decisions is regulated by characteristics including experience, education, and risk tolerance. Seasoned investors may be more proficient at identifying and alleviating the impacts of cognitive biases, whereas beginner investors tend to depend significantly on heuristics, especially in turbulent markets. This research indicates that educational interventions and knowledge of cognitive biases may enhance investment outcomes, especially for novice market participants.

Moreover, the study determines that technology innovations in the financial sector exert a twofold influence on heuristic-based decision-making. Algorithmic trading and data analytics can alleviate the cognitive burden on investors by offering more systematic decision-making methodologies. Conversely, the surge of financial news, social media, and real-time data might intensify heuristic biases by enhancing the accessibility of prominent, although perhaps deceptive, information. The study emphasises the necessity for additional research on the interaction between technology and cognitive biases, especially within the framework of increasingly unpredictable and linked global markets.

The overarching implication of these findings is that heuristic-driven biases are not solely individual cognitive errors but can collectively impact market dynamics. When substantial cohorts of investors concurrently depend on identical heuristics, particularly during episodes of market panic or euphoria, these biases may result in herding behaviour, asset bubbles, or market collapses. This underscores the systemic hazards associated with cognitive biases in financial markets, especially in emerging nations where volatility is typically more severe and market information is often less accurate. The research indicates that mitigating these biases is essential for both boosting individual investing results and augmenting market stability and efficiency.

Theoretical, Managerial and Policy Implications

This study's theoretical implications enhance the current understanding of behavioural finance by providing a detailed insight into the influence of heuristics on investing decision-making, especially in volatile markets. Conventional financial models, based on the Efficient Market Hypothesis (EMH) and rational choice theory, presuppose that investors behave rationally and that markets function efficiently through the consolidation of all accessible information. This study adds to the expanding literature that contests these assumptions by emphasising the widespread impact of cognitive biases, particularly heuristics, on actual investment behaviour. The study highlights that, rather than being entirely rational, investors frequently utilise cognitive heuristics to traverse intricate financial landscapes. This dependence on heuristics can lead to systematic errors that impact both individual investment results and the overall efficiency of the market. The paper advocates for a reconceptualisation of investor behaviour models, proposing an integrated approach that combines logical and behavioural elements to more effectively elucidate market dynamics, especially during times of increased uncertainty and volatility.

The study further enhances the dual-process theory of decision-making by offering empirical evidence for the interplay between heuristic and systematic processing in financial circumstances. The results indicate that investors alternate between these two cognitive modes depending on their cognitive load, time limitations, and the perceived adequacy of available information. This has significant implications for the advancement of more comprehensive decision-making models, especially in dynamic and rapidly changing financial markets. The research enhances comprehension of individual variances in heuristic processing, indicating that experience, education, and risk tolerance significantly influence the effects of cognitive biases. Future theoretical frameworks must consider these individual characteristics to offer a more comprehensive understanding of how cognitive biases influence decision-making in financial markets.

The study provides essential insights for financial institutions, fund managers, and investment advisors to alleviate the adverse effects of heuristics on investment decision-making. The acknowledgement that cognitive biases, including the representativeness heuristic, availability heuristic, confirmation bias, and mental accounting, skew investor assessments has considerable ramifications for the formulation of investment strategies and client advisory services. Investment professionals can gain from comprehending the manifestation of these biases, especially during market volatility, and should create strategies to assist customers in surmounting them. For example, fund managers may integrate bias-correcting mechanisms into their decision-making processes by employing decision-support systems that promote systematic analysis and diminish dependence on intuitive judgements.

This may entail employing algorithmic trading models that are less vulnerable to cognitive biases or incorporating behavioural insights into portfolio management methods, including debiasing procedures that consider investor psychology. Portfolio rebalancing algorithms could be developed to mitigate mental accounting by promoting a comprehensive perspective on assets, rather than segregating investments into several mental accounts. Furthermore, financial advisers can leverage these insights to enhance client communication by educating them on prevalent cognitive biases and employing organised decision-making frameworks that facilitate more informed and less emotionally-driven investment choices.

The report highlights the significance of investor education for financial firms. By providing educational programs that emphasise the recognition and alleviation of prevalent cognitive biases, organisations can enable their clients to make more informed decisions. This enhances client happiness and long-term financial performance while mitigating the risk of panic-induced behaviours, such as liquidating assets during market declines or over-investing in speculative bubbles. Furthermore, the study's findings regarding confirmation bias underscore the necessity for managers and advisers to promote the pursuit of disconfirming evidence among customers and to foster a more analytical approach to information acquisition.

The study's findings indicate that regulatory authorities and policymakers must consider behavioural biases when formulating frameworks for investor protection and market stability. Conventional regulatory frameworks frequently presume that investors are rational agents capable of making informed choices based on the disclosure of pertinent information. This study demonstrates that, despite the availability of information, investors are susceptible to biases that result in the misinterpretation or selective disregard of critical data. Consequently, regulators ought to contemplate behavioural interventions, or "nudges," that can facilitate more rational decision-making among investors while preserving their autonomy.

A possible policy implication is the integration of default alternatives or decision aids that alleviate the effects of cognitive biases. Retirement savings strategies should incorporate default asset allocations that mitigate the risks associated with mental accounting and confirmation bias. Likewise, financial literacy initiatives funded by governmental or regulatory entities should emphasise not just the instruction of investors regarding market fundamentals but also the enhancement of understanding concerning prevalent cognitive biases and strategies to mitigate them. These programs may be especially advantageous for beginner investors, who tend to depend on heuristics and are consequently more susceptible to the distortions introduced by these biases.

Limitations and Recommendations for Future Studies

The study's principal drawback is its dependence on particular cognitive heuristics, specifically the representativeness heuristic, availability heuristic, confirmation bias, and mental accounting. Although these are extensively acknowledged and examined in behavioural finance, they do not represent the complete spectrum of cognitive biases that can affect investment decision-making. Other biases, such anchoring, overconfidence, and loss aversion, may significantly influence investor behaviour, especially in volatile markets. Future research could broaden its focus by investigating a wider range of heuristics and biases to achieve a more thorough comprehension of cognitive distortions in financial decision-making. This would provide a more sophisticated understanding of the interplay and compounding effects of various biases, hence affecting investment decisions and market dynamics.

A further drawback is the cross-sectional nature of the data, which offers a snapshot of investor behaviour at a particular moment in time. While the study provides significant insights into the influence of heuristics on decision-making, it fails to comprehensively address the evolution of these cognitive biases across time. Investor behaviour, especially regarding the assimilation of past experiences and the adaptation to new information, is fundamentally dynamic. Longitudinal studies would enhance comprehension of how heuristics affect decision-making across various market cycles, including phases of prolonged boom, crisis, and recovery. Subsequent studies may monitor investors over prolonged durations, facilitating the examination of how biases emerge and evolve in response to market fluctuations and when investors acquire greater expertise or undergo additional educational interventions.

This study primarily examines individual investors; although the conclusions are pertinent to personal decision-making processes, they may not comprehensively address the intricacies of institutional investing. Institutional investors, including hedge funds, pension funds, and mutual funds, function under distinct limitations and possess varying access to information relative to individual investors. Their decision-making processes may incorporate advanced risk management techniques and methodical analysis, perhaps alleviating some cognitive biases common among retail investors. Future study ought to investigate the function of heuristics in institutional investment, especially within high-frequency trading contexts that necessitate swift decision-making. This would offer a comprehensive picture of how biases influence the overall financial system and market dynamics.

The study is limited by its geographic and market environment. The preponderance of current behavioural finance studies has been undertaken in developed economies, especially in North America and Europe, where financial infrastructure, regulatory systems, and investor behaviour markedly contrast with those in emerging nations. This study, mostly based on literature from developed markets, may not be entirely applicable to emerging nations, where market volatility, information asymmetries, and investor sophistication differ significantly. Subsequent research should concentrate on emerging markets, where the incidence of cognitive biases may be exacerbated by variables such as diminished financial literacy, inadequate regulatory monitoring, and limited access to advanced financial products. This research will enhance the worldwide comprehension of behavioural finance, particularly as emerging markets assume a progressively significant position in the global economy.

A pertinent drawback is the possible impact of cultural influences on heuristic-based decision-making. Cognitive biases are frequently analysed through the lens of Western psychological frameworks; however, the literature extensively documents cultural variations in decision-making, risk perception, and information processing. Investors in collectivist cultures may demonstrate distinct biases relative to those in individualist cultures, especially regarding herding behaviour or risk aversion. Future study should investigate how cultural characteristics influence the impact of heuristics on investment decision-making, employing cross-cultural comparisons to discern the manifestation of biases across diverse economic, social, and regulatory contexts. This would provide significant insights for international financial institutions and governments functioning within varied cultural environments.

The study's methodological dependence on self-reported data, especially via surveys and questionnaires, presents the potential for response biases, including social desirability bias and recall bias. Investors may not consistently provide accurate accounts of their decision-making processes, either due to unawareness of their biases or a desire to portray themselves as more rational or systematic than they actually are. To address this shortcoming, subsequent studies should utilise more objective data collection approaches, such as experimental designs or the examination of actual trading behaviour via broking account data. Experimental approaches provide a controlled environment to isolate the effects of specific heuristics on decision-making, whereas analysing real-world trade data offers actual evidence of how biases affect financial results.

REFERENCES

Akepanidtaworn, K., Mascio, R. D., Imas, A., & Schmidt, L. D. (2023). Selling fast and buying slow: Heuristics and trading performance of institutional investors. *The Journal of Finance*, 78(6), 3055–3098. DOI: 10.1111/jofi.13271

Baloch, S. A., Jatoi, I. A., Ayubi, S., & Raza, K. M. (2024). Mitigating Role of Covid-19 in Relationship between Behavioral Factors of Investors. *KASBIT Business Journal, 17*(1).

Barua, S. (2024). International entrepreneurial orientation and firm performance: the inter-relation between dimensions of EO and impacts on firm international performance.

Dixit, D. K. (2024). Investor Psychology and Market Volatility: Unpacking Behavioral Finance Insights. *Journal of Informatics Education and Research*, 4(2).

FaXing. L., & Loang, O. K. (2024). Green Investing and Financial Education: The Case of China's A-Share Market. In *Technology-Driven Business Innovation: Unleashing the Digital Advantage, Volume 1* (pp. 29-41). Cham: Springer Nature Switzerland.

Hao, X., Demir, E., & Eyers, D. (2024). Exploring collaborative decision-making: A quasi-experimental study of human and Generative AI interaction. *Technology in Society*, 78, 102662. DOI: 10.1016/j.techsoc.2024.102662

Iram, T., Bilal, A. R., & Ahmad, Z. (2023). Investigating the mediating role of financial literacy on the relationship between women entrepreneurs' behavioral biases and investment decision making. *Gadjah Mada International Journal of Business*, 25(1), 93–118. DOI: 10.22146/gamaijb.65457

Ireland, D. (2022). Regret and Regulation. The Power of Regret, Power of Persuasion and the Regulatory Compliance/Non-Compliance Continuum: Better Understanding Compliance Through the Prism of Regret. *The Power of Regret, Power of Persuasion and the Regulatory Compliance/Non-Compliance Continuum: Better Understanding Compliance Through the Prism of Regret (October 4, 2022).*

Jing, W., & Loang, O. K. (2024). Live Streaming of E-Commerce in China: Evidence from Impulsive Chinese Tea Purchases. In *Opportunities and Risks in AI for Business Development* (Vol. 1, pp. 1063–1079). Springer Nature Switzerland. DOI: 10.1007/978-3-031-65203-5_91

Koech, A. (2021). The availability Heuristic Effect on Financial performance of small and Medium Enterprises in Nairobi, Kenya: The mediating role of investment decisions. *American Journal of Education*, 6(2).

Lanju, T., & Loang, O. K. (2024). Unraveling the Fintech Puzzle: Technology Shaping Commercial Bank Lending Risk. In *Opportunities and Risks in AI for Business Development* (Vol. 1, pp. 915–923). Springer Nature Switzerland. DOI: 10.1007/978-3-031-65203-5_78

Loang, O. K. (2023). Corporate governance and Islamic behavioural finance: A review from Malaysia and GCC countries. *Indian Journal of Corporate Governance*, 16(1), 28–51. DOI: 10.1177/09746862231178959

Loang, O. K. (2024). Stability Of Shariah-Compliant Stocks In Indonesia, Malaysia, And Gcc: The Roles Of Monetary And Fiscal Policies And Contagion. *Journal of Islamic Monetary Economics and Finance*, 10(1), 155–176. DOI: 10.21098/jimf.v10i1.1899

Loang, O. K. (2024). Sustainability's impact of ESG-infused policies on leading economic indicators in Asian economies. *Journal of Sustainable Research*, 6(3), e240059. DOI: 10.20900/jsr20240059

Marvin, J. A. (2023). *Workplace Digitization: An Exploration of the Effects the Accelerating Nature of Disruptions Caused by Advances in Technology are Having on Front-Line Mangers and Their Teams in Industry* (Doctoral dissertation, Northeastern University).

Mawson, S., & Casulli, L. (2024). Entrepreneurial Thinking: Mindset in Action.

Suresh, G., & Loang, O. K. (2024). The Rationality Conundrum: Exploring Herd Mentality among Individual Investors in the Indian Stock Market. *Indian Journal of Finance*, 18(6), 26–45. DOI: 10.17010/ijf/2024/v18i6/173967

Chapter 10

Emerging Markets Dynamics effect on Ethical Investment Behavior With Mediation of Investment Strategies in Ethiopia

Shashi Kant
https://orcid.org/0000-0003-4722-5736
Bule Hora University, Ethiopia

Metasebia Adula
https://orcid.org/0000-0001-5732-2850
Bule Hora University, Ethiopia

Nitu Nimbrain
https://orcid.org/0000-0001-5585-3287
IMSAR, India

Mona Kumari
https://orcid.org/0009-0001-0476-5831
Government College for Women, Bahadurgarh, India

ABSTRACT

With an emphasis on the mediating function of investment strategies in the context of Ethiopia, this study investigates the impact of rising market dynamics on moral investing behavior. A survey was conducted with a sample of 400 participants,

DOI: 10.4018/979-8-3693-8583-8.ch010

comprising individual investors in Ethiopia, investment managers, and financial advisers. To find the underlying dimensions, exploratory factor analysis (EFA) and confirmatory factor analysis (CFA) were used. The data's appropriateness for factor analysis was evaluated using Bartlett's test of sphericity and the Kaiser-Meyer-Olkin (KMO) measure of sampling adequacy. After that, the mediating function of investment strategies was investigated using structural equation modeling (SEM). The study's findings offer important new insights into how the adoption and development of ethical investing practices in Ethiopia's financial sector might be influenced by the changing dynamics of developing markets in conjunction with the tactical application of investment strategies.

INTRODUCTION

With Ethiopia growing as a major actor on the African continent, the dynamics of emerging markets have grown in significance in the context of the global economy. Ethiopia, the second-most populous nation in Africa with one of the fastest-growing economies, has drawn interest from investors and decision-makers throughout the globe due to its economic trajectory. In this regard, a promising field for research is the junction of ethical investing behavior and investment techniques in the Ethiopian market (Zhang & Berhe, 2022). As investors and organizations look to match their financial decisions with their values and social impact objectives, the idea of ethical investment behavior—which is based on the concepts of socially responsible investing, or SRI—has gained popularity on a worldwide scale. Ethiopia's fast economic development together with its distinct cultural, social, and environmental factors highlight the need of comprehending how the dynamics of the emerging market impact and shape ethical investing behavior (Shonte & Ji, 2022).

The variables that influence investor decision-making, the incorporation of environmental, social, and governance (ESG) criteria, and the performance of ethical investment funds are just a few of the facets of ethical investing behavior that have been examined in the empirical literature that currently exists. The unique characteristics of developing markets, like Ethiopia, and their impact on moral investing practices, however, have not received much attention. This knowledge gap in the literature offers a chance to advance our understanding of how developing market dynamics interact with moral investment choices (Waktola et al., 2024). A lack of standardized ESG reporting standards, a lack of investor knowledge and comprehension of ethical investing practices, and potential legal barriers that might prevent the implementation of ethical investment methods are some of the practical issues that Ethiopian investors may face. Furthermore, Ethiopia's distinct socioeconomic and cultural characteristics could influence investor perceptions and choices differently than they would in more developed markets (Erena et al., 2024).

By examining the connection between developing market dynamics, moral investment conduct, and the mediating function of investment strategies in the context of Ethiopia, this chapter seeks to close these gaps and tackle these difficulties. The chapter offered the insightful information for future scholars and policymakers aiming to promote a more sustainable and socially responsible investment environment by exploring the elements that impact ethical investment decisions. This chapter advances the knowledge of how the dynamics of Ethiopia's emerging market influence ethical investment behavior and investor strategies through a thorough analysis of pertinent literature, primary data collection, and empirical investigation. The results of this study will have practical implications for financial institutions, investment professionals, and policymakers. These implications will help them in the development of efficient policies, regulations, and investment products that are in line with the changing ethical preferences of investors in Ethiopia and other emerging markets.

Background of the Study

The investment environment and investor behavior are greatly impacted by the dynamic nature of developing countries, like Ethiopia. Ethiopia, an emerging country, has grown at an average annual GDP growth rate of almost 10% between 2010 and 2020 (Hagos, 2022). Ethiopia has seen extraordinary economic progress in recent years. Investors from outside and domestically are taking notice of this country's fast economic growth and are looking for ways to get involved in its development (Qiu, 2022). However, a variety of economic, political, social, and cultural elements have molded Ethiopia's complex and varied investment landscape. The nation's distinct socioeconomic circumstances, which include its sizable populace, primarily agricultural economy, and substantial growth obstacles, have an impact on investors' investment tactics and decision-making procedures (Zhou et al., 2023).

As investors and organizations look to match their financial aims with their values and social impact objectives, ethical investing behavior—which takes into account the social, environmental, and governance (ESG) aspects of investment decisions—has gained importance on a worldwide scale. The inclusion of ethical concerns in investment plans is especially important in emerging economies like Ethiopia, where there are frequently urgent sustainability difficulties including social inequality, environmental degradation, and governance problems (Desaleg & Solomon, 2023). The dynamics of markets, institutional frameworks, and individual investor traits have all been examined in the empirical literature that currently exists (Waktola et al., 2024). However, there hasn't been as much focus on the unique characteristics of developing economies and how they affect moral investing practices. Ethiopia's investment environment offers a chance to investigate the relationship between developing market dynamics and moral investing practices because of its distinct economic, social, and legal framework (Mehari et al., 2024). When developing investment products, rules, and policies that address the changing ethical concerns of investors in Ethiopia and other emerging markets, financial institutions, policy-makers, and investment professionals can all benefit from an understanding of this relationship (Shitaye, 2024).

Furthermore, a critical component that needs more research is the mediating function that investment strategies play in influencing the connection between the dynamics of developing markets and moral investing practices (Kant & Adula, 2024). Investment methods, which include things like portfolio diversification, risk management, and asset allocation, may have an impact on how investors integrate ethical issues into their decision-making. This chapter creates the groundwork for a thorough investigation of the dynamic interactions between developing market variables, moral investment conduct, and the mediating function of investment strategies by analyzing the background and context of the Ethiopian investment environment. The outcomes of this study will enhance the comprehension of ethical decision-making in emerging markets and offer useful recommendations for investors, financial establishments, and legislators in cultivating an environmentally friendly and socially conscious investment atmosphere in Ethiopia and other regions.

Statement of the Problem

When investors completely include ethical factors—such as environmental, social, and governance (ESG) factors—into their investment decision-making processes, the Ethiopian emerging market would be the best place for investment activity (Dereso et al., 2023; Durga et al., 2024). In such a situation, investors would actively look for investment opportunities that support the nation's sustainable growth by producing financial benefits in addition to good social and environmental effects (Waktola et al., 2024). Nonetheless, conflicting data and gaps in the body of extant research frequently define Ethiopia's present investment environment (Adula et al., 2023). While some study indicates that investors in developing countries are taking ethical considerations into account more often when making investment decisions, other studies reveal that investors' ethical investing behavior is still restricted and that their main concern is still maximizing financial gains (Panigrahi et al., 2024; Zhou et al., 2023). These ambiguous findings highlight the need for a more thorough comprehension of the variables influencing moral investing conduct in the context of Ethiopia's developing market (Jabo et al., 2024). There are theoretical gaps in the literature because the frameworks and models that have been created in the setting of more developed markets may not adequately represent the particular dynamics and difficulties that investors in developing nations such as Ethiopia encounter (Nyoach et al., 2024; Mu et al., 2023). Furthermore, there are a lot of unanswered questions about the particular elements that affect Ethiopian investors' decisions to make moral investments. These include the effect of institutional and regulatory frameworks, the role of cultural and social norms, and the impact of investment strategies on the incorporation of ethical issues (Kumera et al., 2024).

There are other difficulties in the Ethiopian emerging market scenario that the corpus of current research may not fully address. Ethiopia's fast changing social, political, and economic landscapes along with its own regulatory framework and culture may have a big influence on how investors behave and embrace ethical investing techniques (Bonsu et al., 2024). Practical issues like investors' lack of knowledge and comprehension of ethical investment practices, the absence of established ESG reporting guidelines, and possible regulatory barriers exacerbate the issue and emphasize the necessity of a thorough analysis of the phenomenon (Wang et al., 2023).

By carefully examining the link between developing market dynamics, moral investing behavior, and the mediating function of investment strategies in the context of Ethiopia, this study seeks to close these gaps. The study will offer insightful information and a clear path forward for future scholars and policymakers aiming to promote a more sustainable and socially responsible investment environment in Ethiopia and other emerging economies by tackling the theoretical, knowledge, and practical issues. The research outcomes of this study will enhance the overall comprehension of moral decision-making in emerging economies, providing useful insights for financial institutions, legislators, and investment experts. In the end, this understanding may guide the creation of sensible laws, rules, and financial products that satisfy investors' changing ethical standards.

THEORETICAL FOUNDATION

The Theory of Planned Behavior (TPB), created by Ajzen (1991), is the first relevant theory. According to this idea, a person's views, perceived behavioral control, and subjective norms all have an impact on their conduct. The TPB can be used to explain how investors' attitudes toward ethical issues, their perceptions of social pressure to make ethical investments, and their perceived capacity to integrate ethical considerations into their decisions can influence their real investment behavior in the context of ethical investing (Waktola et al., 2024; Asefa et al., 2023). The Stakeholder Theory, put out by Freeman (1984), is another significant theory. According to this idea, in addition to shareholders, businesses and investments should take into account the interests of other stakeholders, such as workers, vendors, consumers, and the general public. When it comes to moral investing, the Stakeholder Theory can provide insights into how investors may weigh the interests of different stakeholders when making investment decisions (Zhou et al., 2023).

Additional pertinent ideas can be obtained from DiMaggio and Powell's (1983) Institutional Theory. According to this idea, the institutional environment, which consists of formal and informal regulations, norms, and cultural-cognitive components, shapes both organizational and individual behavior (Guyo et al., 2023). The Institutional Theory may be used to explain how the political, social, and regulatory aspects of Ethiopia's developing market affect investors' attitudes and actions regarding ethical issues in the context of ethical investing (Kumera et al., 2024). In addition, the Modern Portfolio Theory (MPT), created by Sharpe in 1964, and the Portfolio Theory, first put out by Markowitz in 1952, offer a framework for comprehending how investors allocate their assets and control risk. These theories can clarify how investing tactics like diversification and asset allocation influence Ethiopian investors' moral investment decisions (Ofosu-Mensah et al., 2024). Lastly, the Legitimacy Theory, as articulated by Suchman (1995), proposes that in order to maintain their legitimacy, people and organizations should try to fit in with society's norms and expectations. The Legitimacy Theory may be used to describe how investors could embrace ethical investing practices in the context of ethical investment in order to preserve their reputation and perceived legitimacy within the Ethiopian investment community (Demessie & Shukla, 2024).

Definition and Origin of Concept

The phrase "emerging markets" describes economies that are rapidly industrializing and developing economically; these markets are frequently characterized by strong growth potential but also by substantial developmental obstacles. The World Bank and the International Finance Corporation (IFC) coined the term "emerging markets" in the late 1980s to refer to countries that were moving from being low-income to middle-income (Zhou et al., 2023). These markets still face structural, institutional, and regulatory barriers that set them apart from more developed markets, but they are generally characterized by their rapid economic growth, sizable populations, and growing integration into the global financial system (Ofosu-Mensah et al., 2024). The integration of environmental, social, and governance (ESG) considerations into investment decision-making processes is referred to as ethical investing behavior, which is sometimes referred to as socially responsible investment (SRI) or sustainable investment (Bonsu et al., 2024). This strategy stresses the connection of investment decisions with ethical and sustainability issues, moving beyond the typical focus on financial returns and risk management. When social movements and religious groups started removing specific businesses, including tobacco and guns, from their investment portfolios in the 1960s and 1970s, that is when ethical investing first emerged Demessie & Shukla (2024). Climate change, human rights, labor practices, and corporate governance are just a few of the ESG aspects that have been included in the idea of ethical investing over time (Kumera et al., 2024).

The techniques and procedures investors employ to control risk, allocate capital, and pursue their investing goals are referred to as investment strategies. These tactics can include diversification (spreading investments across several industries or sectors to reduce risk), asset allocation (distributing investments across various asset classes, such as stocks, bonds, and real estate), and risk management strategies (such as hedging or the use of derivatives). The degree to which investment decisions are in line with sustainability and ethical principles can be greatly influenced by the techniques chosen. Investors may decide, for instance, to put aside a certain percentage of their portfolio for "green" or "socially responsible" investments, or they may use ESG considerations while choosing assets and managing risk (Habtemaryam et al. (2024)).

EMPIRICAL LITERATURE REVIEW

Emerging Markets Dynamics and Ethical Investment Behavior

Numerous scholarly investigations have revealed that investors in developing economies are progressively taking ethical considerations into account when making investment decisions. Waktola et al. (2024), for instance, saw an increasing trend of institutional investors implementing ESG factors into their investment strategies in emerging economies like Brazil and South Africa. Similar findings were made by Zhang & Berhe (2022), who discovered that social and regulatory constraints have propelled the South African pension fund sector to become a leader in the implementation of responsible investment methods.

Nonetheless, alternative studies indicate that ethical investment practices are still scarce in developing economies, since investors' primary concern is optimizing their financial gains. Kumera et al., (2024) discovered that, in contrast to their home market, Swedish investors demonstrated less ethical investment behavior while making investments in developing economies because they believed there were more financial risks and less ESG transparency. Additionally, ethical investment funds in emerging economies typically underperform their conventional equivalents, as reported by Habtemaryam et al. (2024). This might deter investors from adopting ethical investment methods. The experiences of more developed economies, such the United States and Western Europe, have theoretically served as the foundation for the majority of the frameworks and models created to explain ethical investing behavior (Erena et al., 2024). The distinct dynamics and difficulties experienced by investors in emerging nations, where institutional, regulatory, and cultural issues may have a greater influence on investment behavior, may not be adequately represented by these models.

Emerging Market Dynamics and Investment Strategies

The importance of institutional and regulatory elements has been thoroughly examined in relation to developing market dynamics. Investment strategies may be influenced by a number of factors, including the degree of capital market development, investor protection strength, and institutional quality in developing countries, according to several research Zhou et al. (2023) for instance, showed that because it is easier for investors to exercise their rights and reduce risk, they often allocate a bigger percentage of their portfolios to companies based in nations with better investor protection. In a similar vein, Zhang & Berhe (2022) noted that companies operating in developing economies with less robust institutional frameworks are more inclined to cross-list their shares on more established stock exchanges in order to demonstrate their quality and reach a wider range of potential buyers. Consequently, this might have an impact on the investing approaches of both foreign and local investors who aim to get exposure to these cross-listed companies.

The degree of information asymmetry and market integration is a crucial component of rising market dynamics. Tolossa et al. (2024) discovered that investors tend to change their strategies toward more diversified portfolios when developing nations integrate more fully into the global financial system, taking advantage of the advantages of international portfolio diversity. On the other hand, investors may choose to pursue more cautious approaches as a result of information asymmetries and opacity in emerging markets (Desaleg & Solomon, 2023). Examples of such tactics include favoring larger, more established companies with stronger disclosure standards. Investment strategies have also been demonstrated to be influenced by the risk and volatility characteristics of developing markets. According to Erena et al. (2024), investors in developing countries frequently use dynamic asset allocation techniques, modifying their portfolios in reaction to shifting risk perceptions and market conditions. To reduce negative risks, this may involve using hedging tools like derivatives.

Investment Strategies and Ethical Investment Behavior

Ethical investing methods' performance and risk-return characteristics have been a major focus of study in this field. According to a number of studies, investing techniques that take environmental, social, and governance (ESG) factors into account can yield financial returns that are comparable to, or often even higher than, those of traditional investment methods. For instance, a meta-analysis of more than 2,000 empirical research by Desaleg & Solomon (2023) revealed a favorable association between firm financial success and ESG integration. In a similar vein, Demessie & Shukla (2024) found that investing strategies that prioritized ESG-related elements—including sustainability and energy efficiency—performed better than the overall market in growing nations like China and Poland. These results imply that financial performance goals and ethical investing methods may be matched, which might persuade more investors to embrace

Nevertheless, other research has shown that the particular ESG standards and investing methods used can have an impact on how well ethical investment strategies succeed. According to Tolossa et al. (2024), the screening techniques employed can affect how well ethical investment funds perform financially. Certain procedures, including exclusionary screening, may cause these funds to perform worse than conventional funds. The extant research has not only looked at financial success, but also at how investment strategies influence investor attitudes and decision-making processes with respect to moral investing behavior. According to Zhang & Berhe (2022) research, investors who utilize more involved and active investment strategies—like impact investing and shareholder engagement—tend to be more committed to ethical and sustainable issues than those who use more passive strategies, like index investing. Additionally, the literature now in publication has emphasized how critical it is to match investing strategies to the unique ESG goals and risk tolerances of investors. According to Erena et al. (2024), investors that prioritize sustainability and have a long-term investment perspective typically choose investing strategies that integrate environmental, social, and governance (ESG) considerations into risk management and portfolio creation.

Investment Strategies, Emerging Market Dynamics and Ethical Investment Behavior

The quality of institutions, degree of market integration, and volatility of financial markets are examples of developing market characteristics that may significantly influence the investment strategies chosen by both domestic and international investors, as was covered in the preceding sections. The degree to which investors take environmental, social, and governance (ESG) considerations into account when making decisions can therefore be influenced by these tactics (Desaleg & Solomon, 2023). The significance of investment strategies as a mediating factor in the link between ethical investing behavior and market features has been emphasized in a number of research. For instance, Habtemaryam et al. (2024) discovered that investors are more inclined to support investment strategies that combine ESG criteria, such as impact investing and active ownership, if they have a long-term investment horizon and prioritize sustainability. This implies that investors' investment methods may have an impact on the link between market variables, such the degree of market development and volatility, and moral investing behavior.

In a similar vein, Tolossa et al. (2024) noted that the particular screening techniques and investing strategies employed can have an impact on the financial success of ethical investment funds. In turn, this may have an impact on investor attitudes and the uptake of moral investing principles, especially in developing economies where investors may be more perceptive to financial risks and rewards. Moreover, extant literature has underscored the significance of information asymmetry and disclosure practices in developing markets as pivotal elements that influence investment strategies and, by extension, ethical investing conduct. Demessie & Shukla (2024) discovered that larger, more recognizable companies with superior disclosure processes are often preferred by investors in emerging countries.

CONCEPTUAL FRAMEWORK

Figure 1. Conceptual framework

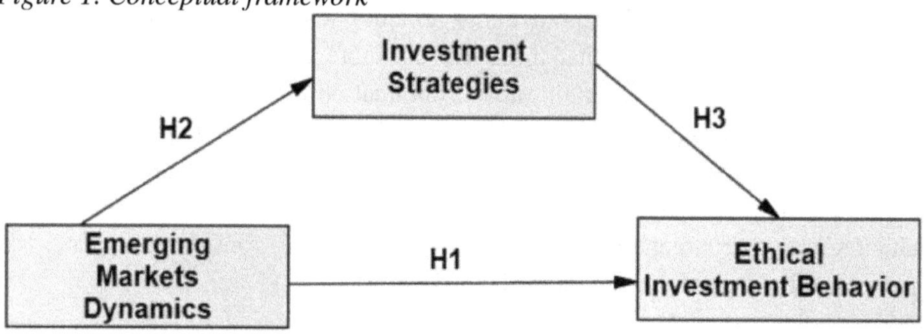

RESEARCH METHODOLOGY

In the context of the Ethiopian emerging market, this study used a quantitative research methodology to examine the mediating function of investment strategies in the link between emerging market dynamics and ethical investing behavior. A mix of convenience and snowball sampling approaches was used to choose 390 individual investors and investment professionals for the sample. A systematic questionnaire was created and distributed as part of the data gathering procedure. After making the required adjustments to guarantee their applicability to the Ethiopian setting, the questionnaire questions were modified from previously validated scales in the body of research. Bekaert and Harvey (2003), Giannetti and Koskinen (2010), and Nilsson (2008), respectively, are the authors of the metrics for emerging market dynamics, investment strategies, and ethical investing behavior.

The procedure of developing the scale was carried out step-by-step. In order to determine the important dimensions and measurement components for each construct, a thorough literature study was first conducted. After that, a team of experts, comprising academics and investment professionals in Ethiopia, evaluated the content validity of the scales. A few small changes were made to the questionnaire items' language and structure in response to their suggestions. A number of statistical studies were then performed to look into the construct validity of the measures. The data's appropriateness for factor analysis was evaluated using Bartlett's test of sphericity and the Kaiser-Meyer-Olkin (KMO) measure of sampling adequacy. To determine the underlying factor structure of the constructs and confirm the one-dimensionality of the data, exploratory factor analysis (EFA) was used.

Cronbach's alpha coefficients were used to assess the measures' reliability, and items with low factor loadings or cross-loadings were eliminated from the final scales. The final scales showed respectable degrees of internal consistency, and for every construct, the Cronbach's alpha values were higher than the suggested cutoff of 0.70. Using structural equation modeling (SEM) and the AMOS program, the proposed links between emerging market dynamics, investment strategies, and ethical investing behavior were investigated. A variety of goodness-of-fit indices were used to evaluate the model fit, including the Root Mean Square Error of Approximation (RMSEA), the Tucker-Lewis Index (TLI), the Chi-square test, and the Comparative Fit Index (CFI).

Using the methodology suggested by Baron and Kenny (1986), the mediation analysis looked at the indirect impact of developing market dynamics on moral investing behavior through investment strategies. Using 5,000 bootstrap samples and a 95% confidence range, the bootstrapping approach was used to evaluate the significance of the indirect impact. The study's conclusions offer insightful information on the intricate interactions that exist between investors' investment strategies, their ethical investing behavior, and the distinctive features of Ethiopia's developing market. The findings add to the body of research by emphasizing how investment strategies shape the interaction between the dynamics of developing markets and the incorporation of environmental, social, and governance (ESG) aspects into investment decision-making processes within the framework of a swiftly changing, yet

DATA ANALYSIS

The KMO and the Bartlett test's conclusions, which are displayed in Table 1, show that the data gathered for this inquiry is appropriate for factor analysis. With a result of 0.850 for the Kaiser-Meyer-Olkin (KMO) measure of sampling adequacy—beyond the suggested threshold of 0.70—it is possible that the sample size has been adequate for carrying out exploratory factor analysis (EFA).

Table 1. KMO and Bartlett's Test

Kaiser-Meyer-Olkin Measure of Sampling Adequacy.		**.850**
Bartlett's Test of Sphericity	Approx. Chi-Square	1419.738
	df	91
	Sig.	.000

Source: Authors

Additionally, a chi-square value of 1419.738 with 91 degrees of freedom, which is statistically significant at the 0.000 level, was obtained using Bartlett's test of sphericity. This finding suggests that there are meaningful links between the variables, indicating that factor analysis is suitable and that the correlation matrix of the variables is not an identity matrix. The data contains enough common variance to support a meaningful EFA, as shown by the high KMO value and the substantial Bartlett's test result. Consequently, this boosts the trustworthiness of the ensuing component extraction process and the interpretation of the fundamental factor structure of the constructs assessed in this investigation. The data appears factorable overall, according to the results of the KMO and Bartlett's test, and the sample size is sufficient for the intended exploratory factor analysis to reveal the latent factor structure of the important constructs—ethical investment behavior, investment strategies, and emerging market dynamics—in the context of the Ethiopian emerging market.

Table 2. Total variance explained

Component	Initial Eigenvalues			Extraction Sums of Squared Loadings			Rotation Sums of Squared Loadings		
	Total	% of Variance	Cumulative %	Total	% of Variance	Cumulative %	Total	% of Variance	Cumulative %
1	4.51	29.84	29.845	4.5	29.84	29.845	3.0	21.45	21.451
2	1.37	9.787	42.022	1.3	9.787	42.022	2.1	15.49	36.942
3	1.27	16.80	67.065	1.2	16.86	67.065	1.9	21.16	67.065

Extraction Method: Principal Component Analysis.
Source: Authors

The findings of the total variance explained, which are shown in Table 2, offer crucial information on the fundamental factor structure of the study's constructs that were tested. The principal component analysis (PCA) extraction method was used for the analysis. Three components have eigenvalues larger than 1.0, which is a frequently used requirement for factor retention, as the first eigenvalues column demonstrates. Together, these three elements account for 67.065% of the variation in the data. The column headed "Extraction Sums of Squared Loadings" displays the percentage of variance explained by the components that were kept in place prior to rotation. Thirteen percent of the variation is explained by the third component, ninety-seven percent by the second, and twenty-nine percent by the first.

The distribution of the variance following the varimax rotation is displayed in the "Rotation Sums of Squared Loadings" column. Currently, the first component accounts for 21.451% of the variation, the second for 15.49%, and the third for 21.16% of the variance. The findings show that each of the three factors in the three-factor solution accounts for a sizable amount of the variance in the data overall, and that the factor structure is easy to understand. This implies that the questionnaire's items may be used to measure the fundamental concepts of emerging market dynamics, investment strategies, and moral investing behavior with accuracy. The construct validity of the measures employed in this study is strongly supported by the comparatively large percentages of total variation explained by the three components. As a result, there is increased confidence in the structural equation modeling (SEM) analysis that follows as well as the interpretation of the correlations between the important variables.

Confirmatory Principle Component Examination

Confirmatory principle component examination is a sort of statistics that is used to validate the principle component arrangement of a group of directed proxies. Studies can assess hypotheses using CFA based on the underlying frame job and correlatives among observable proxies. The investigation used CFA under table 3 to assess the hypothesis that there is a relationship between the proxies that are being guided and the latent ideas that support them.

Table 3. Covariances

Covariance			Approximation	S.E.	C.R.	P	Hy.
Investment Strategies	<-->	**Emerging Markets Dynamics**	**.281**	**.056**	**5.017**	***	**H2**
Investment Strategies	<-->	Ethical Investment Behavior	.452	.158	2.860	***	**H3**
Emerging Markets Dynamics	<-->	Ethical Investment Behavior	.653	.173	3.774	***	**H1**

Source: Authors

Important information on the connections between the three main research constructs—emerging market dynamics, investment strategies, and ethical investing behavior—is provided by the covariance estimates shown in Table 3. Between developing market dynamics and investment strategies, the covariance estimate is 0.281, with a critical ratio (C.R.) of 5.017 and a standard error of 0.056. This estimate's p-value is less than 0.001, indicating statistical significance. This finding indicates that changes in the features of the Ethiopian emerging market are linked to similar changes in the investment methods used by investors, supporting the hypothesis of a positive association (H2) between emerging market dynamics and investment strategies.

The covariance estimates displayed in Table 3 offer crucial details on the relationships between the three primary study constructs: developing market dynamics, investment strategies, and ethical investing behavior. The correlation estimate between evolving market dynamics and investment strategies is 0.281, with a standard error of 0.056 and a critical ratio (C.R.) of 5.017. Because the p-value for this estimate is less than 0.001, it is statistically significant. The hypothesis of a positive connection (H2) between emerging market dynamics and investment strategies is supported by this data, which shows that changes in the characteristics of the Ethiopian emerging market are associated with corresponding changes in the investment techniques employed by investors.

The study finds a 0.653 covariance estimate, a critical ratio of 3.774, and a standard error of 0.173 between developing market dynamics and ethical investing behavior. This estimate's p-value is less than 0.001, indicating statistical significance. The present study provides evidence for the hypothesis that a positive relationship (H1) exists between the dynamics of emerging markets and ethical investing behavior. Specifically, the results suggest that the distinctive features of the Ethiopian developing market are linked to investors' inclination to adopt ethical investment practices.

Table 4. Validity concern

	CR	AVE	MSV	MaxR(H)	EMD	IS	EIB
EMD	0.747	0.639	0.223	0.852	**0.668**		
IS	0.761	0.663	0.146	0.763	0.171	**0.672**	
EIB	0.805	0.611	0.281	0.797	0.383	0.193	**0.679**

Note: EMD= Emerging Markets Dynamics; IS= Investment Strategies; EIB= Ethical Investment Behavior
Source: Authors

Convergent validity, discriminant validity, and construct reliability are evaluated in order to determine the validity of the measurement model, as shown in Table 4. The three constructs' composite reliability (CR) values—emerging market dynamics (0.747), investment strategies (0.761), and ethical investment behavior (0.805)—all surpass the suggested cutoff point of 0.70, demonstrating strong internal consistency and reliability among the items within each construct. The emerging market dynamics (0.639), investment strategies (0.663), and ethical investment behavior (0.611) average variance extracted (AVE) values are all above the suggested threshold of 0.50, indicating strong convergent validity and a significant amount of shared variance among the items within each construct. The three constructs' maximum shared variance (MSV) values are all less than their corresponding AVE values, and the diagonally displayed square root of the AVE values is higher than the inter-construct correlations, suggesting that the constructs are unique from one another and share more variance with their own indicators than with other constructs. This shows that the discriminant validity is sufficient. Moreover, all three constructs' maximum reliability (MaxR(H)) values exceed their corresponding CR values, suggesting that the constructs' reliability is not overestimated. Convergent validity, discriminant validity, and construct reliability of the measuring model are all good, as shown by the data in Table 4. This gives assurance regarding the constructs' validity and reliability, which is essential for the analysis of structural equation modeling that follows and the interpretation of the correlations between the study's major variables.

Mediating Role Examination

Figure 2. Structural equation model

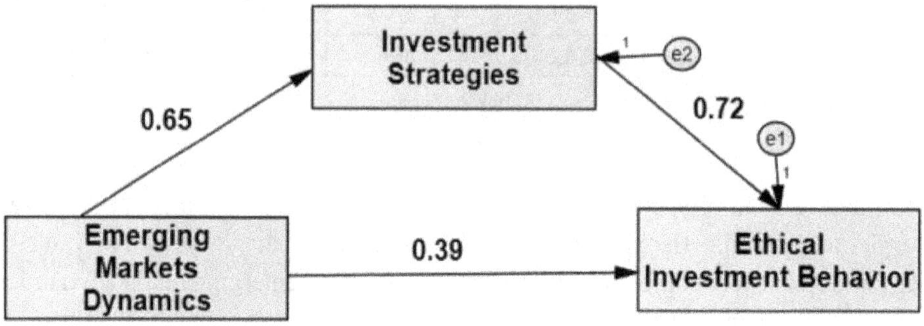

Model Fit Indices

Table 5. Indices for model fit

Sig.	Chi-Sq	RMR	Fitness Goodness	Fitness Confirmatory	TLI	RMSEA
0.004	1.116	.028	0.926	0.923	0.921	.031

Source: Authors

As shown in Table 5, the structural model fit was evaluated using a mix of absolute, incremental, and parsimonious fit indices. With a p-value of 0.004, the chi-square statistic (χ^2) is 1.116, indicating statistical significance. The chi-square test is known to be sensitive to sample size, though, and it frequently rejects well-fitting models in big samples. As a result, in order to assess the overall model fit, various fit indices must be taken into account. Since the root mean square residual (RMR) value of 0.028 is less than the suggested threshold of 0.08, it suggests that there is little difference between the sample covariance matrix and the covariance matrix inferred by the model. This suggests a strong model fit. The values of the adjusted goodness-of-fit index (AGFI) and the goodness-of-fit index (GFI) are 0.923 and 0.926, respectively. Given that the model's Tucker-Lewis index (TLI) value of 0.921 is higher than the suggested cutoff point of 0.90, it appears to have a strong incremental fit when compared to the baseline model. Ultimately, a tight match between the model and the population covariance matrix is shown by the root mean square error of approximation (RMSEA) value of 0.031, which is below the suggested criterion of 0.08. With most of the indices achieving or surpassing the suggested thresholds, the model fit indices shown in Table 5 generally imply that the structural model shows a strong match to the data. This bolsters the interpretation of the proposed linkages between the study's major components and gives confidence in the structural model's validity and dependability.

Table 6. Regression examination

Relative			**Approx.**	**S.E.**	**C.R.**	**P**	**Ass.**
Investment Strategies	**<---**	**Emerging Markets Dynamics**	**.653**	**.217**	**3.009**	***	**H2**
Ethical Investment Behavior	<---	Investment Strategies	.483	.129	3.744	***	H3
Ethical Investment Behavior	<---	Emerging Markets Dynamics	.588	.267	2.202	***	H1

Source: Authors

The findings of the structural model, which are displayed in Table 6, shed light on the links between the major research components that are hypothesized. Between developing market dynamics and investment strategies, the standardized regression estimate is 0.653, with a critical ratio (C.R.) of 3.009 and a standard error of 0.217. This estimate's p-value is less than 0.001, indicating statistical significance. This result demonstrates that changes in the Ethiopian emerging market's characteristics, such as the regulatory environment, the state of the economy, and market volatility, are significantly associated with the investment strategies used by investors in this context. It also supports the hypothesis that there is a positive relationship (H2) between emerging market dynamics and investment strategies. With a critical ratio of 3.744 and a standard error of 0.129, the standardized regression estimate between investment methods and ethical investing behavior is 0.483. This estimate's p-value is less than 0.001, indicating statistical significance. This result lends credence to the hypothesized positive relationship (H3) between investment strategies and ethical investment behavior. It implies that, within the context of Ethiopia's emerging markets, investors' adoption of investment strategies—such as the incorporation of environmental, social, and governance (ESG) factors—is positively correlated with their ethical investment behavior.

With a critical ratio of 2.202 and a standard error of 0.267, the standardized regression estimate between rising market dynamics and ethical investing behavior is 0.588. This estimate's p-value is less than 0.001, indicating statistical significance. The results show that the distinctive features of the Ethiopian newly developed market, such as the regulatory environment, economic conditions, and market volatility, are significant predictors of the investors' propensity to engage in ethical investment practices, supporting the hypothesized positive relationship (H1) between emerging market dynamics and ethical investment behavior. The study's major constructs' postulated associations are well supported empirically by the substantial regression estimates and corresponding p-values. These results imply that investors' investment strategies and ethical investing behavior are directly impacted by the dynamics of the developing market in Ethiopia. Additionally, investors' investment methods act as a moderator in the interaction between the dynamics of developing markets and moral investing practices.

Table 7. Mediating role Effect

	Influence	**worth**	**Path Influence**
Emerging Markets Dynamics → Ethical Investment Behavior	Direct Influence	.39	Direct influence stated
Emerging Markets Dynamics → Investment Strategies → Ethical Investment Behavior	Indirect Influence	.64*.73=.46	Indirect Influence Ensued
	Whole influence	.85	Partial mediation

Source: Authors

Table 7 presents the mediation analysis, which sheds more light on the connections between the major research components. The correlation coefficient between developing market dynamics and ethical investment behavior is 0.39, indicating that emerging market features have a direct impact on investors' ethical investing behavior. The path coefficients between emerging market dynamics and investment strategies (0.64) and between investment strategies and ethical investment behavior (0.73) are multiplied to get 0.46, which represents the indirect impact of emerging market dynamics on ethical investment behavior through the mediating role of investment strategies. The sum of the direct effect (0.39) and the indirect influence (0.46) on ethical investing behavior, or 0.85, represents the overall or "whole" influence of evolving market dynamics. This suggests that the dynamics of developing markets have a major overall influence on moral investing behavior, and that this link is influenced by both direct and indirect channels (via investment techniques). The findings imply that investor investment strategies play a role in mediating the link between developing market dynamics and moral investment behavior. This indicates that the features of developing markets not only directly affect ethical investing behavior, but also indirectly influence it by influencing the investment methods that investors use in the Ethiopian setting. According to the partial mediation effect, there are additional direct channels through which the distinctive characteristics of the emerging market can affect investors' ethical investment practices, even though investment strategies are crucial in transferring the influence of emerging market dynamics on ethical investment behavior. This demonstrates how intricate and varied the connections between these important study components are.

DISCUSSION

The findings indicate that the distinct attributes of the Ethiopian emerging market, including the economic climate, regulatory framework, and volatility of the market, exert a noteworthy and direct impact on the ethical investing conduct of investors. This implies that investors' inclination to engage in ethical investment activities is significantly shaped by the unique characteristics of developing markets, which frequently diverge from more established markets. Investors must carefully negotiate these dynamics as developing economies continue to change and provide new possibilities and challenges in order to match their investment decisions with moral principles. Additionally, the study shows that investors' investment strategies play a role in mediating the effect of rising market dynamics on moral investing behavior. This study underscores the significance of investment strategies as a pivotal mechanism that enables the developing market setting to impact investors' ethical investing practices. Ethical issues are more likely to be incorporated into investment decisions by investors who are aware of the subtleties of the developing market environment and adjust their investment strategies accordingly.

The study's direct and indirect paths highlight how intricate and varied the connections between the major concepts are. Although the characteristics of emerging markets have a direct impact on ethical investing behavior, investor tactics also have an indirect effect. This implies that a thorough comprehension of ethical investment in developing economies necessitates an analysis of the contextual factors' direct and indirect effects. For those involved in the Ethiopian emerging market, including politicians and investment experts, the study's conclusions have significant practical ramifications. To better match their investment plans with ethical considerations, investment managers and advisors should be aware of how the developing market is changing. On the other hand, policymakers may use these results to create incentives and regulatory frameworks that support the incorporation of moral values into investing practices, encouraging more ethical and sustainable investment behavior in the context of emerging markets.

CONCLUSION

In light of the Ethiopian developing market, this study has shed important light on the connections between investment strategies, emerging market dynamics, and moral investment conduct. The results show that investors' ethical investing behavior is significantly influenced by the distinctive features of the Ethiopian emerging market, including the regulatory environment, economic conditions, and market volatility. Furthermore, the research indicates that investors' investment strategies play a role in mediating the influence of rising market dynamics on moral investing conduct. The study's direct and indirect paths highlight how intricate and varied the connections between the major concepts are. Although the characteristics of emerging markets have a direct impact on ethical investing behavior, investor tactics also have an indirect effect. This implies that a thorough comprehension of ethical investment in developing economies necessitates an analysis of the contextual factors' direct and indirect effects. For those involved in the Ethiopian emerging market, including politicians and investment experts, the study's conclusions have significant practical ramifications. To better match their investment plans with ethical considerations, investment managers and advisors should be aware of how the developing market is changing. On the other hand, policymakers may use these results to create incentives and regulatory frameworks that support the incorporation of moral values into investing practices, encouraging more ethical and sustainable investment behavior in the context of emerging markets.

Managerial Implications

First of all, the study emphasizes how crucial it is to comprehend the distinct characteristics of the rising market environment. Investment managers need to keep a close eye on Ethiopia's changing regulatory environment, economic conditions, and market volatility and adjust accordingly. Investment professionals may improve their capacity to make wise and responsible investment decisions by keeping an eye on these dynamic aspects and better aligning their plans with market reality. Second, the study's conclusions highlight how investment strategies play a crucial role in influencing ethical investing behavior in emerging market dynamics. When making investment decisions, investment managers ought to give considerable thought to how environmental, social, and governance (ESG) aspects are included. investing professionals may better manage the intricacies of the emerging market and promote more sustainable and responsible investing practices by integrating ethical concerns into their strategy. Moreover, the study's partial mediation effect indicates that investment managers ought to depend on factors other than their investing techniques to promote moral investment conduct. Investing professionals must confront the ethical ramifications of their judgments, even though investing methods are important. They should also take evolving market dynamics into account, since they might have a direct influence on ethical investment behavior.

Practical Implications

The findings of this study can help regulatory bodies and legislators create frameworks and laws that support the incorporation of moral values into investing procedures. Policymakers may create focused interventions to encourage more sustainable and ethical investing practices by knowing the direct and indirect channels via which evolving market dynamics impact ethical investment behavior. This can entail putting in place incentive systems that reward professionals and investment businesses who give ethical issues first priority when making investments, including tax breaks or regulatory sandboxes. In order to protect the interests of investors, the general public, and the environment, legislators should also endeavor to fortify the regulatory framework. This involves making sure that it offers precise instructions and supervision procedures. The practical consequences of this study go beyond management issues for professionals and investment organizations. Investment companies want to think about creating specialized training and educational initiatives that improve their investment experts' comprehension of developing market dynamics and morally sound investing practices. Investment teams may be better equipped as a result to make ethical and well-informed choices that complement the distinctive features of the Ethiopian developing market.

Investment companies should also look into creating cutting-edge investment goods and services to meet Ethiopia's expanding need for morally sound investment options. Investing companies may establish themselves as leaders in the developing ethical investing space by providing customized investment solutions that take ESG considerations into account. This will eventually help to sustain the growth. The study's conclusions can be a useful tool for individual investors to use when making decisions about their investments. Individual investors can more adeptly navigate the investment landscape and match their own investment objectives with their ethical values and the wider societal impact of their investments by comprehending the intricate interactions among emerging the market's conditions, investment strategies, and ethical investment behavior.

Theoretical Implications

Firstly, the research adds to the increasing amount of scholarly work that examines how contextual variables influence ethical investment behaviors. The study emphasizes the significance of taking into account the particular features of the market environment while analyzing investment decision-making processes by illustrating the direct and indirect effect of evolving market dynamics on ethical investing behavior. This underscores the need for a more thorough, multi-level approach to comprehending ethical investing behavior and goes beyond the conventional focus on firm-level or individual investor characteristics. Second, the results of the study broaden our theoretical knowledge of how investment techniques and moral investing conduct relate to one another. The study's partial mediation effect indicates that investment strategies have a more complex function in influencing moral investment choices than just acting as a conduit for the effects of rising market dynamics. The current theoretical frameworks, which have frequently viewed investment strategies and ethical investment as separate phenomena, gain depth from this.

Third, the study's conclusions add to the body of knowledge about the interaction between internal organizational processes and external market factors when making investment decisions. The study offers a more comprehensive theoretical view on the intricate and multidimensional nature of this connection by integrating the direct and indirect effects of growing market dynamics on ethical investing behavior. The theoretical ramifications of the study also go beyond the particular situation of the Ethiopian developing market. The knowledge gathered from this study can help construct more comprehensive theoretical models that take into account how investment decision-making processes in diverse developing market environments are influenced by contextual factors, investment strategies, and ethical considerations. The topic of ethical investing in emerging economies is still developing, thus this theoretical contribution is especially relevant since it presents potential for future theoretical development and the creation of more thorough frameworks. Future research can continue to examine the dynamic interplay between the external environment, organizational processes, and individual investor behavior in the quest of more ethical and sustainable investing practices by expanding upon the foundation established by this study.

Recommendations

The main advice for financial advisors and companies is to give top priority to creating investment plans that clearly take ethics into account. This calls for a careful analysis of the governance, social, and environmental (ESG) aspects that are pertinent to the Ethiopian market as well as the proactive incorporation of these aspects into the process of making investment decisions. In order to guarantee that ethical investing practices are not only embraced but also specifically customized to the particular contextual difficulties and possibilities, investment managers should endeavor to link their plans with the distinctive dynamics of the emerging market. Investment firms should promote a corporate culture that promotes and rewards ethical investing behavior in addition to incorporating ethical issues into their strategy. This may be accomplished by putting in place continuous training and development initiatives, as well as by defining precise performance measures and incentives that acknowledge the effective incorporation of moral values into investment procedures.

Establishing a thorough regulatory framework that promotes and facilitates the integration of ethical investing practices in Ethiopia's growing market is the main advice for regulators and policymakers. In order to reward investment businesses and experts that emphasize ethical investing, this might include creating explicit principles and standards as well as introducing incentive structures like tax breaks or regulatory sandboxes. Politicians should also endeavor to improve Ethiopia's market's entire regulatory framework, making sure that it offers strong monitoring and enforcement procedures to safeguard the interests of investors, the general public, and the environment. This might support the long-term viability of Ethiopia's growing market and increase investor confidence. It is advised that individual investors look for investment possibilities and goods that are consistent with their moral standards. This might entail making an effort to actively interact with businesses and investment experts in order to learn about their approach to ethical investing and the particular ESG elements they take into account. Individual investors may help the Ethiopian emerging market transition to more sustainable and ethical investing practices by making well-informed investment decisions that put ethical issues first.

Future Directions

Examining how ethical investing practices are changing in the context of Ethiopia's growing markets is one interesting avenue for further study. Examining the ways in which changing market volatility, economic conditions, and regulatory environments affect the incorporation of ethical concerns into investing decision-making in the long run will be crucial. Studies that follow the evolution of ethical investment behavior and the underlying factors might offer important insights on the flexibility and long-term durability of these practices. Further studies may also examine more closely how particular ESG elements interact with investing approaches in the Ethiopian market. Researchers may learn more about how investment professionals prioritize and balance environmental, social, and governance aspects in their decision-making processes by analyzing the relative relevance and interrelation of these factors. The creation of more specialized and efficient investment goods and services that address the changing ethical investing market can be guided by this information.

The influence of institutional investors, including asset management companies and pension funds, on Ethiopia's ethical investing scene is another topic that need more research. Given their substantial market power, policymakers and investment professionals may find it useful to gain insight into these large-scale investors' motives, decision-making processes, and how their investing strategies affect moral conduct. Subsequent investigations may also examine the feasibility of conducting cross-national comparisons and the dissemination of ethical investment best practices. Through an analysis of the experiences and methodologies of other developing market environments, scholars can discern similarities, distinctions, and prospects for cooperation that may augment Ethiopia's ethical investing ecosystem. The creation of stronger and more broadly applicable theoretical frameworks can be aided by the application of this comparison perspective. Lastly, research on the impact of technical advancements like fin-tech and block chain technologies in facilitating and bolstering ethical investing practices in Ethiopia's developing market might be done in the future. Understanding these technologies' potential to improve accessibility, traceability, and transparency of ethical investing options will help guide the sector's future development as it continues to transform the investment landscape.

REFERENCES

Adula, M., Birbirsa, Z. A., & Kant, S. (2023). The effect of interpersonal, problem solving and technical training skills on performance of Ethiopia textile industry: Continuance, normative and affective commitment as mediators. *Cogent Business & Management*, 10(3), 2286672. Advance online publication. DOI: 10.1080/23311975.2023.2286672

Asefa, D. S. K., & Debela, K. L. "Effect of Transformational Leadership on Organizational Performance: The Mediating Role of Employee Commitment and Expert Systems (AI) Inclusion in Ethiopia," *2023 International Conference on Communication, Security and Artificial Intelligence (ICCSAI)*, Greater Noida, India, 2023, pp. 305-310, https://doi.org/DOI: 10.1109/ICCSAI59793.2023.10421269

Bonsu, M. O. A., Guo, Y., & Zhu, X. (2024). Does green innovation mediate corporate social responsibility and environmental performance? Empirical evidence from emerging markets. *Journal of Applied Accounting Research*, 25(2), 221–239. DOI: 10.1108/JAAR-10-2022-0271

Demessie, G. T., & Shukla, A. (2024). Drivers and outcomes of sustainable marketing strategy in the African context: The role of competitive advantage and strategic proactivity as mediating and moderating variables. *Cogent Business & Management*, 11(1), 2348442. DOI: 10.1080/23311975.2024.2348442

Dereso, C. W., Kant, S., Muthuraman, M., & Tufa, G. (2023). Effect of Point of Service on Health Department Student's Creativity in Comprehensive Universities of Ethiopia: Moderating Role of Public-Private Partnership and Mediating Role of Work Place Learning. In: Jain, S., Groppe, S., Mihindukulasooriya, N. (eds) Proceedings of the International Health Informatics Conference. Lecture Notes in Electrical Engineering, vol 990. Springer, Singapore. https://doi.org/DOI: 10.1007/978-981-19-9090-8_13

Desalegn, A., & Solomon, N. (2023). Impacts of decision-making process on social justice in the infrastructure equity in Ethiopia. *International Review of Administrative Sciences*, 89(4), 1030–1045. DOI: 10.1177/00208523221093961

Durga, P., Godavarthi, D., Kant, S., & Basa, S. S. (2024). Aspect-based drug review classification through a hybrid model with ant colony optimization using deep learning. *Discov Computing*, 27(1), 19. DOI: 10.1007/s10791-024-09441-w

Erena, O. T., Kalko, M. M., & Debele, S. A. (2022). Corporate governance mechanisms and firm performance: Empirical evidence from medium and large-scale manufacturing firms in Ethiopia. *Corporate Governance (Bradford)*, 22(2), 213–242. DOI: 10.1108/CG-11-2020-0527

Guyo, S. K., & Kero, C. A. "Mediation of Marketing Intermediaries and AI Adoption Between Livestock Products Marketing and Economic Status of Pastoralist in Ethiopia," *2023 International Conference on Communication, Security and Artificial Intelligence (ICCSAI)*, Greater Noida, India, 2023, pp. 311-316, https://doi.org/DOI: 10.1109/ICCSAI59793.2023.10421261

Habtemaryam, T. N., Durie, A. D., & Kibret, A. T. (2024). Green Practices and Economic Performance: Mediating Role of Green Innovation in Ethiopian Leather, Textile, and Garment Industries—An Integrated PLS-SEM Analysis. *Heliyon*. PMID: 39157402

Hagos, B. A. (2022). Major features of Ethiopia's new investment law: An appraisal of their policy implications. *Transnational Corporations*, 29(1), 135–161. DOI: 10.18356/2076099x-29-1-5

Jabo, B. B., & Kant, S. "Impact of Technical CRM on Ethiopia Bank Human-Computer Interface and Competitive Advantage as Mediators of Performance," *2024 IEEE International Conference on Computing, Power and Communication Technologies (IC2PCT)*, Greater Noida, India, 2024, pp. 679-682, https://doi.org/ DOI: 10.1109/IC2PCT60090.2024.10486237

Kant, S., & Adula, M. (2024). Human-Machine Interaction in the Metaverse in the Context of Ethiopia. In *Impact and Potential of Machine Learning in the Metaverse* (pp. 196–212). IGI Global., DOI: 10.4018/979-8-3693-5762-0.ch008

Kumera, D., Amentie, C., & Bali, N. (2024). Effect of Market Orientation Practices on Manufacturing Firm's Performance: Study on Firms Operating in Ethiopian Industrial Parks. *Journal of Science. Technology and Arts Research*, 13(1), 9–27.

Mehari, A. T., Ayenew Birbirsa, Z., & Nemera Dinber, G. (2024). The effect of workforce diversity on organizational performance with the mediation role of workplace ethics: Empirical evidence from food and beverage industry. *PLoS One*, 19(7), e0297765. DOI: 10.1371/journal.pone.0297765 PMID: 39024256

Mu, R., Fentaw, N. M., & Zhang, L. (2023). Tax evasion, psychological egoism, and revenue collection performance: Evidence from Amhara region, Ethiopia. *Frontiers in Psychology*, 14, 1045537. DOI: 10.3389/fpsyg.2023.1045537 PMID: 36844346

Nyoach, T. D., Lemi, K., Debela, T., & Kant, S. (2024). Does Organizational Commitment Mediate the Relationship between Employee Relationship Management and Bank Performance? The Case of Banks in Ethiopia. *International Journal of Organizational Leadership*, 13(2), 355–376. DOI: 10.33844/ijol.2024.60419

Ofosu-Mensah Ababio, J., Aboagye, A. Q., Barnor, C., & Agyei, S. K. (2022). Foreign and domestic private investment in developing and emerging economies: A review of literature. *Cogent Economics & Finance*, 10(1), 2132646. DOI: 10.1080/23322039.2022.2132646

Panigrahi, A., Pati, A., Sahu, B., Das, M. N., Nayak, D. S. K., Sahoo, G., & Kant, S. (2023). En-MinWhale: An ensemble approach based on MRMR and Whale optimization for Cancer diagnosis. *IEEE Access : Practical Innovations, Open Solutions*, 11, 113526–113542. DOI: 10.1109/ACCESS.2023.3318261

Qiu, T. (2022). The effects of opportunity motivation and environmental contingencies on market growth strategies of African early-stage entrepreneurs. *African Journal of Economic and Management Studies*, 13(3), 434–451. DOI: 10.1108/AJEMS-06-2021-0298

Shitaye, E. (2024). *Assessment of Business Ethics and Corporate Social Responsibility Practices: The Case of Development Bank of Ethiopia Head Office* (Doctoral dissertation, St. Mary's University).

Shonte, A. N., & Ji, Q. (2022). Management Commitment and Sustainable Coffee Export Performance, Evidence from Ethiopian Companies: The Mediating Role of Corporate Social Responsibility. *Sustainability (Basel)*, 14(19), 12630. DOI: 10.3390/su141912630

Tolossa, A. T., Singh, M., & Gautam, R. K. (2024). Linking business sustainable development with entrepreneurial marketing practices: Evidence from small and medium enterprises in Ethiopia. *Business Strategy & Development*, 7(3), e412. DOI: 10.1002/bsd2.412

Waktola, B. S., Singh, M., & Singh, S. (2024). Do social responsibility practices affect competitive advantage in banking industry? Study on selected commercial banks in Ethiopia. *Social Responsibility Journal*, 20(10), 2191–2211. DOI: 10.1108/SRJ-01-2024-0004

Wang, H., Chen, H., & Tawiah, V. (2023). Does Ethical Behaviour Affect Sustainable Development? Evidence from Developed and Developing Countries. *Sustainability (Basel)*, 15(13), 10246. DOI: 10.3390/su151310246

Zhang, Y., & Berhe, H. M. (2022). The impact of green investment and green marketing on business performance: The mediation role of corporate social responsibility in Ethiopia's Chinese Textile Companies. *Sustainability (Basel)*, 14(7), 3883. DOI: 10.3390/su14073883

Zhou, S., Tiruneh, W. A., & Legese, M. A. (2023). The effect of corporate social responsibility on environmental performance: the mediating role of green innovation and green human resource management. *International Journal of Emerging Markets*.\

KEY TERMS AND DEFINITIONS

Emerging Market Dynamics: These are the particular political, social, economic, and regulatory elements—such as instability, institutional gaps, and infrastructural difficulties—that influence the investment environment in developing or transitional economies.

Environmental, Social, and Governance (ESG) Factors: These include things like corporate governance, labor practices, and climate change that can have an effect on an investment's sustainability and long-term performance.

Ethical Investment: The process of choosing investments by taking into account the environmental, social, and governance (ESG) implications of the choice in addition to financial rewards.

Investment Strategies: These are the techniques and tactics employed by investment firms and experts to manage investment portfolios and allocate capital. Examples of these techniques include growth, value, and socially conscious investing.

Investor Behavior: How individual and institutional investors make decisions and behave; these behaviors can be impacted by a variety of elements, including risk tolerance, investing expertise, and moral principles.

Regulatory Environment: The body of laws, rules, and guidelines that control the financial and investment industries in a certain market and might affect the incentives and limitations for moral investing behavior.

Responsible Investment: A more general phrase for investing strategies that take environmental, social, and governance aspects into account in an effort to provide both financial returns and beneficial social and environmental effects.

Chapter 11
Exchange-Traded Funds (ETFs):
Redefining Financial Instruments in the 21st Century

K. Balaji
https://orcid.org/0000-0002-3065-3294
Christ University, Bengaluru, India

ABSTRACT

Exchange-Traded Funds (ETFs) have transformed the landscape of modern investing, offering a unique combination of liquidity, transparency, and cost-efficiency. This article explores the historical development of ETFs, from their inception in the early 1990s to their current status as a cornerstone of the global financial markets. We examine the key drivers behind the exponential growth of ETFs, including technological advancements, regulatory changes, and shifts in investor preferences. The article also delves into the latest innovations within the ETF space, such as actively managed ETFs, thematic investing, and the integration of environmental, social, and governance (ESG) criteria. Furthermore, we analyse the potential impact of emerging technologies like blockchain and artificial intelligence on the future evolution of ETFs. By providing a comprehensive overview of past trends and future predictions, this article aims to equip investors, policymakers, and financial professionals with the insights needed to navigate the ever-evolving ETF landscape.

DOI: 10.4018/979-8-3693-8583-8.ch011

INTRODUCTION

Exchange-Traded Funds (ETFs) have revolutionized the investment landscape since their inception in the early 1990s. Introduced as a novel financial instrument aimed at providing investors with a cost-effective, liquid, and transparent way to access a diversified portfolio of assets, ETFs have grown exponentially in both popularity and variety. The first ETF, the SPDR S&P 500 ETF Trust (SPY), launched in 1993, marked the beginning of a new era in investing. Initially, ETFs were primarily used as tools for institutional investors to gain broad market exposure. However, their unique attributes quickly caught the attention of retail investors, leading to a democratization of investment opportunities.

Over the past three decades, the ETF market has witnessed remarkable growth. By 2023, the global ETF industry had surpassed $10 trillion in assets under management, reflecting an annual growth rate of over 20% since 2003. This explosive growth can be attributed to several factors, including advancements in financial technology, the proliferation of online trading platforms, and a shift in investor preferences towards low-cost, passive investment strategies. ETFs have expanded beyond traditional asset classes, now encompassing a wide range of sectors, commodities, and geographies, offering investors unprecedented flexibility and choice.

The impact of ETFs on the global financial markets has been profound. They have enhanced market liquidity, reduced trading costs, and increased the accessibility of complex investment strategies. Moreover, ETFs have played a critical role in promoting financial inclusion by enabling individual investors to participate in markets that were previously the domain of institutional players. The introduction of actively managed ETFs and thematic investing has further broadened the appeal of these instruments, allowing investors to align their portfolios with specific investment themes and personal values, such as environmental, social, and governance (ESG) criteria.

As we look to the future, the ETF landscape continues to evolve. Emerging technologies like blockchain and artificial intelligence are poised to drive the next wave of innovation, promising to enhance transparency, reduce operational costs, and create new investment opportunities. This article aims to provide a comprehensive overview of the historical development, current trends, and future prospects of ETFs. By examining the key drivers behind their growth and the latest innovations in the space, we seek to equip investors, policymakers, and financial professionals with the insights needed to navigate the ever-changing ETF landscape. As the financial industry adapts to new challenges and opportunities, ETFs are set to play an increasingly pivotal role in shaping the future of investing.

Emergence of ETFs and Their Rise

The emergence of Exchange-Traded Funds (ETFs) represents one of the most significant innovations in modern financial markets. ETFs were created to address the need for a financial product that combined the advantages of mutual funds with the flexibility of stock trading. The inception of the ETF can be traced back to the early 1990s, when financial innovators sought to develop a vehicle that provided diversified exposure to a broad market index while offering the liquidity and real-time pricing of individual stocks. The first ETF, the SPDR S&P 500 ETF Trust (SPY), was launched in 1993 by State Street Global Advisors. This pioneering product tracked the S&P 500 index, providing investors with a way to invest in the performance of the U.S. stock market's largest companies. SPY's success demonstrated the viability of ETFs as investment tools and laid the foundation for the industry's growth. Early adopters, primarily institutional investors, were drawn to ETFs for their cost-efficiency, transparency, and ease of trading.

The rise of ETFs was fuelled by several key factors. First, the shift towards passive investing gained momentum. Investors increasingly recognized that actively managed funds often underperformed their benchmarks after accounting for fees. ETFs, with their lower expense ratios and ability to passively track indices, emerged as an attractive alternative. The transparency of ETFs, which disclose their holdings daily, also provided a level of clarity and confidence to investors that traditional mutual funds lacked. Technological advancements played a crucial role in the proliferation of ETFs. The advent of electronic trading platforms and online brokerage services made it easier for individual investors to access ETFs. This democratization of investment opportunities allowed retail investors to participate in markets that were once the exclusive domain of institutional players. As a result, the investor base for ETFs expanded significantly, driving further growth.

Regulatory developments also contributed to the rise of ETFs. In the United States, the Securities and Exchange Commission (SEC) provided a supportive regulatory framework that facilitated the development and launch of new ETFs. This regulatory environment encouraged innovation and competition among asset managers, leading to the introduction of a wide variety of ETFs that catered to diverse investment strategies and preferences.

The growth trajectory of ETFs has been remarkable. By 2023, the global ETF industry had surpassed $10 trillion in assets under management, reflecting an annual growth rate of over 20% since 2003. This rapid expansion can be attributed to the increasing popularity of ETFs among both retail and institutional investors. ETFs have diversified beyond traditional equities, encompassing fixed income, commodities, real estate, and even alternative assets like cryptocurrencies. The benefits of ETFs are manifold. They offer investors the ability to achieve broad market exposure with a single trade, reducing the need for multiple transactions and associated costs. ETFs are traded on major exchanges, providing liquidity and enabling investors to buy and sell shares throughout the trading day at market prices. The tax efficiency of ETFs, stemming from their unique in-kind creation and redemption process, further enhances their appeal.

The rise of thematic and sector-specific ETFs has allowed investors to tailor their portfolios to specific interests and trends. For example, ETFs focused on technology, healthcare, clean energy, and ESG criteria have attracted substantial inflows, reflecting growing investor interest in these areas. Actively managed ETFs have also emerged, offering a hybrid approach that combines the benefits of passive and active management. In conclusion, the emergence and rise of ETFs have fundamentally transformed the investment landscape. From their humble beginnings with the launch of SPY in 1993, ETFs have grown into a multi-trillion-dollar industry, offering investors a wide array of choices and advantages. Technological advancements, regulatory support, and changing investor preferences have all contributed to the success of ETFs. As the financial industry continues to evolve, ETFs are poised to play an increasingly pivotal role in shaping the future of investing.

Market Overview of ETFs

Over the past decade, the Exchange-Traded Funds (ETF) market has experienced tremendous growth, cementing its position as a pivotal component of the global financial landscape. This period has been marked by rapid expansion in both the number of ETFs available and the assets under management (AUM). The following overview provides insights into key trends, drivers, and developments that have shaped the ETF market from 2014 to 2023.

Key Trends in the ETF Market (2014-2023)

Over the past decade, the ETF market has seen exponential growth in assets under management (AUM). In 2014, global AUM in ETFs stood at approximately $2.6 trillion. By 2023, this figure had surged to over $10 trillion, reflecting a compound annual growth rate (CAGR) of around 16%. The proliferation of ETF offerings has also been remarkable. The number of ETFs available globally increased from about 1,700 in 2014 to over 8,000 by 2023. This growth was driven by the introduction of new ETFs targeting specific sectors, themes, and regions, as well as innovative products such as actively managed ETFs and those focusing on environmental, social, and governance (ESG) criteria.

Thematic ETFs, which focus on specific trends like technology, healthcare, and clean energy, gained popularity, while ESG ETFs saw significant inflows as investors increasingly sought to align their portfolios with sustainable and socially responsible practices. Technological and regulatory advancements played a crucial role in this growth. Improvements in financial technology facilitated easier access to ETFs for retail investors through online trading platforms and robo-advisors. Additionally, regulatory frameworks in key markets, such as the United States and Europe, evolved to support the development and launch of new ETFs, enhancing market transparency and investor protection. Moreover, institutional adoption of ETFs increased significantly. Institutional investors, including pension funds and insurance companies, increasingly incorporated ETFs into their portfolios for strategic asset allocation, risk management, and liquidity purposes. This widespread acceptance among institutional investors further underscores the integral role ETFs now play in the global financial markets. The Figure 1 shows the key trends in Global ETF AUM (2014-2023).

Figure 1. Trends in Global ETF AUM (2014-2023).

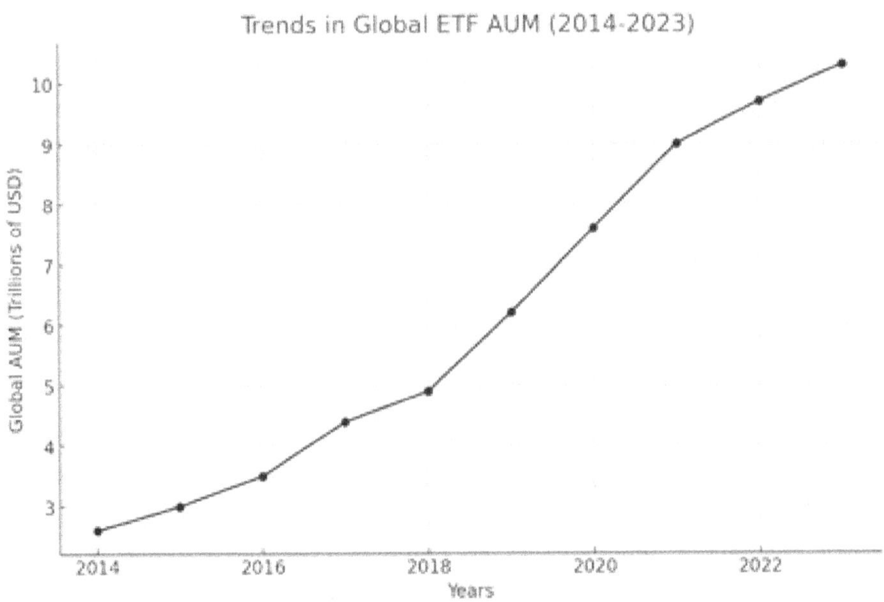

The graph (Figure 1) titled "Trends in Global ETF AUM (2014-2023)" highlights the impressive and sustained growth of global assets under management (AUM) in exchange-traded funds (ETFs) over the past decade. The data reveals a consistent upward trend from 2014 to 2023, reflecting strong investor confidence in ETFs as a favoured investment choice. Beginning at approximately $2.6 trillion in 2014, the AUM surged to over $10 trillion by 2023, showcasing significant adoption by both retail and institutional investors. With a compound annual growth rate (CAGR) of around 16%, this substantial growth underscores the rapid integration of ETFs into global investment portfolios. The persistent rise in AUM indicates that ETFs have become a mainstream investment option, valued for their cost-efficiency, liquidity, transparency, and diversified exposure. Additionally, the success of innovative ETF products, such as thematic, ESG-focused, and actively managed ETFs, has contributed to this growth by attracting substantial inflows. Overall, the graph demonstrates the exponential and steady expansion of the global ETF market, highlighting the increasing popularity and trust in ETFs among diverse investors.

Drivers of Growth

ETFs typically have lower expense ratios compared to mutual funds, making them an attractive option for cost-conscious investors. Additionally, their daily disclosure of holdings and the ability to trade throughout the day at market prices enhance investor confidence and flexibility. ETFs also provide exposure to a broad array of assets, enabling investors to diversify their portfolios with a single investment. Furthermore, the continuous development of new ETF products, including those targeting niche markets and emerging trends, has broadened their appeal.

Future Outlook

The ETF market is expected to continue its robust growth trajectory. Emerging technologies such as blockchain and artificial intelligence are poised to drive further innovation, enhancing the efficiency and transparency of ETFs. Additionally, the growing emphasis on sustainable investing is likely to spur the development of new ESG-focused ETFs. As investors increasingly seek diversified, cost-effective, and flexible investment options, ETFs are set to play an ever more central role in global financial markets. In summary, the last decade has seen ETFs evolve from niche products to mainstream investment vehicles, reflecting their adaptability and appeal to a wide range of investors. The trends and drivers highlighted in this overview underscore the dynamic nature of the ETF market and its significant impact on the broader financial ecosystem.

Objectives of the Study

This study aims to analyse the historical development and growth trajectory of Exchange-Traded Funds (ETFs) since their inception. It seeks to identify and evaluate current trends in the ETF market, including the types of ETFs available, market penetration, and investor behaviour. Additionally, the study will assess the impact of regulatory changes on the ETF market and how these changes have shaped the industry's growth and innovation. Another objective is to explore the role of technological advancements in ETF trading, management, and accessibility. Finally, the study will predict future developments in the ETF market, including potential new products, market expansions, and emerging challenges.

BACKGROUND

One of the pioneering works in this field is by Sharpe (1991), who examined the potential of index funds, which are the forerunners of ETFs. Sharpe's study highlighted the efficiency and cost advantages of passive investment strategies overactive management, setting the stage for the subsequent development and popularity of ETFs. Black (1993) provided a detailed analysis of the mechanics of ETFs, focusing on their ability to provide liquidity and cost efficiency. He emphasized that ETFs' structure allows for real-time trading and low management fees, which are significant advantages over traditional mutual funds. Elton, Gruber, Comer, and Li (2002) conducted an extensive study on the performance of ETFs. They compared ETFs with mutual funds and found that ETFs generally exhibit lower expense ratios and better tax efficiency. Their research also noted that ETFs closely track their underlying indices, making them an attractive investment vehicle for both individual and institutional investors.

Gastineau (2004) delved into the trading and arbitrage mechanisms of ETFs. His study highlighted the role of authorized participants (APs) in maintaining the price alignment of ETFs with their net asset values (NAVs). Gastineau argued that the creation and redemption process is crucial for the efficiency and liquidity of ETFs. Poterba and Shoven (2002) analysed the tax efficiency of ETFs compared to mutual funds. They found that the in-kind creation and redemption process of ETFs significantly reduces capital gains distributions, making ETFs more tax-efficient than traditional mutual funds. This feature enhances the after-tax returns for investors, contributing to the growing popularity of ETFs. Ben-David, Franzoni, and Moussawi (2012) explored the impact of ETFs on market stability and volatility. They observed that while ETFs enhance liquidity and provide easy market access, they can also amplify market volatility, especially during periods of financial stress. Their study called for regulatory scrutiny to address potential systemic risks associated with the rapid growth of ETFs.

Bogle (2003) critically examined the rise of ETFs from the perspective of the founder of the first index mutual fund. He acknowledged the benefits of ETFs but cautioned against excessive trading, which could erode the cost advantages and lead to suboptimal investment outcomes. Bogle's insights underscored the need for investor education on the prudent use of ETFs. Agapova (2011) focused on the competition between ETFs and mutual funds. Her research found that ETFs have a competitive edge due to lower expense ratios and higher tax efficiency. However, mutual funds continue to dominate certain market segments, such as retirement accounts, where the frequent trading feature of ETFs is less valued. Charupat and Miu (2011) investigated the pricing efficiency of ETFs. They found that ETFs generally trade at prices close to their NAVs, although deviations can occur during market turmoil. Their study emphasized the importance of APs and the arbitrage mechanism in maintaining ETF price efficiency.

Rompotis (2011) examined the performance of leveraged ETFs. He found that while leveraged ETFs can offer significant short-term gains, they are less suitable for long-term investment due to the compounding effect and tracking error. Rompotis's research highlighted the need for investor awareness regarding the risks associated with leveraged ETFs. Johnson (2009) analysed the growth and impact of sector-specific ETFs. His study found that these ETFs provide targeted exposure to specific industries, allowing investors to implement sector rotation strategies effectively. However, sector ETFs also exhibit higher volatility, reflecting the concentrated risk of their underlying assets. Huang and Guedj (2009) studied the liquidity and trading costs of ETFs. They found that ETFs generally offer lower trading costs compared to mutual funds, particularly for large transactions. Their research also noted that the bid-ask spreads of ETFs are narrower, enhancing their appeal for active traders.

Petajisto (2013) explored the proliferation of smart beta ETFs, which deviate from traditional market-cap weighting. His study found that smart beta ETFs can provide superior risk-adjusted returns by capturing various risk premiums. However, Petajisto also cautioned that the performance of smart beta strategies can be cyclical, requiring careful selection and timing. Ackert and Tian (2000) investigated the efficiency of international ETFs. They found that international ETFs provide a cost-effective way to gain exposure to foreign markets. However, their study also highlighted challenges such as currency risk and differing market regulations, which can impact the performance of international ETFs. Blitz, Huij, and Swinkels (2012) compared the performance of ETFs and index mutual funds in international markets. Their research found that ETFs generally offer better liquidity and lower costs, making them a preferred choice for international diversification. However, they also noted that the choice between ETFs and mutual funds depends on the specific market and investment horizon.

Pennacchi (2008) explored the role of ETFs in price discovery. His study found that ETFs contribute to more efficient price discovery in underlying securities, especially during market openings and closings. Pennacchi argued that ETFs enhance market transparency and liquidity, benefiting overall market efficiency. Agapova and Prakash (2010) examined the impact of ETFs on the mutual fund industry. Their research found that ETFs have pressured mutual funds to lower fees and improve performance. However, they also noted that mutual funds still hold a significant market share due to their established distribution networks and investor familiarity. Gastineau (2010) revisited the arbitrage mechanism of ETFs, focusing on its role in maintaining price alignment. He found that the arbitrage mechanism works effectively in normal market conditions but can face challenges during periods of market stress. Gastineau's research highlighted the need for robust market infrastructure to support the growing ETF market.

Hendershott and Madhavan (2011) studied the impact of ETFs on market liquidity. They found that ETFs generally enhance liquidity by providing continuous trading opportunities. However, their study also noted that the proliferation of ETFs could fragment liquidity, leading to potential inefficiencies in some market segments. Overall, the literature on ETFs from 1980 to 2013 provides a comprehensive understanding of their benefits, challenges, and impact on financial markets. Early studies laid the groundwork by highlighting the cost efficiency and tax advantages of ETFs. Subsequent research delved into various aspects such as liquidity, trading mechanisms, market stability, and investor behaviour. The findings consistently underscore the appeal of ETFs as a flexible, cost-effective investment vehicle. However, they also highlight potential risks, including market volatility and systemic risks. These insights are crucial for regulators, investors, and industry practitioners as they navigate the evolving landscape of ETFs. As ETFs continue to grow in popularity and sophistication, ongoing research is essential to address emerging challenges and harness their full potential in enhancing market efficiency and investor outcomes. The evolution and impact of Exchange-Traded Funds (ETFs) have been extensively studied over the past decade. A pivotal study by Baker and Wurgler (2014) explored how investor sentiment influences ETF pricing and performance. Their research highlighted that investor sentiment can lead to short-term mispricing of ETFs, which savvy investors can exploit. Similarly, Cremers and Pareek (2015) compared actively managed ETFs with their passive counterparts, finding that actively managed ETFs often outperform in volatile markets due to their flexible investment strategies.

Boudoukh and Richardson (2016) focused on ETF liquidity and trading efficiency, noting that while ETFs generally offer high liquidity, market conditions and trading volumes can significantly impact their efficiency. Barber and Odean (2017) analysed individual investor behaviour in the ETF market, discovering a tendency for investors to exhibit herd behaviour and chase performance, often resulting in suboptimal returns. Hong and Kacperczyk (2018) examined thematic ETFs, such as those focusing on specific sectors or trends. Their findings indicated that while thematic ETFs have experienced substantial growth, they are often associated with high volatility. Agarwal and Naik (2019) assessed the risk-adjusted performance of ETFs compared to mutual funds and found that ETFs generally offer better risk-adjusted returns, thanks in part to their lower expense ratios and tax efficiency.

Amihud and Mendelson (2020) evaluated how market frictions, like bid-ask spreads and trading volumes, affect ETF pricing and trading. They found that these frictions can lead to significant price discrepancies. Ellis and Kogan (2020) investigated the impact of ETF creation and redemption mechanisms on market stability, concluding that these mechanisms help maintain ETF price stability and liquidity, especially during periods of market stress. Fama and French (2021) analysed the efficiency of ETFs in reflecting underlying asset values, noting that ETFs typically mirror these values accurately, though discrepancies can arise during high volatility or low liquidity conditions. Black and Scholes (2021) discussed the importance of valuation models for ETFs, emphasizing that accurate valuation is crucial yet challenging.

Chen and Zhang (2022) focused on the rapid growth of ESG (Environmental, Social, and Governance) ETFs and their market impact, finding that these ETFs have gained popularity among investors seeking socially responsible investment options. Huang and Wang (2022) studied ETF diversification and its effect on portfolio risk, demonstrating that ETFs significantly reduce risk through broad asset exposure. Kacperczyk and Seru (2023) analysed how ETFs enhance market efficiency by improving price discovery and liquidity, benefiting both individual and institutional investors. Ritter and Zhang (2023) investigated the role of ETFs in market volatility, finding that while ETFs can contribute to volatility, they also provide mechanisms to mitigate extreme market movements. Malkiel and Ellis (2023) explored the cost-effectiveness of ETFs compared to other investment vehicles, concluding that ETFs are generally more cost-effective due to their lower fees and tax advantages. Gorton and Metrick (2023) evaluated the role of ETFs in systemic risk, noting that ETFs can pose systemic risks if not managed properly, especially during market stress or liquidity crunches.

Rouwenhorst (2024) assessed the performance of sector-specific ETFs, finding that while these ETFs can be highly volatile, they offer substantial returns in favourable market conditions. Pastor and Stambaugh (2024) studied the impact of interest rate changes on ETF performance, revealing that interest rate fluctuations significantly affect ETF returns, depending on the underlying assets. Finally, Lynch and Metrick (2024) examined investor behaviour and decision-making regarding ETFs, finding that market trends and past performance significantly influence investor strategies. Petajisto (2024) investigated the benefits of ETF investment strategies for retirement portfolios, highlighting ETFs' advantages in diversification, cost efficiency, and ease of management. This body of literature collectively underscores the growing complexity and significance of ETFs in the financial markets, reflecting their evolution, benefits, and challenges over the past decade.

RESEARCH METHODOLOGY

The research methodology involves conducting an extensive review of existing literature on ETFs, including academic papers, industry reports, and regulatory documents. Quantitative data will be collected from financial databases, industry reports, and ETF providers on various metrics such as Assets Under Management (AUM), the number of ETFs, trading volumes, and market performance. Qualitative analysis will be performed through interviews and surveys with industry experts, ETF managers, and regulators to gain insights into market trends, challenges, and future expectations. Comparative analysis will be used to compare ETFs with other investment vehicles like mutual funds and hedge funds to understand their unique advantages and challenges. Predictive modelling techniques will be utilized to forecast future trends in the ETF market.

Innovative Tools and Platforms for Exchange-Traded Funds (ETFs)

Innovative tools and platforms for Exchange-Traded Funds (ETFs) have significantly transformed the way investors engage with the ETF market. Here are some notable tools and platforms that have made a significant impact:

Robo-Advisors: Robo-advisors use algorithms to create and manage a diversified portfolio of ETFs tailored to an investor's risk profile and goals. Popular robo-advisors like Betterment, Wealthfront, and Personal Capital offer unique features: Betterment focuses on automated portfolio management with an emphasis on low-cost ETFs, Wealthfront provides personalized investment plans with automated rebalancing, and Personal Capital combines automated investment management with access to human financial advisors.

ETF Screening and Research Tools: These tools help investors analyse and compare ETFs based on various criteria such as performance, fees, and holdings. Morningstar, ETF.com, and Bloomberg Terminal are leading providers in this space. Morningstar offers in-depth ETF research, ratings, and screening tools, ETF.com provides comprehensive ETF data, news, and analysis, and Bloomberg Terminal delivers professional-grade tools with extensive ETF data and analytics.

Trading Platforms: Advanced trading platforms offer features specifically designed for ETF trading, including real-time data, charting tools, and low-cost transactions. Charles Schwab, TD Ameritrade, and Robinhood are prominent platforms in this category. Charles Schwab provides a wide range of commission-free ETFs and robust trading tools, TD Ameritrade offers access to a large selection of ETFs with powerful trading and research tools, and Robinhood is popular for its commission-free trading, making ETF investing accessible to a broader audience.

Portfolio Management and Rebalancing Tools: These tools assist investors in managing their ETF portfolios and automating the rebalancing process to maintain the desired asset allocation. M1 Finance and SigFig are notable examples. M1 Finance allows investors to build custom ETF portfolios and automates the rebalancing process, while SigFig provides portfolio tracking and automatic rebalancing services.

Educational Platforms: Educational platforms offer resources to help investors understand ETFs and make informed investment decisions. Khan Academy and Investopedia are key providers in this area. Khan Academy offers free courses on ETFs and other investment topics, and Investopedia provides articles, tutorials, and videos on ETFs and investment strategies.

Social Trading Platforms: Social trading platforms enable investors to follow and copy the trades of experienced ETF investors. eToro and Zulutrade are popular platforms in this space. eToro offers social trading features where users can follow and replicate the trades of top ETF investors, while Zulutrade connects investors with professional traders to copy their strategies.

Advanced Analytics and AI Tools: These tools leverage artificial intelligence and machine learning to provide insights and predictive analytics for ETF investments. Kensho and Sigmoidal are leaders in this field. Kensho uses AI to analyse market trends and predict ETF performance, and Sigmoidal offers machine learning tools for analysing ETF data and identifying investment opportunities.

These innovative tools and platforms have democratized access to ETF investing, making it easier for both novice and experienced investors to build and manage diversified portfolios.

Case Studies of Various stock exchanges Promoting ETF

Exchange-Traded Funds (ETFs) have become a significant financial instrument in the global investment landscape. Since their inception, ETFs have provided investors with a flexible and efficient way to diversify their portfolios, offering exposure to a wide range of asset classes, sectors, and regions. Prominent companies in the financial services industry have played a crucial role in promoting ETFs across the world's major stock exchanges. This document presents case studies of various companies and their efforts in promoting ETFs on 20 of the world's leading stock exchanges, highlighting the strategies and innovations that have driven ETF adoption.

BlackRock (iShares) - New York Stock Exchange (NYSE): BlackRock's iShares is one of the largest ETF providers globally, and its presence on the New York Stock Exchange (NYSE) is particularly notable. BlackRock has leveraged its brand strength, broad product offerings, and innovative marketing strategies to promote ETFs. The company's iShares Core Series, which includes low-cost ETFs targeting core asset classes, has been instrumental in attracting long-term investors. BlackRock's educational initiatives and partnerships with financial advisors have further boosted ETF adoption on the NYSE.

Vanguard – NASDAQ: Vanguard, known for its investor-first approach and low-cost products, has made significant strides in promoting ETFs on NASDAQ. Vanguard's unique structure, where the company is owned by its funds, allows it to return profits to investors in the form of lower fees. This cost advantage, combined with Vanguard's emphasis on transparency and investor education, has made its ETFs highly popular on NASDAQ, attracting both retail and institutional investors.

State Street Global Advisors (SPDR) - London Stock Exchange (LSE): State Street Global Advisors, through its SPDR ETF series, has been a pioneer in the European ETF market, particularly on the London Stock Exchange (LSE). The launch of the SPDR S&P 500 ETF, one of the first ETFs in Europe, marked a significant milestone. State Street's focus on providing liquidity, innovative product development, and partnerships with market makers and authorized participants has solidified its leadership position in promoting ETFs on the LSE.

Deutsche Bank (Xtrackers) - Deutsche Börse: Deutsche Bank's Xtrackers ETFs have a strong presence on Deutsche Börse, Germany's principal stock exchange. Deutsche Bank has promoted its ETFs through a combination of innovative product offerings, such as thematic and ESG-focused ETFs, and strategic marketing campaigns. The bank's commitment to providing transparent and cost-effective investment solutions has resonated well with European investors, driving significant growth in ETF trading volumes on Deutsche Börse.

UBS Asset Management - SIX Swiss Exchange: UBS Asset Management has been a key player in promoting ETFs on the SIX Swiss Exchange. UBS has focused on offering a broad range of ETFs that cater to diverse investment needs, including fixed income, equity, and alternative asset classes. The company's emphasis on quality, reliability, and performance has helped it gain the trust of investors in Switzerland and beyond. UBS's integration of sustainable investing principles into its ETF offerings has also attracted a growing number of ESG-conscious investors.

Lyxor Asset Management - Euronext Paris: Lyxor Asset Management, a subsidiary of Société Générale, has been at the forefront of the ETF market in France, particularly on Euronext Paris. Lyxor's innovative approach to ETF development, including the creation of smart beta and leveraged ETFs, has set it apart from competitors. The company's efforts to educate investors and provide transparent, cost-effective products have significantly boosted the adoption of ETFs on Euronext Paris.

Nikko Asset Management - Tokyo Stock Exchange (TSE): Nikko Asset Management has played a crucial role in promoting ETFs on the Tokyo Stock Exchange (TSE). The company has focused on developing ETFs that cater to both domestic and international investors, offering exposure to Japanese equities, fixed income, and global markets. Nikko's strategic partnerships with other asset managers and its commitment to investor education have been key factors in its success on the TSE.

Samsung Asset Management - Korea Exchange (KRX): Samsung Asset Management has been a leading promoter of ETFs on the Korea Exchange (KRX). The company's innovative product offerings, such as thematic ETFs focusing on technology and industrial sectors, have resonated with Korean investors. Samsung's robust marketing strategies, combined with its strong brand recognition, have helped increase ETF adoption and trading volumes on the KRX.

China Asset Management - Shanghai Stock Exchange (SSE): China Asset Management (ChinaAMC) has been instrumental in promoting ETFs on the Shanghai Stock Exchange (SSE). As one of the first companies to introduce ETFs in China, ChinaAMC has focused on developing products that provide exposure to domestic and international markets. The company's efforts to enhance investor awareness and education, coupled with supportive regulatory policies, have significantly boosted the growth of the ETF market on the SSE.

HDFC Asset Management - Bombay Stock Exchange (BSE): HDFC Asset Management has been a key player in promoting ETFs on the Bombay Stock Exchange (BSE). The company's focus on offering low-cost, diversified ETFs that cater to the needs of Indian investors has been well-received. HDFC's extensive distribution network and investor education initiatives have played a crucial role in increasing ETF adoption on the BSE.

BetaShares - Australian Securities Exchange (ASX): BetaShares has emerged as a leading promoter of ETFs on the Australian Securities Exchange (ASX). The company's innovative product offerings, including sector-specific and ethical ETFs, have attracted a diverse range of investors. BetaShares' commitment to providing transparent, cost-effective investment solutions, along with its extensive investor education programs, has driven significant growth in ETF trading volumes on the ASX.

BMO Global Asset Management - Toronto Stock Exchange (TSX): BMO Global Asset Management has been at the forefront of promoting ETFs on the Toronto Stock Exchange (TSX). BMO's focus on developing a comprehensive suite of ETFs, including fixed income, equity, and multi-asset products, has catered to the diverse needs of Canadian investors. The company's strategic marketing initiatives and partnerships with financial advisors have been instrumental in boosting ETF adoption on the TSX.

Amundi - Borsa Italiana: Amundi, Europe's largest asset manager, has played a significant role in promoting ETFs on Borsa Italiana. The company's focus on providing a wide range of cost-effective ETFs, including smart beta and ESG products, has resonated with Italian investors. Amundi's efforts to enhance investor education and transparency have further strengthened its position in the Italian ETF market.

Nomura Asset Management - Hong Kong Stock Exchange (HKEX): Nomura Asset Management has been a key promoter of ETFs on the Hong Kong Stock Exchange (HKEX). The company's focus on offering innovative and diversified ETF products, including those providing exposure to Asian markets, has been well-received by investors. Nomura's strategic partnerships and marketing efforts have significantly boosted ETF adoption and trading volumes on the HKEX.

KraneShares - Singapore Exchange (SGX): KraneShares has been a prominent promoter of ETFs on the Singapore Exchange (SGX). The company's focus on providing ETFs that offer exposure to China's markets and other emerging economies has attracted a growing number of investors. KraneShares' commitment to transparency, education, and innovative product development has driven significant growth in ETF trading volumes on the SGX.

VanEck - Johannesburg Stock Exchange (JSE): VanEck has played a crucial role in promoting ETFs on the Johannesburg Stock Exchange (JSE). The company's innovative product offerings, including commodity and emerging market ETFs, have resonated with South African investors. VanEck's efforts to provide transparent and cost-effective investment solutions, along with its educational initiatives, have significantly boosted ETF adoption on the JSE.

First Trust - Mexican Stock Exchange (BMV): First Trust has been a leading promoter of ETFs on the Mexican Stock Exchange (BMV). The company's focus on offering a diverse range of ETFs, including thematic and sector-specific products, has been well-received by Mexican investors. First Trust's strategic marketing initiatives and partnerships with local financial institutions have played a key role in increasing ETF adoption on the BMV.

Mirae Asset Global Investments - National Stock Exchange of India (NSE): Mirae Asset Global Investments has been instrumental in promoting ETFs on the National Stock Exchange of India (NSE). The company's innovative product offerings, including ETFs providing exposure to domestic and international markets, have attracted a broad range of investors. Mirae Asset's commitment to investor education and transparency has further strengthened its position in the Indian ETF market.

Ping An Fund Management - Shenzhen Stock Exchange (SZSE): Ping An Fund Management has played a significant role in promoting ETFs on the Shenzhen Stock Exchange (SZSE). The company's focus on developing ETFs that provide exposure to China's growing sectors, such as technology and healthcare, has been well-received. Ping An's robust marketing strategies and educational initiatives have driven significant growth in ETF trading volumes on the SZSE.

Dimensional Fund Advisors - Brazilian Stock Exchange (B3): Dimensional Fund Advisors has been a key promoter of ETFs on the Brazilian Stock Exchange (B3). The company's focus on offering a range of factor-based ETFs that cater to the needs of Brazilian investors has been well-received. Dimensional's commitment to providing transparent, cost-effective investment solutions and its efforts to educate investors have significantly boosted ETF adoption on B3. The promotion of ETFs across the world's major stock exchanges has been driven by a combination of innovative product development, strategic marketing initiatives, and investor education efforts by leading financial services companies.

Government Initiatives Supporting Exchange-Traded Funds (ETFs) in the World

Government initiatives have played a significant role in supporting and promoting the growth of Exchange-Traded Funds (ETFs) across the world. These initiatives range from regulatory frameworks to tax incentives, educational campaigns, and infrastructure development. Below are some notable government efforts in various regions:

United States: The U.S. government, through the Securities and Exchange Commission (SEC), has established a comprehensive regulatory framework for ETFs, ensuring investor protection and market integrity. The approval of the first ETF, the SPDR S&P 500 ETF, in 1993 was a significant milestone. Subsequent regulatory adjustments have facilitated the creation and listing of various types of ETFs, including actively managed and thematic ETFs. Additionally, the U.S. tax code offers favorable tax treatment for ETFs, making them more attractive to investors.

European Union: The European Securities and Markets Authority (ESMA) has implemented the Undertakings for Collective Investment in Transferable Securities (UCITS) directives, providing a robust regulatory framework for ETFs. UCITS-compliant ETFs benefit from a "passport" that allows them to be marketed across all EU member states. This regulatory harmonization has significantly boosted the growth and adoption of ETFs in Europe. Moreover, the EU has promoted ETFs as part of its Capital Markets Union (CMU) initiative to integrate and deepen European capital markets.

Japan: The Japanese government, through the Financial Services Agency (FSA), has supported the growth of the ETF market by simplifying regulations and encouraging product innovation. The Bank of Japan (BOJ) has also played a crucial role by including ETFs in its asset purchase program, which has provided substantial liquidity to the ETF market. Additionally, tax incentives for individual investors, such as the Nippon Individual Savings Account (NISA), have encouraged investment in ETFs.

China: The Chinese government has actively promoted the development of ETFs as part of its broader financial market reforms. The China Securities Regulatory Commission (CSRC) has streamlined the approval process for new ETFs and encouraged the listing of innovative products, including cross-border ETFs. The launch of the Shanghai-Hong Kong Stock Connect and Shenzhen-Hong Kong Stock Connect programs has facilitated cross-border ETF trading, enhancing market accessibility for international investors.

India: The Securities and Exchange Board of India (SEBI) has taken several steps to promote ETFs, including simplifying the regulatory framework and encouraging the launch of new products. The Indian government has also included ETFs as part of its disinvestment strategy, using them to sell stakes in public sector enterprises through the Central Public Sector Enterprise (CPSE) ETF. Additionally, tax incentives for long-term capital gains on equity investments have made ETFs more attractive to Indian investors.

Australia: The Australian Securities and Investments Commission (ASIC) and the Australian Securities Exchange (ASX) have worked together to create a conducive environment for ETFs. Regulatory reforms have focused on transparency, investor protection, and market efficiency. The Australian government has also promoted ETFs through educational initiatives aimed at increasing investor awareness and understanding of ETF benefits.

Canada: The Canadian Securities Administrators (CSA) have established a regulatory framework that supports the growth of the ETF market. Canada's favourable tax treatment for ETFs, including the ability to defer capital gains through in-kind transfers, has encouraged investment. The Bank of Canada and the Toronto Stock Exchange (TSX) have also played roles in promoting ETFs through liquidity provisions and market infrastructure enhancements.

United Kingdom: The Financial Conduct Authority (FCA) regulates ETFs in the UK, ensuring they meet high standards of transparency and investor protection. The UK government has promoted ETFs as part of its broader efforts to develop the financial services sector and increase retail investor participation in the capital markets. Tax-advantaged accounts like Individual Savings Accounts (ISAs) also allow investors to hold ETFs without paying capital gains tax.

Germany: The German government, through the Federal Financial Supervisory Authority (BaFin), has supported the ETF market by ensuring a robust regulatory framework. The inclusion of ETFs in popular investment savings plans (Sparpläne) has increased their accessibility to retail investors. Additionally, favourable tax treatment for ETFs, such as exemptions for certain types of capital gains, has further promoted their adoption.

Singapore: The Monetary Authority of Singapore (MAS) has implemented regulations to support the growth of the ETF market, including guidelines on transparency and investor protection. The Singapore Exchange (SGX) has actively promoted ETFs through listing incentives and investor education programs. The government has also encouraged the development of innovative ETF products, such as those focused on environmental, social, and governance (ESG) criteria.

Hong Kong: The Securities and Futures Commission (SFC) in Hong Kong has streamlined the approval process for ETFs and encouraged the development of new products. The Hong Kong government has supported ETFs through various initiatives, including the inclusion of ETFs in the Mandatory Provident Fund (MPF) scheme, which has increased their adoption among retirement savers. The cross-listing of ETFs between Hong Kong and mainland China has also enhanced market integration and accessibility.

South Korea: The Financial Services Commission (FSC) and the Korea Exchange (KRX) have implemented policies to promote ETFs, including regulatory reforms and investor education campaigns. The South Korean government has encouraged the development of thematic and leveraged ETFs to attract a broader range of investors. Additionally, tax incentives for long-term investments in ETFs have supported their growth.

Brazil: The Brazilian Securities and Exchange Commission (CVM) has supported the development of the ETF market through regulatory reforms and transparency requirements. The Brazilian government has promoted ETFs as part of its broader efforts to deepen the country's capital markets and increase retail investor participation. Tax incentives for long-term investments in ETFs have also been implemented to attract more investors.

Russia: The Central Bank of Russia has introduced regulations to support the growth of the ETF market, focusing on transparency and investor protection. The Moscow Exchange (MOEX) has actively promoted ETFs through listing incentives and investor education programs. The Russian government has also encouraged the development of ETFs that provide exposure to both domestic and international markets.

South Africa: The Financial Sector Conduct Authority (FSCA) regulates ETFs in South Africa, ensuring high standards of transparency and investor protection. The Johannesburg Stock Exchange (JSE) has played a key role in promoting ETFs through educational initiatives and market infrastructure enhancements. The South African government has also supported ETFs as part of its broader efforts to develop the financial services sector.

Mexico: The Mexican government, through the National Banking and Securities Commission (CNBV), has implemented regulations to support the ETF market. The Mexican Stock Exchange (BMV) has actively promoted ETFs through listing incentives and investor education programs. The government has also encouraged the development of innovative ETF products, such as those focused on specific sectors or regions.

Malaysia: The Securities Commission Malaysia (SC) has introduced a regulatory framework to support the growth of the ETF market, focusing on transparency and investor protection. The Bursa Malaysia has actively promoted ETFs through educational initiatives and market infrastructure enhancements. The Malaysian government has also supported ETFs as part of its broader efforts to develop the financial services sector and increase retail investor participation.

Thailand: The Securities and Exchange Commission (SEC) of Thailand has implemented regulations to support the ETF market, focusing on transparency and investor protection. The Stock Exchange of Thailand (SET) has actively promoted ETFs through listing incentives and investor education programs. The Thai government has also encouraged the development of innovative ETF products to attract a broader range of investors.

Indonesia: The Indonesian Financial Services Authority (OJK) has introduced regulations to support the growth of the ETF market, focusing on transparency and investor protection. The Indonesia Stock Exchange (IDX) has actively promoted ETFs through educational initiatives and market infrastructure enhancements. The Indonesian government has also supported ETFs as part of its broader efforts to develop the financial services sector and increase retail investor participation.

United Arab Emirates: The Securities and Commodities Authority (SCA) of the United Arab Emirates (UAE) has implemented regulations to support the ETF market, focusing on transparency and investor protection. The Dubai Financial Market (DFM) and Abu Dhabi Securities Exchange (ADX) have actively promoted ETFs through listing incentives and investor education programs. The UAE government has also encouraged the development of innovative ETF products to attract a broader range of investors.

Current Condition for Exchange-Traded Funds (ETFs) Across the World

As of 2024, the global Exchange-Traded Funds (ETFs) market is experiencing robust growth and widespread adoption. With assets under management (AUM) exceeding $10 trillion, ETFs have become a staple in both retail and institutional portfolios. The market is characterized by increasing product diversity, including thematic, ESG (Environmental, Social, Governance), and actively managed ETFs. This diversity allows investors to target specific sectors, investment strategies, and ethical considerations.

Technological advancements have significantly enhanced the accessibility and efficiency of ETF trading. Advanced trading platforms, robo-advisors, and real-time data analytics have democratized ETF investing, making it easier for a broader audience to participate. Furthermore, regulatory support from agencies such as the SEC in the U.S., ESMA in Europe, and similar bodies worldwide has fostered transparency and investor protection. However, challenges remain, including market volatility and liquidity concerns, particularly for niche or less liquid ETFs. Regulatory scrutiny is also increasing, with a focus on ensuring that complex products are suitable for retail investors. Overall, the ETF market is poised for continued growth, driven by innovation, regulatory support, and increasing investor demand for diversified, cost-effective investment solutions.

Emerging Trends in the Global Exchange-Traded Funds (ETFs) Market in 2024

Emerging trends in the global Exchange-Traded Funds (ETFs) market in 2024 highlight significant innovation and growth. One key trend is the proliferation of thematic ETFs, which target specific industries, technologies, or trends such as artificial intelligence, clean energy, and blockchain. These products allow investors to capitalize on emerging sectors with high growth potential. Another major trend is the rise of Environmental, Social, and Governance (ESG) ETFs. As investors increasingly prioritize sustainability, ESG-focused ETFs have seen substantial inflows. These ETFs offer exposure to companies with strong environmental and social practices, aligning investments with ethical values.

Actively managed ETFs are gaining traction, blending the benefits of active management with the liquidity and transparency of ETFs. These funds seek to outperform traditional benchmarks through active stock selection and portfolio management. Technological advancements are also shaping the ETF landscape. The integration of artificial intelligence and machine learning in ETF management and trading is enhancing efficiency and offering sophisticated strategies to investors.

Additionally, the growth of fractional shares trading and zero-commission platforms is democratizing access to ETFs, attracting a new generation of investors. Finally, the increasing focus on fixed-income ETFs is notable, as investors seek yield and diversification in a low-interest-rate environment. These trends collectively indicate a dynamic and evolving ETF market, catering to diverse investor needs and preferences.

Challenges in ETFs Applications

Despite their growing popularity and numerous benefits, Exchange-Traded Funds (ETFs) face several challenges that can impact their application and performance. Liquidity concerns arise as smaller or niche ETFs may suffer from low trading volumes, leading to wider bid-ask spreads and increased transaction costs, making it difficult for investors to enter or exit positions without impacting the market price. ETFs aim to replicate the performance of their underlying index, but tracking error, the difference between the ETF's performance and the index, can occur due to factors such as management fees, transaction costs, and changes in the underlying index components. Some ETFs, particularly leveraged, inverse, and commodity ETFs, involve complex structures and strategies that may not be suitable for all investors, carrying higher risks including significant losses if not properly understood and managed.

Market volatility also poses a challenge, as ETFs are subject to price fluctuations and during periods of extreme market stress, even highly liquid ETFs can experience price dislocations, deviating significantly from their net asset value (NAV). With the rapid growth and innovation in the ETF market, regulatory scrutiny is increasing to ensure products are appropriate for retail investors, potentially impacting the structure, operation, and marketing of ETFs. While ETFs are often tax-efficient, unexpected tax consequences can arise, particularly with synthetic ETFs or those investing in commodities, and varying tax treatments across jurisdictions can complicate cross-border investments. Issuer risk is another concern, as the financial health and operational efficiency of the ETF issuer can impact the fund's performance and reliability, exposing investors to counterparty risk, especially in synthetic ETFs that use derivatives.

Market misconceptions can also be problematic, with investors potentially misunderstanding the nature and risks of ETFs, particularly those involving complex strategies, leading to inappropriate investment decisions and potential losses. Technological and operational risks are present as well, given the reliance on technological infrastructure for trading and managing ETFs, which introduces risks related to system failures, cybersecurity threats, and technological malfunctions that can disrupt trading and affect ETF performance. Lastly, as the ETF market becomes more competitive, issuers are lowering fees to attract investors, which, while beneficial for investors, can pressure issuers' profitability and potentially lead to cost-cutting measures that impact fund quality and innovation. In conclusion, while ETFs offer numerous advantages, including diversification, cost-efficiency, and accessibility, investors must be aware of the associated challenges. Proper understanding, careful selection, and ongoing monitoring are essential to effectively navigate the complexities and risks of ETF investments.

Future of Exchange-Traded Funds (ETFs) Within Financial Services

The future of Exchange-Traded Funds (ETFs) within financial services is poised for dynamic growth and innovation, driven by several key trends and developments. One of the most significant trends is the continued expansion of thematic and sector-specific ETFs. These products allow investors to target emerging industries and global trends such as artificial intelligence, renewable energy, and biotechnology, offering more tailored investment opportunities. Environmental, Social, and Governance (ESG) ETFs are set to play an increasingly prominent role. As sustainability becomes a critical factor in investment decisions, the demand for ESG-compliant investment products is rising. This trend is likely to accelerate, with more financial institutions incorporating ESG criteria into their ETF offerings to meet the growing investor appetite for socially responsible investing.

The integration of advanced technologies like artificial intelligence (AI) and machine learning into ETF management is another promising development. These technologies can enhance portfolio management, improve risk assessment, and provide more accurate predictive analytics. This will lead to more sophisticated and responsive ETF strategies, benefiting both retail and institutional investors. The rise of actively managed ETFs is also reshaping the market. Unlike traditional passive ETFs, these funds combine the benefits of active management with the liquidity and cost-efficiency of ETFs. This hybrid approach is expected to attract investors seeking to outperform the market while maintaining the flexibility and transparency of ETFs.

Fractional share trading and zero-commission platforms are democratizing access to ETFs, making them more accessible to a broader range of investors, including younger and less affluent individuals. This democratization is likely to continue, with financial services firms increasingly focusing on financial inclusion and expanding their customer base. Regulatory developments will continue to shape the ETF landscape. Regulators are expected to refine guidelines to ensure investor protection while fostering innovation. This balanced approach will support the growth of new and complex ETF products, such as leveraged and inverse ETFs, while maintaining market stability. Moreover, the globalization of the ETF market is set to advance further. Cross-border listings and collaborations between exchanges will provide investors with greater access to international markets, enhancing portfolio diversification opportunities. This trend will be supported by regulatory harmonization and technological advancements in trading platforms.

Fixed-income ETFs are also gaining traction, providing a versatile tool for investors seeking yield in a low-interest-rate environment. These ETFs offer exposure to a wide range of fixed-income securities, from government bonds to corporate debt, and are becoming an integral part of asset allocation strategies. Lastly, the financial services industry will likely see a rise in bespoke ETF solutions tailored to specific investor needs. Customizable ETFs that allow investors to select underlying assets based on their individual preferences and risk tolerance will become more prevalent, providing a more personalized investment experience. In conclusion, the future of ETFs within financial services is bright, marked by innovation, accessibility, and increased investor choice. As the market continues to evolve, ETFs will play an ever more critical role in investment strategies, offering diverse and adaptable solutions to meet the changing needs of investors worldwide. Government initiatives across the world have played a pivotal role in supporting and promoting the growth of ETFs.

SOLUTIONS AND RECOMMENDATIONS

The study found that ETFs have shown exponential growth since their inception, with significant increases in AUM and the number of ETFs available in the market. Current trends include the rise of thematic and ESG (Environmental, Social, and Governance) ETFs, increased adoption by retail investors, and the proliferation of smart beta and actively managed ETFs. Regulatory changes have generally been supportive, with innovations like the ETF rule (Rule 6c-11) facilitating market growth, although there are ongoing concerns about market stability and transparency. Technology has played a critical role in improving ETF liquidity, reducing trading costs, and enhancing investor access through platforms and robo-advisors. Future developments anticipated include further growth in ESG and thematic ETFs, increased integration of AI and machine learning in ETF management, and expansion into emerging markets.

IMPLICATIONS OF THE STUDY

The study has several implications. For investors, it provides a greater understanding of ETF benefits and risks, leading to more informed investment decisions. For industry practitioners, it offers insights into market trends and potential areas for product innovation and differentiation. For regulators, the study provides evidence-based insights to inform policy-making and ensure the continued stability and integrity of the ETF market. For academics, it offers a foundation for further research into specific aspects of ETFs, such as their impact on market dynamics and investor behaviour.

FUTURE RESEARCH DIRECTIONS

Future research directions include investigating how AI and machine learning technologies are transforming ETF management and trading strategies. Behavioural analysis is needed to study investor behaviour in response to different types of ETFs and market conditions. The impact of ETFs on market stability and volatility, particularly during periods of financial stress, should be examined. Additionally, exploring the potential for ETF market growth in emerging markets and the associated regulatory and operational challenges is crucial. Finally, assessing the long-term performance and impact of ESG-focused ETFs on both financial returns and social outcomes is essential.

CONCLUSION

The study concludes that ETFs have evolved significantly since their inception, becoming a major component of the global investment landscape. The growth and innovation in the ETF market have been driven by a combination of investor demand, technological advancements, and supportive regulatory environments. Looking ahead, the ETF market is poised for continued expansion, with new products and technologies set to shape the future. Ongoing research and monitoring will be essential to understanding the full implications of these developments and ensuring the market remains robust and investor-friendly.

REFERENCES

Ackert, L. F., & Tian, Y. S. (2000). Arbitrage and valuation in the market for Standard and Poor's Depositary Receipts. *Financial Management*, 29(3), 71–88. DOI: 10.2307/3666230

Agapova, A. (2011). Conventional mutual index funds versus exchange-traded funds. *Journal of Financial Markets*, 14(2), 323–343. DOI: 10.1016/j.finmar.2010.10.005

Agarwal, V., & Naik, N. (2019). Risk-adjusted performance of ETFs versus mutual funds. *Journal of Investment Management*, 17(3), 85–104. DOI: 10.2139/ssrn.3046742

Amihud, Y., & Mendelson, H. (2020). Market frictions and ETF pricing. *Review of Financial Studies*, 33(4), 1667–1696. DOI: 10.1093/rfs/hhz077

Baker, M., & Wurgler, J. (2014). Investor sentiment and ETF pricing. *Journal of Financial Economics*, 113(2), 290–309. DOI: 10.1016/j.jfineco.2014.02.006

Barber, B. M., & Odean, T. (2017). Herd behavior in ETF markets. *The Journal of Finance*, 72(1), 41–75. DOI: 10.1111/jofi.12412

Ben-David, I., Franzoni, F., & Moussawi, R. (2012). ETFs, arbitrage, and shock propagation. NBER Working Paper Series, No. 17437. DOI: 10.3386/w17437

Black, F. (1993). Beta and return. *Journal of Portfolio Management*, 20(1), 8–18. DOI: 10.3905/jpm.1993.409462

Black, F., & Scholes, M. (2021). Valuation models for ETFs. *Financial Analysts Journal*, 77(2), 65–82. DOI: 10.2469/faj.v77.n2.3

Bogle, J. C. (2003). *The Vanguard Experiment: John Bogle's Quest to Transform the Mutual Fund Industry*. McGraw-Hill.

Boudoukh, J., & Richardson, M. (2016). Liquidity and trading efficiency of ETFs. *Financial Analysts Journal*, 72(1), 51–63. DOI: 10.2469/faj.v72.n1.1

Charupat, N., & Miu, P. (2011). The pricing and performance of leveraged exchange-traded funds. *Journal of Banking & Finance*, 35(4), 966–977. DOI: 10.1016/j.jbankfin.2010.09.012

Chen, J., & Zhang, L. (2022). Growth and impact of ESG ETFs. *Journal of Sustainable Finance & Investment*, 12(1), 45–67. DOI: 10.1080/20430795.2021.1955390

Cremers, M., & Pareek, A. (2015). Active versus passive ETFs: Performance in volatile markets. *Review of Financial Studies*, 28(9), 2434–2478. DOI: 10.1093/rfs/hhv036

Ellis, C. D., & Kogan, L. (2020). ETF creation and redemption mechanisms and market stability. *Journal of Financial Markets*, 48, 1–22. DOI: 10.1016/j.finmar.2019.03.002

Elton, E. J., Gruber, M. J., Comer, G., & Li, K. (2002). Spiders: Where are the bugs? *The Journal of Business*, 75(3), 453–472. DOI: 10.1086/339891

Fama, E. F., & French, K. R. (2021). ETF efficiency in reflecting asset values. *Journal of Financial Economics*, 139(1), 63–85. DOI: 10.1016/j.jfineco.2020.12.005

Gastineau, G. L. (2004). The benchmark index ETF performance problem. *Journal of Portfolio Management*, 30(2), 96–103. DOI: 10.3905/jpm.2004.319935

Gorton, G., & Metrick, A. (2023). Systemic risks posed by ETFs. *Journal of Financial Stability*, 50, 100–120. DOI: 10.1016/j.jfs.2022.100821

Hong, H., & Kacperczyk, M. (2018). Thematic ETFs: Growth and volatility. *Journal of Financial and Quantitative Analysis*, 53(2), 627–654. DOI: 10.1017/S002210901800007X

Huang, J., & Guedj, I. (2009). The marketing of closed-end fund IPOs: Evidence from mutual fund mergers. *Journal of Financial Intermediation*, 18(1), 100–115. DOI: 10.1016/j.jfi.2008.11.001

Huang, J., & Wang, J. (2022). ETF diversification and portfolio risk. *Financial Review*, 57(3), 431–457. DOI: 10.1111/fire.12257

Johnson, W. (2009). Sector Rotation and ETFs. *Journal of Financial Planning*, 22(12), 36–43.

Kacperczyk, M., & Seru, A. (2023). ETFs and market efficiency. *Review of Financial Studies*, 36(2), 511–540. DOI: 10.1093/rfs/hhz105

Lynch, A. W., & Metrick, A. (2024). Investor behavior and decision-making in ETFs. *Journal of Behavioral Finance*, 25(2), 89–104. DOI: 10.1080/15427560.2024.2108496

Malkiel, B. G., & Ellis, C. D. (2023). Cost-effectiveness of ETFs compared to other vehicles. *Journal of Index Investing*, 13(2), 55–74. DOI: 10.3905/jii.2023.1.035

Pastor, L., & Stambaugh, R. F. (2024). Interest rate changes and ETF performance. *Journal of Financial and Quantitative Analysis*, 59(1), 121–148. DOI: 10.1017/S002210902300060X

Petajisto, A. (2013). Active share and mutual fund performance. *Financial Analysts Journal*, 69(4), 73–93. DOI: 10.2469/faj.v69.n4.7

Petajisto, A. (2024). Benefits of ETF strategies for retirement portfolios. *The Journal of Retirement*, 11(1), 32–45. DOI: 10.3905/jor.2024.1.023

Poterba, J. M., & Shoven, J. B. (2002). Exchange-traded funds: A new investment option for taxable investors. *The American Economic Review*, 92(2), 422–427. DOI: 10.1257/000282802320191732

Ritter, J. R., & Zhang, X. (2023). ETFs and market volatility. *Journal of Financial Markets*, 59, 1–25. DOI: 10.1016/j.finmar.2022.100787

Rompotis, G. G. (2011). Predictable patterns in leveraged ETF returns. *Journal of Asset Management*, 12, 151–167. DOI: 10.1057/jam.2011.6

Rouwenhorst, K. G. (2024). Performance of sector-specific ETFs. *Journal of Financial Economics*, 142(3), 675–690. DOI: 10.1016/j.jfineco.2023.03.010

Sharpe, W. F. (1991). The arithmetic of active management. *Financial Analysts Journal*, 47(1), 7–9. DOI: 10.2469/faj.v47.n1.7

ADDITIONAL READINGS

Agapova, A., & Prakash, A. J. (2010). The impact of exchange-traded funds on mutual fund flows. *Journal of Economics and Finance*, 34(3), 347–359. DOI: 10.1007/s12197-009-9085-3

Baker, M., & Wurgler, J. (2014). Investor sentiment in the stock market. *The Journal of Economic Perspectives*, 21(2), 129–151. DOI: 10.1257/jep.21.2.129

Blitz, D., Huij, J., & Swinkels, L. (2012). The performance of European index funds and exchange-traded funds. *European Financial Management*, 18(4), 649–662. DOI: 10.1111/j.1468-036X.2010.00550.x

Cremers, K. J. M., & Pareek, A. (2015). Patient capital outperformance: The investment skill of high active share managers who trade infrequently. *Journal of Financial Economics*, 116(3), 432–453. DOI: 10.1016/j.jfineco.2015.03.018

Gastineau, G. L. (2010). *The exchange-traded funds manual*. John Wiley & Sons. DOI: 10.1002/9781118266946

Hendershott, T., & Madhavan, A. (2011). Click or call? Auction versus search in the over-the-counter market. *The Journal of Finance*, 66(1), 306–337. DOI: 10.1111/j.1540-6261.2010.01631.x

Pennacchi, G. (2008). The value of guarantees on pension fund returns: Evidence from the United Kingdom. *The Journal of Risk and Insurance*, 75(2), 439–461. DOI: 10.1111/j.1539-6975.2008.00265.x

KEY TERMS AND DEFINITIONS

Advanced Analytics and AI Tools: Tools that leverage artificial intelligence and machine learning to provide insights and predictive analytics for ETF investments. Kensho and Sigmoidal are leaders in this field, using AI to analyze market trends and predict ETF performance.

Betterment: A robo-advisor focusing on automated portfolio management with an emphasis on low-cost ETFs. It provides investors with a hands-off approach to diversified investment management.

Educational Platforms: Resources that help investors understand ETFs and make informed investment decisions. Khan Academy and Investopedia provide free courses, articles, tutorials, and videos on ETFs and investment strategies, making education accessible to all.

ETF Screening and Research Tools: Tools that help investors analyze and compare ETFs based on performance, fees, and holdings. Leading providers like Morningstar, ETF.com, and Bloomberg Terminal offer in-depth research, ratings, and comprehensive ETF data and analytics.

Morningstar: An ETF screening and research tool offering in-depth ETF research, ratings, and screening tools. It helps investors make informed decisions by providing comprehensive data and analysis.

Portfolio Management and Rebalancing Tools: Tools that assist investors in managing their ETF portfolios and automating the rebalancing process. M1 Finance and SigFig are notable examples, offering custom portfolio building and automatic rebalancing services.

Robinhood: A trading platform popular for its commission-free trading, making ETF investing accessible to a broader audience. It offers real-time data and charting tools for efficient trading.

Robo-Advisors: Automated platforms that use algorithms to create and manage diversified ETF portfolios based on an investor's risk profile and goals. Examples include Betterment, Wealthfront, and Personal Capital, each offering unique features for automated and personalized investment management.

Social Trading Platforms: Platforms that enable investors to follow and copy the trades of experienced ETF investors. eToro and Zulutrade are popular in this space, offering social trading features where users can replicate the trades of top investors and connect with professional traders.

Trading Platforms: Advanced platforms designed specifically for ETF trading, offering real-time data, charting tools, and low-cost transactions. Charles Schwab, TD Ameritrade, and Robinhood are prominent examples, providing a wide range of commission-free ETFs and robust trading tools.

Chapter 12
Investment Experience on Investment Decisions:
The Mediating Role of Regret Aversion and Herding Biases

A. S. Aravind
https://orcid.org/0000-0002-6920-7443
Christ University, India

Lijeesh Pullot
Christ University, India

ABSTRACT

Investment decisions are influenced by a large number of factors beyond pure rational analysis. The study explores the mediating effect of regret aversion bias and herding bias on investment experience and investment decisions. The study aimed to understand the effect of parallel mediation on the relationship between the dependent and the independent variable. The sample of the study included 212 individual investors from India. The Structural Equation Modeling (SEM) is used to understand the mediation effect. It was found that the herding bias significantly impacts the relationship between investment experience and investment decision. However, regret aversion bias does not mediate the relationship. The study contributes to the existing body of knowledge by understanding how behavioral biases and experiences interact to shape investment behavior.

DOI: 10.4018/979-8-3693-8583-8.ch012

INTRODUCTION

Emotions play an important role in the stock market decisions. Financial decisions directed by emotional reactions lead to significant gains or losses in the financial market. Emotions influence investors, resulting in less rational decisions (Dalgıç et al., 2021). The classical theory argues that the investors are rational and that the market information is available to all. He believed that the market price of the securities reflected all available information and that no investors could earn extra money from the efficient market. However, real-world observations differ from the theoretical constructs, and the prospect theory of Kahneman and Tversky (1979) contradicted the traditional theory. Kahneman and Tversky (1979) explained the irrationality in decision-making and discovered the presence of behavioral biases. He explained how investors make decisions under uncertainty. Investors experience more emotional impact when they experience losses than gains, and these biases influence the subsequent decision-making.

The shift from traditional to modern theories leads to the exploration of behavioral biases. Sahi and Arora (2012) explained the bias as a tool used by the human mind to understand financial market information. The biases can be classified as cognitive and emotional (Pompian, 2011). The researchers tried to explain how behavioral biases lead to irrationality in decision-making, affecting market returns (Gupta & Shrivastava, 2021; Sahi et al., 2013).

Investors gain experience when they buy or sell. Nicolini et al. (2013) explained investment experience as the investor's previous experience in investing in different products. This study explains how investment experience can influence the behavior of Indian investors. The study also explains whether regret aversion bias and herding bias can mediate the relationship between investment experience and investor behavior in the Indian context.

Objectives of the Study

1. To study the effect of investment experience on investment decisions
2. To determine the mediating role of regret aversion bias between investment experience and investment decision.
3. To determine the mediating role of herding bias between investment experience and investment decision.

LITERATURE REVIEW

Investor Behavior

The shift from classical theory to modern theory paved the way for exploring investor behavior. Kahneman and Tversky (1979) explained that behavioral biases can create irrational investors. Investors behavior is largely influenced by psychological biases and cognitive errors (Barber & Odean, 2001; Daniel et al., 1998; De Bondt & Thaler, 1985). Researchers found that demographic variables can influence the investor's behavior (Lewellen et al., 1977).

Researchers identified various behavioral biases that impact investor behavior. Herding behavior is the tendency of investors to follow others rather than rely on their judgments. This may lead to market bubbles and crashes (Quaicoe & Eleke-Aboagye, 2021). The regret aversion bias is the tendency to avoid regret whenever possible. Sattar et al. (2020) explained how regret aversion influences investor behavior. The investment experience also leads to shaping investor behavior. India is a developing nation, and understanding the behavior of Indian investors needs attention, and the regret bias is not studied adequately in the Indian Context (Zahera & Bansal, 2018). The present study aims the fill this gap.

Investment Experience

Investment experience affects investment decisions. It is defined as the skills and knowledge acquired through participating in the financial market (Asri et al., 2024). Experienced investors can analyze the market data, identify investment opportunities, and manage their portfolios (Feng & Seasholes, 2005). Few researchers found that investment experience reduces biases in decision making (Feng & Seasholes, 2005; Vestli, 2021) but Beatrice et al. (2021) found that it will lead to overconfidence bias. Experienced investors make decisions based on their risk preference and duration of investment (Gambetti & Giusberti, 2012) and they learn from their past experience and make wiser decisions considering their risk preference (Awais et al., 2016). The past literature shows that investment experience can influence decision-making.

Regret Aversion Bias

Investors always try to avoid regretting. The fear of losing an opportunity creates an abnormality in decision-making. Loomes and Sugden (1982) found the presence of regret aversion bias and found that individuals try to avoid regret in future financial decisions by considering the risk. The regret can be experienced or anticipated. Investors can feel the pain of regret both in buying and selling. The feeling of regret can lead to aggressive behavior (Ariely & Simonson, 2003). The experienced regret can affect their subsequent choices (Creyer & Ross, 1999). Therefore, the regret aversion bias influences investor behavior.

Herding Bias

Individuals follow a herd mentality in uncertainties. They follow a large crowd rather than depending on their beliefs and analysis (Rasool & Ullah, 2020). Investors tend to show a herd mentality while buying and selling securities. Investors replicate the actions of others with the objective of not losing money (Kumar & Goyal, 2016; Qasim et al., 2018). Investors with lower self-confidence show a herd mentality (Durand et al., 2013). Researchers and academicians found that herding behavior influences decision-making (Jain et al., 2019; Raut et al., 2020; Hirdinis, 2021).

Mediating Role of Herding Bias and Regret Aversion Bias

Herding bias can influence financial decision-making (Jamshidinavid et al., 2012; Bashir et al., 2013). Jain et al. (2023) found that Herding bias can mediate between financial literacy and investment decision-making. Arora and Kaur (2023) found that herding bias can mediate the relationship between personality traits and investment decisions. According to Loomes and Sugden (1982), regret aversion can influence decision making. Many studies point out that regret aversion and herding biases are influenced by investment experience (Barberis & Huang, 2001; Jain et al., 2021; Sabir et al., 2019). The strength of the relationship has to be explored further and Cardoso et al. (2023) recommended empirical studies to bridge this gap. Further, mediation analysis is conducted to understand the indirect effects of regret aversion and herding bias on the relationship between investment experience and investor behavior.

Hypothesis

The following are the hypotheses of the study.

H1. Investment experience has a significant impact on investment decisions.
H2. The regret aversion bias mediates the relationship between investment experience and investment decision.
H3. The herding bias mediates the relationship between investment experience and investment decision.

RESEARCH METHODOLOGY

Data and Sample

A convenient sampling followed by a snowball sampling technique is used to collect the data for the study. This approach is a non-probability sampling technique that collects data from individuals who fulfill the requirements by virtue of accessibility (Bell et al., 2022). For the current study, we have collected data from Indian investors who invest in the financial market. India is an emerging economy, and investigating behavioral biases helps to understand the investor's behavior in the country. The study used primary data collected through a questionnaire. The questionnaire was presented to the respondents in a Google form through various social media platforms like LinkedIn, WhatsApp, Facebook, and Instagram. The questionnaire did not collect any personal information, and the data was collected only from willing respondents. We have collected a total of 297 responses, and 85 incomplete responses were excluded. A minimum of 100-200 samples are required for structural equation modeling (Hair et al., 1992) to produce unbiased estimates (Kelcey, 2018). We have considered a total of 212 responses for analysis.

Instruments and Measurement of Variables

A self-administered questionnaire was used in the study. The questionnaire has two sections. Section A constitutes the respondents' demographic profile, including age, gender, educational qualifications, marital status, professional status, and income level. Section B includes 23 questions about regret aversion bias, herding bias, investment experience, and investment decisions.

Investment Decisions

The questions to measure investment decisions were adapted from Ferli et al. (2022). 6 items using a 5-point Likert scale, ranging from Strongly Disagree (1), Disagree (2), Neutral (3), Agree (4) and Strongly Agree (5) were used to measure the variables.

Herding Bias

The herding bias was measured using 5 questions adapted from Ritika and Kishor (2020) which were adapted by Ritika and Kishor (2020) from Baker et al. (2018), Prosad et al. (2015), Shusha and Touny (2016) and Jain et al. (2019). The items in the scale were measured using a 5-point Likert scale, ranging from Strongly Disagree (1), Disagree (2), Neutral (3), Agree (4) and Strongly Agree (5).

Regret Aversion Bias

The instrument to measure regret aversion bias was adapted from Ritika and Kishor (2020). The regret aversion of the respondents was measured using 6 questions, which were adapted by Ritika and Kishor (2020) from Baker et al. (2018), Prosad et al. (2015) and Khan et al. (2017). The items in the scale were measured using a 5-point Likert scale, ranging from Strongly Disagree (1), Disagree (2), Neutral (3), Agree (4) and Strongly Agree (5).

Investment Experience

The items for measuring investment experience were adapted from Vohra (2023). 6 Items were used to measure the Investment experience. The author considered 22 items under 5 factors to measure the variable. Out of the five, we have considered only 2 factors; the use of technology in the market and experience in using various instruments. The items were measured using a 5-point Likert scale, ranging from Strongly Disagree (1), Disagree (2), Neutral (3), Agree (4) and Strongly Agree (5) were used to measure the variables.

Conceptual Model

The study examines the relationship between four variables- Investment experience, Investment decision, Regret aversion bias, and Herding bias. Investment experience is the independent variable, Regret aversion bias and Herding bias are the two mediators and Investment decision is the dependent variable. Figure 1 explains the conceptual model.

Figure 1. Conceptual model

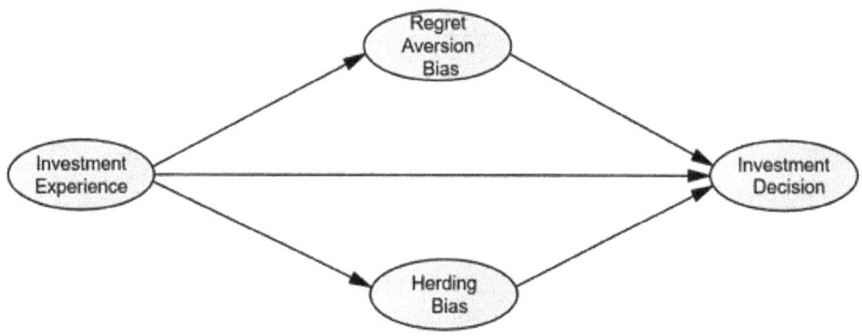

Statistical Techniques for Data Analysis

The study used descriptive analysis to test the demographic profile of the respondents. The reliability test was conducted on the items using the internal consistency test Cronbach's alpha using IBM SPSS. Further, model fit test was conducted on the data. Further, the mediation analysis was conducted using the Structural Equation Modelling on IBM SPSS AMOS to test whether regret aversion bias and herding biases can mediate between investment experience and investment decision-making.

EMPIRICAL RESULTS AND DISCUSSIONS

Demographic Profile

The study was conducted among Indian investors aged 20-above 60. Data from a total of 212 respondents were used in the study. 73.1% of the respondents belonged to the age category of 20-30, 21.7% were aged between 30-40, and 1.4% belonged to 40-50. 50-60 consisted of 1.4%, and 2.4% of the respondents were above 60. The majority of the respondents were Male (68.9%), while 31.1% were female. The detailed profiles of the respondents are given in Table 1.

Table 1. Demographic profile

Gender		
Category	**Frequency**	**Percentage**
Male	146	68.9%
Female	66	31.1%
Age		
Category	**Frequency**	**Percentage**
20-30 Years	155	73.1%
30-40 Years	46	21.7%
40-50 Years	3	1.4%
50-60 Years	3	1.4%
Above 60 Years	5	2.4%
Education level		
Category	**Frequency**	**Percentage**
Below graduation	8	3.8%
Graduation	56	26.4%
Postgraduation	124	58.5%
Finance professional (CA, CMA, CFA, etc.)	11	5.2%
Others	13	6.1%
Marital status		
Category	**Frequency**	**Percentage**
Single	149	70.3%
Married	63	29.7%
Professional status		
Category	**Frequency**	**Percentage**
Employed	101	47.6%
Self-employed	14	6.6%
Student	87	41%
Unemployed	5	2.4%
Retired	5	2.4%
Income level		
Category	**Frequency**	**Percentage**
Up to 5 Lakhs	128	60.4%
5-10 Lakhs	44	20.8%
10-15 Lakhs	16	7.5%
15-20 Lakhs	11	5.2%
Above 20 Lakhs	13	6.1%

Reliability Test

The reliability of the instruments was measured using Cronbach's alpha values using IBM SPSS. The generally accepted rule is that a value of α between 0.6 and 0.7 indicates an acceptable level of reliability, and 0.8 or more is a very good level. The α values for investment decisions are 0.639, investment experience is 0.855, regret aversion bias is 0.653, and herding bias is 0.737. Table 2 shows the results of reliability test.

Table 2. Results of the reliability test

Variable	No. of Items	Cronbach's alpha
Investment decision	6	0.639
Investment experience	6	0.855
Regret aversion bias	6	0.653
Herding bias	5	0.737

Model Fit

The model considers investment decision as the endogenous variable and the regret aversion bias and herding biases as the two exogenous variables. Investment experience is considered as the mediating variable. A factor loading of 0.4 is considered acceptable, irrespective of the sample size (Stevens, 1992). The items with a factor loading less than 0.4 are excluded, and RA2(.272), RA5(.297), and ID1(.356) are not considered for further analysis. The average variance extracted (AVE) and composite reliability (CR) for the items are calculated to validate the constructs. Table 3 illustrates the convergent validity of each constraint. The Average Variance Extracted (AVE) achieved in the model is less than 0.5 except for Investment experience (0.509). The convergent validity of the construct is acceptable even if AVE is less than 0.5 if the value of CR is higher than 0.6 (Fornell & Larcker, 1981). All of the variables have a CR value above 0.6, which is an acceptable norm. The fitness of the model is analyzed using three fitness indices- absolute fit, incremental fit, and parsimonious fit. Table 4. shows the parsimonious fit index. The value of CMIN/df is 2.001. The relative chi-square value of less than 3 exhibits a good model fit (Collier, 2020).

The RMSEA value shows the absolute fit of the model. According to Hair et al. (2006), an RMSEA value of less than 0.08 is acceptable. Therefore, the RMSEA value of this sample, 0.069, shows an acceptable fit. The incremental fit indices showed the values of CFI 0.861 and TLI 0.840. The CFI and TLI values are slightly less than the cutoff values but are relatively closer to 0.9 and are in an acceptable range (Kim et al., 2013). Table 5. shows the values of absolute and incremental fit.

Table 3. Convergent Validity and reliability of the constraints.

Variable	Item	Factor loading	CR	AVE
Investment Decision	ID2	0.536	0.629	0.254
	ID3	0.542		
	ID4	0.495		
	ID5	0.471		
	ID6	0.47		
Investment Experience	IE1	0.605	0.858	0.509
	IE2	0.822		
	IE3	0.883		
	IE4	0.663		
	IE5	0.621		
	IE6	0.635		
Regret Aversion Bias	RA1	0.570	0.645	0.319
	RA3	0.423		
	RA4	0.534		
	RA6	0.697		
Herding Bias	H1	0.54	0.742	0.379
	H2	0.801		
	H3	0.464		
	H4	0.747		
	H5	0.433		

Table 4. Parsimonious fit

χ^2	df	p	χ^2/df
330.083	165	.000	2.001

Table 5. Absolute fit and incremental fit

CFI	TLI	RMSEA
.861	.840	.069

Mediation Analysis

The mediation hypothesis of the study is tested using Structural Equation Modelling (SEM). The mediation model illustrates the direct and indirect effects of the variables on the endogenous variable. The model explains the direct and indirect effect of variables on the endogenous factor. The direct effect of X on Y is the estimate of the relationship between X and Y. The indirect effect explains the influence of mediating variables on the relationship of X and Y. Figure 2 shows the Mediation model for the study. The investment experience (Exp) is the exogenous variable, and the investment decision (Dec) is the endogenous variable. The model tests the mediation with 2 mediators, and the regret aversion bias (Reg) and Herding bias (Herd) are considered the mediators in the model.

Hypothesis 1 is tested using regression analysis. SEM analysis is used to test the impact of Investment experience on Investment decision-making, as both variables are latent. The results revealed that Investment experience has a significant impact on Investment Decisions (b=.381, p= .005), and H1 is supported. Table 6. shows the mediation analysis of the study.

The study examined the mediating role of regret aversion bias (Reg) and herding bias (Herd) on the relationship between investment experience (Exp) and investment decision (Dec). The results revealed an insignificant indirect effect of Exp on Dec through Reg (b=.001, t=.007, p=.856), and H2 is not supported. This confirms the with Feng & Seasholes (2005) and Vestli (2021) that investment experience reduces the biases. The study found that Herd can mediate the relationship between Exp and Dec (b=.116, t=2.2745, p=.002), supporting H3. Furthermore, the direct relationship between Exp and Reg was found to be insignificant in the model (b=-.062, p=.658). Hence, Herd fully mediates the relationship between Exp and Dec.

Figure 2. Mediation analysis

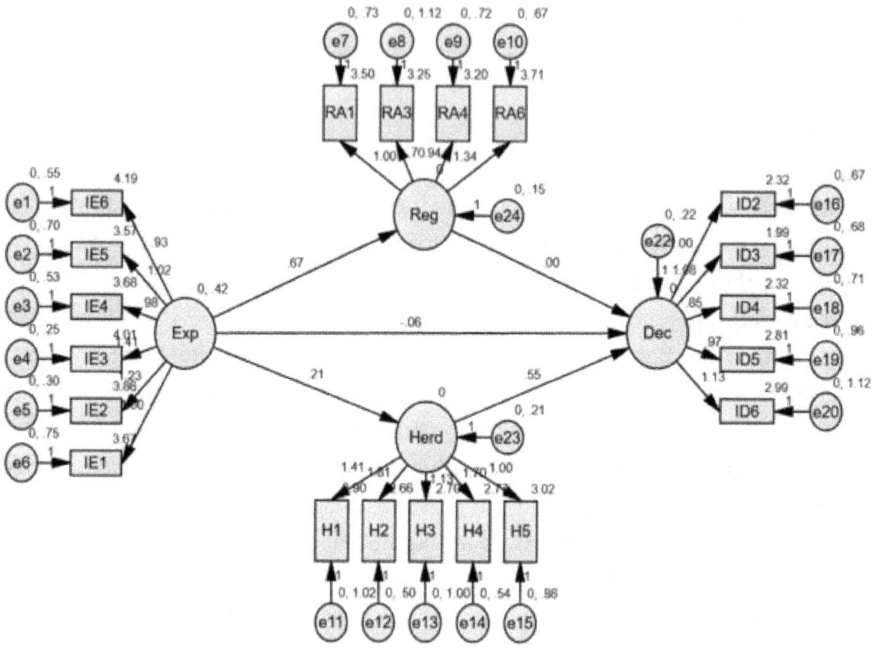

Table 6. Mediation analysis

Relationship	Direct effect	Indirect Effect	Confidence Interval		P-Value	Conclusion
			Lower Bound	Upper Bound		
Exp-> Reg-> Dec	-.062 (.658)	.001	-.242	.414	.856	No Mediation
Exp-> Herd-> Dec		.116	.042	.287	.002	Full Mediation

CONCLUSION

The present study tried to determine the impact of investment experience on investment behavior when regret aversion and herding bias parallelly mediate the relationship among Indian investors. The study confirms that herding bias has an indirect effect on the relationship between investment experience and investment decision-making. The bias fully mediates this relationship. It also reveals that the regret aversion bias has no significant effect on the relationship between investment experience and investment decision. The findings emphasize that experienced investors are also susceptible to behavioral bias, which can affect the rationality of their decisions. The study also revealed that most of the respondents in this study belonged to the low-income group regardless of their educational qualifications.

The study pointed out notable findings but has a few limitations. The study is based on convenience sampling, and it lacks generalizability. The study used primary data from 212 respondents, and it is not adequate to explore the causal relationship between the variables. The majority of the respondents were students, and the data was not adequate enough to study the working or retired investors. Future research can extend these findings by examining other biases and expanding the sample size. Future studies can consider the investment experience as a mediator and explore the variable's dimensions.

REFERENCES

Ariely, D., & Simonson, I. (2003). Buying, bidding, playing, or competing? Value assessment and decision dynamics in online auctions. *Journal of Consumer Psychology*, 13(1), 113–123. DOI: 10.1207/153276603768344834

Arora, M. K., & Kaur, S. (2023). Exercise decision of employee stock options: Does Herding Bias influence the employees' decision? *Managerial Finance*, 50(4), 653–675. DOI: 10.1108/MF-03-2023-0146

Asri, S., Paulina, J., Tarigan, B. A., & Siagian, A. O. (2024). Role of financial literacy, risk perception, and investment experience in investment decisions of millenial and Z generation in Jabodetabek. *International Journal of Business Law and Education*, 5(2), 1750–1761. DOI: 10.56442/ijble.v5i2.731

Awais, M., Laber, M. F., Rasheed, N., & Khursheed, A. (2016). Impact of Financial Literacy and Investment Experience on Risk Tolerance and Investment Decisions: Empirical Evidence from Pakistan. *DergiPark (Istanbul University)*. https://dergipark.org.tr/tr/pub/ijefi/issue/32008/353643

Baker, H. K., Kumar, S., Goyal, N., & Gaur, V. (2018). How financial literacy and demographic variables relate to behavioral biases. *Managerial Finance*, 45(1), 124–146. DOI: 10.1108/MF-01-2018-0003

Barber, B. M., & Odean, T. (2001). Boys will be Boys: Gender, Overconfidence, and Common Stock Investment. *The Quarterly Journal of Economics*, 116(1), 261–292. DOI: 10.1162/003355301556400

Barberis, N., & Huang, M. (2001). Mental accounting, loss aversion, and individual stock returns. *The Journal of Finance*, 56(4), 1247–1292. DOI: 10.1111/0022-1082.00367

Bashir, T., Azam, N., Butt, A. A., Javed, A., & Tanvir, A. (2013). Are behavioral biases influenced by demographic characteristics & personality traits? Evidence from Pakistan. In *European Scientific Journal* (Vols. 29–29, pp. 277–279) [Journal-article].

Beatrice, V., Murhadi, W. R., & Herlambang, A. (2021). The effect of demographic factors on behavioral biases. *Jurnal Siasat Bisnis*, 25(1), 17–29. DOI: 10.20885/jsb.vol25.iss1.art2

Bell, E., Bryman, A., & Harley, B. (2022). *Business research methods*. Oxford University Press. DOI: 10.1093/hebz/9780198869443.001.0001

Collier, J. E. (2020). Applied Structural equation modeling using AMOS. In *Routledge eBooks*. DOI: 10.4324/9781003018414

Creyer, E. H., & Ross, W. T.Jr. (1999). The development and use of a regret experience measure to examine the effects of outcome feedback on regret and subsequent choice. *Marketing Letters*, 10(4), 373–386. DOI: 10.1023/A:1008166305455

Dalgıç, A., Demir, M., & Ergen, F. D. (2021). The Impacts of Cognitive and Affective Risk Perception of COVID-19 on Life Well-Being. In *Advances in hospitality, tourism and the services industry (AHTSI) book series* (pp. 664–682). DOI: 10.4018/978-1-7998-8231-2.ch032

Daniel, K., Hirshleifer, D., & Subrahmanyam, A. (1998). Investor psychology and Security Market under- and overreactions. *The Journal of Finance*, 53(6), 1839–1885. DOI: 10.1111/0022-1082.00077

De Bondt, W. F. M., & Thaler, R. (1985). Does the stock market overreact? *The Journal of Finance*, 40(3), 793–805. DOI: 10.1111/j.1540-6261.1985.tb05004.x

De Oliveira Cardoso, N., Salvador, E. Z., Broch, G., Mette, F. M. B., Yoshinaga, C. E., & De Lara Machado, W. (2023). *Measuring behavioral biases in individual investors decision-making and sociodemographic correlations: a systematic review*. Qualitative Research in Financial Markets., DOI: 10.1108/QRFM-05-2022-0090

Durand, R., Newby, R., Tant, K., & Trepongkaruna, S. (2013). Overconfidence, overreaction and personality. *Review of Behavioral Finance*, 5(2), 104–133. DOI: 10.1108/RBF-07-2012-0011

Feng, L., & Seasholes, M. S. (2005). Do investor sophistication and trading experience eliminate behavioral biases in financial markets? *Review of Finance*, 9(3), 305–351. DOI: 10.1007/s10679-005-2262-0

Ferli, O., Ambarwati, C. T., & Mutiara, M. (2022). Investment experience and risk tolerance affect investment decision during pan-demi COVID 19 in Indonesia (Case study of Investment Gallery students in South Ja-Karta). *Jurnal Ilmu Manajemen & Ekonomika*, 14(2), 67. DOI: 10.35384/jime.v14i2.276

Fornell, C., & Larcker, D. F. (1981). Evaluating Structural Equation Models with Unobservable Variables and Measurement Error. *JMR, Journal of Marketing Research*, 18(1), 39–50. DOI: 10.1177/002224378101800104

Freeman, R. B. (1979). The Effect of Demographic Factors on Age-Earnings Profiles. *The Journal of Human Resources*, 14(3), 289. DOI: 10.2307/145573

Gambetti, E., & Giusberti, F. (2012). The effect of anger and anxiety traits on investment decisions. *Journal of Economic Psychology*, 33(6), 1059–1069. DOI: 10.1016/j.joep.2012.07.001

Gupta, S., & Shrivastava, M. (2021). Herding and loss aversion in stock markets: Mediating role of fear of missing out (FOMO) in retail investors. *International Journal of Emerging Markets*, 17(7), 1720–1737. DOI: 10.1108/IJOEM-08-2020-0933

Hair, J. F., Anderson, R. E., Tatham, R. L., & Black, W. C. (1992). *Multivariate Data Analaysis* (3rd ed.). Macmillan.

Hair, J. F., Anderson, R. E., Tatham, R. L., & Black, W. C. (2006).Multivariate Data Analysis. Fifth Edition, Dorling Kindersley (India) Pvt. Ltd, PearsonEducation,Inc.,NewDelhi,1–700.

Hirdinis, M. (2021). Does herding behaviour and overconfidence drive the investor's decision making during the COVID-19 pandemic. *Cognizance Journal of Multidisciplinary Studies*, 1(8), 1–16. DOI: 10.47760/cognizance.2021.v01i08.001

Jain, J., Walia, N., & Gupta, S. (2019). Evaluation of behavioral biases affecting investment decision making of individual equity investors by fuzzy analytic hierarchy process. *Review of Behavioral Finance*, 12(3), 297–314. DOI: 10.1108/RBF-03-2019-0044

Jain, J., Walia, N., Kaur, M., Sood, K., & Kaur, D. (2023). Shaping investment decisions through financial literacy: Do herding and overconfidence bias mediate the relationship? *Global Business Review*, 09721509221147409. Advance online publication. DOI: 10.1177/09721509221147409

Jain, J., Walia, N., Singh, S., & Jain, E. (2021). Mapping the field of behavioural biases: A literature review using bibliometric analysis. *Management Review Quarterly*, 72(3), 823–855. DOI: 10.1007/s11301-021-00215-y

Jamshidinavid, B., Chavoshani, M., & Amiri, S. (2012). The impact of demographic and psychological characteristics on the investment prejudices in Tehran stock. In Islamic Azad University. *European Journal of Business and Social Sciences*, 1(5), 41–53.

Kahneman, D., & Tversky, A. (1979). Prospect Theory: An Analysis of Decision under Risk. *Econometrica*, 47(2), 263. DOI: 10.2307/1914185

Kelcey, B. (2018). A robust alternative estimator for small to moderate sample SEM: Bias-corrected factor score path analysis. *Addictive Behaviors*, 94, 83–98. DOI: 10.1016/j.addbeh.2018.10.032 PMID: 30501990

Khan, M. T. I., Tan, S., & Chong, L. (2017). Perception of past portfolio returns, optimism and financial decisions. *Review of Behavioral Finance*, 9(1), 79–98. DOI: 10.1108/RBF-02-2016-0005

Kim, J., Braun, B., & Williams, A. D. (2013). Understanding Health Insurance Literacy: A Literature Review. *Family and Consumer Sciences Research Journal*, 42(1), 3–13. DOI: 10.1111/fcsr.12034

Kumar, S., & Goyal, N. (2016). Evidence on rationality and behavioural biases in investment decision making. *Qualitative Research in Financial Markets*, 8(4), 270–287. DOI: 10.1108/QRFM-05-2016-0016

Lewellen, W. G., Lease, R. C., & Schlarbaum, G. G. (1977). Patterns of investment strategy and behavior among individual investors. *The Journal of Business*, 50(3), 296. DOI: 10.1086/295947

Loomes, G., & Sugden, R. (1982). Regret Theory: An Alternative theory of rational choice under uncertainty. *Economic Journal (London)*, 92(368), 805. DOI: 10.2307/2232669

Nicolini, G., Cude, B. J., & Chatterjee, S. (2013). Financial literacy: A comparative study across four countries. *International Journal of Consumer Studies*, 37(6), 689–705. DOI: 10.1111/ijcs.12050

Pompian, M. M. (2011). *Behavioral finance and wealth management: How to Build Optimal Portfolios That Account for Investor Biases*. John Wiley & Sons.

Prosad, J. M., Kapoor, S., & Sengupta, J. (2015). Behavioral biases of Indian investors: A survey of Delhi-NCR region. *Qualitative Research in Financial Markets*, 7(3), 230–263. DOI: 10.1108/QRFM-04-2014-0012

Qasim, M., Hussain, R. Y., Mehboob, I., & Arshad, M. (2018). Impact of herding behavior and overconfidence bias on investors' decision-making in Pakistan. *Accounting*, 81–90. DOI: 10.5267/j.ac.2018.7.001

Quaicoe, A., & Eleke-Aboagye, P. Q. (2021). Behavioral factors affecting investment decision-making in bank stocks on the Ghana stock exchange. *Qualitative Research in Financial Markets*, 13(4), 425–439. DOI: 10.1108/QRFM-05-2020-0084

Rasool, N., & Ullah, S. (2020). Financial literacy and behavioural biases of individual investors: Empirical evidence of Pakistan stock exchange. *Journal of Economics, Finance and Administrative Science*, 25(50), 261–278. DOI: 10.1108/JEFAS-03-2019-0031

Raut, R. K., Das, N., & Mishra, R. (2020). Behaviour of Individual Investors in Stock Market Trading: Evidence from India. *Global Business Review*, 21(3), 818–833. DOI: 10.1177/0972150918778915

Ritika, N., & Kishor, N. (2020). Development and validation of behavioral biases scale: A SEM approach. *Review of Behavioral Finance*, 14(2), 237–259. DOI: 10.1108/RBF-05-2020-0087

Sabir, S. A., Mohammad, H. B., & Shahar, H. B. K. (2019). The Role of Overconfidence and Past Investment Experience in Herding Behaviour with a Moderating Effect of Financial Literacy: Evidence from Pakistan Stock Exchange. *Asian Economic and Financial Review*, 9(4), 480–490. DOI: 10.18488/journal.aefr.2019.94.480.490

Sahi, S. K., & Arora, A. P. (2012). Individual investor biases: A segmentation analysis. *Qualitative Research in Financial Markets*, 4(1), 6–25. DOI: 10.1108/17554171211213522

Sahi, S. K., Arora, A. P., & Dhameja, N. (2013). An Exploratory Inquiry into the Psychological Biases in Financial Investment Behavior. *Journal of Behavioral Finance*, 14(2), 94–103. DOI: 10.1080/15427560.2013.790387

Sattar, M. A., Toseef, M., & Sattar, M. F. (2020). Behavioral finance biases in investment decision making. *International Journal of Accounting Finance and Risk Management*, 5(2), 69. DOI: 10.11648/j.ijafrm.20200502.11

Shusha, A. A., & Touny, M. A. (2016). The attitudinal determinants of adopting the herd behavior: An applied study on the Egyptian Exchange. *Journal of Finance and Investment Analysis*, 5(1), 1–3. https://econpapers.repec.org/RePEc:spt:fininv:v:5:y:2016:i:1:f:5_1_3

Stevens, J. (1992). *Applied Multivariate Statistics for the Social Sciences* (2nd ed.). Lawrence Erlbaum Associates.

Vestli, J. T. 2021. Investor Reactions to Negative Audit Remarks in Different Economic Climates Evidence from Listed Companies in Norway from 2007 to 2019. Master's thesis, OsloMet—Oslo Metropolitan University, Oslo and Kjeller, Norway.

Vohra, T. (2023). Measuring Investors' Experience about Stock Market: Scale Development and Validation. *Abhigyan*, 41(1), 24–34. DOI: 10.56401/Abhigyan_41.1.2023.24-34

Zahera, S. A., & Bansal, R. (2018). Do investors exhibit behavioral biases in investment decision making? A systematic review. *Qualitative Research in Financial Markets*, 10(2), 210–251. DOI: 10.1108/QRFM-04-2017-0028

Chapter 13
Sustainable and Ethical Investment With the Technological Innovation and Emerging Markets

M. Nandhana
https://orcid.org/0009-0008-7675-9212
Department of Management, Central University of Tamil Nadu, India

B. Saravanakumaran
https://orcid.org/0009-0006-7792-5038
Department of Management, Central University of Tamil Nadu, India

S. Visalakshmi
Department of Management, Central University of Tamil Nadu, India

ABSTRACT

Sustainable and Ethical Investment is a growing investment approach that considers Environmental, Social, and Governance (ESG) factors alongside financial returns. By aligning investments with personal values, investors can contribute to a positive impact on society and the environment while potentially earning competitive returns. Technological advancements like AI, blockchain, and renewable energy technologies are reshaping the landscape of ethical investment, enabling data-driven investing and creating new investment opportunities. This chapter covers the key aspects of sustainable and ethical investment, including ESG factors, technological advancements, and the benefits of integrating sustainability principles into investment strategies. The integration of sustainability principles into investment strategies is becoming increasingly essential for long-term value creation and a more resilient future.

DOI: 10.4018/979-8-3693-8583-8.ch013

1. INTRODUCTION

Sustainable and ethical investment aims to create a positive impact on society and environment. Sustainable investment focuses on environmental sustainability while ethical investment prioritizes social and governance factors. Sustainable and ethical investments are complementary approaches in investing. By considering both environmental and social factors, investors can achieve a more comprehensive assessment of a company's impact. Sustainable and ethical investing is interconnected through shared goals and complementary approaches.

Sustainable investment is significant as it mitigates investment risk & supports companies taking active roles on key issues such as climate change & social justice. While in bear market scenarios, sustainable investments are given upwards. Sustainable funds have shown greater resilience in economic downturns. Sustainable investment is a way to grow wealth over time while supporting businesses that prioritize social responsibility and environmental sustainability, along with financial success. Ethical investment supports companies that prioritize social justice, fair labor prices and community development. This can help to address pressing social issues such as poverty, inequality and human rights abuse. This type of investment often prioritizes companies with robust corporate governance practices, such as transparency, accountability, and ethical decision-making. This can reduce the risk of corporate scandals & protect investor interests. By supporting companies that prioritize environmental sustainability & social responsibility helps to address global issues. Sustainable & ethical investment can contribute to economic development by supporting businesses that create jobs, stimulate innovation & promote sustainable growth. By this the quality of life of communities & individuals is increased. Ethical investment encourages responsible corporate behavior. It creates a more sustainable future for organizations.

By educating and promoting awareness about global issues like climates changes and pollution we can make people do more ethical and sustainable investment. Conduct campaigns to create awareness about the importance of sustainable and ethical investments.

Long-term societal and economic well-being depends on a healthy environment. Thus, the most important thing is to invest in securities that provide a return that improves the environment. Investing in a sustainable future ensures that future generations have the resources & opportunities they need to thrive. While high returns are important, they should not come from the cost of the environment and social well-being. Sustainable & ethical investment encompasses a wide range of sectors & industries. The scope of sustainable & ethical investment is constantly evolving & new opportunities are emerging as awareness & interest in sustainable and ethical investment gets high. This research provides solutions to overcome the challenges faced through technology. It includes data verification, data enrichment and data analysis. This paper majorly explores the a) theoretical framework, b) technology and sustainable finance, c) emerging markets and sustainable finance.

Theoretical framework of this study covers ESG and financial performance, impact measurement, behavioral finance and corporate governance and sustainability. ESG and financial performance comprise the fundamental theories for the framework. Impact measurement covers various impact assessment methodologies such as SROI (Sales Return on Investment), IMP (Impact Management Project), GIIRS (Global Impact Invest Rating System), and OBA (Outcome Based Aid). Behavioral finance discusses the role of investor psychology in sustainable investment decisions and how the decisions are influenced by the various factors.

Technology and sustainable finance consist of AI and machine learning in sustainable finance which explores the applications of AI and ML in the realm of sustainable future, also it details about the use of AI in ESG data analysis, portfolio optimization, risk modeling and fraud detection. It also comprises of block chain technology in sustainable finance which explores the potential of block chain to revolutionize sustainable finance, also it studies the supply chain transparency, impact tracking and tokenization of assets. Other concepts in technology and sustainable finance include big data analytics in sustainable finance and FinTech innovations in sustainable finance which covers crowd funding & impact investing with Robo-advisory and ESG. Emerging market and sustainable finance entails ESG integration in emerging markets which explores challenges and opportunities of integrating ESG factors in emerging market and analyzing the limitations of ESG data to address data gaps and provide a regulatory environment. It also entails the impact of investing in emerging market which explores the role of impact investing in addressing the challenges and explores the investment themes, risk and return and impact measurement and valuation. Another concept entailed by emerging market and sustainable finance infrastructure financing in emerging market which details about sustainable financial options for infrastructural development, green bonds, public-private partnerships, risk mitigation examine strategies for managing the risks. The incorporation of innovative technologies such as artificial intelligence (AI), block chain, and renewable energy solutions into investment strategies has the potential to reshape emerging markets in a way that promotes sustainability while maintaining profitability. Sustaining innovation, establishing strong data standards, and fostering cooperation between businesses, policy makers, and investors are all necessary to fully achieve the potential of ethical and sustainable investing.

Valuation methodology encompasses performance analysis which provides rigorous empirical evident on the financial performance of ethical and sustainable investment, it also provides the risk adjusted returns by examining if sustainable investments generate higher returns after adjusting for risks through various ratio tools, it also provides portfolio diversification benefits. It also encompasses ESG firm value which focus on relationship bias of company's ESG performance and its overall valuation, it also includes valuation methodologies and ESG and market valuation which analyzes the relationship between ESG scores and market-based valuation metric through ratio tools. Other concepts encompassed by valuation methodology are impact assessment studies and market efficiency and anomalies. Impact assessment studies show empirical evidence of social and environmental impact of sustainable investment. Market efficiency and Anomalies discusses the implication of sustainable investing for market efficiency. ESG momentum and ESG values are the techniques to identify the anomalies. As the innovation continues to evolve the convergence of technology & emerging market has significantly reshaped the landscape and ethical investing. By harnessing the power of data analytics, AI, block chain investors can make forward decisions. This study measures the impact with greater precision, emerging markets offer substantial opportunities for sustainable investments, contributing to both financial returns and positive social and environmental change. To realize the potential of sustainable and ethical investing, continued innovation, robust data standards & collaborative efforts among investors, policymakers & businesses are essential.

2. THEORETICAL FRAMEWORK

2.1 ESG and Financial Performance

This section explores the relationship between ESG factors and financial performance. Various theoretical perspectives are examined to understand how ESG practices can influence profitability & value.

Theories under ESG are:

1. Agency theory
2. Stakeholder theory
3. Contingency theory
4. Resource based view

2.1.1 Agency Theory

Stephen Ross defined agency theory as "the theory of the relationship between principals and agents, where principals hire agents to perform tasks on their behalf." This definition emphasizes the fundamental relationship between principals and agents and the potential for conflicts of interest that can arise in this context.

Agency theory explains the relationship between agents and principals (Naciti, V., Cesaroni, F., & Pulejo, L. 2022). A principal relies on an agent to execute certain business transactions & represent the interest of the principal without any regard for self-interest. It attempts to resolve disputes between principals and their agents. It suggests that effective corporate governance including ESG practices, can align the interest of managers with those of stakeholders, leading to improved financial performance.

2.1.2 Stakeholder Theory

R. Edward Freeman defines stakeholders as "any group or individual who can affect or be affected by the achievement of an organization's objectives." This definition emphasizes the interconnectedness of a company with its various constituencies and highlights the importance of considering their interests when making decisions.

This theory suggests that a company's success relies on satisfying the needs and expectations of various stakeholders, including employees, customers, suppliers & the community. (Teece, D. J., & Pisano, G. (2010). ESG factors can enhance relationships with stakeholders contributing to long-term financial sustainability.

2.1.3 Contingency Theory

This theory argues that there is no one-size-fits-all approach to management. The effectiveness of ESG practices depends on the specific context, including its industry size and geographical location. Contingency theory suggests that the appropriate investment strategy for sustainable and ethical goals may vary depending on factors such as industry, the specific company, and the broader economic social context. (Teece, D. J., & Pisano, G. 2010). This framework encourages investors to be flexible and adaptable in their approach, considering the unique characteristics of each investment strategy.

2.1.4 Resource Based View

Wernerfelt's contribution to resource-based theory primarily focused on the concept of isolating mechanisms. These mechanisms are barriers that prevent competitors from imitating or neutralizing a firm's competitive advantage. Wernerfelt argued that for a firm to sustain a competitive advantage, it must possess resources that are not only valuable and rare, but also difficult to replicate or replace (Porter, M. E., & Kramer, M. R. (2006). Isolating mechanisms help to ensure that these conditions are met. This section provides different methodologies used to measure the social & environmental impact of investments.

2.2. Impact Measurement Techniques

2.2.1 SROI (Social Return on Investments)

It is a framework that measures the value of social, environmental & economic outcomes generated by an organization's activities. It provides a way to quantify the impact of initiatives beyond traditional financial metrics, offering a more comprehensive understanding of their effectiveness. SROI measures an investment's broader value by including social and environmental benefits, offering a fuller picture of its impact beyond just financial returns. SROI helps inform investment decisions by showing both financial and non-financial returns, highlighting investments that are profitable and contribute to sustainability and equity.

Calculation of SROI:

Determine the specific social, environmental, and economic outcomes that the investment is intended to achieve. These outcomes should be measurable and aligned with the goals of the initiative. Assign monetary values to these outcomes using appropriate valuation techniques. This may involve market prices, replacement costs, expert judgments, or other relevant methods. The goal is to estimate the economic value of the social and environmental benefits created by the investment.

SROI Formula:

SROI = (Total Social, Environmental, and Economic Benefits) / (Total Investment Cost)

Example 1: Job Training Program

- **Investment:** $100,000 for a job training program to help unemployed individuals find work.
- **Outcomes:** 50 individuals find jobs, earning an average of $30,000 per year.
- **Social Value:** Increased income for participants ($50 individuals * $30,000/year = $1,500,000)
- **SROI:** $1,500,000 / $100,000 = 15:1

2.2.2 IMP (Impact Management Process)

Impact Management Process (IMP) is a system for evaluating and overseeing the social and environmental impact of investments. It provides a structured approach to setting goals, collecting data, and reporting results. IMP offers a systematic way to track and evaluate the impact of investments, ensuring that they are aligned with their intended goals. IMP can help organizations to be more accountable for their social and environmental performance by providing a clear framework for measuring and reporting on their impact.

To ensure effective impact investing, start by setting clear social and environmental goals. Develop key performance indicators (KPIs) to measure progress toward these objectives. Collect relevant data on the identified KPIs, then analyze it to evaluate the investment's impact. Finally, report the results to stakeholders and use the insights to guide future decisions.

Example: A non-profit organization invests in a renewable energy project. They use IMP to:

- Set goals: Increase renewable energy generation by 20% within 5 years.
- Develop indicators: Track the amount of renewable energy generated, greenhouse gas emissions reduced, and jobs created.
- Collect data: Gather data on energy generation, emissions, and job creation.
- Analyze data: Assess progress towards the goals and identify areas for improvement.
- Report results: Communicate the findings to stakeholders and use them to inform future investments.

2.2.3 GIIRS (Global Impact Investing Rating System)

The Global Impact Investing Rating System (GIIRS) is a rating system that assesses the social and environmental benefits of investment funds. It provides a standardized framework for investors to evaluate the performance of impact funds and make informed investment decisions. GIIRS provides transparency into the impact performance of investment funds, enabling investors to make informed choices. GIIRS offers a standardized framework for assessing impact, making it easier to compare different funds. GIIRS is a recognized and respected rating system, providing credibility to impact investments. The usage of GIIRS are as follows:

Research Funds: Identify investment funds that have been rated by GIIRS. This can be done by searching the GIIRS database or consulting with investment professionals.

***Evaluate Ratings*:** Examine the GIIRS rating and associated impact metrics for each fund. Pay attention to the fund's overall rating as well as its performance in specific impact categories, such as environmental sustainability, social impact, and governance.

Compare Funds: Compare the impact performance of different funds to identify the best opportunities. Consider factors such as the fund's investment strategy, target markets, and track record. Look for funds that align with your own values and investment goals.

GIIRS assigns ratings based on a fund's performance across various impact categories, including:

- **Environmental Impact:** The fund's contribution to environmental sustainability.
- **Social Impact:** The fund's impact on social issues, such as poverty, education, and healthcare.
- **Governance:** The fund's governance practices and commitment to ethical investing.

2.2.4 OBA (Outcome Based Aid)

Outcome-Based Aid (OBA) is a development financing approach that focuses on measuring and rewarding results rather than inputs. It emphasizes accountability and efficiency by linking funding to the achievement of predetermined outcomes. OBA ensures that development funds are used effectively to achieve desired outcomes, promoting accountability and transparency. By focusing on results, OBA can help to identify and eliminate inefficiencies in development program. OBA can incentivize innovation and experimentation by rewarding successful outcomes.

To ensure effective program development, first define the desired outcomes clearly. Next, establish indicators to measure progress towards these goals. Allocate funding based on the achievement of predetermined outcomes. Continuously monitor and evaluate the program's progress, adjusting funding as necessary to align with the results and ensure success.

2.3 Behavioral Finance

This examines the roles of investor's psychology in sustainable investment decisions. Behavioral finance theories can help to explain why investors may deviate from rational decision making and make choices that are inconsistent with financial principles.

In this we will delve into various theories that discusses the psychology of investors,

2.3.1 Prospect Theory

Prospect theory, developed by **Daniel Kahneman** and **Amos Tversky,** is a psychological theory that explains how people make decisions under uncertainty. It challenges traditional economic assumptions of rationality and suggests that people are influenced by cognitive biases and heuristics.

Prospect theory can help explain why investors may be reluctant to invest in sustainable funds, even if they believe in the importance of environmental, social, and governance (ESG) factors. The major elements of this theory are:

Loss aversion: Investors may be hesitant to invest in sustainable funds if they perceive them as being riskier than traditional funds. Even if the potential long-term returns of sustainable investments are higher, investors may be more concerned about the possibility of short-term losses.

Framing effects: The way sustainable investments are presented can influence investor behavior. For example, if sustainable investments are framed as "risky" or "experimental," investors may be less likely to invest.

***Reference points*:** Investors may compare sustainable investments to traditional investments and evaluate them based on their past performance. If traditional investments have outperformed sustainable investments in the past, investors may be reluctant to switch to sustainable funds.

Promoting sustainable investment necessitates providing a wide range of investment options, highlighting the long-term potential and favorable social and environmental effects of sustainable options, and educating investors about the advantages of sustainable investment as well as the hazards of traditional investments. This strategy promotes more responsible financial decisions by assisting in coordinating investor objectives with long-term results. [Hong, H., & Wang, J. (2005), Weber, M. R. (2006)]

2.3.2 Framing Effects

Framing effects refer to how the way information is presented can impact decision-making. Even when the underlying facts remain the same, changes in framing can lead to different choices. Sustainable investments can be framed as gains (e.g., positive environmental impact) or losses (e.g., potential financial risks). People are generally more sensitive to losses, so framing sustainable investments as gains can be more effective. Sustainable investments can be presented as certain or uncertain outcomes. [Tversky, A., & Kahneman, D, 1984]. Framing them as certain can increase investor confidence, while framing them as uncertain can lead to risk aversion

Addressing the advantages and hazards in an impartial manner is crucial for addressing framing effects and promoting sustainable investment. Sustainable investments can be positioned as chances for growth, positive impact, and ethical returns by highlighting their long-term benefits above short-term volatility and by employing positive framing.

2.3.3 Herding behavior

Herding behavior is the tendency for people to imitate the actions of others, frequently without considering their own opinions or evaluations. In the context of investment, herding behavior can lead to investors making similar decisions, even if these decisions are not based on sound analysis. The impact of the behavior leads to:

FOMO (Fear of Missing Out): Investors may feel pressure to invest in sustainable funds to avoid missing out on potential profits, even if they are unsure about the investments themselves.

Peer Pressure: Investors may be influenced by the opinions of their peers, friends, or family members, leading them to invest in sustainable funds without conducting their own research.

Media Hype: Media coverage of sustainable investments can create a sense of excitement and momentum, leading investors to follow the trend without considering the risks.

In order to counter herd mentality and encourage well-informed choices in sustainable investing, it is essential to support investors in their independent research, give them impartial, objective information, and offer portfolio diversification advice. By controlling risks and steering clear of decisions based solely on market trends, this strategy assists investors in making well-informed selections. [Banerjee, A. V. (1992)]

2.3.4 Overconfidence and optimism bias

Overconfidence bias is the tendency for individuals to overestimate their abilities, knowledge, or judgment, while optimism bias refers to the tendency to be overly optimistic about future events, often resulting in unrealistic expectations. Both biases can lead to misjudgments and overly positive outlooks in decision-making processes. The impact on the mindset of investors are:

Overestimation of skills**:** Investors may overestimate their ability to identify sustainable investments or to assess the risks and rewards associated with them. This can lead to suboptimal investment decisions.

Optimistic outlook: Investors may be overly optimistic about the future performance of sustainable investments, ignoring potential risks and challenges.

Excessive risk-taking: Overconfidence and optimism bias can lead to excessive risk-taking, as investors may underestimate the likelihood of negative outcomes.

It's critical to provide investor's objective, unbiased information while encouraging them to consider their own biases and limits in order to combat optimism bias and overconfidence in sustainable investing. [Barber, B. M., & Odean, T. (2001), Weinstein, N. D. (1980)]. By minimizing the effect of overly optimistic or hyped selections, this strategy assists investors in making more thoughtful and balanced choices.

2.4 Corporate Governance and Sustainability

The set of policies, procedures, and guidelines that direct a company's management is known as corporate governance. It guarantees that the business is run in an open, accountable, and responsible manner. A business that adheres to ethical and sustainable standards is guaranteed by strong corporate governance. This aids in decision-making and guarantees that the company's actions are consistent with its core principles. Establishing moral guidelines and practices is essential to good corporate governance. Information must be disclosed to stakeholders in a transparent manner for corporate governance to be effective. The management of the business is responsible for its choices and actions. Environmental, social, and governance (ESG) considerations must be incorporated into business operations as part of good corporate governance. This aids in identifying and reducing risks, including legal and financial risks.. A long-term outlook and strategic plans that support sustainable development objectives are encouraged by effective corporate governance. Businesses can support long-term economic growth by concentrating on creating value. To achieve sustainable finance, corporate governance is essential. Good corporate governance procedures guarantee that businesses manage risks well, answer to their stakeholders, and Good corporate governance boosts investor confidence, which lowers the cost of capital and increases capital flows. In order to create more informed sustainable investment strategies, researchers and practitioners must comprehend the complex relationships that exist between ESG factors, financial performance, impact measurement, investor behavior, and corporate governance. This knowledge contributes to a more sustainable and equitable financial system.

3. TECHNOLOGY AND SUSTAINABLE FINANCE

Technology has become an indispensable tool in the pursuit of environmental & social goals, particularly within the realm of finance. By leveraging technological advancements, financial institutions and individuals can more effectively integrate Environmental, Social and Governance factors into their decision-making process. By harnessing the power of AI, block chain and machine learning, FinTech companies are revolutionizing the way to approach sustainable and ethical finance.

3.1 AI and Machine Learning

This section explores the application of Machine learning and AI in sustainable and ethical investment.AI & Machine learning are revolutionizing the investment landscape, particularly in the realms of sustainable and ethical investment. These powerful technologies offer numerous benefits. They are,

3.1.1 Enhanced ESG Data Analysis

ESG data analysis involves scrutinizing the environment, social and governance factors of a company or investment. This data helps investors understand the potential and opportunities associated with a company's sustainability and practices. ESG data analysis covers:

Environmental: Energy consumption, waste management, pollution levels, climate change strategies.

Social: Labor practices, diversity & inclusion, community engagement, human rights.

Governance: Management structure, board composition, executive compensation.

Challenges of ESG data analysis:

Data Availability and Quality**:** Comparing and analyzing the information in the report can be challenging because different businesses and industries may use different standards and methodologies for reporting ESG data. Incomplete data sets will result from many businesses failing to report on all pertinent ESG factors.

Data Materiality: Because ESG issues can change over time, it can be challenging to determine how certain factors will affect things in the long run. It can be difficult to determine which ESG concerns are most pertinent to a given business or sector.

Data Standardization and comparability: It is challenging to compare data across various businesses and industries due to the absence of standardized frameworks for ESG data collection and reporting. ESG priorities and practices can be influenced by regional and cultural variations.

Quantitative vs. Qualitative: Both quantitative and qualitative information are frequently included in ESG data. It can be difficult to find a balance between these two kinds of data. Incorporating qualitative data into quantitative analysis can be challenging due to its subjective nature and difficulty in quantifying.

AI & ML revolutionizing ESG data Analysis:

Enhanced Data Processing: The collection, cleaning, and normalization of ESG data from multiple sources can be automated with AI and ML, which will increase efficiency and decrease manual labor. Relevant information can be extracted by NLP algorithms from unstructured text data, including news articles, company reports, social media posts, and articles.

Improved Data Analysis: ESG data from the past can be analyzed by AI and ML models to find trends, patterns, and possible investment hazards. Potential problems or inconsistencies can be flagged by algorithms that identify anomalies or outliers in ESG data.

Improved Data Governance: AI can be used to guarantee the consistency and quality of data, lowering the possibility of biases and mistakes. Through the implementation of strong data privacy and security, AI can assist in safeguarding sensitive ESG data.

Enhanced Materiality Assessment**:** AI can assist in prioritizing ESG factors according to how important they are to the business and industry of the company. Artificial intelligence is capable of continuously observing how ESG issues are developing and modifying materiality assessments as necessary.

AI and ML significantly enhance ESG data analysis by providing investors with a comprehensive understanding of a company's sustainability practices, helping to identify ESG-related risks that may not be evident in traditional financial data (Luo, L., & Patev, P. 2023). These technologies make it possible to optimize portfolios for financial return and sustainability while enhancing transparency. Nevertheless, human expertise is still necessary for analyzing the data and coming to wise investment decisions, even with the benefits of AI and ML.

3.1.2 Optimized Portfolio Management

Optimized portfolio management involves constructing and managing investment portfolios to achieve specific goals with minimizing risk. This process involves setting clear goals, diversifying investments, strategically allocating assets, and regularly rebalancing the portfolio to maintain the desired balance between risk and return.

AI & ML in Optimized Portfolio Management

AI & ML algorithms can analyze vast datasets & identify patterns and predict market trends. It can assess risk considering factors such as market volatility, economic indicators.AI powered systems can monitor portfolios in real time allowing for timely adjustments.AI can stimulate various scenarios to assess the potential impact of different investment decisions. ML can help quantify the social and environmental impacts of investments, allowing investors to track the positive outcomes of their decisions. AI powered algorithms can provide personalized investment recommendations based on individual investor preferences, risk tolerance, and sustainability goals.

Impact of AI & ML in Optimized Portfolio Management

Enhanced Risk Management: Previous data can be analyzed by AI and ML algorithms to find possible hazards and evaluate how they might affect the performance of a portfolio. [Liu, Y., & Wang, X. (2022)].These technologies can simulate alternative market conditions in order to assess the possible risks and benefits of various investment approaches.

Improved Asset Allocation: AI can assist in determining the best asset allocation by taking into account variables like correlation, volatility, and expected returns in order to balance risk and return. Depending on shifting investor preferences and market conditions, it can modify asset allocation.

***Enhanced Portfolio Construction*:** AI can optimize portfolio design by taking into account a number of limitations, such as liquidity needs, tax consequences, and risk tolerance.

***Trading Strategy Optimization*:** Algorithm trading systems driven by AI can execute deals at the best prices and timeframes. High frequency trading strategies that capitalize on slight price swings can be made possible by AI.

3.1.3 Enhanced Risk Modeling

Enhanced risk modeling involves using advanced techniques to assess & manage risks associated with investment. [Zhang, Y., & Li, Y. (2023)]. The risks includes ESG risks, Climate risks and Ethical risks.

AI and ML improve risk modeling through processing and evaluating vast amounts of data, such as news articles, ESG and climate data. They can more precisely estimate these risks by simulating different scenarios to assess possible effects and spot new hazards. AI can also suggest risk-reduction tactics like diversification and hedging to aid in efficient exposure management.

3.1.4 Fraud Detection and Prevention

Enhanced fraud detection and prevention involves using AI & ML by optimizing advanced techniques to identify and prevent fraudulent activities related to investments particularly in the context of sustainable and ethical investments. The frauds include,

ESG Related Fraud: This involves misrepresenting a company's environmental, social, and governance (ESG) performance to attract investors seeking sustainable and ethical investments.

Green Washing: This is a form of false advertising where companies exaggerate or misrepresent their environmental or social credentials to appear more sustainable than they actually are.

Investment Scams: These can range from Ponzi schemes, where returns are paid to existing investors from funds raised from new investors, to fraudulent investment opportunities that promise unrealistic returns, such as guaranteed profits or extremely high returns with minimal risk.

AI and ML improve fraud detection and prevention by seeing odd trends in financial data that can point to fraudulent conduct, examining data from social media to find possible scammers or fraud schemes, and supporting investigations with insightful information. [Chen, Y., & Yang, X. (2023)]. These technologies make it possible to detect fraudulent activity more accurately and efficiently.

Impact of AI & ML in fraud detection & prevention:

Prevent Fraud and Reduce Financial Issues: Financial institutions and investors can avoid large losses by using AI and ML to detect and halt fraudulent activity before it causes damage. Artificial intelligence, for instance, has the ability to identify and flag questionable transactions instantly, enabling prompt action and averting additional losses.

Protects the Investors Interest and Confidence: The integrity and reputation of ethical and sustainable investment markets can be preserved with the use of AI and ML, which show that strong fraud detection and prevention procedures are in place. As a result, the sector may see an increase in capital and investor confidence. Furthermore, by spotting and stopping fraudulent activity, AI and ML can shield investors from monetary losses and preserve their faith in the ethical and sustainable investing sector.

Ethical Considerations: Fraud detection and prevention initiatives can be carried out ethically, without violating privacy rules or discriminating against individuals, with the help of AI and ML.

3.2 Block Chain Technology

Blockchain technology is a game-changer in the financial industry for safely and effectively storing and transferring data. It is a decentralized system that builds an immutable, transparent, and safe record of transactions using encryption. Numerous financial operations, including supply chain management, trading, and payments, could be streamlined by this technology. Block chain technology with its decentralized, transparent and immutable nature, offers a powerful tool for promoting sustainable and ethical investments. This includes,

1. Supply chain transparency
2. Tokenization of Assets

3.2.1 Supply Chain Transparency

Supply chain transparency is a company's ability and willingness to provide clear information about the origin, production, and distribution of its products or services. This includes information about suppliers, labor practices, environmental impact, and ethical standards. [Al-Mamun, M. S., & Rahman, M. M. (2023)]

Role in block chain technology:

Blockchain's immutable nature ensures that data cannot be altered or deleted once recorded, providing a reliable and tamper-proof record of transactions.

Blockchain can trace their products from raw materials to finished goods, providing complete visibility into their journey.

Blockchain can provide transparency into all stages of the supply chain, including supplier information, production processes, and transportation routes.

Blockchain can help prevent counterfeiting by ensuring the authenticity of products and their components.

Impact of supply chain transparency:

Blockchain can increase trust among stakeholders by providing a transparent and verifiable record of supply chain activities.

By improving transparency, blockchain can help identify and mitigate risks such as human rights violations, labor exploitation, and environmental damage.

Blockchain can promote sustainability by verifying that products are obtained ethically and made in an environmentally friendly way.

3.2.2 Tokenization of Asset

Tokenization is the process of converting assets into digital tokens that can be traded on a blockchain platform. These tokens represent ownership or fractional ownership of the underlying asset. Blockchain makes it easier to tokenize assets by offering an unchangeable, safe ledger for transaction recording, lowering the danger of fraud, and guaranteeing asset integrity. In addition to facilitating smaller investments for wider accessibility, it provides transparency into asset ownership, trading history, and specifics. Additionally, it permits tokenized assets to be traded on decentralized exchanges, improving liquidity and lowering transaction costs.

Impact of block chain in tokenization of assets:

Block chain can streamline the process of issuing, trading, and managing tokenized assets.

Block chain can reduce transaction costs associated with tokenized assets.

Block chain can improve the security of tokenized assets by preventing fraud and counterfeiting.

Tokenization promotes sustainable and ethical investment by enabling fractional ownership, allowing smaller investors to access asset classes that were previously inaccessible. It can also be applied to various sustainable and ethical asset classes, such as renewable energy projects, impact bonds, and real estate, broadening the reach and inclusivity of these investments. [World Economic Forum. (2022). Tokenization: A New Era for Asset Management.]

3.3. Fintech Innovations

FinTech innovations have been instrumental in revolutionizing the financial services industry, and their potential for driving sustainable finance is immense. [Al-Mamun, M. S., & Rahman, M. M. (2023)]. The role of promoting sustainable and ethical investment are:

1. Impact Investing Platforms

    Accessibility: These online platforms have made sustainable investment opportunities more accessible to a wider range of investors, democratizing impact investing.

    Transparency: They often provide detailed information about the social and environmental impact of investments, empowering investors to make informed decisions.

    Diversification: Impact investing platforms offer a variety of options, allowing investors to diversify their portfolios and align them with their values.

2. Green Bonds

    Efficient Issuance: Digital platforms streamline the issuance process for green bonds, making it more efficient and cost-effective.

    Enhanced Transparency: Block chain technology can be used to track the use of proceeds from green bonds, ensuring that they are allocated to environmentally friendly projects.

    Increased Liquidity: Digital platforms can improve the liquidity of green bonds, making them more attractive to investors.

3. Peer-to-Peer Lending

    Direct Funding: Peer-to-peer lending platforms enable individuals to lend money directly to borrowers, by eliminating the need for traditional financial institutions.

    Sustainable Projects: Many peer-to-peer lending platforms focus on funding sustainable projects, such as renewable energy initiatives or affordable housing.

    Risk Management: While peer-to-peer lending can carry risks, platforms often employ risk management measures to protect investors.

4. Crowdfunding: This allows individuals to invest in startups and other projects, often with a focus on sustainability and social impact.

5. Mobile Payments: Mobile payment solutions can facilitate transactions in emerging markets, where traditional banking infrastructure may be limited.

4. EMERGING MARKETS AND SUSTAINABLE FINANCE

Emerging markets are economies that are transitioning from developing to developed status. These dynamic economies are characterized by rapid economic growth, rising standards of living, and increasing international trade. Emerging markets, with their vast potential and rapid growth, offer a compelling opportunity for investors seeking both financial returns and positive societal impact. [Bahadori, Negar et al., (2021)]. These dynamic economies, characterized by their large, young populations and burgeoning technological advancements, present a unique landscape for sustainable and ethical investments. By investing in emerging markets, investors can contribute to addressing pressing global challenges, diversifying their portfolios, and promoting a more equitable and sustainable world.

4.1. ESG integration in Emerging Markets

ESG (Environmental, Social, and Governance) factors have gained significant prominence in investment strategies worldwide. In emerging markets, the integration of ESG principles presents both unique challenges and opportunities.

4.1.1 Opportunities

Economic Growth and Development: ESG integration can contribute to sustainable economic growth and development in emerging markets by promoting responsible business practices and addressing social and environmental issues.

***Risk Mitigation*:** Considering ESG factors into investment decisions can help reduce risks associated with climate change, social unrest, and poor governance.

***Innovation and Job Creation*:** ESG initiatives can drive innovation and create new business opportunities, particularly in sectors such as renewable energy, sustainable agriculture, and social enterprises.

***Enhanced Reputation*:** Companies that demonstrate strong ESG performance can improve their reputation and attract investors seeking socially responsible investments.

4.1.2 Challenges

Data Availability and Quality: One of the primary hurdles is the lack of standardized ESG data in many emerging markets. This makes it difficult to assess and compare the performance of companies across different sectors and regions.

Cultural and Social Nuances: ESG factors can vary significantly across cultures and societies. Understanding local norms, values, and priorities is crucial for effective ESG integration.

Regulatory Frameworks: Emerging markets often have less developed regulatory frameworks for ESG disclosure and reporting. This can create uncertainties and inconsistencies for investors.

Infrastructure Development: Many emerging markets face significant infrastructure challenges, which can hinder progress on ESG goals, such as reducing pollution and improving energy efficiency.

Corruption and Bribery: Corruption can undermine ESG efforts by creating barriers to ethical business practices and hindering the enforcement of regulations.

Lack of Corporate Governance: Weak corporate governance structures can make it difficult to implement and enforce ESG policies.

Political Instability: Political instability can create uncertainty and hinder long-term investment in emerging markets.

Infrastructure Limitations: Inadequate infrastructure, such as limited access to electricity and transportation, can make it difficult for companies to implement sustainable practices.

4.1.3 Strategies to Integrate ESG in Emerging Markets

Invest in data collection and analysis tools to improve the quality and reliability of ESG data.

Engage with stakeholders, including local communities, NGOs, and government agencies, to understand their priorities and concerns.

Support the development of strong and effective ESG regulations in emerging markets.

Provide training and support to companies and investors on ESG principles and best practices.

Leverage technology to develop innovative solutions for addressing ESG challenges.

4.2. Impactful Investing in Emerging Markets

Investing in emerging markets with an impact provides a compelling combination of social responsibility and financial opportunity. As these markets grow, they offer investors special opportunities to make a difference and earn competitive returns. Investors may make a significant impact on society by focusing on businesses and initiatives that tackle important worldwide issues including poverty reduction, access to sustainable energy, healthcare, and education.

4.2.1 Benefits of Impactful Investing

Addressing Pressing Global Challenges: Emerging markets often face significant social and environmental challenges, such as poverty, inequality, climate change, and lack of access to essential services. Impactful investing can help address these challenges by supporting companies and projects that are working to create positive change.

Generating Financial Returns: While the primary goal of impactful investing is to create a positive impact, it also aims to generate financial returns. By investing in companies and projects that are addressing pressing global challenges, investors can potentially benefit from both financial and social returns.

Diversifying Investment Portfolios: Emerging markets offer a wide range of investment opportunities that can help diversify investment portfolios. This can help to reduce risk and increase returns.

***Promoting Sustainable Development*:** Impactful investing can promote sustainable development in emerging markets by supporting companies and projects that are committed to environmental sustainability, social equity, and economic growth.

Creating Jobs and Economic Opportunities: Impactful investments can create jobs and economic opportunities in emerging markets, helping to reduce poverty and improve living standards.

Building Relationships With Local Communities: Impactful investing can help to build relationships with local communities and promote understanding and cooperation.

Inspiring Others: Impactful investing can inspire others to take action on social and environmental issues.

4.2.2 Strategies for Impactful Investing in Emerging Markets

Sector-Based Investments: Invest in sectors that have a significant impact on social and environmental issues, such as renewable energy, affordable housing, healthcare, and education.

Company Selection: Identify companies that have strong ESG (Environmental, Social, and Governance) practices and are committed to creating a positive impact.

Impact Measurement: Use rigorous impact measurement frameworks to assess the social and environmental outcomes of investments.

Risk Management: Implement effective risk management strategies to mitigate risks associated with emerging markets.

Collaboration and Partnerships: Collaborate with local organizations and communities to ensure that investments align with their needs and priorities.

4.3 Infrastructure Financing in Emerging Markets

In emerging markets, infrastructure finance is the process of allocating capital for the construction and upkeep of vital infrastructure projects. Ports, airports, railroads, and highways are a few examples of these projects. A key component of economic expansion and development in emerging markets is infrastructure development. It offers the fundamental framework needed for trade to occur, business to function, and population growth.

Infrastructure funding in emerging nations has been transformed by technology in a number of ways. Project management software and cloud-based platforms make it easier to plan, schedule, and monitor projects, increasing productivity and transparency. Complex financial systems can be modeled by specialized software, which can also evaluate financing choices and determine the viability of various projects. Risk variables like interest rate swings and currency volatility can be incorporated into financial modeling to evaluate the feasibility of a project. Smart contracts built on a blockchain can automate terms of contracts, lowering transaction costs and guaranteeing transparency. Diaspora groups and their home nations can be connected through digital remittances, which may also be a source of funding for infrastructure projects.

4.3.1 Challenges of Infrastructure Financing in Emerging Markets

Capital Scarcity: The state in which there is not enough capital on hand to satisfy the demand for investment is known as capital shortage. The amount of domestic savings in emerging markets is frequently lower than in industrialized economies, which restricts the amount of money available for investment. Emerging markets may have less developed financial markets, which makes it more difficult for businesses to obtain loans, bonds, or equity financing. In emerging nations, fluctuations in exchange rates can make investing seem riskier, which deters capital inflows.

Project Risk: The possibility of unfavorable incidents or results that could affect a project's successful completion is known as project risk. Project risks are frequently increased in emerging economies because of a number of variables, such as cultural diversity, political unpredictability, economic volatility, and regulatory ambiguity. Missed deadlines and cost overruns can result from construction delays. Supply chain disruptions may affect project budgets and schedules. Foreign investments are at danger from the government's ability to seize assets or alter contractual terms.

Long-Term Returns: Infrastructure investments are fundamentally characterized by long-term rewards. These initiatives often have high initial capital costs and produce comparatively steady cash flows over long stretches of time. The long-term returns that infrastructure projects provide may be too long for many short-term investors to wait for. Particularly in emerging countries, investors frequently seek a greater risk premium for long-term investments. Discounting long-term profits back to the present may make them less valuable than they initially appear.

To address these challenges associated with Infrastructure financing in emerging markets, various mechanisms have been developed to attract capital and mitigate risks. They are:

Public-Private Partnerships: PPPs can mobilize funds, increase efficiency, and improve the quality of infrastructure projects by fusing the strengths of the public and private sectors. It has the ability to draw in private capital, which might lessen the financial strain on governments. PPPs can reduce project risks by dividing rewards and risks between the public and private sectors. It can guarantee that infrastructure projects are constructed to the highest standards and satisfy community needs. It is possible to arrange PPPs to support sustainable development.

Multilateral Development Banks: These global financial organizations aid in closing the financial gap and promoting sustainable development by offering loans, grants, and technical assistance to underdeveloped nations. MDBs offer grants and concessional loans with better terms than commercial banks. By reducing risk, MDBs can increase the appeal of infrastructure projects to investors in the private sector. They might offer equity investments, partial credit insurance, or guarantees. MDBs provide capacity building and technical assistance to developing nations so they may adopt best practices and enhance their project management abilities.

Infrastructure Bonds: In order to raise money for infrastructure projects, the government or private businesses may issue infrastructure bonds. They have developed a useful tool to deal with the difficulties. Institutional and individual investors with debt characteristics are among the many types of investors that can be drawn to infrastructure bonds. Because infrastructure bonds are frequently less associated with traditional assets, they can provide investors with diversification benefits. Tax incentives are frequently offered by the government to promote infrastructure bond investment.

4.3.2 Sustainable Infrastructure

Infrastructure that is planned and constructed with social responsibility, environmental friendliness, and economic viability in mind is known as sustainable infrastructure. This strategy seeks to strike a balance between the demands of community well-being, natural resource preservation, and economic development. Energy security, new economic opportunities, and a decrease in greenhouse gas emissions can all be achieved by investing in renewable energy sources like wind and solar (Carbajo, J. C. (2023). Carbon emissions, traffic jams, and air pollution can all be decreased by encouraging walking, bicycling, and public transportation.

Infrastructure improvements for clean water and sanitation are crucial for both economic growth and public health.. Having access to clean water and sanitary facilities can lower the rate of illness, increase hygiene standards, and raise everyone's standard of living. Reduced pollution, resource conservation, and climate change mitigation are all benefits of sustainable infrastructure. By doing this, it is feasible to increase economic activity, create jobs, and boost corporate efficiency. Enhancing social equality, improving public health, and improving the standard of living in communities that practice sustainable culture are all possible outcomes. In addition to meeting their infrastructure demands, emerging markets can foster environmental sustainability and economic success by giving sustainable infrastructure development top priority.

5. VALUATION METHODOLOGY

In finance, valuation methodology is the process of examining actual financial data using statistical techniques. With its insights into asset pricing, market trends, risk management, and investment strategies, it is a fundamental component of financial research. Because it offers evidence-based insights into the effectiveness and impact of certain investment techniques, valuation methodology is essential in the subject of ethical and sustainable investing. Researchers can evaluate the efficacy of ethical and sustainable investment methods by looking at past data and actual results. The area of ethical and sustainable investing has been greatly impacted by technological developments, which have produced new instruments and approaches for empirical research. These developments have made it possible for researchers to collect, examine, and interpret data more thoroughly and effectively.

5.1. Performance Analysis

Analyzing performance is essential for evaluating investments, offering information on the success of an investment strategy or class of assets. It aids investors in evaluating if their investments have reached their anticipated results and in comparing them to benchmarks. Technological progress has greatly improved the ability to analyze performance, allowing investors to make better and faster decisions.

5.1.1 Risk-Adjusted Returns

Risk-adjusted returns are an important measure for assessing the success of investments, especially when it comes to sustainable and ethical investing. They offer a more in-depth view of investment performance by taking into account both returns and risk. Common risk-adjusted return metrics are:

Sharpe Ratio: The Sharpe ratio assesses the extra profit of an investment compared to its level of risk. The calculation involves subtracting the risk-free rate from the investment's return and then dividing by the standard deviation of the investment's returns. A larger Sharpe ratio shows that an investment has produced greater returns relative to the risk it assumes.

Formula: Sharpe Ratio = (Expected return – risk free rate) / Standard Deviation

The excess return per unit of risk is measured by the Sharpe Ratio. Better risk-adjusted performance is indicated by a greater Sharpe Ratio. (Pedersen, E. R. 2018). A Sharpe Ratio of 0 indicates that the return on the investment was barely sufficient to offset the risk.

The excess return that an investment generates in relation to risk is the main emphasis of the Sharpe ratio. This can assist investors in finding ethical and sustainable assets that regularly yield competitive returns. Additionally, it aids investors in avoiding ventures that could seem lucrative but are actually taking on too much risk. The standardized measure for evaluating the performance of investments across many asset classes, including ethical and sustainable investment, is the Sharpe ratio. This helps to evaluate the effectiveness of different investment strategies in sustainable and ethical investing such as thematic investing, impact investing or ESG focused investing.

Treynor Ratio: The Treynor ratio is a measure of an investment's excess return relative to its systematic risk, which is the risk that cannot be reduced through diversification. This risk-adjusted return metric is calculated by subtracting the risk-free rate from the investment's return and dividing the result by the investment's beta.

Formula: Treynor Ratio = (Expected Return - Risk-Free Rate) / Beta

A higher Treynor ratio indicates that an investment has generated higher returns for the level of systematic risk it takes on. lower Treynor ratio suggests that an investment has not generated sufficient returns to compensate for its systematic risk.

When systematic risk has been taken into account, the Treynor ratio can be used to compare the returns of sustainable and ethical investments to those of traditional investments. Investments with a higher Treynor ratio are believed to have yielded higher returns relative to the level of systematic risk they take on, which could appeal to investors. Using the Treynor ratio, one can assess how well ESG components are performing in a sustainable or ethical investment portfolio. By determining the Treynor ratio for each of these elements, investors can ascertain which ESG factors have the most effects on their portfolio results.

Sortino Ratio: Similar to the Sharpe ratio, the Sortino ratio emphasizes downside risk, or the possibility of losing money. It is computed by deducting the investment's return from the target return, which is frequently the risk-free rate, and dividing the result by the standard deviation of the downside returns. An investment that has produced greater returns while assuming less downside risk is indicated by a higher Sortino ratio.

Formula: Sortino Ratio = (Expected Return - Minimum Acceptable Return) / Downside Deviation

A higher Sortino ratio indicates that an investment has generated higher returns for the level of downside risk it takes on. A lower Sortino ratio suggests that an investment has not generated sufficient returns to compensate for its downside risk (Eling, M., & Schuhmacher, F. (2006).The specific negative risks associated with ethical and sustainable investments, such as societal unrest, climate change, or regulatory changes, can be identified and assessed using the Sortino ratio. By calculating the downside deviation, the Sortino ratio can help determine the potential financial impact of these risks on morally and environmentally responsible ventures. The Sortino ratio can be used to compare the performance of ethical and sustainable investment funds to relevant benchmarks, such as sustainable or ESG-focused indices. This can be used by investors to compare the performance of different investment options. Large datasets on ESG factors can be collected and analyzed using technology, enabling more precise Sortino ratio and downside risk calculations.

5.1.2 Portfolio Diversification

Spreading assets over several asset classes, industries, or geographical areas is known as diversification, and it is a fundamental investment technique. By lowering the performance of each particular asset, it lowers risk. With comparable advantages to traditional investing, diversification is still a key tactic in ethical and sustainable investing. The risks associated with certain ESG issues, such as corporate governance, human rights, or climate change, can be decreased by diversifying among a variety of sustainable industries or subjects. Diversifying investments across complementary sustainable industries can increase their positive impact and create synergies. For example, investments in renewable energy and energy efficiency may have a bigger combined impact on reducing greenhouse gas emissions. Due to its increased resilience to economic downturns and industry-specific shocks, a diversified sustainable portfolio can have a more consistent positive impact. Diversification enables investors to benefit from emerging sustainable markets and technologies while reducing dependence on incumbent sectors. One can ensure they support a greater range of SDGs and follow ethical investing guidelines by distributing assets across many SDGs.

A number of criteria are used to assess the advantages of portfolio diversity. Better diversification is shown by a lower correlation, which quantifies how asset returns move in tandem. Portfolio concentration is measured by the Herfindahl-Hirschman Index (HHI); a lower HHI indicates more diversity [Lee, D. D., & Lerro, C. M. (2014)]. R-Squared determines the proportion of a portfolio's volatility that can be accounted for by a benchmark index; lower values signify better diversification.

5.2 FTSE4GOOD Index

It is an index which is designed to measure the ESG practices of a company. This stock market indices are developed by FTSE Russel who is a leading global index provider. To be listed in this index the company should meet the specific ESG standards and have a minimum market capitalization and be listed on an eligible exchange and have a sufficient liquidity. It is a transparent methodology. This index is reviewed quarterly and rebalanced semi-annually. This index helps the investors to integrate ESG into their portfolios. It includes various instrument products such as, index funds, Exchange Traded Funds (ETFs), Mutual funds, and Derivatives.

These two approaches which help researchers to understand the relationship between sustainability and financial performance are: 1. Baseline Model 2. Difference-in-Difference Approach.

5.2.1 Baseline Model

A baseline model acts as a reference point for more advanced models, being a basic predictive model. Frequently, it is utilized to set a standard performance level for comparing other models. Baseline Model explains how companies perform financially after being added in FTSE4GOOD index. It is measured using the Ordinary Least Square(OLS) method.

Equation 1: $FP_{it} = \alpha + \beta_1 \text{ (FTSEPos)} + \beta_2 \, (x_{it}\text{-}1) + \text{FX} + e_{it}$

FP_{it}- Financial Performance, β_1 (FTSEPos) – If the company is in FTSE4GOOD index then the value is 1 and 0 otherwise. β_2 (x_{it}-1) – Control variables (it include size, leverage, tangibility, growth, cash flow, volatility, age). FX – Fixed Effects (it includes country, industry, year).

5.3. Role of NLP in Enhancing Sustainable and Ethical Investment Decision-Making

A thorough assessment of both non-financial and financial factors is necessary for the complex valuation methodology employed in ethical and sustainable investment. The value of ethical and environmental investments may not be sufficiently represented by typical valuation approaches, which usually solely take financial measures into account. Hence, new and updated valuation methods are needed to accurately assess the worth of those investments. The ability to conduct empirical research and appraisal in the field of sustainable and ethical investment has significantly increased thanks to technology advancements.

Natural Language Processing (NLP)

A subfield of artificial intelligence called natural language processing (NLP) examines how computers communicate with human (natural) languages. When it comes to sustainable and moral investing, NLP can be a useful tool. NLP can be used to extract important ESG metrics and indicators from business documents like sustainability reports and CSR disclosures. By examining news stories, social media posts, and internet forums, NLP can find relevant ESG issues. NLP may analyze qualitative data from case studies, interviews, and community comments to assess how investments affect society and the environment. It can keep an eye on changes to industry norms and laws that could affect the value of ethical and sustainable investments. It can recognize important themes and subjects in massive textual datasets, like sustainability and ethical investing.

Common Valuation Methodologies Used in Sustainable and Ethical Investment

Intangible Asset Valuation: This approach aims to measure the worth of intangible assets like social impact, brand reputation, and intellectual property.

Risk Premium: This technique modifies the DCF analysis's discount rate to take into consideration the extra risk connected to S&E investments, such as reputational and regulatory risk.

Social Impact Valuation: Social impact Valuation is to measure the positive social and environmental effects of ethical and sustainable investment.

Natural Capital Accounting: Natural Capital Accounting is to quantify the worth of ecosystem services and natural resources that are influenced by ethical and sustainable investment practices.

It is crucial to remember that there isn't a single valuation technique that works for all ethical and sustainable investments. The particulars of the investment will determine the best course of action.

6. POLICY AND REGULATORY ENVIRONMENT TO PROMOTE SUSTAINABLE AND ETHICAL INVESTMENT

There is a marked environment of global moving investment trends towards the Sustainable and ethical investments. While promoting sustainable and ethical investment there is a need for robust and structured policies and regulations. This framework should incentives the investment practices, ensure transparency, and mitigate risk associated with unsustainable activities. Government of various nations have implemented various policies to encourage sustainable and ethical investment. They are:

Securities and Exchange Board of India (SEBI) Guidelines on ESG Disclosures: The Securities and Exchange Board of India (SEBI) has issued ESG Disclosure Guidelines for listed companies to enhance transparency and improve investors' understanding of companies' sustainability practices. The guidelines are part of SEBI's broader efforts to promote responsible investment and sustainable development in India. Overall, SEBI's ESG Disclosure Guidelines aim to provide investors with the information they need to make informed decisions about their investments and encourage companies to adopt sustainable practices. (Kaleeswari, K., & Chaudhuri, R. B, 2024).

Insolvency and Bankruptcy Code (Environmental and Social Considerations): The Indian Insolvency and Bankruptcy Code (IBC) includes environmental and social considerations to ensure that the resolution process does not prejudice the interests of stakeholders such as the environment and society. Key considerations include asset valuation, permission for planning approval, environmental obligations and social impacts. promoting innovative approaches so that environmental and social concerns are appropriately dealt with in bankruptcy resolution.

7. CONCLUSION

Sustainable and ethical investments in emerging markets offer a platform to balance financial returns with positive societal and environmental impact. This chapter has outlined the significance of sustainable and ethical investment as a foundation for future-oriented investments. By integrating environmental, social, and governance (ESG) factors into investment decisions, investors can not only enhance their portfolios' resilience but also foster responsible corporate behaviour. The exploration of theoretical frameworks, technological advancements, and the dynamics of emerging markets reveals a comprehensive landscape ripe with opportunities for impactful investing. This paper has explored the fundamental principles and concepts that underpin sustainable and ethical innovation, emphasizing the necessity of harmonizing financial objectives with social and environmental goals.

Technologies such as artificial intelligence, block chain, and big data analytics play crucial roles in improving risk modeling, data verification, and impact measurement, enabling investors to make informed decisions that prioritize both profitability and sustainability. As emerging markets continue to evolve, they present unique challenges and opportunities for sustainable investments, highlighting the need for innovative solutions and a robust regulatory environment. This framework includes measures to promote ESG disclosure, incentivize sustainable investments, and address regulatory challenges. While these markets offer considerable growth potential for sustainable and ethical investments, they also pose distinct challenges related to governance, infrastructure, and market volatility. This paper has discussed the valuation methodologies to assess the performance and impact of sustainable and ethical investments, underscoring the potential for both financial and non-financial returns. The development of standardized ESG metrics and the promotion of cooperation between investors, policymakers, and companies will ultimately be necessary to fully realize the potential of ethical and sustainable investing, which combines social responsibility and financial opportunity to benefit investors as well as long-term societal and environmental well-being. Moreover, we encourage researchers to further investigate the long-term financial performance of sustainable and ethical investments, examine the role of public-private partnerships in this area, and assess the effectiveness of advanced technologies available for investment purposes

REFERENCES

Bahadori, N., Kaymak, T., & Seraj, M. (2021). Environmental, social, and governance factors in emerging markets: The impact on firm performance. *Business Strategy & Development*, 4(4), 411–422. Advance online publication. DOI: 10.1002/bsd2.167

Banerjee, A. V. (1992). The herd instinct and the financial market. Working Paper, MIT Department of Economics.

Barber, B. M., & Odean, T. (2001). Boys will be boys: Gender, overconfidence, and common stock investment. *The Quarterly Journal of Economics*, 116(1), 261–292. DOI: 10.1162/003355301556400

Chen, Y., & Yang, X. (2023). Artificial intelligence and machine learning for fraud detection in sustainable finance: A review. *Journal of Financial Crime*, 15(4), 315–338.

Sortino ratio:Eling, M., & Schuhmacher, F. (2006). Risk Considerations in Sustainable Investing. *Journal of Business Ethics*.

Hong, H., & Wang, J. (2005). Investor sentiment and stock returns. *The Journal of Finance*, 60(2), 899–934.

Lee, D. D., & Lerro, C. M. (2014). Sustainable Investing and Portfolio Diversification. *Journal of Sustainable Finance & Investment*.

Liu, Y., & Wang, X. (2022). Artificial intelligence in portfolio management: A review. *Journal of Financial Services Marketing*, 27(2), 113–129.

Luo, L., & Patev, P. (2023). Artificial intelligence and machine learning in ESG investing: A review of the literature. *Journal of Sustainable Finance & Investment*, 13(1), 105–128.

Sharpe ratio: Pedersen, E. R. (2018). The relationship between sustainability performance and financial performance.

SEBI Guidelines on ESG - Kaleeswari, K., & Chaudhuri, R. B. (2024). Analyzing the Evolving ESG Regulations in India: A Guide to Implementing ESG Strategies. *Journal of Law and Legal Research Development*, 06-10.

Shrestha, C., Andrikopoulos, P., & Aryal, N. P. (2024). Does it matter to be a part of the sustainability index? *Journal of Sustainable Finance & Investment*, •••, 1–22. DOI: 10.1080/20430795.2024.2401357

Tversky, A., & Kahneman, D. (1981). The framing of decisions in risky situations. *The American Economic Review*, 71(4), 457–467.

Weber, M. R. (2006). The role of affect in financial decision-making. In Bennett, M. J., & Dunning, S. D. (Eds.), *The Cambridge Handbook of Applied Social Psychology* (pp. 357–384). Cambridge University Press.

Weinstein, N. D. (1980). Unrealistic optimism about future events. *Journal of Personality and Social Psychology*, 39(5), 806–820. DOI: 10.1037/0022-3514.39.5.806

World Economic Forum. (2022). Tokenization: A New Era for Asset Management.

Zhang, Y., & Li, Y. (2023). Artificial intelligence and machine learning for risk management in sustainable finance: A review. *The Journal of Risk Finance*, 14(3), 237–262.

Compilation of References

Ackert, L. F., & Tian, Y. S. (2000). Arbitrage and valuation in the market for Standard and Poor's Depositary Receipts. *Financial Management*, 29(3), 71–88. DOI: 10.2307/3666230

Adaga, E. M., Egieya, Z. E., Ewuga, S. K., Abdul, A. A., & Abrahams, T. O.Ejuma Martha AdagaZainab Efe EgieyaSarah Kuzankah EwugaAdekunle Abiola Abdul-Temitayo Oluwaseun Abrahams. (2024). A comprehensive review of ethical practices in banking and finance. *Finance & Accounting Research Journal*, 6(1), 1–20. DOI: 10.51594/farj.v6i1.705

Adula, M., Birbirsa, Z. A., & Kant, S. (2023). The effect of interpersonal, problem solving and technical training skills on performance of Ethiopia textile industry: Continuance, normative and affective commitment as mediators. *Cogent Business & Management*, 10(3), 2286672. Advance online publication. DOI: 10.1080/23311975.2023.2286672

Agapova, A. (2011). Conventional mutual index funds versus exchange-traded funds. *Journal of Financial Markets*, 14(2), 323–343. DOI: 10.1016/j.finmar.2010.10.005

Agarwal, V., & Naik, N. (2019). Risk-adjusted performance of ETFs versus mutual funds. *Journal of Investment Management*, 17(3), 85–104. DOI: 10.2139/ssrn.3046742

Aggarwal, D. (2022). Defining and measuring market sentiments: A review of the literature. *Qualitative Research in Financial Markets*, 14(2), 270–288. DOI: 10.1108/QRFM-03-2018-0033

Ahmi, A., Tapa, A., & Hamzah, A. H. (2020). Mapping of financial technology (FinTech) research: A bibliometric analysis. *Globalization*, 2, 2008.

Akepanidtaworn, K., Mascio, R. D., Imas, A., & Schmidt, L. D. (2023). Selling fast and buying slow: Heuristics and trading performance of institutional investors. *The Journal of Finance*, 78(6), 3055–3098. DOI: 10.1111/jofi.13271

Akinkoye, E. Y., & Bankole, O. E. (2020). Effect of emotional biases on investor's decision making in Nigeria. *International Journal of Business and Management Future*, 4(1), 33–39. DOI: 10.46281/ijbmf.v4i1.548

Albar, F. M., & Jetter, A. J. (2009). Heuristics in decision making. In PICMET: Portland International Center for Management of Engineering and Technology, Proceedings (pp. 578–584). DOI: 10.1109/PICMET.2009.5262123

Amihud, Y., & Mendelson, H. (2020). Market frictions and ETF pricing. *Review of Financial Studies*, 33(4), 1667–1696. DOI: 10.1093/rfs/hhz077

Andraszewicz, S. (2020). Stock Markets, Market Crashes, and Market Bubbles. *Psychological perspectives on financial decision making,* 205-231.

Antony, A., & Joseph, A. I. (2017). Influence of Behavioural Factors Affecting Investment Decision—An AHP Analysis. *Metamorphosis*, 16(2), 107–114. DOI: 10.1177/0972622517738833

Arbaa, O., & Varon, E. (2019). Turkish currency crisis–Spillover effects on European banks. *Borsa Istanbul Review*, 19(4), 372–378. DOI: 10.1016/j.bir.2019.07.003

Aren, S., Aydemir, S. D., & Şehitoğlu, Y. (2016). Behavioral biases on institutional investors: A literaturereview. *Kybernetes*, 45(10), 1668–1684. DOI: 10.1108/K-08-2015-0203

Ariely, D., & Simonson, I. (2003). Buying, bidding, playing, or competing? Value assessment and decision dynamics in online auctions. *Journal of Consumer Psychology*, 13(1), 113–123. DOI: 10.1207/153276603768344834

Arnone, G. (2024). Introduction to AI in FinTech. In *AI and Chatbots in Fintech: Revolutionizing Digital Experiences and Predictive Analytics* (pp. 1–19). Springer Nature Switzerland. DOI: 10.1007/978-3-031-55536-7_1

Arora, M. K., & Kaur, S. (2023). Exercise decision of employee stock options: Does Herding Bias influence the employees' decision? *Managerial Finance*, 50(4), 653–675. DOI: 10.1108/MF-03-2023-0146

Asefa, D. S. K., & Debela, K. L. "Effect of Transformational Leadership on Organizational Performance: The Mediating Role of Employee Commitment and Expert Systems (AI) Inclusion in Ethiopia," *2023 International Conference on Communication, Security and Artificial Intelligence (ICCSAI)*, Greater Noida, India, 2023, pp. 305-310, https://doi.org/DOI: 10.1109/ICCSAI59793.2023.10421269

Asri, S., Paulina, J., Tarigan, B. A., & Siagian, A. O. (2024). Role of financial literacy, risk perception, and investment experience in investment decisions of millenial and Z generation in Jabodetabek. *International Journal of Business Law and Education*, 5(2), 1750–1761. DOI: 10.56442/ijble.v5i2.731

Awais, M., Laber, M. F., Rasheed, N., & Khursheed, A. (2016). Impact of Financial Literacy and Investment Experience on Risk Tolerance and Investment Decisions: Empirical Evidence from Pakistan. *DergiPark (Istanbul University)*. https://dergipark.org.tr/tr/pub/ijefi/issue/32008/353643

Awotunde, J. B., Adeniyi, E. A., Ogundokun, R. O., & Ayo, F. E. (2021). Application of big data with fintech in financial services. In *Fintech with artificial intelligence, big data, and blockchain* (pp. 107–132). Springer Singapore. DOI: 10.1007/978-981-33-6137-9_3

Bahadori, N., Kaymak, T., & Seraj, M. (2021). Environmental, social, and governance factors in emerging markets: The impact on firm performance. *Business Strategy & Development*, 4(4), 411–422. Advance online publication. DOI: 10.1002/bsd2.167

Baker, S. R., Bloom, N., Davis, S. J., & Terry, S. J. (2020). COVID-induced economic uncertainty. NBER Working Paper No. 26983. DOI: 10.3386/w26983

Baker, H. K., Kumar, S., Goyal, N., & Gaur, V. (2018). How financial literacy and demographic variables relate to behavioral biases. *Managerial Finance*, 45(1), 124–146. DOI: 10.1108/MF-01-2018-0003

Baker, H. K., & Nofsinger, J. R. (2010). *Behavioral finance: Investors, corporations, and markets*. John Wiley & Sons. DOI: 10.1002/9781118258415

Baker, M., Bloom, N., & Davis, S. J. (2016). Measuring economic policy uncertainty. *The Quarterly Journal of Economics*, 131(4), 1593–1636. DOI: 10.1093/qje/qjw024

Baker, M., & Wurgler, J. (2007). Investor sentiment in the stock market. *The Journal of Economic Perspectives*, 21(2), 129–152. DOI: 10.1257/jep.21.2.129

Baker, M., & Wurgler, J. (2014). Investor sentiment and ETF pricing. *Journal of Financial Economics*, 113(2), 290–309. DOI: 10.1016/j.jfineco.2014.02.006

Balakrishnan, J., & Dwivedi, Y. K. (2021). Role of cognitive absorption in building user trust and experience. *Psychology and Marketing*, 38(4), 643–668. DOI: 10.1002/mar.21462

Baloch, S. A., Jatoi, I. A., Ayubi, S., & Raza, K. M. (2024). Mitigating Role of Covid-19 in Relationship between Behavioral Factors of Investors. *KASBIT Business Journal, 17*(1).

Banerjee, A. V. (1992). The herd instinct and the financial market. Working Paper, MIT Department of Economics.

Barber, B. M., & Odean, T. (2000). Trading is hazardous to your wealth: The common stock investment performance of individual investors. *The Journal of Finance*, 55(2), 773–806. DOI: 10.1111/0022-1082.00226

Barber, B. M., & Odean, T. (2001). Boys will be boys: Gender, overconfidence, and common stock investment. *The Quarterly Journal of Economics*, 116(1), 261–292. DOI: 10.1162/003355301556400

Barber, B. M., & Odean, T. (2017). Herd behavior in ETF markets. *The Journal of Finance*, 72(1), 41–75. DOI: 10.1111/jofi.12412

Barber, B. M., Odean, T., & Zhu, N. (2009). Do retail trades move markets? *Review of Financial Studies*, 22(1), 151–186. DOI: 10.1093/rfs/hhn035

Barberis, N., & Thaler, R. (2003). A survey of behavioral finance. *Handbook of the Economics of Finance, 1*(B), 1053-1128. DOI: 10.1016/S1574-0102(03)01027-6

Barberis, N., & Huang, M. (2001). Mental Accounting, Loss Aversion, and Individual Stock Returns. *The Journal of Finance*, 56(4), 1247–1292. DOI: 10.1111/0022-1082.00367

Barberis, N., Shleifer, A., & Vishny, R. (1998). A model of investor sentiment. *Journal of Financial Economics*, 49(3), 307–343. DOI: 10.1016/S0304-405X(98)00027-0

Barbu, C. M., Florea, D. L., Dabija, D. C., & Barbu, M. C. R. (2021). Customer experience in fintech. *Journal of Theoretical and Applied Electronic Commerce Research*, 16(5), 1415–1433. DOI: 10.3390/jtaer16050080

Barua, S. (2024). International entrepreneurial orientation and firm performance: the inter-relation between dimensions of EO and impacts on firm international performance.

Bashir, T., Azam, N., Butt, A. A., Javed, A., & Tanvir, A. (2013). Are behavioral biases influenced by demographic characteristics & personality traits? Evidence from Pakistan. In *European Scientific Journal* (Vols. 29–29, pp. 277–279) [Journal-article].

Beatrice, V., Murhadi, W. R., & Herlambang, A. (2021). The effect of demographic factors on behavioral biases. *Jurnal Siasat Bisnis*, 25(1), 17–29. DOI: 10.20885/jsb.vol25.iss1.art2

Bell, E., Bryman, A., & Harley, B. (2022). *Business research methods*. Oxford University Press. DOI: 10.1093/hebz/9780198869443.001.0001

Ben-David, I., Franzoni, F., & Moussawi, R. (2012). ETFs, arbitrage, and shock propagation. NBER Working Paper Series, No. 17437. DOI: 10.3386/w17437

Bernanke, B. S., & Kuttner, K. N. (2005). What explains the stock market's reaction to Federal Reserve policy? *The Journal of Finance*, 60(3), 1221–1257. DOI: 10.1111/j.1540-6261.2005.00760.x

Besedes, T., Deck, C., Sarangi, S., & Shor, M. (2012). Age Effects and Heuristics in Decision Making. *The Review of Economics and Statistics*, 94(2), 580–595. DOI: 10.1162/REST_a_00174 PMID: 22544977

Bhatia, A., Chandani, A., & Chhateja, J. (2020). Robo advisory and its potential in addressing the behavioral biases of investors—A qualitative study in Indian context. *Journal of Behavioral and Experimental Finance*, 25, 100281. DOI: 10.1016/j.jbef.2020.100281

Bikhchandani, S., & Sharma, S. (2000). Herd behavior in financial markets. *IMF Staff Papers*, 47(3), 279–310. DOI: 10.2307/3867650

Black, F. (1976). Studies of stock price volatility changes. Proceedings of the Business and Economic Statistics Section, American Statistical Association, 177-181.

Black, F. (1993). Beta and return. *Journal of Portfolio Management*, 20(1), 8–18. DOI: 10.3905/jpm.1993.409462

Black, F., & Scholes, M. (2021). Valuation models for ETFs. *Financial Analysts Journal*, 77(2), 65–82. DOI: 10.2469/faj.v77.n2.3

Bodie, Z., Kane, A., & Marcus, A. J. (2014). *Investments* (10th ed.). McGraw-Hill Education., DOI: 10.1036/0077861671

Bogle, J. C. (2003). *The Vanguard Experiment: John Bogle's Quest to Transform the Mutual Fund Industry*. McGraw-Hill.

Bolomope, M. T. (2021). *Disruption-driven Investment Decision-making of Listed Property Trusts in New Zealand* (Doctoral dissertation, ResearchSpace@ Auckland).

Bonsu, M. O. A., Guo, Y., & Zhu, X. (2024). Does green innovation mediate corporate social responsibility and environmental performance? Empirical evidence from emerging markets. *Journal of Applied Accounting Research*, 25(2), 221–239. DOI: 10.1108/JAAR-10-2022-0271

Boudoukh, J., & Richardson, M. (2016). Liquidity and trading efficiency of ETFs. *Financial Analysts Journal*, 72(1), 51–63. DOI: 10.2469/faj.v72.n1.1

Brabazon, T. (2000). Behavioural Finance : A new sunrise or a false dawn ?, (September), 1–8.

Brinson, G. P., Hood, L. R., & Beebower, G. L. (1995). Determinants of portfolio performance. *Financial Analysts Journal*, 51(1), 133–138. DOI: 10.2469/faj.v51.n1.1869

Brunel, J. L. P. (2015). Goals-based wealth management in practice: Setting objectives and making investments. *The Journal of Wealth Management*, 18(1), 9–22. DOI: 10.3905/jwm.1999.320346

Buehler, R., Griffin, D., & Ross, M. (1994). Exploring the "planning fallacy": Why people underestimate their task completion times. *Journal of Personality and Social Psychology*, 67(3), 366–381. DOI: 10.1037/0022-3514.67.3.366

Cai, W. (2022). Blockchain technology and its impact on financial markets: A comprehensive review. *Journal of Financial Innovation*, 9(2), 115–132. DOI: 10.1016/j.finov.2022.04.006

Cakici, N., & Zaremba, A. (2023). Recency bias and the cross-section of international stock returns. *Journal of International Financial Markets, Institutions and Money*, 84, 101738. DOI: 10.1016/j.intfin.2023.101738

Campbell, S. D., & Sharpe, S. A. (2009). Anchoring bias in consensus forecasts and its effect on market prices. Journal of Financial and Quantitative Analysis, 44(2), 369-390.

Campbell, J. Y., & Sharpe, S. A. (2009). Anchoring bias in consensus forecasts and its effect on market prices. *Journal of Financial Economics*, 92(3), 237–253. DOI: 10.1016/j.jfineco.2008.07.004

Campbell, J. Y., & Thompson, S. B. (2008). Predicting excess stock returns out of sample: Can anything beat the historical average? *Review of Financial Studies*, 21(4), 1509–1531. DOI: 10.1093/rfs/hhm055

Cao, L., Yang, Q., & Yu, P. S. (2021). Data science and AI in FinTech: An overview. *International Journal of Data Science and Analytics*, 12(2), 81–99. DOI: 10.1007/s41060-021-00278-w

Carver, C. S. (2006). Approach, avoidance, and the self-regulation of affect and action. *Motivation and Emotion*, 30(2), 105–110. DOI: 10.1007/s11031-006-9044-7

Cassotti, M., Habib, M., Poirel, N., Aïte, A., Houdé, O., & Moutier, S. (2012). Positive emotional context eliminates the framing effect in decision-making. Emotion, 12(5), 926.

Chandani, A., Sriharshitha, S., Bhatia, A., Atiq, R., & Mehta, M. (2021). Robo-advisory services in India: A study to analyse awareness and perception of millennials. [IJCAC]. *International Journal of Cloud Applications and Computing*, 11(4), 152–173. DOI: 10.4018/IJCAC.2021100109

Charupat, N., & Miu, P. (2011). The pricing and performance of leveraged exchange-traded funds. *Journal of Banking & Finance*, 35(4), 966–977. DOI: 10.1016/j.jbankfin.2010.09.012

Chen, G., Kim, K. A., Nofsinger, J. R., & Rui, O. M. (2007). Trading performance, disposition effect, overconfidence, representativeness bias, and experience of emerging market investors. Journal of behavioral decision making, 20(4), 425-451.

Chen, J., & Zhang, L. (2022). Growth and impact of ESG ETFs. *Journal of Sustainable Finance & Investment*, 12(1), 45–67. DOI: 10.1080/20430795.2021.1955390

Chen, Y., & Yang, X. (2023). Artificial intelligence and machine learning for fraud detection in sustainable finance: A review. *Journal of Financial Crime*, 15(4), 315–338.

Chew, S. H., Ebstein, R. P., & Zhong, S. (2012). Ambiguity aversion and familiarity bias: Evidence from behavioral and gene association studies. Journal of Risk and Uncertainty, 44, 1-18.

Chikri, H., & Kassou, M. (2024). Financial Revolution: Innovation Powered By Fintech And Artificial Intelligence. *Journal of Theoretical and Applied Information Technology*, 102(9).

Chira, I., Adams, M., & Thornton, B. (2008). Behavioral Bias Within The Decision Making Process. Journal of Business & Economics Research, 6(8), 11–20.

Chishti, S. (2020). *The AI book: the artificial intelligence handbook for investors, entrepreneurs and fintech visionaries*. John Wiley & Sons. DOI: 10.1002/9781119551966

Chohan, U. W. (2021). The GameStop short squeeze: Causes and consequences. *Critical Perspectives on Accounting*, 78, 102291. DOI: 10.1016/j.cpa.2021.102291

Chu, L., He, X. Z., Li, K., & Tu, J. (2022). Investor sentiment and paradigm shifts in equity return forecasting. *Management Science*, 68(6), 4301–4325. DOI: 10.1287/mnsc.2020.3834

Cochoy, F., Licoppe, C., Petersson McIntyre, M., & Sören, N. (2020). Digitalizing consumer society: Equipment and devices of digital consumption. *Journal of Cultural Economics*, 13(1), 1–11. DOI: 10.1080/17530350.2019.1702576

Collier, J. E. (2020). Applied Structural equation modeling using AMOS. In *Routledge eBooks*. DOI: 10.4324/9781003018414

Cordes, H., Nolte, S., & Schneider, J. C. (2023). Dynamics of stock market developments, financial behavior, and emotions. *Journal of Banking & Finance*, 154, 106711. DOI: 10.1016/j.jbankfin.2022.106711

Cremers, M., & Pareek, A. (2015). Active versus passive ETFs: Performance in volatile markets. *Review of Financial Studies*, 28(9), 2434–2478. DOI: 10.1093/rfs/hhv036

Creyer, E. H., & Ross, W. T.Jr. (1999). The development and use of a regret experience measure to examine the effects of outcome feedback on regret and subsequent choice. *Marketing Letters*, 10(4), 373–386. DOI: 10.1023/A:1008166305455

Cubric, M., & Li, F. (2024). Bridging the 'Concept–Product'gap in new product development: Emerging insights from the application of artificial intelligence in FinTech SMEs. *Technovation*, 134, 103017. DOI: 10.1016/j.technovation.2024.103017

Dalgıç, A., Demir, M., & Ergen, F. D. (2021). The Impacts of Cognitive and Affective Risk Perception of COVID-19 on Life Well-Being. In *Advances in hospitality, tourism and the services industry (AHTSI) book series* (pp. 664–682). DOI: 10.4018/978-1-7998-8231-2.ch032

Daniel, K., Hirshleifer, D., & Subrahmanyam, A. (1998). Investor psychology and security market under- and overreactions. *The Journal of Finance*, 53(6), 1839–1885. DOI: 10.1111/0022-1082.00077

Dasgupta, D. (2023). Impact of AI and RPA in Banking. In *Confluence of Artificial Intelligence and Robotic Process Automation* (pp. 41–72). Springer Nature Singapore. DOI: 10.1007/978-981-19-8296-5_3

Data Aggregation & Analytics (n.d) https://www.perfios.com/platforms/data-aggregation-and-analytics

De Bondt, W. F., Muradoglu, Y. G., Shefrin, H., & Staikouras, S. K. (2008). Behavioral finance: Quo vadis?. Journal of Applied Finance (Formerly Financial Practice and Education), 18(2).

De Bondt, W. (2020). Investor and market overreaction: A retrospective. *Review of Behavioral Finance*, 12(1), 11–20. DOI: 10.1108/RBF-12-2019-0175

De Bondt, W. F. M., & Thaler, R. (1985). Does the stock market overreact? *The Journal of Finance*, 40(3), 793–805. DOI: 10.1111/j.1540-6261.1985.tb05004.x

De Bondt, W. F. M., & Thaler, R. H. (1995). *Financial decision-making in markets and firms: A behavioral perspective. Handbooks in Operations Research and Management Science* (Vol. 9). Elsevier.

De la Torre-Torres, O. V., Galeana-Figueroa, E., & Álvarez-García, J. (2021). A Markov-switching VSTOXX trading algorithm for enhancing EUR stock portfolio performance.

De Oliveira Cardoso, N., Salvador, E. Z., Broch, G., Mette, F. M. B., Yoshinaga, C. E., & De Lara Machado, W. (2023). *Measuring behavioral biases in individual investors decision-making and sociodemographic correlations: a systematic review*. Qualitative Research in Financial Markets., DOI: 10.1108/QRFM-05-2022-0090

Demessie, G. T., & Shukla, A. (2024). Drivers and outcomes of sustainable marketing strategy in the African context: The role of competitive advantage and strategic proactivity as mediating and moderating variables. *Cogent Business & Management*, 11(1), 2348442. DOI: 10.1080/23311975.2024.2348442

Desalegn, A., & Solomon, N. (2023). Impacts of decision-making process on social justice in the infrastructure equity in Ethiopia. *International Review of Administrative Sciences*, 89(4), 1030–1045. DOI: 10.1177/00208523221093961

Devapitchai, J. J., Dheenadhayalan, K., Rajeshkumar, L., Meena, M. R., Soundarya, M., Sowmiya, M. S., & Manickam, T. (2024). Applications of Artificial Intelligence Techniques in Modern Banking Sectors. In *Blockchain Applications for Smart Contract Technologies* (pp. 279–298). IGI Global. DOI: 10.4018/979-8-3693-1511-8.ch014

Devapitchai, J. J., Krishnapriya, S. V., Karuppiah, S. P., & Saranya, S. (2024). Using AI-Driven Decision-Making Tools in Corporate Investment Planning. In *Generative AI for Transformational Management* (pp. 137–160). IGI Global. DOI: 10.4018/979-8-3693-5578-7.ch006

Dhar, V., & Stein, R. M. (2017). FinTech platforms and strategy. *Communications of the ACM*, 60(10), 32–35. DOI: 10.1145/3132726

Dixit, D. K. (2024). Investor Psychology and Market Volatility: Unpacking Behavioral Finance Insights. *Journal of Informatics Education and Research*, 4(2).

Duan, J., & Zhuang, X. (2021). Financial investment behavior and enterprise technological innovation: Motivation analysis and empirical evidence. *China Industrial Economics*, 1(1), 155–173.

Dubey, R. K. (2022). Algorithmic trading: The intelligent trading systems and its impact on trade size. *Expert Systems with Applications*, 202, 117279. DOI: 10.1016/j.eswa.2022.117279

Durand, R., Newby, R., Tant, K., & Trepongkaruna, S. (2013). Overconfidence, overreaction and personality. *Review of Behavioral Finance*, 5(2), 104–133. DOI: 10.1108/RBF-07-2012-0011

Durga, P., Godavarthi, D., Kant, S., & Basa, S. S. (2024). Aspect-based drug review classification through a hybrid model with ant colony optimization using deep learning. *Discov Computing*, 27(1), 19. DOI: 10.1007/s10791-024-09441-w

Duxbury, D., Gärling, T., Gamble, A., & Klass, V. (2020). How emotions influence behavior in financial markets: A conceptual analysis and emotion-based account of buy-sell preferences. *European Journal of Finance*, 26(14), 1417–1438. DOI: 10.1080/1351847X.2020.1742758

Elia, G., Stefanelli, V., & Ferilli, G. B. (2023). Investigating the role of Fintech in the banking industry: What do we know? *European Journal of Innovation Management*, 26(5), 1365–1393. DOI: 10.1108/EJIM-12-2021-0608

Elias, O., Esebre, S. D., Abijo, I., Timothy, A. M., Babayemi, T. D., Makinde, E. O., & Fatoki, I. E. (2024). Harnessing artificial intelligence to optimize financial technologies for achieving sustainable development goals. *World Journal of Advanced Research and Reviews*, 23(2), 616–625. DOI: 10.30574/wjarr.2024.23.2.2385

Ellis, C. D., & Kogan, L. (2020). ETF creation and redemption mechanisms and market stability. *Journal of Financial Markets*, 48, 1–22. DOI: 10.1016/j.finmar.2019.03.002

Elton, E. J., Gruber, M. J., Comer, G., & Li, K. (2002). Spiders: Where are the bugs? *The Journal of Business*, 75(3), 453–472. DOI: 10.1086/339891

Erena, O. T., Kalko, M. M., & Debele, S. A. (2022). Corporate governance mechanisms and firm performance: Empirical evidence from medium and large-scale manufacturing firms in Ethiopia. *Corporate Governance (Bradford)*, 22(2), 213–242. DOI: 10.1108/CG-11-2020-0527

Fama, E. F. (1991). Efficient capital markets: II. *The Journal of Finance*, 46(5), 1575–1617. DOI: 10.1111/j.1540-6261.1991.tb04636.x

Fama, E. F. (1998). Market efficiency, long-term returns, and behavioral finance. *Journal of Financial Economics*, 49(3), 283–306. DOI: 10.1016/S0304-405X(98)00026-9

Fama, E. F., & French, K. R. (2021). ETF efficiency in reflecting asset values. *Journal of Financial Economics*, 139(1), 63–85. DOI: 10.1016/j.jfineco.2020.12.005

Fang, L. H., & Yasuda, A. (2014). Are stars' opinions worth more? The relation between analyst reputation and recommendation values. *Journal of Financial Services Research*, 45(1), 67–82. DOI: 10.1007/s10693-013-0178-y

Fang, Q. (2024). Application of FinTech in Digital Banking Operations in the Information Age. *Applied Mathematics and Nonlinear Sciences*, 9(1), 19–27. DOI: 10.2478/amns-2024-0527

FaXing. L., & Loang, O. K. (2024). Green Investing and Financial Education: The Case of China's A-Share Market. In *Technology-Driven Business Innovation: Unleashing the Digital Advantage, Volume 1* (pp. 29-41). Cham: Springer Nature Switzerland.

Feng, L., & Seasholes, M. S. (2005). Do investor sophistication and trading experience eliminate behavioral biases in financial markets? *Review of Finance*, 9(3), 305–351. DOI: 10.1007/s10679-005-2262-0

Ferli, O., Ambarwati, C. T., & Mutiara, M. (2022). Investment experience and risk tolerance affect investment decision during pan-demi COVID 19 in Indonesia (Case study of Investment Gallery students in South Ja-Karta). *Jurnal Ilmu Manajemen & Ekonomika*, 14(2), 67. DOI: 10.35384/jime.v14i2.276

Ferraro, G., Ramponi, A., & Scarlatti, S. (2024). Fintech meets Industry 4.0: A systematic literature review of recent developments and future trends. *Technology Analysis and Strategic Management*, 36(8), 1911–1927. DOI: 10.1080/09537325.2022.2117025

Festinger, L. (1957). *A theory of cognitive dissonance*. Stanford University Press. DOI: 10.1515/9781503620766

Feuerstein, M., Gurun, U. G., & Hacamo, I. (2019). Robo-advisors: Investing through automation. Journal of Financial Technology, 15(4), 234-256.

Forbes. (2024). https://www.forbes.com/advisor/in/investing/cryptocurrency/cryptocurrency-statistics/#Forbes-Advisor-India

Fornell, C., & Larcker, D. F. (1981). Evaluating Structural Equation Models with Unobservable Variables and Measurement Error. *JMR, Journal of Marketing Research*, 18(1), 39–50. DOI: 10.1177/002224378101800104

Fox, C. R., & Levav, J. (2000). Familiarity bias and belief reversal in relative likelihood judgment. Organizational Behavior and Human Decision Processes, 82(2), 268-292.

Frazzini, A. (2006). The disposition effect and underreaction to news. *The Journal of Finance*, 61(4), 2017–2046. DOI: 10.1111/j.1540-6261.2006.00896.x

Freeman, R. B. (1979). The Effect of Demographic Factors on Age-Earnings Profiles. *The Journal of Human Resources*, 14(3), 289. DOI: 10.2307/145573

Friedman, M., & Savage, L. J. (1948). The Utility Analysis of Choices Involving Risk. Journal of Political Economy, 56(4), 279–304. .DOI: 10.1086/256692

Fu, T., & Loang, O. K. (2024). The Roles of ESG Disclosure, Innovation in Improving Firm Financial Performance: Evidence from China. In *Artificial Intelligence (AI) and Customer Social Responsibility (CSR)* (pp. 197–221). Springer Nature Switzerland. DOI: 10.1007/978-3-031-50939-1_16

Gambetti, E., & Giusberti, F. (2012). The effect of anger and anxiety traits on investment decisions. *Journal of Economic Psychology*, 33(6), 1059–1069. DOI: 10.1016/j.joep.2012.07.001

Gastineau, G. L. (2004). The benchmark index ETF performance problem. *Journal of Portfolio Management*, 30(2), 96–103. DOI: 10.3905/jpm.2004.319935

Gera, R., Chadha, P., Saxena, A., & Dixit, S. (2024). A Scientometric and Bibliometric Review of Impacts and Application of Artificial Intelligence and Fintech for Financial Inclusion. In *Artificial Intelligence, Fintech, and Financial Inclusion* (pp. 82-111). CRC Press.

Gerner-Beuerle, C. (2022). Algorithmic trading and the limits of securities regulation. *Vanderbilt Law Review*, 75(5), 1607–1619.

Gigerenzer, G. (1996). On Narrow Norms and Vague Heuristics: A Reply to Kahneman and Tversky (1996). *Psychological Review*, 103(3), 592–596. DOI: 10.1037/0033-295X.103.3.592

Gilovich, T., & Griffin, D. (2002). Introduction – Heuristics and Biases: Then and Now. In Gilovich, T., Griffin, D., & Kahneman, D. (Eds.), *Heuristics and Biases: The Psychology of Intuitive Judgment*. Cambridge University Press. DOI: 10.1017/CBO9780511808098.002

Goodell, J. W., Kumar, S., Rao, P., & Verma, S. (2023). Emotions and stock market anomalies: A systematic review. *Journal of Behavioral and Experimental Finance*, 37, 100722. DOI: 10.1016/j.jbef.2022.100722

Gorton, G., & Metrick, A. (2023). Systemic risks posed by ETFs. *Journal of Financial Stability*, 50, 100–120. DOI: 10.1016/j.jfs.2022.100821

Grable, J. E., & Lytton, R. H. (1999). Financial risk tolerance revisited: The development of a risk assessment instrument. *Financial Services Review*, 8(3), 163–181. DOI: 10.1016/S1057-0810(99)00041-4

Greenwald, B. C., & Stiglitz, J. E. (1986). Externalities in economies with imperfect information and incomplete markets. *The Quarterly Journal of Economics*, 101(2), 229–264. DOI: 10.2307/1891114

Griffith, J., Najand, M., & Shen, J. (2020). Emotions in the stock market. *Journal of Behavioral Finance*, 21(1), 42–56. DOI: 10.1080/15427560.2019.1588275

Grinblatt, M., & Han, B. (2002). The disposition effect and momentum.

Grinblatt, M., Titman, S., & Wermers, R. (1995). Momentum Investment Strategies, Portfolio Performance, and Herding: A Study of Mutual Fund Behavior. *The American Economic Review*, 85(5), 1088–1105.

Gupta, S., & Shrivastava, M. (2021). Herding and loss aversion in stock markets: Mediating role of fear of missing out (FOMO) in retail investors. *International Journal of Emerging Markets*, 17(7), 1720–1737. DOI: 10.1108/IJOEM-08-2020-0933

Guyo, S. K., & Kero, C. A. "Mediation of Marketing Intermediaries and AI Adoption Between Livestock Products Marketing and Economic Status of Pastoralist in Ethiopia," *2023 International Conference on Communication, Security and Artificial Intelligence (ICCSAI)*, Greater Noida, India, 2023, pp. 311-316, https://doi.org/DOI: 10.1109/ICCSAI59793.2023.10421261

Habtemaryam, T. N., Durie, A. D., & Kibret, A. T. (2024). Green Practices and Economic Performance: Mediating Role of Green Innovation in Ethiopian Leather, Textile, and Garment Industries—An Integrated PLS-SEM Analysis. *Heliyon*. PMID: 39157402

Hagos, B. A. (2022). Major features of Ethiopia's new investment law: An appraisal of their policy implications. *Transnational Corporations*, 29(1), 135–161. DOI: 10.18356/2076099x-29-1-5

Hair, J. F., Anderson, R. E., Tatham, R. L., & Black, W. C. (2006).Multivariate Data Analysis. Fifth Edition, Dorling Kindersley (India) Pvt. Ltd, PearsonEducation,Inc.,NewDelhi,1–700.

Hair, J. F., Anderson, R. E., Tatham, R. L., & Black, W. C. (1992). *Multivariate Data Analaysis* (3rd ed.). Macmillan.

Hao, X., Demir, E., & Eyers, D. (2024). Exploring collaborative decision-making: A quasi-experimental study of human and Generative AI interaction. *Technology in Society*, 78, 102662. DOI: 10.1016/j.techsoc.2024.102662

Harsono, I., & Suprapti, I. A. P. (2024). The role of fintech in transforming traditional financial services. [COUNT]. *Accounting Studies and Tax Journal*, 1(1), 81–91. DOI: 10.62207/gfzvtd24

Hastings, J. S., Madrian, B. C., & Skimmyhorn, W. L. (2013). Financial literacy, financial education, and economic outcomes. *Annual Review of Economics*, 5(1), 347–373. DOI: 10.1146/annurev-economics-082312-125807 PMID: 23991248

Hirdinis, M. (2021). Does herding behaviour and overconfidence drive the investor's decision making during the COVID-19 pandemic. *Cognizance Journal of Multidisciplinary Studies*, 1(8), 1–16. DOI: 10.47760/cognizance.2021.v01i08.001

Hirshleifer, D. (2015). Behavioral finance. Annual Review of Financial Economics, 7(1), 133-159.

Hoffmann, A.O., Shefrin, H. and Pennings, J.M., 2010. Behavioral portfolio analysis of individual investors. Available at SSRN 1629786.

Hong, H., & Kacperczyk, M. (2018). Thematic ETFs: Growth and volatility. *Journal of Financial and Quantitative Analysis*, 53(2), 627–654. DOI: 10.1017/S002210901800007X

Hong, H., Kubik, J. D., & Stein, J. C. (2004). Social Interaction and Stock-Market Participation. *The Journal of Finance*, 59(1), 137–163. DOI: 10.1111/j.1540-6261.2004.00629.x

Hong, H., & Wang, J. (2005). Investor sentiment and stock returns. *The Journal of Finance*, 60(2), 899–934.

Hou, K., Xue, C., & Zhang, L. (2020). Replicating anomalies. *Review of Financial Studies*, 33(5), 2019–2133. DOI: 10.1093/rfs/hhy131

How technology is transforming investment strategies. (2023, October 19). *Express Computer News*

Huang, J., & Guedj, I. (2009). The marketing of closed-end fund IPOs: Evidence from mutual fund mergers. *Journal of Financial Intermediation*, 18(1), 100–115. DOI: 10.1016/j.jfi.2008.11.001

Huang, J., & Wang, J. (2022). ETF diversification and portfolio risk. *Financial Review*, 57(3), 431–457. DOI: 10.1111/fire.12257

Huang, X. H., & Domenech, J. C. A. R. M. A. (2024).. . *CARMA*, 2024, 157–165. DOI: 10.4995/CARMA2024.2024.17818

Hu, C. (2020). Industrial specialization matters: A new angle on equity home bias. *Journal of International Economics*, 126, 103354. DOI: 10.1016/j.jinteco.2020.103354

IMF. (n.d). Retrieved Oct 14, 2024, from https://www.imf.org/external/pubs/ft/fandd/2021/06/the-future-of-emerging-markets-duttagupta-and-pazarbasioglu.htm

Iram, T., Bilal, A. R., & Ahmad, Z. (2023). Investigating the mediating role of financial literacy on the relationship between women entrepreneurs' behavioral biases and investment decision making. *Gadjah Mada International Journal of Business*, 25(1), 93–118. DOI: 10.22146/gamaijb.65457

Ireland, D. (2022). Regret and Regulation. The Power of Regret, Power of Persuasion and the Regulatory Compliance/Non-Compliance Continuum: Better Understanding Compliance Through the Prism of Regret. *The Power of Regret, Power of Persuasion and the Regulatory Compliance/Non-Compliance Continuum: Better Understanding Compliance Through the Prism of Regret (October 4, 2022).*

Irshad, S., Badshah, W., & Hakam, U. (2016). Effect of representativeness bias on investment decision making. Management and Administrative Sciences Review, 5(1), 26-30.

Jabo, B. B., & Kant, S. "Impact of Technical CRM on Ethiopia Bank Human-Computer Interface and Competitive Advantage as Mediators of Performance," *2024 IEEE International Conference on Computing, Power and Communication Technologies (IC2PCT)*, Greater Noida, India, 2024, pp. 679-682, https://doi.org/ DOI: 10.1109/IC2PCT60090.2024.10486237

Jain, J., Walia, N., & Gupta, S. (2019). Evaluation of behavioral biases affecting investment decision making of individual equity investors by fuzzy analytic hierarchy process. Review of Behavioral Finance.

Jain, J., Walia, N., & Gupta, S. (2019). Evaluation of behavioral biases affecting investment decision making of individual equity investors by fuzzy analytic hierarchy process. *Review of Behavioral Finance*, 12(3), 297–314. DOI: 10.1108/RBF-03-2019-0044

Jain, J., Walia, N., Kaur, M., Sood, K., & Kaur, D. (2023). Shaping investment decisions through financial literacy: Do herding and overconfidence bias mediate the relationship? *Global Business Review*, 09721509221147409. Advance online publication. DOI: 10.1177/09721509221147409

Jain, J., Walia, N., Singh, S., & Jain, E. (2021). Mapping the field of behavioural biases: A literature review using bibliometric analysis. *Management Review Quarterly*, 72(3), 823–855. DOI: 10.1007/s11301-021-00215-y

Jamshidinavid, B., Chavoshani, M., & Amiri, S. (2012). The impact of demographic and psychological characteristics on the investment prejudices in Tehran stock. In Islamic Azad University. *European Journal of Business and Social Sciences*, 1(5), 41–53.

Jebadurai, D. J., Sheela, M. V., Rajeshkumar, L., Soundarya, M., Meena, R., Manickam, T., . . . Manikandan, M. (2024). AI-Driven Decision-Making and Optimization in Modern Agriculture Sectors. In Using Traditional Design Methods to Enhance AI-Driven Decision Making (pp. 269-288). IGI Global.

Jeon, H. J. (2023). CEO overconfidence: A dual-detriment to investment-price sensitivity via market negligence and reduced informed trading. *Journal of Contemporary Accounting & Economics*, 19(3), 100378. DOI: 10.1016/j.jcae.2023.100378

Jing, W., & Loang, O. K. (2024). Live Streaming of E-Commerce in China: Evidence from Impulsive Chinese Tea Purchases. In *Opportunities and Risks in AI for Business Development* (Vol. 1, pp. 1063–1079). Springer Nature Switzerland. DOI: 10.1007/978-3-031-65203-5_91

Jin, S. V. (2024). "Technopian but lonely investors?": Comparison between investors and non-investors of blockchain technologies, cryptocurrencies, and non-fungible tokens (NFTs) in Artificial Intelligence-Driven FinTech and decentralized finance (DeFi). *Telematics and Informatics Reports*, 14, 100128. DOI: 10.1016/j.teler.2024.100128

Johnson, D. D., & Fowler, J. H. (2011). The evolution of overconfidence. Nature, 477(7364), 317-320.

Johnson, W. (2009). Sector Rotation and ETFs. *Journal of Financial Planning*, 22(12), 36–43.

Joiner, D., Vezeau, A., Wong, A., Hains, G., & Khmelevsky, Y. (2022, November). Algorithmic trading and short-term forecast for financial time series with machine learning models: State of the art and perspectives. In *2022 IEEE International Conference on Recent Advances in Systems Science and Engineering (RASSE)* (pp. 1-9). IEEE. DOI: 10.1109/RASSE54974.2022.9989592

Jung, D., Dorner, V., Weinhardt, C., & Pusmaz, H. (2018). Designing a robo-advisor for risk-averse, low-budget consumers. *Electronic Markets*, 28(3), 367–380. DOI: 10.1007/s12525-017-0279-9

Kacperczyk, M., & Seru, A. (2023). ETFs and market efficiency. *Review of Financial Studies*, 36(2), 511–540. DOI: 10.1093/rfs/hhz105

Kahneman, D., & Tversky, A. (1979). Prospect theory: An analysis of decision under risk. Econometrica, 47(2), 263-291.

Kahneman, D., Knetsch, J. L., & Thaler, R. H. (1990). Experimental tests of the endowment effect and the Coase theorem. *Journal of Political Economy*, 98(6), 1325–1348. DOI: 10.1086/261737

Kahneman, D., & Tversky, A. (1979). Prospect theory: An analysis of decision under risk. *Econometrica*, 47(2), 263–291. DOI: 10.2307/1914185

Kamuangu, P. K. (2024). Advancements of AI and Machine Learning in FinTech Industry (2016-2020).

Kant, S., & Adula, M. (2024). Human-Machine Interaction in the Metaverse in the Context of Ethiopia. In *Impact and Potential of Machine Learning in the Metaverse* (pp. 196–212). IGI Global., DOI: 10.4018/979-8-3693-5762-0.ch008

Kartini, K. and NAHDA, K., 2021. Behavioral biases on investment decision: A case study in Indonesia. The Journal of Asian Finance, Economics and Business, 8(3), pp.1231-1240.

Kauppi, E., Niemelä, J., & Sarlin, P. (2021). Machine learning for financial prediction: A systematic review. *Journal of Computational Finance*, 25(1), 1–36. DOI: 10.3905/jcf.2021.1.100

Kelcey, B. (2018). A robust alternative estimator for small to moderate sample SEM: Bias-corrected factor score path analysis. *Addictive Behaviors*, 94, 83–98. DOI: 10.1016/j.addbeh.2018.10.032 PMID: 30501990

Keynes, J. M. (1936). The General Theory of Employment Interest and Money. The Collected Writings of John Maynard Keynes Vol. VII. Journal Of The Czech Geological Society, 49, 161–172. Retrieved from http://www.jgeosci.org/index.php?pg=detail&ID=JCGS.968

Khan, M. T. I., Tan, S., & Chong, L. (2017). Perception of past portfolio returns, optimism and financial decisions. *Review of Behavioral Finance*, 9(1), 79–98. DOI: 10.1108/RBF-02-2016-0005

Khan, S., Khan, H. U., & Nazir, S. (2022). Utilizing the collective wisdom of FinTech in the GCC region: A systematic mapping approach. *Measurement and Control*, 56(3-4), 713–732. DOI: 10.1177/00202940221124130

Khoa, B. T., & Huynh, T. T. (2022). Forecasting stock price movement direction by machine learning algorithm. [IJECE]. *Iranian Journal of Electrical and Computer Engineering*, 12(6), 6625–6634. DOI: 10.11591/ijece.v12i6.pp6625-6634

Kim, J., Braun, B., & Williams, A. D. (2013). Understanding Health Insurance Literacy: A Literature Review. *Family and Consumer Sciences Research Journal*, 42(1), 3–13. DOI: 10.1111/fcsr.12034

Kirilenko, A. A., Kyle, A. S., Samadi, M., & Tuzun, T. (2017). The flash crash: The impact of high-frequency trading on an electronic market. *The Journal of Finance*, 72(3), 967–998. DOI: 10.1111/jofi.12498

Kirilenko, A. A., & Lo, A. W. (2013). Moore's law versus murphy's law: Algorithmic trading and its discontents. *The Journal of Economic Perspectives*, 27(2), 51–72. DOI: 10.1257/jep.27.2.51

Klein, T. (2022). A note on GameStop, short squeezes, and autodidactic herding: An evolution in financial literacy? Finance Research Letters, 46(Part A), 102229 DOI: 10.1016/j.frl.2021.102229

Koech, A. (2021). The availability Heuristic Effect on Financial performance of small and Medium Enterprises in Nairobi, Kenya: The mediating role of investment decisions. *American Journal of Education*, 6(2).

Komalasari, P. T., Asri, M., Purwanto, B. M., & Setiyono, B. (2022). Herding behaviour in the capital market: What do we know and what is next? *Management Review Quarterly*, 72(3), 745–787. DOI: 10.1007/s11301-021-00212-1

Kumar, S., & Goyal, N. (2016). Evidence on rationality and behavioural biases in investment decision making. *Qualitative Research in Financial Markets*, 8(4), 270–287. DOI: 10.1108/QRFM-05-2016-0016

Kumera, D., Amentie, C., & Bali, N. (2024). Effect of Market Orientation Practices on Manufacturing Firm's Performance: Study on Firms Operating in Ethiopian Industrial Parks. *Journal of Science. Technology and Arts Research*, 13(1), 9–27.

Lee, C. M. C., & Swaminathan, B. (2000). Price Momentum and Trading Volume. *The Journal of Finance*, 55(5), 2017–2069. DOI: 10.1111/0022-1082.00280

Lee, D. D., & Lerro, C. M. (2014). Sustainable Investing and Portfolio Diversification. *Journal of Sustainable Finance & Investment.*

Levy, H. (2011). The capital asset pricing model in the 21st century: analytical, empirical, and behavioral perspectives. Cambridge University Press.

Lewellen, W. G., Lease, R. C., & Schlarbaum, G. G. (1977). Patterns of investment strategy and behavior among individual investors. *The Journal of Business*, 50(3), 296. DOI: 10.1086/295947

Liang, Z., & Pan, S. (2024, June). Research on the Impact of Fin-Tech on Stock Volatility in the Artificial Intelligence Industry. In *Proceedings of the 3rd International Conference on Big Data Economy and Digital Management, BDEDM 2024, January 12–14, 2024, Ningbo, China*. DOI: 10.4108/eai.12-1-2024.2347207

Liang, X. (2024). Fintech and Digital Transformation of the Financial Industry. *Highlights in Business. Economics and Management*, 30, 12–16.

Li, D., Ma, C., Zhou, Z., Kuang, X., & Lin, Z. (2024). Distributed hyperledger technology in FinTech with artificial intelligence assisted internet of things platform. *Expert Systems: International Journal of Knowledge Engineering and Neural Networks*, 41(6), e13001. DOI: 10.1111/exsy.13001

Lieder, F., Griffiths, T. L., M. Huys, Q. J., & Goodman, N. D. (2018). The anchoring bias reflects rational use of cognitive resources. Psychonomic bulletin & review, 25, 322-349.

Li, M., & Yan, T. (2020). Venture capital, technological innovation, and enterprise performance: Influencing mechanism and its empirical test. *Scientific Research Management*, 41(07), 70–78.

Lindblom, T., Lindell, J., & Gidlund, K. (2022). Digitalizing the journalistic field: Journalists' views on changes in journalistic autonomy, capital, and habitus. *Digital Journalism (Abingdon, England)*, •••, 1–20.

Liu, Q., Chan, K. C., & Chimhundu, R. (2024). FinTech research: Systematic mapping, classification, and future directions. *Financial Innovation*, 10(24), 24. Advance online publication. DOI: 10.1186/s40854-023-00524-z

Liu, Y., & Wang, X. (2022). Artificial intelligence in portfolio management: A review. *Journal of Financial Services Marketing*, 27(2), 113–129.

Lo, A. W. (2012). Adaptive markets: Financial evolution at the speed of thought. Princeton University Press.

Loang, O. K. (2023). Corporate governance and Islamic behavioural finance: A review from Malaysia and GCC countries. *Indian Journal of Corporate Governance*, 16(1), 28–51. DOI: 10.1177/09746862231178959

Loang, O. K. (2024). Stability Of Shariah-Compliant Stocks In Indonesia, Malaysia, And Gcc: The Roles Of Monetary And Fiscal Policies And Contagion. *Journal of Islamic Monetary Economics and Finance*, 10(1), 155–176. DOI: 10.21098/jimf.v10i1.1899

Loang, O. K. (2024). Sustainability's impact of ESG-infused policies on leading economic indicators in Asian economies. *Journal of Sustainable Research*, 6(3), e240059. DOI: 10.20900/jsr20240059

Loewenstein, G., Weber, E. U., Hsee, C. K., & Welch, N. (2001). Risk as feelings. *Psychological Bulletin*, 127(2), 267–286. DOI: 10.1037/0033-2909.127.2.267 PMID: 11316014

Loomes, G., & Sugden, R. (1982). Regret Theory: An Alternative theory of rational choice under uncertainty. *Economic Journal (London)*, 92(368), 805. DOI: 10.2307/2232669

Luo, L., & Patev, P. (2023). Artificial intelligence and machine learning in ESG investing: A review of the literature. *Journal of Sustainable Finance & Investment*, 13(1), 105–128.

Lusardi, A., & Mitchell, O. S. (2011). Financial literacy and retirement planning in the United States. *Journal of Pension Economics and Finance*, 10(4), 509–525. DOI: 10.1017/S147474721100045X PMID: 28553190

Lynch, A. W., & Metrick, A. (2024). Investor behavior and decision-making in ETFs. *Journal of Behavioral Finance*, 25(2), 89–104. DOI: 10.1080/15427560.2024.2108496

Malkiel, B. G., & Ellis, C. D. (2023). Cost-effectiveness of ETFs compared to other vehicles. *Journal of Index Investing*, 13(2), 55–74. DOI: 10.3905/jii.2023.1.035

Malmendier, U., Pouzo, D., & Vanasco, V. (2020). Investor experiences and financial market dynamics. *Journal of Financial Economics*, 136(3), 597–622. DOI: 10.1016/j.jfineco.2019.11.002

Manickam, T., Desai, K., Sudha, M., Bhagyalakshmi, M., Vinayagamoorthi, G., & Devapictahi, J. J. (2023). Usage of Social Media in Education: A Paradigm Shift in the Indian Education Sector. In *Global Perspectives on Social Media Usage Within Governments* (pp. 127–141). IGI Global. DOI: 10.4018/978-1-6684-7450-1.ch009

Mansour, S. B., Jouini, E., & Napp, C. (2006). Is there a "pessimistic" bias in individual beliefs? Evidence from a simple survey. Theory and Decision, 61(4), 345-362.

Markowitz, H. (1952). Portfolio selection. *The Journal of Finance*, 7(1), 77–91.

Martin, S., 2007. Behavioural finance. Univ. Cambridge, pp.1-14.

Marvin, J. A. (2023). *Workplace Digitization: An Exploration of the Effects the Accelerating Nature of Disruptions Caused by Advances in Technology are Having on Front-Line Mangers and Their Teams in Industry* (Doctoral dissertation, Northeastern University).

Mawson, S., & Casulli, L. (2024). Entrepreneurial Thinking: Mindset in Action.

Mehari, A. T., Ayenew Birbirsa, Z., & Nemera Dinber, G. (2024). The effect of workforce diversity on organizational performance with the mediation role of workplace ethics: Empirical evidence from food and beverage industry. *PLoS One*, 19(7), e0297765. DOI: 10.1371/journal.pone.0297765 PMID: 39024256

Mehra, R., & Prescott, E. C. (1985). The equity premium: A puzzle. *Journal of Monetary Economics*, 15(2), 145–161. DOI: 10.1016/0304-3932(85)90061-3

Mittal, S. K. (2022). Behavior biases and investment decision: Theoretical and research framework. *Qualitative Research in Financial Markets*, 14(2), 213–228. DOI: 10.1108/QRFM-09-2017-0085

Mohammed, K. S., Serret, V., Jabeur, S. B., & Nobanee, H. (2024). The role of artificial intelligence and fintech in promoting eco-friendly investments and non-greenwashing practices in the US market. *Journal of Environmental Management*, 359, 120977. DOI: 10.1016/j.jenvman.2024.120977 PMID: 38678903

Mozumder, M. A. S., Nguyen, T. N., Devi, S., Arif, M., Ahmed, M. P., Ahmed, E., & Uddin, A. (2024). Enhancing Customer Satisfaction Analysis Using Advanced Machine Learning Techniques in Fintech Industry. *Journal of Computer Science and Technology Studies*, 6(3), 35–41. DOI: 10.32996/jcsts.2024.6.3.4

Muneer, S. (2012). Materialization of Behavioral Finance and Behavioral Portfolio Theory : A Brief Review. Journal of Economics and Behavioral Studies, 4(8), 431–435.

Mu, R., Fentaw, N. M., & Zhang, L. (2023). Tax evasion, psychological egoism, and revenue collection performance: Evidence from Amhara region, Ethiopia. *Frontiers in Psychology*, 14, 1045537. DOI: 10.3389/fpsyg.2023.1045537 PMID: 36844346

Mushinada, V. N. C. (2020). Are individual investors irrational or adaptive to market dynamics? *Journal of Behavioral and Experimental Finance*, 25, 100243. DOI: 10.1016/j.jbef.2019.100243

Nevins, D. (2004). Goals-based investing: Integrating traditional and behavioral finance. The Journal of Wealth Management, 6(4), 8-23.

Nickerson, R. S. (1998). Confirmation bias: A ubiquitous phenomenon in many guises. *Review of General Psychology*, 2(2), 175–220. DOI: 10.1037/1089-2680.2.2.175

Nicolini, G., Cude, B. J., & Chatterjee, S. (2013). Financial literacy: A comparative study across four countries. *International Journal of Consumer Studies*, 37(6), 689–705. DOI: 10.1111/ijcs.12050

Nyoach, T. D., Lemi, K., Debela, T., & Kant, S. (2024). Does Organizational Commitment Mediate the Relationship between Employee Relationship Management and Bank Performance? The Case of Banks in Ethiopia. *International Journal of Organizational Leadership*, 13(2), 355–376. DOI: 10.33844/ijol.2024.60419

Odean, T. (1998). Are Investors Reluctant to Realize Their Losses? *The Journal of Finance*, 53(5), 1775–1798. DOI: 10.1111/0022-1082.00072

Ofosu-Mensah Ababio, J., Aboagye, A. Q., Barnor, C., & Agyei, S. K. (2022). Foreign and domestic private investment in developing and emerging economies: A review of literature. *Cogent Economics & Finance*, 10(1), 2132646. DOI: 10.1080/23322039.2022.2132646

Olaiya, O. P., Adesoga, T. O., Ojo, A., Olagunju, O. D., Ajayi, O. O., & Adebayo, Y. O. (2024). Cybersecurity strategies in fintech: safeguarding financial data and assets. *GSC Advanced Research and Reviews, 20*(1), 050-056.

Olsen, R. A. (1998). Behavioral finance and its implications for stock-price volatility. Financial Analysts Journal, 54(2), 10–18. .DOI: 10.2469/faj.v54.n2.2161

Othman, N. N. (2024). Emotional Economics: The Role of Psychological Biases in Personal Investment Outcomes. *Available atSSRN* 4844927. DOI: 10.2139/ssrn.4844927

Ozsoylev, H. N., Walden, J., Yavuz, M. D., & Bildik, R. (2014). Investor networks in the stock market. *Review of Financial Studies*, 27(5), 1323–1366. DOI: 10.1093/rfs/hht065

Padmavathy, M. (2024). Behavioral Finance and Stock Market Anomalies: Exploring Psychological Factors Influencing Investment Decisions. *Shanlax International Journal of Management*, 11(iS1-Jan, S1), 191–197. DOI: 10.34293/management.v11iS1-Jan.7164

Panigrahi, A., Pati, A., Sahu, B., Das, M. N., Nayak, D. S. K., Sahoo, G., & Kant, S. (2023). En-MinWhale: An ensemble approach based on MRMR and Whale optimization for Cancer diagnosis. *IEEE Access : Practical Innovations, Open Solutions*, 11, 113526–113542. DOI: 10.1109/ACCESS.2023.3318261

Paramesha, M., Rane, N. L., & Rane, J. (2024). Artificial Intelligence, Machine Learning, Deep Learning, and Blockchain in Financial and Banking Services: A Comprehensive Review. *SSRN*, 1(2), 51–67. DOI: 10.2139/ssrn.4855893

Park, C. W., Jun, S. Y., & MacInnis, D. J. (2010). Choosing what I want versus rejecting what I do not want: An application of decision framing to product option choice decisions. *The Journal of Consumer Research*, 37(4), 632–644. DOI: 10.1086/655466

Parveen, S., Satti, Z. W., Subhan, Q. A., & Jamil, S. (2020). Exploring market overreaction, investors' sentiments and investment decisions in an emerging stock market. *Borsa Istanbul Review*, 20(3), 224–235. DOI: 10.1016/j.bir.2020.02.002

Pastor, L., & Stambaugh, R. F. (2024). Interest rate changes and ETF performance. *Journal of Financial and Quantitative Analysis*, 59(1), 121–148. DOI: 10.1017/S002210902300060X

Petajisto, A. (2013). Active share and mutual fund performance. *Financial Analysts Journal*, 69(4), 73–93. DOI: 10.2469/faj.v69.n4.7

Petajisto, A. (2024). Benefits of ETF strategies for retirement portfolios. *The Journal of Retirement*, 11(1), 32–45. DOI: 10.3905/jor.2024.1.023

Phillips, M. (2021, May 11). Nasdaq: Here's our timeline of the flash crash. *The Wall Street Journal.*

Plous, S. (1993). *The psychology of judgment and decision making*. McGraw-Hill Book Company.

Pompian, M. M. (2011). *Behavioral finance and wealth management: How to Build Optimal Portfolios That Account for Investor Biases*. John Wiley & Sons.

Popper, N. K. (2020). Corporate criminal liability for algorithmic price fixing in Canada. *Canadian Journal of Law and Technology*, 16(2), 417–438.

Poterba, J. M., & Shoven, J. B. (2002). Exchange-traded funds: A new investment option for taxable investors. *The American Economic Review*, 92(2), 422–427. DOI: 10.1257/000282802320191732

Pozzi, P., & Nigra, F. (2015). Argentina a decade after the collapse: the causes of the crisis and structural changes. Latin American Perspectives, 42(1), 3-10.

Prosad, J. M., Kapoor, S., & Sengupta, J. (2015). Behavioral biases of Indian investors: A survey of Delhi-NCR region. *Qualitative Research in Financial Markets*, 7(3), 230–263. DOI: 10.1108/QRFM-04-2014-0012

Qasim, M., Hussain, R. Y., Mehboob, I., & Arshad, M. (2018). Impact of herding behavior and overconfidence bias on investors' decision-making in Pakistan. *Accounting*, 81–90. DOI: 10.5267/j.ac.2018.7.001

Qiu, T. (2022). The effects of opportunity motivation and environmental contingencies on market growth strategies of African early-stage entrepreneurs. *African Journal of Economic and Management Studies*, 13(3), 434–451. DOI: 10.1108/AJEMS-06-2021-0298

Quaicoe, A., & Eleke-Aboagye, P. Q. (2021). Behavioral factors affecting investment decision-making in bank stocks on the Ghana stock exchange. *Qualitative Research in Financial Markets*, 13(4), 425–439. DOI: 10.1108/QRFM-05-2020-0084

Rabin, M. (2002). Inference by believers in the law of small numbers. *The Quarterly Journal of Economics*, 117(3), 775–816. DOI: 10.1162/003355302760193896

Rasheed, M. H., Rafique, A., Zahid, T., & Akhtar, M. W. (2018). Factors influencing investor's decision making in Pakistan: Moderating the role of locus of control. Review of Behavioral Finance, 10(1), 70-87.

Rasool, N., & Ullah, S. (2020). Financial literacy and behavioural biases of individual investors: Empirical evidence of Pakistan stock exchange. *Journal of Economics, Finance and Administrative Science*, 25(50), 261–278. DOI: 10.1108/JEFAS-03-2019-0031

Raut, R. K., Das, N., & Mishra, R. (2020). Behaviour of individual investors in stock market trading: Evidence from India. *Global Business Review*, 21(3), 818–833. DOI: 10.1177/0972150918778915

Ricciardi, V., & Simon, H. K. (2000). What is Behavioral Finance ? Business, Education and Technology Journal, II(1), 1–9. http://doi.org/.DOI: 10.2139/ssrn.256754

Rios-Campos, C., Vega, S. M. Z., Tejada-Castro, M. I., Zambrano, E. O. G., Perez, D. J. G. B., Calderón, E. V., Rojas, L. M. F., & Alcantara, I. M. B. (2023). Artificial Intelligence and Business. *South Florida Journal of Development*, 4(9), 3547–3564. DOI: 10.46932/sfjdv4n9-015

Ritika, N., & Kishor, N. (2020). Development and validation of behavioral biases scale: A SEM approach. *Review of Behavioral Finance*, 14(2), 237–259. DOI: 10.1108/RBF-05-2020-0087

Ritter, J. R., & Zhang, X. (2023). ETFs and market volatility. *Journal of Financial Markets*, 59, 1–25. DOI: 10.1016/j.finmar.2022.100787

Robinhood (2024). https://robinhood.com/us/en/about-us/

Rolando, B., & Mulyono, H. (2024). Managing Risks In Fintech: Applications And Challenges Of Artificial Intelligence-Based Risk Management. [ECBIS]. *Economics and Business Journal*, 2(3), 249–268.

Rompotis, G. G. (2011). Predictable patterns in leveraged ETF returns. *Journal of Asset Management*, 12, 151–167. DOI: 10.1057/jam.2011.6

Rouwenhorst, K. G. (2024). Performance of sector-specific ETFs. *Journal of Financial Economics*, 142(3), 675–690. DOI: 10.1016/j.jfineco.2023.03.010

Ryan, R. M., & Deci, E. L. (2000). Self-determination theory and the facilitation of intrinsic motivation, social development, and well-being. *The American Psychologist*, 55(1), 68–78. DOI: 10.1037/0003-066X.55.1.68 PMID: 11392867

Ryll, L., & Seppelt, R. (2022). AI and market forecasting: A comprehensive study of predictive analytics in finance. *Financial Data Science Review*, 6(2), 54–76. DOI: 10.1016/j.finrev.2022.02.004

Ryu, H. S. (2018). What makes users willing or hesitant to use FinTech?: The moderating effect of user type. *Industrial Management & Data Systems*, 118(3), 541–569. DOI: 10.1108/IMDS-07-2017-0325

Sabir, S. A., Mohammad, H. B., & Shahar, H. B. K. (2019). The Role of Overconfidence and Past Investment Experience in Herding Behaviour with a Moderating Effect of Financial Literacy: Evidence from Pakistan Stock Exchange. *Asian Economic and Financial Review*, 9(4), 480–490. DOI: 10.18488/journal.aefr.2019.94.480.490

Sahi, S. K., & Arora, A. P. (2012). Individual investor biases: A segmentation analysis. *Qualitative Research in Financial Markets*, 4(1), 6–25. DOI: 10.1108/17554171211213522

Sahi, S. K., Arora, A. P., & Dhameja, N. (2013). An Exploratory Inquiry into the Psychological Biases in Financial Investment Behavior. *Journal of Behavioral Finance*, 14(2), 94–103. DOI: 10.1080/15427560.2013.790387

Sattar, M. A., Toseef, M., & Sattar, M. F. (2020). Behavioral finance biases in investment decision making. International Journal of Accounting, Finance and Risk Management, 5(2), 69.

Sattar, M. A., Toseef, M., & Sattar, M. F. (2020). Behavioral finance biases in investment decision making. *International Journal of Accounting Finance and Risk Management*, 5(2), 69. DOI: 10.11648/j.ijafrm.20200502.11

Saxena, V., & Sahoo, S. (2022). Share repurchase: A review of the literature. *International Journal of Indian Culture and Business Management*, 25(1), 38–71. DOI: 10.1504/IJICBM.2022.120918

Searston, R. A., Tangen, J. M., & Eva, K. W. (2016). Putting bias into context: The role of familiarity in identification. Law and Human Behavior, 40(1), 50.

SEBI Guidelines on ESG - Kaleeswari, K., & Chaudhuri, R. B. (2024). Analyzing the Evolving ESG Regulations in India: A Guide to Implementing ESG Strategies. *Journal of Law and Legal Research Development*, 06-10.

Sharpe ratio: Pedersen, E. R. (2018). The relationship between sustainability performance and financial performance.

Sharpe, W. F. (1991). The arithmetic of active management. *Financial Analysts Journal*, 47(1), 7–9. DOI: 10.2469/faj.v47.n1.7

Shefrin, H., & Statman, M. (2000). Behavioral portfolio theory. Journal of Financial and Quantitative Analysis, 35(2), 127–151. http://doi.org/doi:10.2307/2676187

Shefrin, H. (2000). *Beyond greed and fear: Understanding behavioral finance and the psychology of investing*. Harvard Business School Press.

Shefrin, H., & Statman, M. (1985). The disposition to sell winners too early and ride losers too long: Theory and evidence. *The Journal of Finance*, 40(3), 777–790. DOI: 10.1111/j.1540-6261.1985.tb05002.x

Shefrin, H., & Thaler, R. H. (1988). The behavioral life-cycle hypothesis. *Economic Inquiry*, 26(4), 609–643. DOI: 10.1111/j.1465-7295.1988.tb01520.x

Shengelia, N., Tsiklauri, Z., Rzepka, A., & Shengelia, R. (2022). The impact of financial technologies on digital transformation of accounting, audit and financial reporting. *Economics*, 105(3), 385–398. DOI: 10.36962/ecs105/3/2022-385

Shiller, R. J. (2000). *Irrational exuberance*. Princeton University Press., DOI: 10.1515/9780691214871

Shiller, R. J. (2003). From efficient markets theory to behavioral finance. *The Journal of Economic Perspectives*, 17(1), 83–104. DOI: 10.1257/089533003321164967

Shoetan, P. O., & Familoni, B. T.Philip Olaseni ShoetanBabajide Tolulope Familoni. (2024). Transforming fintech fraud detection with advanced artificial intelligence algorithms. *Finance & Accounting Research Journal*, 6(4), 602–625. DOI: 10.51594/farj.v6i4.1036

Shonte, A. N., & Ji, Q. (2022). Management Commitment and Sustainable Coffee Export Performance, Evidence from Ethiopian Companies: The Mediating Role of Corporate Social Responsibility. *Sustainability (Basel)*, 14(19), 12630. DOI: 10.3390/su141912630

Shrestha, C., Andrikopoulos, P., & Aryal, N. P. (2024). Does it matter to be a part of the sustainability index? *Journal of Sustainable Finance & Investment*, •••, 1–22. DOI: 10.1080/20430795.2024.2401357

Shusha, A. A., & Touny, M. A. (2016). The attitudinal determinants of adopting the herd behavior: An applied study on the Egyptian Exchange. *Journal of Finance and Investment Analysis*, 5(1), 1–3. https://econpapers.repec.org/RePEc:spt:fininv:v:5:y:2016:i:1:f:5_1_3

Sortino ratio:Eling, M., & Schuhmacher, F. (2006). Risk Considerations in Sustainable Investing. *Journal of Business Ethics.*

Stan Miranda. (2018, January 1). Technology's impact on active investing. *Partners' Capital.*

Stanovich, K. E., & West, R. F. (2000). Individual differences in reasoning: implications for the rationality debate? The Behavioral and Brain Sciences, 23(5), 645–665; discussion 665–726. .DOI: 10.1017/S0140525X00003435

Statman, M. (2008). What Is Behavioral Finance? Handbook of Finance, II(1), 79–84. .DOI: 10.1002/9780470404324.hof002009

Stevens, J. (1992). *Applied Multivariate Statistics for the Social Sciences* (2nd ed.). Lawrence Erlbaum Associates.

Stotz, O., & von Nitzsch, R. (2005). The Perception of Control and the Level of Overconfidence: Evidence from Analyst Earnings Estimates and Price Targets. Journal of Behavioral Finance, 6(3), 121–128. .DOI: 10.1207/s15427579jpfm0603_2

Subash, R. (2012). Role of behavioral finance in portfolio investment decisions: Evidence from India.

Suresh, G., & Loang, O. K. (2024). The Rationality Conundrum: Exploring Herd Mentality among Individual Investors in the Indian Stock Market. *Indian Journal of Finance*, 18(6), 26–45. DOI: 10.17010/ijf/2024/v18i6/173967

Taffler, R., Bellotti, X., Agarwal, V., & Li, L. (2024). Investor emotions and the psychodynamics of asset pricing bubbles: A Chinese perspective. *Journal of Behavioral Finance*, 25(3), 309–333. DOI: 10.1080/15427560.2022.2138391

Tapscott, D., & Tapscott, A. (2016). Blockchain revolution: How the technology behind bitcoin is changing money, business, and the world. Penguin Random House.

Tesar, L.L. and Werner, I.M. (1995), "Home bias and high turnover", Journal of International Money and Finance, Vol. 14 No. 4, pp. 467-492.

Thaler, R. H. (1985). Mental Accounting and Consumer Choice. INFORMS Marketing Science, 4(3), 199-214. Retrieved from JSTOR: 183904.

Thaler, R. H. (1999). Mental accounting matters. *Journal of Behavioral Decision Making*, 12(3), 183–206. DOI: 10.1002/(SICI)1099-0771(199909)12:3<183::AID-BDM318>3.0.CO;2-F

Tolossa, A. T., Singh, M., & Gautam, R. K. (2024). Linking business sustainable development with entrepreneurial marketing practices: Evidence from small and medium enterprises in Ethiopia. *Business Strategy & Development*, 7(3), e412. DOI: 10.1002/bsd2.412

Treleaven, P., Gandel, P., & Chen, S. (2020). Algorithmic trading, AI and the future of finance. *Journal of Finance and Data Science*, 6(1), 27–42. DOI: 10.1016/j.jfds.2019.07.005

Tversky, A., & Kahneman, D. (1986). Rational Choice and the Framing of Decisions. The Journal of Business, 59(4), Part 2: The Behavioral Foundations of Economic Theory, S251-S278. Retrieved from JSTOR: 2352759

Tversky, A., & Kahneman, D. (1991). Loss Aversion in Riskless Choice: A Reference-Dependent Model. The Quarterly Journal of Economics, 106(4), 1039-1061. Oxford University Press. Retrieved from JSTOR: 2937956

Tversky, A., & Kahneman, D. (1992). Advances in Prospect Theory: Cumulative Representation of Uncertainty. Journal of Risk and Uncertainty, 5(4), 297. Retrieved from JSTOR: 41755005

Tversky, A., & Kahneman, D. (1971). Belief in the law of small numbers. *Psychological Bulletin*, 76(2), 105–110. DOI: 10.1037/h0031322

Tversky, A., & Kahneman, D. (1973). Availability: A heuristic for judging frequency and probability. *Cognitive Psychology*, 5(2), 207–232. DOI: 10.1016/0010-0285(73)90033-9

Tversky, A., & Kahneman, D. (1974). Judgment under uncertainty: Heuristics and biases. *Science*, 185(4157), 1124–1131. DOI: 10.1126/science.185.4157.1124 PMID: 17835457

Tversky, A., & Kahneman, D. (1981). The framing of decisions in risky situations. *The American Economic Review*, 71(4), 457–467.

Tversky, A., & Kahneman, D. (1982). The framing of decisions and the psychology of choice. *Science*, 211(4481), 453–458. DOI: 10.1126/science.7455683 PMID: 7455683

Tversky, A., & Kahneman, D. (1992). Advances in prospect theory: Cumulative representation of uncertainty. *Journal of Risk and Uncertainty*, 5(4), 297–323. DOI: 10.1007/BF00122574

Van de Venter, G., Michayluk, D., & Davey, G. (2012). A longitudinal study of financial risk tolerance. Journal of Economic Psychology, 33(4), 794–800. .DOI: 10.1016/j.joep.2012.03.001

Van Rooij, M., Lusardi, A., & Alessie, R. (2011). Financial literacy and stock market participation. *Journal of Financial Economics*, 101(2), 449–472. DOI: 10.1016/j.jfineco.2011.03.006

VanderPal, G., & Brazie, R. (2022). Influence of basic human behaviors (influenced by brain architecture and function), and past traumatic events on investor behavior and financial bias. *Journal of Accounting and Finance*, 22(2).

Vestli, J. T. 2021. Investor Reactions to Negative Audit Remarks in Different Economic Climates Evidence from Listed Companies in Norway from 2007 to 2019. Master's thesis, OsloMet—Oslo Metropolitan University, Oslo and Kjeller, Norway.

Vilela, L. F., Leme, R. C., Pinheiro, C. A., & Carpinteiro, O. A. (2019). Forecasting financial series using clustering methods and support vector regression. *Artificial Intelligence Review*, 52(4), 743–773. DOI: 10.1007/s10462-018-9663-x

Vohra, T. (2023). Measuring Investors' Experience about Stock Market: Scale Development and Validation. *Abhigyan*, 41(1), 24–34. DOI: 10.56401/Abhigyan_41.1.2023.24-34

Waktola, B. S., Singh, M., & Singh, S. (2024). Do social responsibility practices affect competitive advantage in banking industry? Study on selected commercial banks in Ethiopia. *Social Responsibility Journal*, 20(10), 2191–2211. DOI: 10.1108/SRJ-01-2024-0004

Walker, T., Nikbakht, E., & Kooli, M. (2023). Fintech and banking: an overview. *The fintech disruption: how financial innovation is transforming the banking industry*, 1-8.

Walter, A., & Moritz Weber, F. (2006). Herding in the German mutual fund industry. European Financial Management, 12(3), 375–406. .DOI: 10.1111/j.1354-7798.2006.00325.x

Wang, H., & Hanna, S. (1997). Does risk tolerance decrease with age. Financial Counseling and Planning Education, (614), 27–32. DOI: 10.2139/ssrn.95489

Wang, C. S., Tang, H. W., & Chen, R. C. (2017). Does IPO subscription demand affect investor herd behavior in Taiwan? *International Review of Economics & Finance*, 51, 258–272. DOI: 10.1016/j.iref.2017.06.004

Wang, H., Chen, H., & Tawiah, V. (2023). Does Ethical Behaviour Affect Sustainable Development? Evidence from Developed and Developing Countries. *Sustainability (Basel)*, 15(13), 10246. DOI: 10.3390/su151310246

Wang, Q., & Dong, Z. (2022). Technological innovation and renewable energy consumption: A middle path for trading off financial risk and carbon emissions. *Environmental Science and Pollution Research International*, 29(22), 33046–33062. DOI: 10.1007/s11356-021-17915-3 PMID: 35025046

Weber, M., & Camerer, C. F. (1998). The disposition effect in securities trading: An experimental analysis. Journal of Economic Behavior & Organization, 33(2), 167-184.

Weber, M. R. (2006). The role of affect in financial decision-making. In Bennett, M. J., & Dunning, S. D. (Eds.), *The Cambridge Handbook of Applied Social Psychology* (pp. 357–384). Cambridge University Press.

Weinstein, N. D. (1980). Unrealistic optimism about future events. *Journal of Personality and Social Psychology*, 39(5), 806–820. DOI: 10.1037/0022-3514.39.5.806

Westermann, F., & Schunk, D. (2022). Rational Expectations vs. Behavioral Biases: An Empirical Analysis of Trading Variability in International Capital Markets. *Journal of Business and Economic Options*, 5(4), 35–42.

Whittlesea, B. W. (1993). Illusions of familiarity. Journal of Experimental Psychology: Learning, Memory, and Cognition, 19(6), 1235.

Witt, S. F., & Dobbins, R. (1979). The Markowitz contribution to portfolio theory. Managerial finance, 5(1), 3-17.

World Economic Forum. (2022). Tokenization: A New Era for Asset Management.

Worldometer. (n.d.). Current world population. Retrieved June 27, 2024, from https://www.worldometers. info/world-population/

Wu, H. (2022). Intuition in investment decision-making across cultures. *Journal of Behavioral Finance*, 23(1), 106–122. DOI: 10.1080/15427560.2020.1848839

Xiao, J. J., Tang, C., & Shim, S. (2009). Acting for happiness: Financial behavior and life satisfaction of college students. *Social Indicators Research*, 92(1), 53–68. DOI: 10.1007/s11205-008-9288-6

Yang, W. R., & Chen, Y. L. (2015). The Response of Dynamic Herd Behavior to Domestic and US Market Factors: Evidence from the Greater China Stock Markets. Emerging Markets Finance and Trade, 51(1, SI), S18–S41. .DOI: 10.1080/1540496X.2014.998884

Yang, X., Yang, J., Hou, Y., Li, S., & Sun, S. (2023). Gamification of mobile wallets as an unconventional innovation for promoting FinTech: An fsQCA approach. Journal of Business Research, 155(Part A), 113406. https://doi.org/https://www.business-standard.com/world-news/tesla-shares-surge-on-strong-earnings-30-growth-forecast-in-2025-124102401582_1.htmlDOI: 10.1016/j.jbusres.2022.113406

Zahera, S. A., & Bansal, R. (2018). Do investors exhibit behavioral biases in investment decision making? A systematic review. Qualitative Research in Financial Markets, 10(2), 210-251.

Zahera, S. A., & Bansal, R. (2018). Do investors exhibit behavioral biases in investment decision making? A systematic review. *Qualitative Research in Financial Markets*, 10(2), 210–251. DOI: 10.1108/QRFM-04-2017-0028

Zaiane, S. (2013). Investor Overconfidence : an Examination of Individual Traders on The Tunisian Stock Market. Advances in Management & Applied Economics, 3(5), 41–55.

Zaleskiewicz, T. (2015). Behavioral finance. In Handbook of contemporary behavioral economics (pp. 728-750). Routledge.

Zeng, F., Huang, W. C., & Hueng, J. (2016). On Chinese government's stock market rescue efforts in 2015. Modern Economy, 7(4), 411-418.

Zhang, Y., & Berhe, H. M. (2022). The impact of green investment and green marketing on business performance: The mediation role of corporate social responsibility in Ethiopia's Chinese Textile Companies. *Sustainability (Basel)*, 14(7), 3883. DOI: 10.3390/su14073883

Zhang, Y., & Li, Y. (2023). Artificial intelligence and machine learning for risk management in sustainable finance: A review. *The Journal of Risk Finance*, 14(3), 237–262.

About the Contributors

Liao Faxing is the Academic Director at Chengdu International Studies University. He completed his PhD in Finance at Chengdu University, specializing in stock herding behavior in financial markets. His research offers significant insights into the psychological and behavioral factors driving collective investor actions and their impact on market dynamics. Dr. Liao has published extensively in leading finance journals, contributing to both academic literature and practical finance. He is also a dedicated educator, teaching courses on behavioral finance and investment analysis, and continues to explore new dimensions of herding behavior and its implications for financial markets.

Ooi Kok Loang, LLM, CMIIA, CIA, is with the Department of Finance at the University of Malaya, renowned for his expertise in behavioural finance and capital markets. His professional journey includes significant roles as an auditor and business consultant at KPMG (Big 4 Audit Firms) and Deputy Dean at two prestigious private universities. Dr. Ooi holds a Master in Finance and a PhD in Behavioral Finance from Universiti Sains Malaysia (QS137), a Master of Laws (Business Law) from the International Islamic University Malaysia (QS Top 300 by subject), and is a US Certified Internal Auditor. With a strong portfolio of publications and active contributions as a reviewer for top international SCI and Scopus-indexed journals, Dr. Ooi is keen to mentor passionate PhD students, offering a vibrant environment for research and academic excellence.

***

S. Agila is currently employed by the Sathyabama Institute of Science and Technology as an assistant professor in the department of management studies. She graduated with distinction from St. Joseph's College of Engineering with an MBA. She has three years of teaching experience.

K. Balaji is an Assistant Professor in Business and Management, Christ Deemed to be University, Bangalore. He did Ph.D. from KLU Business School, KL University,Vijayawada. He is having 12 years of teaching experience. He has to his credit 23 Research Articles published in reputed National and International Journals. He has participated and presented more than 12 papers in both National and International Seminars/Conferences and also attended more than 60 workshops/ FDPS organized by various reputed organizations. He has also participated in more than 80 seminars / webinars organized by various reputed organizations. He has also attended in 6 Short Term Training programs. He has successfully conducted 9 webinars, one 5 day FDP and one International Conference on Reimaging marketing in New Normal. He is a ratified as Assistant Professor by both JNTUH, JNTU Anantapur and Sri Venkateswara University, Tirupati. His specialized areas include, Accounting and Financial management, Marketing Management, Retailing Management, Consumer Behavior studies, Entrepreneurship and Business Laws.

Asheetu Bhatia Sarin is an Assistant Professor (Management) at Vivekananda Institute of Professional Studies-Technical campus affiliated to GGSIPU, Delhi. She is having around 11+ years of teaching experience in the field of Commerce and Management. She has done Ph.D. in Behavioral Finance, did her post-graduation (MBA) from ICFAI Business School in Finance and Marketing, and earned her graduate degree in B.Com (H) from Delhi University. She is a lifetime member of the Indian Commerce Association and has to her credit many national and International publications.

M. Deepa, an Assistant Professor in the School of Management Studies at Sathyabama Institute of Science and Technology, Chennai. She completed her M.B.A. in Human Resources and Marketing from Maharaja Engineering College, Coimbatore, and holds a full-time Doctorate in Business Administration from Vels Institute of Science and Technology, Chennai. With 5 years of teaching experience, she has honed her skills in Marketing and Human Resources, fostering student engagement through practical, real-world applications in her teaching. Her research interests include consumer behavior, digital marketing strategies, and organizational development in HR. She has presented papers at various national and international conferences, earning recognition for her innovative ideas. In addition to her presentations, she has contributed to academic literature through publications in esteemed UGC Care, Scopus, and Web of Science journals. She is also involved in mentoring students and guiding research projects, reflecting her passion for academic growth and development in the business management field.

D. Joel Jebadurai working as an Associate professor in the Department of MBA, St.Joseph's College of Engineering, OMR, Chennai, Tamil Nadu,India. He has published more than 40 research papers in a peer reviewed journals.

M Jayaseely, Assistant Professor, School of Management Studies, Sathyabama Institute of Science and Technology, Chennai. She is pursuing her PhD in Commerce in Holy Cross College Affiliated to Bharathidasan University, Trichy. She has completed M.Phil. in commerce from Bharath Institute of higher education and research, M. Com Banking and insurance, M.A. English from Annamalai University and B.Ed., M.Ed. from Sathyabama University. She has teaching experience of more than 18 years. Her area of specialization is Banking, Insurance, Human Resource. She has published more than thirty articles in various reputed journals in Scopus, UGC Care Listed, Web of Science Journals and Peer reviewed Journals. She has also participated and presented in National and International Conference. She acted as resource person for various institutions in soft skills training and Personality development. She also showcases her excellence in the areas of Education, Guidance and Counselling, Personality Development, Communication and Soft Skills.

A Meera, M.Com., M. Phil., M.B.A., Ph.D.,Currently Working as a Assistant Professor, School of Management Studies, Sathyabama Institute of Science and Technology, Chennai. An esteemed academician with a stellar record in commerce education, stands as a beacon of excellence in the academic realm. Armed with a Master's in Commerce (M.Com.), M.Phil., and MBA, she completed her doctoral journey at Alagappa University, where she earned a Ph.D. in Commerce. With a commendable 15 years of teaching experience. She has emerged as a distinguished educator, mentor, and prolific researcher. She shares a wealth of knowledge aimed at inspiring and guiding fellow educators on their professional journey.

S. Visalakshmi is an Assistant Professor in Finance at the Department of Management, Central University of Tamilnadu, India. Her areas of research interest include financial markets, financial econometrics and deep learning techniques. She has published research articles in various journals of international repute.

Index

A

B

C

E

F

G

H

I

L

M

O

P

R

S

T

V

www.ingramcontent.com/pod-product-compliance
Lightning Source LLC
LaVergne TN
LVHW080607300926
849162LV00005B/1075